ADVANCES IN
EXPERIMENTAL
SOCIAL PSYCHOLOGY

VOLUME 4

CONTRIBUTORS TO VOLUME 4

ELLIOT ARONSON

DONN BYRNE

SUSAN M. ERVIN-TRIPP

NICO H. FRIJDA

EDWARD E. SAMPSON

EZRA STOTLAND

HARRY S. UPSHAW

ADVANCES IN

Experimental
Social Psychology

EDITED BY

Leonard Berkowitz
DEPARTMENT OF PSYCHOLOGY
UNIVERSITY OF WISCONSIN
MADISON, WISCONSIN

VOLUME 4

1969

ACADEMIC PRESS   New York San Francisco London

A Subsidiary of Harcourt Brace Jovanovich, Publishers

ACADEMIC PRESS, INC.
111 Fifth Avenue, New York, New York 10003

United Kingdom Edition published by
ACADEMIC PRESS, INC. (LONDON) LTD.
24/28 Oval Road, London NW1

LIBRARY OF CONGRESS CATALOG CARD NUMBER: 64-23452

PRINTED IN THE UNITED STATES OF AMERICA

CONTRIBUTORS

Numbers in parentheses indicate the pages on which the authors' contributions begin.

ELLIOT ARONSON, *Department of Psychology, University of Texas, Austin, Texas* (1)

DONN BYRNE, *Department of Psychology, University of Texas, Austin, Texas* (35)

SUSAN M. ERVIN-TRIPP, *Speech Department, University of California, Berkeley, California* (91)

NICO H. FRIJDA, *Department of Psychology, Amsterdam University, Amsterdam, Holland* (167)

EDWARD E. SAMPSON, *Department of Psychology, University of California, Berkeley, California* (225)

EZRA STOTLAND, *Department of Psychology, University of Washington, Seattle, Washington* (271)

HARRY S. UPSHAW, *Department of Psychology, University of Illinois at Chicago Circle, Chicago, Illinois* (315)

CONTENTS

The Theory of Cognitive Dissonance: A Current Perspective

Elliot Aronson

Attitudes and Attraction

Donn Byrne

Sociolinguistics

Susan M. Ervin-Tripp

Recognition of Emotion

Nico H. Frijda

Studies of Status Congruence

Edward E. Sampson

Exploratory Investigations of Empathy

Ezra Stotland

The Personal Reference Scale:
An Approach to Social Judgment

Harry S. Upshaw

CONTENTS OF OTHER VOLUMES

Volume 3

THE THEORY OF
COGNITIVE DISSONANCE:
A CURRENT PERSPECTIVE[1]

Elliot Aronson
DEPARTMENT OF PSYCHOLOGY
UNIVERSITY OF TEXAS
AUSTIN, TEXAS

[1]Slightly revised from a chapter entitled "Dissonance Theory: Progress and Problems," in *The Cognitive Consistency Theories: a Source Book,* edited by R. Abelson, E. Aronson, W. McGuire, T. Newcomb, M. Rosenberg, and P. Tannenbaum; Chicago: Rand McNally, 1968; reprinted by permission of the author, editors, and publisher. This paper was prepared while the author's research was being supported by the National Institute of Mental Health, grant MH 12357.

I. Introduction

As a formal statement, Festinger's theory of cognitive dissonance (1957) is quite primitive; it lacks the elegance and precision that are commonly associated with scientific theorizing. Yet its impact has been great. As McGuire has observed in his recent survey in the *Annual Review of Psychology* (1966, p. 492), "Over the past three years, dissonance theory continued to generate more research and more hostility than any other one approach." We will allude to the "hostility" part of this statement from time to time throughout this article; but first, let us discuss the research.

The research has been as diverse as it has been plentiful; its range extends from maze running in rats (Lawrence and Festinger, 1962) to the development of values in children (Aronson and Carlsmith, 1963); from the hunger of college sophomores (Brehm *et al.*, 1964) to the proselytizing behavior of religious zealots (Festinger *et al.*, 1956). For descriptive summaries of dissonance experiments, the reader is referred to Festinger (1957); Festinger and Aronson (1960); Brehm and Cohen (1962); Festinger and Bramel (1962); Festinger and Freedman (1964).

The proliferation of research testing and extending dissonance theory results for the most part from the generality and simplicity of the theory. Although it has been applied primarily in social psychological settings, it is not limited to social psychological phenomena such as interpersonal relations or feelings toward a communicator and his communication. Rather, its domain is in the widest of places—the skull of an individual organism.[2]

A. THE THEORY

The core notion of the theory is extremely simple: Dissonance is a negative drive state which occurs whenever an individual simultaneously holds two cognitions (ideas, beliefs, opinions) which are psychologically inconsistent. Stated differently, two cognitions are dissonant if, considering these two cognitions alone, the opposite of one follows from the other. Since the occurrence of dissonance is presumed to be unpleasant, individuals strive to reduce it by adding "consonant" cognitions or by changing one or both cognitions to make them "fit togeth-

---

[2]An additional reason for the great number of experiments on dissonance theory is completely *ad hominem;* Leon Festinger has an unmatched genius for translating interesting hypotheses into workable experimental operations and for inspiring others to do so. He has produced a great deal of research irrespective of any particular theoretical approach.

er" better; i.e., so that they become more consonant with each other.[3] To use Festinger's time-worn (but still cogent) example, if a person believes that cigarette smoking causes cancer and simultaneously knows that he himself smokes cigarettes, he experiences dissonance. Assuming that the person would rather not have cancer, his cognition "I smoke cigarettes" is psychologically inconsistent with his cognition "Cigarette smoking produces cancer." Perhaps the most efficient way to reduce dissonance in such a situation is to stop smoking. But, as many of us have discovered, this is by no means easy. Thus, a person will usually work on the other cognition. There are several ways in which a person can make cigarette smoking seem less absurd. He might belittle the evidence linking cigarette smoking to cancer ("Most of the data are clinical rather than experimental"); or he might associate with other cigarette smokers ("If Sam, Jack, and Harry smoke, then it can't be very dangerous"); or he might smoke filter-tipped cigarettes and delude himself that the filter traps the cancer-producing materials; or he might convince himself that smoking is an important and highly pleasurable activity ("I'd rather have a shorter but more enjoyable life than a longer, unenjoyable one"); or he might actually make a virtue out of smoking by developing a romantic, devil-may-care image of himself, flaunting danger by smoking. All of these behaviors reduce dissonance, in effect, by reducing the absurdity involved in going out of one's way to contract cancer. Thus, dissonance theory does not rest upon the assumption that man is a *rational* animal; rather, it suggests that man is a rational*izing* animal—that he attempts to appear rational, both to others and to himself. To clarify the theoretical statement and to illustrate the kind of research generated by the theory a few experiments will be briefly described.

B. DISSONANCE FOLLOWING A DECISION

One of the earliest experiments testing derivations from dissonance theory was performed by Brehm (1956). Brehm gave individuals their choice between two appliances which they had previously evaluated. He found that following the decision, when the subjects reevaluated the alternatives, they enhanced their liking for the chosen appliance and downgraded their evaluation of the unchosen one. The derivation is

---

[3]Although dissonance theory is an incredibly simple statement, it is not quite as simple as a reading of this article will indicate. Many aspects of the theory (for example, the propositions relevant to the magnitude of dissonance) will not be discussed here because they are peripheral to the major focus of this essay.

clear: Following a difficult choice, people experience dissonance. Cognitions about any negative attributes of the preferred object are dissonant with having chosen it; cognitions about positive attributes of the unchosen object are dissonant with *not* having chosen it. To reduce dissonance, people emphasize the positive aspects and deemphasize the negative aspects of the chosen objects while emphasizing the negative and deemphasizing the positive aspects of the unchosen object (see also Festinger, 1964).

C.   DISSONANCE RESULTING FROM EFFORT

Aronson and Mills (1959) reasoned that if people undergo a great deal of trouble in order to gain admission to a group which turns out to be dull and uninteresting they will experience dissonance. The cognition that they worked hard in order to become a member of the group is dissonant with cognitions concerning the negative aspects of the group. One does not work hard for nothing. To reduce dissonance, they will distort their perception of the group in a positive direction. In the Aronson-Mills experiment, college women underwent an initiation in order to become a member of a group discussion on the psychology of sex. For some of the girls the initiation was very embarrassing—it consisted of reciting a list of obscene words in the presence of the male experimenter. For others the initiation was a mild one. For still others there was no initiation at all. All of the subjects then listened to the same tape recording of a discussion being held by the group they had just joined. As predicted, the girls in the Severe Initiation condition rated the discussion much more favorably than did those in the other two conditions [see also Aronson (1961); Zimbardo (1965); Lewis (1964); Gerard and Mathewson (1966)].

D.   INSUFFICIENT JUSTIFICATION

Aronson and Carlsmith (1963) predicted that if threats are used to prevent people from performing a desired activity, the *smaller* the threat, the greater will be the tendency for people to derogate the activity. If an individual refrains from performing a desired activity, he experiences dissonance: The cognition that he likes the activity is dissonant with the cognition that he is not performing it. One way to reduce dissonance is by derogating the activity—in that way he can justify the fact that he is not performing it. However, any threat provides cognitions that are consonant with not performing the activity; and the more severe the threat, the greater the consonance. In short, a severe threat provides ample justification for not performing the activity; a mild threat provides less justification, leading the individual to add justifications of his own in the form of convincing himself that he *does not like* to perform the activity. In their experiment, Aronson and Carlsmith found that children who were threatened with *mild* punishment for playing with a desired toy *decreased* their liking for the toy to a greater extent than did children who were severely threatened (see also Turner and Wright, 1965; Freedman, 1965).

II. What Is Psychological Inconsistency?

The very simplicity of the core of the theory is at once its greatest strength and its most serious weakness. We have already discussed the heuristic value of its simplicity. It should be emphasized that many of the hypotheses which are obvious derivations from the theory are *unique* to that theory; i.e., they could not be derived from any other theory. This increases our confidence in dissonance theory as an explanation of an important aspect of human behavior. The weakness occurs primarily in the difficulty involved with defining the limits of the theoretical statement. While at the "center" of the theory it is relatively easy to generate hypotheses that are clear and direct, at its "fringes" it is not always clear whether or not a prediction can be made from the theory and, if so, exactly what that prediction will be.[4] Although investigators who have had experience working with the theory seem to have little difficulty intuiting its boundary conditions, they have had considerable difficulty communicating this to other people; indeed, a situation has evolved which can best be described by the statement: "If you want to be sure, ask Leon." This has proved to be both a source of embarrassment for the proponents of the theory as well as a source of annoyance and exasperation to its critics.

Why is it so difficult to make a more precise theoretical statement? Perhaps the most basic reason has to do with the nature of the inconsistency involved in the core definition of dissonance theory. It would be easy to specify dissonant situations if the theory were limited to *logical* inconsistencies. There exist relatively unequivocal rules of logic which can be applied without ambiguity or fear of contradiction. But recall that the inconsistency that produces dissonance, although it can be logical inconsistency, is not necessarily logical. Rather, it is *psychological* inconsistency. While this aspect of the theory increases its

---

[4]Later in this article some attempt will be made to specify exactly what is meant by "center" and "fringes."

power, range, and degree of interest, at the same time it also causes some serious problems. Thus, returning to our friend, the cigarette smoker, the cognition regarding smoking cigarettes is not logically inconsistent with the cognition linking cigarette smoking to cancer; i.e., strictly speaking, having information that cigarette smoking causes cancer does not make it illogical to smoke cigarettes. But these cognitions do produce dissonance because, taken together, they do not make sense psychologically. Assuming that the smoker does not want cancer, the knowledge that cigarettes cause cancer should lead to *not* smoking cigarettes. Similarly, none of the research examples mentioned above deals with logical inconsistency; e.g., it is not illogical to go through hell and high water to gain admission to a dull discussion group; it is not illogical to choose to own an appliance that one considers slightly more attractive than the unchosen alternative; it is not illogical to refrain from playing with a toy at the request of an adult.

Festinger (1957) lists four kinds of situations in which dissonance can arise: (1) logical inconsistency; (2) inconsistency with cultural mores; (3) inconsistency between one cognition and a more general, more encompassing cognition; and (4) past experience.

(1) Logical inconsistency: Suppose a person believed that all men are mortal but also held the belief that he, as a man, would live forever. These two cognitions are dissonant because they are logically inconsistent. The obverse of one follows from the other on strict logical grounds.

(2) Cultural mores: If a college professor loses his patience with one of his students and shouts at him angrily, his knowledge of what he is doing is dissonant with his idea about what is the proper, acceptable behavior of a professor toward his students—in our culture. In some other cultures this might be appropriate behavior and, therefore, would not arouse dissonance.

(3) Inconsistency between a cognition and a more encompassing cognition: In a given election, if a person who has always considered himself to be a Democrat votes for the Republican candidate, he should experience dissonance. The concept "I am a Democrat" encompasses the concept "I vote for Democratic candidates."

(4) Past experience: If a person stepped on a tack while barefoot and felt no pain, he would experience dissonance because he knows from experience that pain follows from stepping on tacks. If he had never had experience with tacks or other sharp objects, he would *not* experience dissonance.

The illustrations presented above are clear examples of dissonance. Similarly, the situations investigated in the experiments described above are clearly dissonant. But there *are* situations where for all practical purposes it is not perfectly clear whether two cognitions are dissonant or merely irrelevant. Because dissonance is *not* limited to logical inconsistencies, it is occasionally difficult to specify *a priori* whether or not a cultural more is being violated, whether or not an event is markedly different from past experience, or whether or not it is different from a more general cognition. Recall the basic theoretical statement: Two cognitions are dissonant if, considering these two cognitions alone, the obverse of one follows from the other. The major source of conceptual ambiguity rests upon the fact that Festinger has not clarified the meaning of the words "follows from."

For example, if I learn that my favorite novelist beats his wife, does this arouse dissonance? It is difficult to be certain. Strictly speaking, being a wife-beater is not incompatible with being a great novelist.[5] However, there may be a sense in which the term "great novelist" implies that such a person is wise, sensitive, empathic, and compassionate — and wise, sensitive, empathic, and compassionate people do not go around beating their wives. This is not a logical inconsistency; nor is it a clear violation of a cultural more; moreover, it may have nothing to do with past experience — and it is not *necessarily* embedded in a more general cognition. Thus, a knowledge of the kinds of situations in which dissonance *can* occur is not always useful in determining whether dissonance *does* occur.

A rule of thumb which we have found useful is to state the situation in terms of the violation of an expectancy. For example, one might issue the following instructions: "Consider Mr. Roy Wilkins of the National Association for the Advancement of Colored People. I'm going to tell you something about his beliefs about the native IQ of Negroes relative to that of Caucasians. What do you expect these beliefs to be?" No doubt most people would have a firm expectancy that Mr. Wilkins would say that there are no innate differences. Consequently, one could then conclude that if individuals were exposed to a statement by Mr. Wilkins to the effect that Negroes were innately stupider than Caucasians, most would experience dissonance. Let's try our difficult example. Suppose we confronted a large number of people with the following proposition: "Consider the great novelist, X. I am about to tell you something about whether or not he beats his wife. What do you expect me to say?" Probably most people would shrug; i.e., they would not have a strong expectancy (but, again, this is an empirical question; there is no certainty that

---

[5] If *I* had beaten my wife I might experience dissonance because of *my* violation of a cultural more. But since I know that many people beat their wives, discovering that a particular person beats his wife is not necessarily inconsistent with my cognition about the world and human nature. More will be said about this later.

it would come out this way). If this occurred, one could conclude that X's wife-beating behavior is irrelevant to his status as a novelist. An empirical rule of thumb may be of practical utility but is, of course, no substitute for a clearer, less ambiguous, more precise theoretical statement. Near the end of the article this rule of thumb will be elaborated upon and it will be indicated how it might be used conceptually.

III. Methodological Problems

Some critics have pointed to the ambiguities inherent in the theoretical statement and have concluded that they make the theory impossible to disprove and, consequently, worthless. As stated above, some conceptual ambiguities do exist and will be elaborated on shortly. But first, we should make it clear that these conceptual ambiguities exist in a very small part of the domain in which the theory has continued to make clear and precise predictions; these predictions have been validated a number of times in a number of different ways. Why, then, does the theory inspire what McGuire (1966) referred to as "... more hostility than any other one approach"? We feel that a good deal of the hostility is misdirected—stemming from a confusion between conceptual and methodological ambiguities. Much of the difficulty in disproving dissonance theory arises from weaknesses in the method of social psychological experimentation. These weaknesses are hardly the fault of the theory. Moreover, these methodological problems are not peculiar to research on dissonance theory but are shared by research on all theories that predict social psychological phenomena. They tend to have been associated with dissonance theory precisely because of the great quantity of research generated (and, therefore, of methodological problems unearthed) by that theory. The major methodological problems stem from the lack of tried and true, standardized techniques for operationalizing conceptual variables in social psychology. Consequently, any single failure in a given experiment can be attributed to a failure in the experimental operations rather than an error of conceptualization. At the same time, repeated failures across a wide variety of techniques would spell the end of dissonance theory or any theory.

THE PROBLEM OF ALTERNATIVE EXPLANATIONS

The lack of a standardized method in social psychology has contributed to another major difficulty with research in this area: It is frequently possible to come up with alternative explanations for empirical results. Thus, like experiments testing other theories in social psychology, many of the experiments testing dissonance theory are subject to alternative explanations. If some of the data can be explained without recourse to dissonance theory, our confidence in the theory is weakened. At the same time, dissonance theory does provide the most parsimonious explanation for the data taken as a whole—as McGuire has argued: "The whole set of dissonance studies would require accepting a tremendous variety of alternative explanations, whereas dissonance theory alone explains a large subset of them" (1966, p. 493). Although this is some recommendation, it is not wholly sufficient. One still wants to be able to determine which explanation is more nearly correct. The best way to distinguish among plausible alternative explanations is through a series of well-controlled systematic experiments which are essentially conceptual replications using markedly different sets of operations to test the same hypothesis. This technique has been referred to as "purification"; the necessity for such procedures as well as a fuller description is provided elsewhere (Aronson and Carlsmith, 1968).

Let us take, as an illustration, the initiation experiment by Aronson and Mills (1959). Recall that the investigators predicted the results on the basis of dissonance theory; specifically, the cognition that one has gone through an unpleasant and embarrassing initiation in order to get into a group was dissonant with the cognition that the discussion group was dull and dreary. In order to reduce dissonance, subjects in the Severe Initiation condition (but not in the Mild Initiation condition) convinced themselves that the "dull" group was really quite exciting. In order to maximize credibility and impact, the investigators constructed a rather novel method for operationalizing "unpleasant effort"; they had the girls in the Severe Initiation condition recite a list of obscene words and some lurid passages from contemporary novels in the presence of a male experimenter. This procedure made sense in terms of the over-all "scenario" of the experiment, thus effectively masking the true purpose of the experiment and reducing the possibility of suspicion. It also seemed to be effective in the sense that the girls appeared to be embarrassed—they tended to hesitate, blush, cast their eyes downward, etc. Nevertheless, the use of sexually related material opened the door for at least two plausible alternative explanations, both offered by Chapanis and Chapanis (1964). One is that while reciting the material the girls did not become embarrassed, but, rather, became sexually aroused; this could have produced pleasure or the expectation of pleasure which supposedly would increase the attractiveness of the discussion group. The second is quite the reverse: The subjects in the Severe Initiation condition felt relief (from sexual anxiety?) when they found the group discussion banal instead of embarrassing. Supposedly, this could lead them to rate the discussion as not banal at all.

Whether these explanations are more or less plausible than the dissonance explanation is not important. The important point is that they are at
least possible. In order to distinguish between the dissonance explanation
and these alternative explanations, the same hypothesis should be tested
using an operational definition of "unpleasant effort" which has nothing to
do with the pleasantness of sexual arousal or relief from sexual anxiety.
Such an experiment has been performed by Gerard and Mathewson
(1966), who replicated the Aronson-Mills (1959) experiment conceptually. In their experiment they advertised their group discussions as
being on the topic of college morals; the actual discussion was a rather
pallid one involving cheating on examinations. The initiation procedure
consisted of electric shocks instead of obscene words as used by Aronson
and Mills. The results paralleled those of Aronson and Mills and confirmed the prediction from dissonance theory: Those subjects who underwent a series of severe electric shocks in order to gain admission to a dull
discussion group came to rate that group more favorably than those who
gained admission after having undergone mild electric shocks.

This single procedure, of course, does not eliminate all alternative
explanations. Let us return to the critique of the Aronson-Mills (1959)
experiment. To quote Chapanis and Chapanis:

> It is interesting to speculate what would have happened if the girls had
> been 'initiated' into the group by the use of a more generally accepted painful
> procedure, such as using electric shock. Somehow it seems doubtful that this
> group would appreciate the group discussion more than the control group, unless
> — and here is the crucial point — the conditions were so manipulated that Ss expe-
> rienced a feeling of successful accomplishment in overcoming the painful obsta-
> cle. It seems to us that if there is anything to the relationship between severity of
> initiation and liking for the group, it lies in this feeling of successful accomplish-
> ment. The more severe the test, the stronger is the pleasurable feeling of success
> in overcoming the obstacle. There is no need to postulate a drive due to disso-
> nance if a *pleasure principle* can account for the results quite successfully
> (1964, p. 5).

Thus, while Chapanis and Chapanis would appear to have been
wrong in their conviction that the effect demonstrated by Aronson and
Mills would *not* replicate if electric shock had been used, they have apparently left themselves an escape hatch. Fortunately, however, there are
some data on this issue also. According to Chapanis and Chapanis (1964),
the more painful the situation one overcomes, the greater the feeling of
successful accomplishment. Although they do not explain how this feeling
of pleasure would make subjects like the discussion group better, one assumes that they are using a rather simple contiguity model: If a person
feels good, contiguous stimuli (e.g., the discussion group) look and feel

good. Dissonance theory, of course, does not make use of such a contiguity explanation; i.e., the group discussion looks good *not* because it is contiguous with pain reduction (dissonance reduction)—rather, it comes to look good as a *means of reducing* dissonance. The crucial aspect of dissonance arousal in this situation is that getting into a group was contingent upon going through a severe initiation; that is, it was an initiation, not simply a stimulus that was contiguous with a pleasant feeling. Consequently, if one simply hears a group discussion after having successfully undergone a severe shock, dissonance theory would make no prediction regarding the attractiveness of the group. It would make a prediction only if the person had experienced dissonance; i.e., if the person had undergone a severe initiation *in order to* get into a dull group.

Thus, a test between the Chapanis and Chapanis "successful accomplishment" explanation and the dissonance explanation can be arranged simply by comparing an initiation (i.e., an "in order to" situation) with a contiguous situation. Such a test was built into the Gerard-Mathewson (1966) study. In this experiment some subjects underwent a severe shock in order to get into a group (Initiation condition) while other subjects simply underwent severe shock (No Initiation condition). If a feeling of success is aroused by getting through the shock situation, both groups had it. All subjects were then exposed to a taped group discussion. Thus, for subjects in both conditions the discussion was contiguous with feelings of "successful accomplishment"; but only those in the Initiation condition experienced dissonance. The results clearly support dissonance theory. Those who went through severe electric shock in order to get into a dull group rated the taped group discussion as more attractive than a "mild shock" control condition. Those who went through a severe shock (without dissonance) and then listened to the same tape rated the discussion as less attractive than those in the Initiation condition—indeed, they tended to rate the taped discussion as *less* attractive than subjects in the parallel (No Initiation) condition who underwent mild electric shock. This latter finding suggests that even in the absence of dissonance, "a feeling of successful accomplishment" does not operate—but something else does; more will be made of this later.[6]

To sum up this point, it should be made clear that neither the receiving of electric shock nor the recitation of obscene words is a perfect empirical realization of the conception "unpleasant effort." Neither, by it-

---

[6]One additional piece of data is of relevance. One-half of the subjects in the Initiation condition were told they passed the test and one-half were not told. The "told—not told" manipulation did not interact with the severity of shock. This provides further evidence against the "successful accomplishment" explanation.

self, is free of alternative explanations. The recitation of obscene words is open to alternative explanations involving sexual matters — electric shock is open to alternative explanations involving pain, fear, pain reduction, and fear reduction. But taken together, they eliminate most possible alternative explanations. Accordingly, many of the results supporting dissonance theory have been and can continue to be strengthened by eliminating alternative explanations through the purification of operations afforded by conceptual replications. As this process continues, our confidence in the validity and viability of the theory increases — in spite of its simplicity and inelegance as a conceptual statement.[7]

Of course, as indicated, not all the problems of dissonance theory are methodological. Several additional conceptual problems will be discussed in a moment.

IV. The "Nothing But" Critique

Scientists tend to be conservative, parsimonious creatures. This is generally a healthy attitude which most frequently manifests itself in a reluctance to accept a new theory or a novel explanation for a phenomenon if the phenomenon can be squeezed (even with great difficulty) into an existing approach. In this regard, dissonance theory has been referred to as "warmed-over soup"; i.e., as nothing but a new name for an old explanation. This has been most persistently stated in regard to that aspect of the theory related to decision making. In this context dissonance theory has been referred to as nothing but another name for conflict theory.

A. DISSONANCE OR CONFLICT?

In fact, there are several differences. Conflict occurs before a decision is made, dissonance occurs after the decision. During conflict it is assumed that an individual will devote his energies to a careful, dispassionate, and sensible evaluation and judgment of the alternatives. He will

---

[7]In struggling toward greater methodological sophistication, investigators working with dissonance theory face the same problems as other experimental social psychologists. Thus, the major critical review of dissonance theory to date (Chapanis and Chapanis, 1964) is largely a methodological critique. Although many of the points made in this review involve reasonable methodological criticisms, the unfortunate illusion is created that, somehow, "dissonance theorists" commit more methodological blunders than the rest of us. In articulating this point, Chapanis and Chapanis attempt to cite examples of good (i.e., nondissonance) methodology in this area. Ironically, their principal example of good methodology is an experiment where the subjects were allowed to assign *themselves* to experimental conditions (p. 19), thus negating the major defining characteristic of an experiment.

gather all of the information, pro and con, about all of the alternatives in order to make a reasonable decision. Following the decision, a person is in a state of dissonance — all negative aspects of X are dissonant with having chosen X; all positive aspects of Y are dissonant with *not* having chosen Y. Far from evaluating the alternatives impartially (as in conflict), the individual experiencing dissonance will seek biased information and evaluations designed to make his decision appear more reasonable. As in Brehm's (1956) experiment, he will seek to spread the alternatives apart. The more difficulty a person had making a decision, the greater the tendency toward this kind of behavior as a means of justifying his decision.

But how can we be certain that the "spreading apart" of the alternatives in Brehm's experiment occurred after the decision? Could it not have occurred during the conflict stage? That is, it is conceivable that, in order to make their decision easier, subjects in Brehm's experiment began to reevaluate the appliances in a biased manner *before* the decision. If this were the case, then there is no essential difference between predecisional and postdecisional processes; if so, this behavior can be considered part of conflict — and there is, indeed, no need to complicate matters by bringing in additional terminology.

Brehm's experiment does not allow us to determine whether the evaluation of chosen and unchosen alternatives was spread apart before or after the decision. Experiments by Davidson and Kiesler (1964) and by Jecker (1964) serve to clarify this issue. In Jecker's experiment, subjects were offered their choice between two phonograph records. In three conditions there was *low conflict*; i.e., subjects were told that there was a very good chance that they would receive *both* records no matter which they chose. In three other conditions, *high conflict* was produced by telling them that the probability was high that they would be given only the record that they chose. All of the subjects rated the records before the instructions; in each of the conflict conditions subjects rerated the records either (*a*) after they discovered that they received both records, (*b*) after they discovered that they received only the one record they chose, or (*c*) before they were certain whether they would get one or both. The results are quite clear: No spreading apart occurred when there was no dissonance; i.e., when the subject actually received both records or when he was not certain whether he would receive one or both, he did *not* reevaluate the alternatives systematically. Where dissonance did occur there was a systematic reevaluation; i.e., subjects spread their evaluation of the alternatives when they received only one record — this occurred independently of the degree of conflict. This experiment provides clear evidence that conflict and dissonance are different processes; whatever else dissonance theory might be, it is *not* "nothing but conflict theory."

B. DISSONANCE OR SELF-JUDGMENT?

An intriguing variation on the "nothing but" theme is Bem's (1965, 1967) analysis of the insufficient justification phenomenon. Speaking from the point of view of "a radical behaviorist," Bem suggested that the experiments involving insufficient justification can be accounted for by a self-judgment model. Accordingly, an aversive motivational state (dissonance) is superfluous to an understanding of these phenomena. Bem's model was based upon an individual's ability to infer what his real attitudes are by merely discriminating the circumstances which control his behavior. According to Bem, each person is the observer of his own behavior. The individual, then, in effect asks himself what the reinforcements were which guided his actions. If the person observes that he performed for a large reward, he is *less* apt to believe that the behavior was a reflection of his real attitudes than if he performed it for a small reward.

To clarify the different approaches, let us examine the experiment by Cohen (1962) in which Yale students were induced to write an essay favoring the repressive actions of the New Haven Police Department in quelling a student riot. Cohen found that those students who were paid 50¢ came to believe in the truth of their statements to a greater extent than did those who were paid $1.00

According to dissonance theory, the cognition that one has written an essay is dissonant with the cognition that one disagrees with the point of view of the essay. The smaller the compensation, the greater the dissonance; the greater the dissonance, the greater the tendency to agree with what one has written.

Bem suggested that what is called "dissonance" is really an instance of self-judgment based upon the subject's simple discrimination of the reinforcement contingencies. According to Bem, the subject says, in effect, "If I wrote the essay for only 50¢, then I must really believe it, whereas if it required $1.00 to get me to write it, then I probably don't believe it as much." This reasoning, in and of itself, is not really different from the way a dissonance theorist would conceptualize the process. But Bem carried his reasoning one step further: He reasoned that an aversive motivational state is unnecessary. Consequently, an observer should be able to arrive at the same inference as the subject himself—if the observer has knowledge of the incentive offered to the subject to induce him to perform a given behavior. Bem tested this prediction by describing to each of his subjects one of the conditions in Cohen's (1962) experiment. He found that these observers could estimate the attitude of Cohen's subjects— even though these observers, of course, were not experiencing dissonance. In short, Bem's observer-subjects estimated that Cohen's subjects who wrote the essay for 50¢ were more favorably disposed to the actions of the New Haven police than those who wrote the essay for $1.00.

But the events experienced by a "real" subject and those experienced by an observer are very different. Taking this position, Jones *et al.* (1968, in press) argue that Bem's results are misleading. Picture the situation: Yale students are asked to write an essay favoring police suppression of Yale students. It seems reasonable to assume that Bem's observers would infer that a typical Yale student would be unwilling to comply with the experimenter's request. But the subject Bem described to an observer *did*, in fact, comply. Because of this, Bem's observers in the 50¢ condition are likely to infer that the behavior of that specific subject was not typical; i.e., since he was quite willing to express an obviously unpopular point of view for such a small sum of money, he must have been more willing to comply than most Yale students. Consequently, it is possible that he favored the actions of the New Haven police in the first place. In Cohen's original experiment, of course, since the subject was himself the complier, if he complied reluctantly and was initially opposed to the actions of the New Haven police, it is more likely that he was aware of it.

This is a subtle distinction, but it may be an important one. In a set of factorial experiments, Jones *et al.* demonstrated that they can replicate Bem's results under Bem's conditions; i.e., observers felt that subjects who wrote the essay for 50¢ were more favorably disposed to the New Haven police than those who wrote the essay for $1.00. But under conditions which effectively eliminated the possibility of observers attributing *a priori* differences to the subjects, the results were opposite to Bem's. Here observers estimated that the original subjects in the $1.00 condition were more favorable to the actions of the New Haven police than were the original subjects in the 50¢ condition. These results, then, cast serious doubt on the contention that the observer (who, of course, is not experiencing dissonance) can effectively infer the attitudes of a subject in a dissonance experiment.

However, this experiment is not completely conclusive because it involves a change in the conditions of Cohen's original experiment. The possibility remains that Cohen's subjects *did* come to feel that they *initially* favored the actions of the New Haven police. Thus, Bem's results may, indeed, be an accurate translation of the Cohen experiment. What must be established in future experiments is whether or not the subject's behavior (writing a counter-attitudinal essay) becomes so very salient that it overwhelms his memory about his original position. This seems unlikely when the issue is as personally involving for the Yale students as the actions of the New Haven police. Nevertheless, the question remains an open one; at this time the most that can be said is that there is no compelling evidence that dissonance-like phenomena can occur in the absence of an aversive motivational state.

V. The Multiple Mode Problem

As indicated earlier, several problems are central to the theoretical statement. One of the knottiest and most interesting conceptual problems in dissonance theory involves the fact that in a given situation there is usually more than one way for a person to reduce dissonance. For example, the cigarette smoker has several techniques at his disposal. He may use any one, or several simultaneously. Experimentally, this problem can be eliminated by the simple device of blocking alternative techniques of dissonance reduction. This is part of the definition of experimental control; any experimenter worth his salt will attempt to control the environment so that the behavior elicited by his independent variable will occur in a manner which is measurable and at a time and place where the measuring instruments have been set up. To illustrate: In a typical communication—persuasion experiment, if a highly credible communicator states a position which is discrepant from the position of the recipient, the recipient experiences dissonance. He can reduce dissonance in one of four ways: (1) he can change his opinion to make it coincide with the communicator's, (2) he can attempt to change the communicator's opinion, (3) he can seek social support from other members of the audience, or (4) he can derogate the communicator. If one is interested in measuring opinion change (1), one can eliminate (2) and (3) by making it impossible for the subject to interact either with the communicator or his fellow subjects. Furthermore, one can reduce the subject's ability to derogate the communicator by assigning the latter high enough prestige so that he becomes virtually nonderogatable. Thus, if these four techniques exhaust the universe, the only way that a subject can reduce dissonance is by changing his attitude on the issue. The prudent experimenter will have built his experiment to make it appear reasonable to measure the subject's attitudes after the communication, and he will use the most sensitive measuring instrument he can construct.

Thus, if the question one asks is "Does dissonance occur in such a situation and does it get reduced?" the answer can be easily determined experimentally. But we may have a different question in mind: "In a given situation, how do people generally reduce dissonance?" And the answer to this question may be strikingly different from the mode found in the laboratory experiment. To illustrate, in the above example, most people might prefer to argue with the communicator rather than change their opinion.

The above argument suggests that the results from carefully controlled laboratory experiments, on occasion, may be somewhat misleading. For example, suppose a young Ph.D. is being considered for a teaching position in a major department at a prestigeous Ivy League university. What happens if the members of that department decide not to hire him? If he feels that he is a good and worthy scholar, he will experience cognitive dissonance: His cognition that he is a good scholar is dissonant with his cognition that he was rejected by members of a good department. Thus, he can reduce dissonance in at least two ways: (1) he can convince himself that his rejectors are, in reality, stupid, defensive, unprofessional, and/or senile people who cannot or will not recognize a good man when they see one; (2) he can convince himself that if they can reject him (as good as he is), then their standards must be astronomically high and therefore they are a fine group of nonsenile professionals. Both of these techniques succeed in reducing dissonance; moreover, they both protect the individual's ego — he leaves for his job at East Podunk State Teacher's College with the conviction that he is a good scholar. But note that the results of his dissonance-reducing behavior can leave him with totally opposite opinions about the members of the staff at the Ivy League university. Thus, if one wanted to arouse dissonance in an individual for the specific purpose of enhancing his impressions of the people at Ivy University, one had better be careful. The same dissonance-producing situation can result in quite the opposite dissonance-reducing behavior.

A. CONSISTENCY WITH OTHER EVENTS

This is a serious conceptual problem. One way that it can be solved is by coming up with a set of specific propositions that can lead one to state the conditions under which one mode or the other is more likely to occur. A possible solution was previously outlined in a specific situation (Aronson, 1961). The situation was one involving alternative modes of dissonance reduction following the unsuccessful expenditure of effort. If a person struggles to reach a goal and fails, he experiences dissonance. His cognition that he exerted effort to attain the goal is dissonant with his cognition that he did not reach it. He could reduce dissonance by convincing himself that the goal was not worth it anyway; recall that this was the way that Aesop's fox reduced dissonance in the fable of the sour grapes. There is another reasonable way to reduce dissonance: by the person's finding something else in the situation to which he can attach value in order to justify his expenditure of effort without achieving his avowed goal. Thus, the fox might convince himself that he got some much-needed exercise while leaping for the grapes, and that even though he failed to get those luscious, sweet grapes, it was worth the effort because of the muscles he developed while trying.

Under what conditions will an individual take one path rather than the other? The first solution (Aronson, 1961) is probably easier, but only in a situation where the effort expended is of short duration. However, if the situation consists of a long and repeated expenditure of effort, it becomes a less viable solution. To use the previous illustration, if the fox made a few leaps at the grapes and failed, he could convince himself that they were probably sour anway; but if he spent the entire afternoon struggling to reach the grapes, it would not effectively reduce dissonance to maintain that the grapes were sour—for if that were the case, why in the world did he try to reach them over and over and over again? The data from the above-mentioned experiment indicated that after the repeated expenditure of effort people *do* attach value to an incidental stimulus; however, the definitive factorial experiment remains to be done.

It is encouraging to note that experimenters are beginning to focus their efforts on this kind of problem. A good example of this trend is described in a very recent article by Walster *et al.* (1967), who hypothesize that individuals will choose that mode of dissonance reduction which is least likely to be challenged by future events. In their experiment, children were given their choice between two toys. In a situation like this, individuals can reduce dissonance in two ways: by cognitively increasing the attractiveness of the chosen alternative and/or by cognitively decreasing the attractiveness of the unchosen alternative. One-half of the children were led to expect that they would subsequently hear objective information about the toy they chose; one-half of the children were led to expect that they would hear objective information about the rejected toy. The investigators found, as predicted, that individuals reduced dissonance by distorting the attractiveness of that toy which they were not going to hear information about; that is, they opted to reduce dissonance in a manner which was less likely to run up against objective reality.

B. COMMITMENT AND VOLITION

In order to be of maximum use, such specific solutions should be restated into more general propositions, where possible, and incorporated into the theory. An important step in this direction was taken by Brehm and Cohen (1962) in emphasizing the importance of commitment and volition in determining not only the strength of the dissonance involved, but also, perhaps more important, in determining the nature of the dissonance and, hence, the nature of the mechanisms needed to reduce dissonance. Whether or not a high degree of volition is present can change the nature of the prediction even though both situations may involve cognitive dissonance. For example, in a minor part of their experiment, Aronson *et al.* (1963) reasoned that disagreement with a highly credible source produces more dissonance then disagreement with a source having low credibility. The cognition that a highly sentient person believes X is dissonant with the cognition that I believe *not X*. The higher the credibility of the source, the greater the dissonance — because the less sense it makes to be in disagreement with him. This should lead to greater attitude change in the Highly Credible condition — to reduce dissonance. The results of their experiment were consistent with this reasoning. On the other hand, Zimbardo (1960) and Brehm and Cohen (1962) reasoned that under certain conditions a source having low credibility would produce greater attitude change than one having high credibility. Specifically, if a person had chosen of his own volition to go to hear a speech by a low credibility source, he would experience a great deal of dissonance. The cognition involving volition and commitment is dissonant with the cognition that the credibility of the communicator is low; after all, it is absurd to choose to go out of one's way to hear a low prestige source make a speech which is discrepant with one's own opinion. In order to reduce dissonance, one might convince oneself that there was no essential discrepancy — that one always held the position espoused by the low credibility source. Thus, Zimbardo and Brehm and Cohen suggested that under conditions of high commitment one might get greater agreement with a low credibility source than with a high credibility source. This prediction made by Zimbardo and by Brehm and Cohen is consistent with other data involving choice and commitment. For example, Smith (1961) found that soldiers who volunteered to eat grasshoppers when induced by an unpleasant leader, came to like the grasshoppers better than did those who volunteered to eat them when induced by an affable leader. Similar results are reported by Zimbardo (1964a,b).

It should be clear that the prediction made by Aronson *et al.* and that made by Zimbardo and by Brehm and Cohen are not mutually exclusive; rather, they apply to a crucially different set of circumstances. Although both predictions are derived from dissonance theory, they involve different aspects of the theory; the crucial distinction is whether or not a high degree of volition is present. Nonetheless, to avoid confusion, these distinctions should be articulated with even greater clarity.

To sum up this section, dissonance theory, as originally stated, *does* have some areas of conceptual fuzziness. Much of this fuzziness can be eliminated by empirical research. Again, this research should be focused on the conditions and variables which maximize and minimize the occurrence of dissonance and dissonance reduction as well as the conditions which lead to one or another mode of dissonance reduction. This position will be elaborated upon in a moment.

VI. Dissonance Theory and Reward-Incentive Theory

A. NOT WHICH BUT WHEN

One of the intriguing aspects of dissonance theory is that it frequently leads to predictions which stand in apparent contradiction to those made by other theoretical approaches, most notably, to a general reward-incentive theory. The words "stand in apparent contradiction" were carefully chosen, for as we shall see, these theories are not mutually exclusive on a conceptual level. No advocate of dissonance theory would take issue with the fact that people frequently perform behaviors in order to obtain rewards or that activities associated with rewards tend to be repeated. What they would suggest is that under certain carefully prescribed conditions, cognitive events are set in motion which result in behaviors quite different from what one would expect from reward-incentive theories. Moreover, they might also suggest that such situations are not rare and, therefore, such behaviors are not flukey. Rather, they are quite common; one reason that they seem strange or "uncommonsensical" to us is that total reliance on other theoretical approaches (explicitly or implicitly) have blinded us to alternative possiblities or have made us disinclined to look beyond the obvious events generated by reward-reinforcement theories. The much discussed "nonobvious" predictions generated by dissonance theory are nonobvious only in an apparent sense; they become obvious and make sense once we gain an understanding of the dissonance-reducing process.

In the previous section, when discussing alternative ways of reducing dissonance, the author tried to make the point that it is not very fruitful to ask what the mode of dissonance reduction is; rather, it is far more meaningful and instructive to isolate the various modes of reducing dissonance and to ask what the optimum conditions are for each. Similarly, rather than ask whether dissonance theory or reward-incentive theory is the more valid, one should attempt to determine the optimal conditions for the occurrence of processes and behaviors predicted by each theory.

One example of this approach has already been discussed. Recall that in the Gerard and Mathewson (1966) conceptual replication of the Aronson-Mills (1959) experiment, they found that when dissonance was eliminated from the experimental situation (in the No Initiation condition) subjects tended to rate the group discussion as being less attractive if it followed severe electric shock. Recall also that this is opposite to the feelings of "successful accomplishment" interpretation proposed by Chapanis and Chapanis (1964); rather, it can be considered as consistent with a general reward theory; i.e., stimuli contiguous with severe shock are considered to be unattractive. Similar findings relevant to reward theory are reported by Aronson (1961).

Another example of this approach can be found in an experiment by Freedman (1963), who had subjects perform a dull task after first informing them that either (*a*) the data would definitely be of no value to the experimenter since his experiment was already complete, or (*b*) the data would be of *great* value to the experimenter. According to dissonance theory, performing a dull task is dissonant with the fact that it is not very valuable; in order to reduce dissonance, subjects should attempt to convince themselves that they actually enjoyed performing the task for its own sake. However, if the data are valuable, there is little dissonance, hence, little need to convince one's self that the task was enjoyable. Freedman's results confirmed his prediction: Subjects in the No-Value condition enjoyed the task to a greater extent than did subjects in the High-Value condition. In addition, he ran a parallel set of conditions except that he withheld information about how valuable the task performance was for the experimenter until *after* the subjects had completed the task. With this modification he found the opposite effect: Those who were told the task was valuable enjoyed it more than those who were told it was useless.

A moment's reflection should indicate that there is little or no dissonance in the above situation. No subject can have any reason to suspect that an experimenter is observing him for no reason at all. If the subject performed the task in good faith, he had no way of knowing his data would not be used by the experimenter; that is, experimenters do not generally collect data that they have no intention of using. Accordingly, the subject does not need to seek justification for performing the task—the fact that his performance turned out to be futile was nothing that he could have possibly foreseen. On the other hand, if, in advance, he had some reason for believing that his efforts might be futile (as in the previous condition), he *does* need additional justification—he must convince himself that he chose to do it for its own sake. The point stressed here is that where little or no dissonance exists, an incentive effect emerges: The more valuable the task, the "better" it is; the "better" it is, the more the subjects enjoyed doing it. This experiment clearly demonstrates that dissonance effects and incentive effects can exist side by side. Moreover, it helps define some of the limiting conditions of each.

In a similar vein, a recent experiment by Carlsmith *et al.* (1966) has taken us a long way toward an understanding of the conditions optimal for the emergence of incentive and dissonance phenomena following counter-attitudinal advocacy. According to dissonance theory, if a person says something he feels is untrue, he experiences dissonance: The cognition "I said X" is dissonant with the cognition "I believe not X." In order to reduce dissonance, he might attempt to convince himself that what he said was not so very untrue. Thus, dissonance theory suggests that advocating an opposite position increases one's tendency to believe in that position. However, if one is provided with a great deal of justification for advocating an opposite position (for example, if one is paid a great deal of money for telling a lie), one experiences less dissonance; that is, if I told a small lie for $53,000, I would have ample justification for having lied: The cognition that I received $53,000 is consonant with having lied. Consequently, I would have less need to justify my action by convincing myself that I really believed what I said than if I had been paid a mere 53¢ for lying. This general prediction has been confirmed by several experiments (e.g., Festinger and Carlsmith, 1959; Cohen, 1962; Nuttin, 1964; Lependorf, 1964), These experiments have shown greater attitude change for less reward across a wide range of topics; moreover, it has been confirmed across a wide range of rewards, from $20.00 (high) and $1.00 (low) in the Festinger-Carlsmith experiment, to 50¢ (high)[8] and 5¢ (low) in the Lependorf experiment. Thus, it would appear that this is a sturdy finding. On the other hand, there is some evidence that under certain conditions the opposite effect might emerge (Janis and Gilmore, 1965; Elms and Janis, 1965; Rosenberg, 1965).[9] Briefly, under certain conditions, offering a high incentive for advocating a given position may lead to a better performance, i.e., thinking up more and better arguments. This could lead to greater attitude change; i.e., a person changes his attitude *because* he has exposed himself to more arguments *because* he has looked harder *because* he was paid more money.

B. COMMITMENT AND COMPLEXITY

But what are these conditions? Or, better still, what conditions are optimum for the dissonance effect and what conditions are optimum for the incentive effect? The experiment by Carlsmith *et al.* (1966) provides

---

[8]"High" and "low" means, of course, relative to the other conditions; thus, 50¢ is high because it is higher than 5¢.

[9]For a more detailed critical analysis of all of these experiments, see Aronson (1966).

us with a solid clue. In their experiment subjects were put through a dull task and were then asked to describe the task as interesting. The dependent variable was the extent to which the subjects convinced themselves that the task really was interesting. The results showed a dissonance effect (the smaller the reward, the greater the opinion change) only under conditions where subjects lied to another person in a highly committing face-to-face situation. In other conditions, subjects wrote an essay, were assured complete anonymity, and were told that only bits and pieces of their argument would be used. Here an incentive effect emerged: The greater the reward, the greater the opinion change. In the early experiments (e.g., Festinger and Carlsmith, 1959) the importance of the face-to-face situation was not fully appreciated by the investigators because this variable was not systematically manipulated. In a recent analysis of this area (Aronson, 1966) it was suggested that the important distinction between the above conditions is "degree of commitment"; i.e., in the face-to-face situation the subject was saying things to a person which he himself believed were untrue. In our opinion, this situation involves much more commitment and, hence, arouses much more dissonance than the writing of an anonymous essay which the subject has been told would not be used in its original form.

At the same time, it should be noted that the complexity of the experimental operations employed by Carlsmith et al. (1966) allow for alternative explanations. One of the most serious of these alternative explanations is in terms of the complexity of the counter-attitudinal task involved. Rosenberg (1966) has argued that dissonance theory may be limited to situations where not much cognitive elaboration is required; he contended that where the task is more complex, incentive effects might occur. In analyzing the study by Carlsmith et al., Rosenberg made the reasonable point that writing an essay and telling a lie not only differ in degree of commitment but also may differ in the degree of cognitive complexity required. Consequently, this experiment cannot be taken as offering unambiguous support for our suggestion that degree of commitment is the decisive factor.

Two very recent experiments shed some additional light on this problem. In one, Linder et al. (1967) were careful to hold the complexity of the task constant. The task was a complex one in all conditions: College students were asked to write an essay favoring more stringent paternalistic supervision of students by the college administration. The experimenters varied (a) the degree of commitment (in terms of whether or not the subjects were allowed to feel that they had a clear choice as to whether or not to write the essay) and (b) the magnitude of monetary incentive for writing the essay. The results are quite clear: When commitment was high there was a dissonance effect; i.e., the smaller the incentive, the greater the opinion change. When commitment was relatively low there was an incentive effect. A different experiment (Helmreich and Collins, 1968) produced similar results. Here the task was also held constant, but instead of being complex (as in the study by Linder *et al.*) it was a simple one. Subjects were asked to record a statement which would be played to a large classroom of other students. In two relatively high commitment conditions the subject's simple statement was put on *video* tape along with his name, class, major, and hometown. In a low-commitment condition the subjects made statements anonymously on *audio* tape. The results paralleled those obtained by Linder *et al.* In the high-commitment conditions the smaller the incentive, the greater the opinion change (dissonance effect); in the low-commitment condition the greater the incentive, the greater the opinion change (incentive effect).

VII. The "Underlying Cognition" Problem

The importance of commitment emerges most clearly when we scrutinize the phenomenon of the white lie more thoroughly. Clearly, every time we say something that we do not believe, we do *not* experience dissonance. Under certain conditions there are some underlying cognitions which serve to prevent the occurrence of dissonance. For example, if we stated a counter-attitudinal position in the context of a formal debate, we would not experience dissonance (see Scott, 1957, 1959; Aronson, 1966). It is clearly understood both by the speaker and the audience that a debater's own personal views have nothing to do with the opinions he expresses. The rules of the game of debating are an underlying cognition which prevents the occurrence of dissonance. Similarly, as teachers we frequently get exposed to a great many stupid ideas from our students. Unless we know the student well—know that he is capable of better ideas and know that he is capable of "taking it"—most teachers refrain from tearing the idea to pieces. Instead, we tend to give the student our attention, nod and smile, and suggest that it is not such a bad idea. We do this because we have a general underlying cognition that we should not discourage students early in their careers and that it is wrong to be unkind to people who are relatively powerless to fight back. It would be ludicrous to suggest that teachers begin to believe that a student's poor idea is really a pretty good one simply because the teacher had said "pretty good idea" to the student. The underlying cognition prevents the occurrence of dissonance. But observe how commitment can make it a dissonant situation: If, on the basis of the teacher's statement, the student had decided to read his paper at an APA convention, the teacher might begin to convince himself that it was not such a bad idea—because the teacher has now been committed—he has misled the student into taking some action. This increases the teacher's commitment to the situation and is probably more powerful than the underlying consonant cognition "this is how we treat students." The teacher now seeks additional justification for having misled the student, perhaps by convincing himself that it was not such a bad idea after all.

The general point to be made here is an important one. Inconsistency is said to arise between two cognitive elements if "considering these two alone, the obverse of one element follows from the other" (Festinger, 1957, pp. 260–261). But we know that in most situations two cognitions are almost never taken by themselves. Occasionally, two cognitions, which in the abstract would appear to be dissonant, fail to arouse dissonance because of the existence of a "neutralizing" underlying cognition. For example, suppose I know a brilliant fellow who is married to an incredibly stupid woman. These cognitions are inconsistent but I would contend that they do not necessarily produce dissonance; i.e., I can tolerate this inconsistency—it does not cause me pain, it does not necessarily lead me to change my opinion about the brilliant fellow or his wife. I do not conclude that he is dumber than I thought or that she is smarter. Why? Because I have a general, underlying, pervasive cognition that there are a multitude of factors which determine mate selection—similarities of intelligence being only one of them. Moreover, I know that it is extremely rare for all of these to be matched in a marital relationship. Therefore, although taken by themselves, the above two cognitions are incompatible, I simply do not ever take them by themselves.

Festinger suggested that one way to reduce dissonance is to martial consonant cognitions; thus, he might say that the above reasoning is one way of reducing dissonance. But it is a moot yet important point whether I martialed the above cognitions as a result of the inconsistency, or whether I walked around with these cognitions about mate selection before the fact. If the latter is the case, then it can hardly be said that I dredged up this overriding cognition as a means of reducing dissonance. For example, let us look at the finding (Aronson and Carlsmith, 1963; Turner and Wright, 1965; Freedman, 1965) that children threatened with mild punishment for playing with a toy tend to derogate that toy after refraining from playing with it. Suppose that many children entered the situation with the strong feeling that adults must be obeyed always, even when commands are arbitrary and threats are nonexistent ("My mother, right or wrong!"). Put another way (which will become important in a moment), suppose that part of the self-concept of these children involved "obedience to adult authority." If this were the case there would have been no dissonance even though, *taken by itself,* the cognition "I like that toy" is dissonant with the cognition "I'm not playing with it." If this were *not* already a part of the person's self-concept, it might have become one as a function of the experiment; i.e., developing a belief in the importance of obedience is one way of reducing dissonance in the above situation. But if it were already there, there would have been no dissonance to begin with.

This added complexity should not lead us to throw up our hands in despair. Rather, it should lead us to a more careful analysis of the situations we are dealing with and perhaps even to a greater concern with individual differences.

VIII. The Importance of the Self-Concept and Other Expectancies

In discussing the difficulties involved in making precise predictions from dissonance theory in some situations, we have purposely tiptoed around the problem of individual differences. The fact that all people are not the same presents intriguing problems for dissonance theory as it does for all general motivational theories. Of course, one man's problem is another man's primary datum; i.e., psychologists who are interested in personality regard individual differences as being of great interest. For those who are primarily interested in establishing nomothetic laws, individual differences usually constitute nothing more than an annoying source of error variance. Nevertheless, whether or not we are interested in individual differences per se, an understanding of the way people differ in dissonant situations can be an important means of clarifying and strengthening the theory. Basically, there are three ways that individuals differ which should be of concern to people investigating dissonance theory:

(1) People differ in their ability to tolerate dissonance. It seems reasonable to assume that some people are simply better than others at shrugging off dissonance; i.e., it may take a greater *amount* of dissonance to bring about dissonance-reducing behavior in some people than in others.

(2) People probably differ in their preferred mode of dissonance reduction; e.g., some people may find it easier to derogate the source of a communication than to change their own opinion. Others may find the reverse resolution easier.

(3) What is dissonant for one person may be consonant for someone else; i.e., people may be so different that certain events are regarded as dissonant for some but not for others.

The first two possibilities are covered in depth elsewhere (see Abelson *et al.*, 1968). We shall not dwell on them here except to say that earlier in this article we underscored the difficulty of ascertaining the proper conditions for establishing whether or not dissonance exists for *most people* and the conditions for determining which mode of dissonance reduction *most people* will use; the existence of individual differences complicates matters further by adding another important dimension which should eventually be specified. The third case will be discussed here because it is of great relevance for the general theory. Furthermore, it is prior to the other two, for before one can determine whether (*a*) an individual is experiencing *enough* dissonance to reduce it or (*b*) *how* he will reduce it, we must first determine whether the events are indeed dissonant, consonant, or irrelevant to him.

Dissonant or consonant with what? Recall the earlier discussion wherein a rule of thumb based upon an expectancy was described (e.g., the Mr. Roy Wilkins of the NAACP and wife-beating novelist illustrations). Dissonance theory makes a clear prediction when a firm expectancy is involved as one of the cognitions in question. Thus, our cognition about Roy Wilkin's *behavior* can be dissonant with our expectancy about how he *will* behave. Dissonance theory is clearer still when that firm expectancy involves the individual's self-concept, for—almost by definition—our expectancies about our own behavior are firmer than our expectancies about the behavior of another person. Thus, at the very heart of dissonance theory, where it makes its clearest and neatest prediction, we are not dealing with any two cognitions; rather, we are usually dealing with the self-concept and cognitions about some behavior. If dissonance exists it is because the individual's behavior is inconsistent with his self-concept.

As we suggested several years ago (Aronson, 1960), this point has been elusive because almost all of the experiments testing dissonance theory have made predictions based upon the tacit assumption that people have a high self-concept. Why do people who buy new cars selectively expose themselves to advertisements about their own make of car (Ehrlich *et al.*, 1957) and try to convince themselves that they made the right choice? Because the knowledge that one has bought a junky car is dissonant with a high self-concept. But suppose a person had a low self-concept? Then the cognition that he bought a junky car would *not* be dissonant. Indeed, if the theory holds, such a person should engage in all kinds of "bizarre" behavior such as exposing himself to advertisements about other cars, hearing squeaks and rattles that are not even there, and saying, in effect, "Just my luck, I bought a lemon—these things are always happening to me." In short, if a person conceives of himself as a "schnook," he will expect to behave like a "schnook"; consequently, wise, reasonable, successful, "un-schnooky" behavior on his part should arouse dissonance. One of the advantages of this kind of statement is that it allows us to separate the effects of dissonance from other hedonic effects; that is, people with *high* self-concepts who fail *do* experience dissonance, but they experience many other negative feelings as well simply because failure is unpleasant. No one can deny that success brings pleasant consequences for people with high and low self-concepts alike; that is, regardless of a person's self-concept, successful achievement is often accompanied by such pleasant things as acclaim, money, fame, admiration, and popularity. But dissonance theory allows us to predict that for people with low self-concepts the "good feelings" aroused by the products of success will be tempered by the discomfort caused by dissonance – the dissonance between a low self-concept and cognitions about high performance. Several experiments have demonstrated that people who expect failure are somewhat discomforted by success (Aronson and Carlsmith, 1962; Cottrell, 1965; Brock *et al.*, 1965), but the data are by no means unequivocal (see Abelson *et al.*, 1968).

Thus, although we were not fully aware of it at the time, in the clearest experiments performed to test dissonance theory, the dissonance involved was between a self-concept and cognitions about a behavior that violated this self-concept. In the experiments on counter-attitudinal advocacy, for example, we maintain that it is incorrect to say that dissonance existed between the cognition "I believe the task is dull" and "I told someone that the task was interesting." This is not dissonant for a psychopathic liar – indeed, it is perfectly consonant. What is dissonant is the cognition "I am a decent, truthful human being" and the cognition "I have misled a person; I have conned him into believing something which just isn't true; he thinks that I really believe it and I cannot set him straight because I probably won't see him again." In the initiation experiment, in our opinion dissonance does not exist between the cognition "I worked hard to get into a group" and the cognition "The group is dull and stupid." Recall that for a "schnook" these cognitions are not at all dissonant. What is dissonant in this situation is the cognition "I am a reasonable and intelligent person" and the cognition "I have worked hard for nothing." Reasonable, intelligent people usually get a fair return for their investment – they usually do not buy a pig in a poke (unless there is some reasonably implicit guarantee, as in Freedman's [1963] experiment discussed above).

As an empirical refinement this self-concept notion is probably trivial. Experimenters have made the tacit assumption that people have high self-concepts – and these experimenters achieved positive results; this implies that the assumption is valid for most people in these situations.

But the self-concept notion may constitute a valuable and interesting *theoretical* refinement. A theory becomes infinitely more meaningful when its domain is clearly demarcated; i.e., when it states clearly where it does not apply. If it is the case that dissonance theory makes unequivocal predictions only when the self-concept or another strong expectancy is involved, then an important set of boundary conditions has been drawn. What we have described earlier as a rule of thumb may actually be a conceptual clarification.

It was stated early in this article that "at the center of the theory" predictions are unequivocal, but at the "fringes" they are somewhat fuzzy. At this point, we can assert that "at the center" means situations in which the self-concept or other firm expectancies are involved — and in which most people share the same self-concepts or other firm expectancies. Thus, most people have self-concepts about being truthful and honest so that we can make clear predictions intuitively, as in the Carlsmith *et al.* (1966) experiment. Most people have self-concepts involving making reasonable and wise decisions so that we can intuit clear predictions, as in the Brehm (1956) or Jecker (1964) experiments. Also, most people have firm expectancies about what Mr. Wilkins might say about Negro intelligence, so that a dissonance theory prediction makes sense and can be made clearly, even though a self-concept is not involved. The prediction about the great novelist who beats his wife gives the theory trouble precisely because people differ tremendously with regard to whether or not they expect a particular novelist to be a gentle and considerate man. In a specific instance, the knowledge of whether or not individual X has this expectancy would increase the accuracy of the prediction. In our opinion, this is of no great importance. What we consider important is the recognition of the fact that dissonance theory may be best suited for making general predictions in situations where expectancies are firm and nearly universal.

Several years ago, Zajonc (1960) raised a very interesting and reasonable question: If dissonance is bothersome, why do we enjoy magicians? That is, magicians can be thought of as people who arouse dissonance. Should we not experience pain and discomfort when we see rabbits pulled from hats, women sawed in half, or dimes turned into quarters? Perhaps the reason that we are not upset by magicians is because the behavior of a magician is consonant with our expectancy regarding magicians. That is, since we know in advance that a magician uses tricks and sleight-of-hand techniques to produce interesting illusions, why should we experience dissonance when we see him do these things? Is this not akin to the "schnook" who expects to purchase an inferior car?

Before the reader dismisses this as mere sophistry, it should be remarked that this is an empirical question. What is suggested is that we enjoy magicians *only* when they are billed as magicians. If they were not billed as magicians, they would cause quite a bit of discomfort. If the fellow sitting next to us at the bar suddenly "became" a fat woman, this would be very upsetting—unless the bartender had forewarned us that we were sitting next to a professional quick-change artist known as "Slippery Sam, the man of a thousand faces." If he then "became" a fat woman, we would be thrilled and delighted. It is interesting to note that the bartender could have produced a similar result if he had forewarned us that he had placed some LSD in our drink. In short, either being told a man is a magician or being told we were fed a halucinogen is consistent with seeing a man "become" a fat woman.

Empirically, this can be tested by finding some young children or some people from a different culture who have never seen or heard of magicians. Without the expectancy regarding magicians that Zajonc and the author share, these subjects might be quite upset by the goings on.

IX. Man Cannot Live by Consonance Alone

The implication of this article is that dissonant situations are ubiquitous and that man expends a great deal of time and energy attempting to reduce dissonance. It should be obvious that man does many other things as well. Festinger never intended dissonance theory to be imperial or monolithic. In 1957, he emphasized the fact that dissonance reduction is only one of many motives and can be counteracted by more powerful drives. We have already discussed how dissonance effects and reward-incentive effects can both occur in the same experimental design. Even more basic is the confrontation that occurs when consonance needs meet utility needs head-on. An extremely high drive to reduce dissonance would lead man to weave a cocoon about himself; he would never admit his mistakes and would distort reality to make it compatible with his behavior. But if a person is ever going to grow, improve, and avoid repeating the same errors, he must sooner or later learn to profit from past mistakes. One cannot profit from one's mistakes without first admitting that one has *made* a mistake. And yet, the admission of error almost always arouses some dissonance. The fact is, people frequently *do* profit from their mistakes; thus, people occasionally do not avoid or reduce dissonance.

To illustrate, if a man spends $50,000 for a home, dissonance theory would suggest that he may be the last to notice that during the rainy season there is water in the basement. Noticing water would arouse dissonance by making his purchase appear to have been a mistake. But to notice the water has great utility—for he must notice it in order to repair it, or at least to prepare for the flood. Moreover, if he does not take cognizance of his leaky basement he may walk into the same problem the next time he purchases a house. Thus, dissonance and utility are in constant tension by virtue of the fact that under certain conditions dissonant information may be extremely useful and, conversely, useful information can arouse dissonance. This phenomenon was discussed by Mills *et al.* (1959), who suggested that one reason why people frequently do not avoid dissonant information is that it often has great utility. In their experiment, they found that many subjects who had recently committed themselves to taking essay examinations as opposed to multiple-choice examinations opted to read articles explaining why essay examinations were more difficult, anxiety-provoking, etc. In this situation, apparently, the utility of the information was considered worth the price to be paid in dissonance. More recent experiments by Canon (1964) and Aronson and Ross (in preparation) have begun to indicate the requisite conditions for these effects. Precise predictions can be made by manipulating the strength of the opposing drive. As utility increases and dissonance becomes weaker, individuals begin to show a preference for dissonance-arousing but useful information. But as dissonance increases (i.e., immediately after a decision or when commitment is high, etc.), individuals tend to manifest dissonance-reducing behavior in spite of the fact that the future consequences of such behavior tend to be unpleasant.

X. Epilogue

The theory of cognitive dissonance is much more complicated than we thought it was some 10 years ago. A good deal of research has been done since then. Many of the problems which were specified earlier have been solved; many new problems have been unearthed, some of which remain to be solved. Hopefully, future research will lead to the emergence of still new problems, which will lead to still more research, which will continue to yield an increased understanding of human behavior. Perhaps this is what the scientific enterprise is all about.

In their critique of five years of dissonance theory, Chapanis and Chapanis (1964) concluded with the pronouncement "Not proven." Happily, after more than 10 years, it is still not proven; all the theory ever does is generate research.

REFERENCES

Abelson, R., Aronson, E., McGuire, W., Newcomb, T., Rosenberg, M., and Tannenbaum, P. (Eds.), *The cognitive consistency theories: a source book.* Chicago: Rand McNally, 1968.

Aronson, E. The cognitive and behavioral consequences of the confirmation and disconfirmation of expectancies. Proposal to the National Science Foundation, 48 pp., August, 1960.

Aronson, E. The effect of effort on the attractiveness of rewarded and unrewarded stimuli. *Journal of Abnormal and Social Psychology,* 1961, 63, 375-380.

Aronson, E. The psychology of insufficient justification: An analysis of some conflicting data. In S. Feldman (Ed.), *Cognitive consistency.* New York: Academic Press, 1966. Pp. 115-133.

Aronson, E., and Carlsmith, J. M. Performance expectancy as a determinant of actual performance. *Journal of Personality and Social Psychology,* 1962, 65, 178-182.

Aronson, E., and Carlsmith, J. M. Effect of the severity of threat on the devaluation of forbidden behavior. *Journal of Abnormal and Social Psychology,* 1963, 66, 584-588.

Aronson, E., and Carlsmith, J. M. Experimentation in social psychology. In G. Lindzey and E. Aronson (Eds.), *Handbook of social psychology.* (Rev. ed.), Vol. II. Reading, Mass.: Addison-Wesley, 1968.

Aronson, E., and Mills, J. The effect of severity of initiation on liking for a group. *Journal of Abnormal and Social Psychology,* 1959, 59, 177-181.

Aronson, E., and Ross, A. The effect of support and criticism on interpersonal attractiveness. In preparation.

Aronson, E., Turner, Judith, and Carlsmith, J. M. Communicator credibility and communication discrepancy as determinants of opinion change. *Journal of Abnormal and Social Psychology,* 1963, 67, 31-36.

Bem, D. J. An experimental analysis of self-persuasion. *Journal of Experimental Social Psychology,* 1965, 1, 199-218.

Bem, D. J. Self-perception: An alternative interpretation of cognitive dissonance phenomena. *Psychological Review,* 1967, 74, 183-200.

Brehm, J. W. Postdecision changes in the desirability of alternatives. *Journal of Abnormal and Social Psychology,* 1956, 52, 384-389.

Brehm, Mary L., Back, K. W., and Bogdonoff, M. D. A physiological effect of cognitive dissonance under stress and deprivation. *Journal of Abnormal and Social Psychology,* 1964, 69, 303-310.

Brehm, J. W., and Cohen, A. R. *Explorations in cognitive dissonance.* New York: Wiley, 1962.

Brock, T. C., Adelman, S. K., Edwards, D. C., and Schuck, J. R. Seven studies of performance expectancy as a determinant of actual performance. *Journal of Experimental Social Psychology,* 1965, 1, 295-310.

Canon, L. K. Self-confidence and selective exposure to information. In L. Festinger (Ed.) *Conflict, decision and dissonance.* Stanford University Press, 1964. Pp. 83-96.

Carlsmith, J. M., Collins, B. E., and Helmreich, R. L. Studies in forced compliance: I. The effect of pressure for compliance on attitude change produced by face-to-face role playing and anonymous essay writing. *Journal of Personality and Social Psychology,* 1966, 4, 1-3.

Chapanis, Natalia P., and Chapanis, A. Cognitive dissonance: Five years later. *Psychological Bulletin,* 1964, 61, 1-22.

Cohen, A. R. An experiment on small rewards for discrepant compliance and attitude change. In J. W. Brehm and A. R. Cohen, *Explorations in cognitive dissonance.* New York: Wiley, 1962. Pp. 73-78.

Collins, B. E. An experimental study of satisfaction, productivity, turnover, and comparison levels. Unpublished paper, Northwestern University, 1963.

Cottrell, N. B. Performance expectancy as a determinant of actual performance: A replication with a new design. *Journal of Personality and Social Psychology*, 1965, 2, 685-691.

Davidson, J. R., and Kiesler, Sara B. Cognitive behavior before and after decision. In L. Festinger ,Ed.., *Conflict, decision and dissonance*. Stanford University Press, 1964. Pp. 10-21.

Ehrlich, D., Guttman, I., Schonbach, P., and Mills, J. Post-decision exposure to relevant information. *Journal of Abnormal and Social Psychology*, 1957, 54, 98-102.

Elms, A. C., and Janis, I. L. Counter-norm attitudes induced by consonant versus dissonant conditions of role-playing. *Journal of Experimental Research in Personality*, 1965, 1, 50-60.

Festinger, L. *A theory of cognitive dissonance*. Evanston, Ill.: Row, Peterson, 1957.

Festinger, L. (Ed.), *Conflict, decision and dissonance*. Stanford University Press, 1964.

Festinger, L., and Aronson, E. The arousal and reduction of dissonance in social contexts. In D. Cartwright and A. Zander (Eds.), *Group dynamics: research and theory*. Evanston, Ill.: Row, Peterson, 1960. Pp. 214-231.

Festinger, L. and Bramel, D. The reactions of humans to cognitive dissonance. In Bachrach, A. J. (Ed.), *Experimental foundations of clinical psychology*. New York: Basic Books, 1962.

Festinger, L., and Carlsmith, J. M. Cognitive consequences of forced compliance. *Journal of Abnormal and Social Psychology*, 1959, 58, 203-210.

Festinger, L., and Freedman, J. L. Dissonance reduction and moral values. In P. Worchel and D. Byrne (Eds.), *Personality change*. New York: Wiley, 1964, Pp. 220-243.

Festinger, L., Riecken, H. W., and Schachter, S. *When prophecy fails*. Minneapolis: University of Minnesota Press, 1956.

Freedman, J. L. Attitudinal effects of inadequate justification. *Journal of Personality*, 1963, 31, 371-385.

Freedman, J. L. Long-term behavioral effects of cognitive dissonance. *Journal of Experimental Social Psychology*, 1965, 1, 145-155.

Gerard, H. B., and Mathewson, G. C. The effects of severity of initiation on liking for a group: A replication. *Journal of Experimental Social Psychology*, 1966, 2, 278-287.

Helmreich, R., and Collins, B. E. Studies in forced compliance: IV. Commitment and incentive magnitude as determinants of opinion change. *Journal of Personality and Social Psychology,* in press.

Janis, I. L., and Gilmore, J. B. The influence of incentive conditions on the success of role playing in modifying attitudes. *Journal of Personality and Social Psychology*, 1965, 1, 17-27.

Jecker, J. D. The cognitive effects of conflict and dissonance. In L. Festinger ,Ed.., *Conflict, decision and dissonance*. Stanford University Press, 1964.

Jones, R. A., Linder, D. E., Kiesler, C. A., Zanna, M., and Brehm, J. W. Internal states or external stimuli: Observers' attitude judgments and the dissonance theory-self-persuasion controversy. *Journal of Experimental Social Psychology*, 1968, in press.

Lawrence, D. H., and Festinger, L. *Deterrents and reinforcement*. Stanford University Press, 1962.

Lependorf, S. The effects of incentive value and expectancy on dissonance resulting from attitude-discrepant behavior and disconfirmation of expectancy. Unpublished doctoral dissertation, State University of New York at Buffalo, 1964.

Lewis, M. Some nondecremental effects of effort. *Journal of Comparative and Physiological Psychology*, 1964, 57, 367-372.

Linder, D. E., Cooper, J., and Jones, E. E. Decision freedom as a determinant of the role of incentive magnitude in attitude change. *Journal of Personality and Social Psychology,* 1967, **6**, 245-254.

McGuire, W. J. Attitudes and opinions. In P. R. Farnsworth, Olga McNemar, and Q. McNemar (Eds.), *Annual Review of Psychology,* 1966, **17**, 475-514.

Mills, J., Aronson, E., and Robinson, H. Selectivity in exposure to information. *Journal of Abnormal and Social Psychology,* 1959, **59**, 250-253.

Nuttin, J. M., Jr. Dissonant evidence about dissonance theory. For Second Conference of Experimental Social Psychologists in Europe, Frascati, 1964.

Rosenberg, M. J. When dissonance fails: On eliminating evaluation apprehension from attitude measurement. *Journal of Personality and Social Psychology,* 1965, **1**, 28-42.

Rosenberg, M. J. Some limits of dissonance: toward a differential view of counter-attitudinal performance. In S. Feldman ,Ed.., *Cognitive consistency.* New York: Academic Press, 1966. Pp. 135-170.

Scott, W. A. Attitude change through reward of verbal behavior. *Journal of Abnormal and Social Psychology,* 1957, **55**, 72-75.

Scott, W. A. Attitude change by response reinforcement: Replication and extension. *Sociometry,* 1959, **22**, 328-335.

Smith, E. E. The power of dissonance techniques to change attitudes. *Public Opinion Quarterly,* 1961, **25**, 626-639.

Turner, Elizabeth A., and Wright, J. C. Effects of severity of threat and perceived availability on the attractiveness of objects. *Journal of Personality and Social Psychology,* 1965, **2**, 128-132.

Walster, Elaine, Berscheid, Ellen, and Barclay, A. M. A determinant of preference among modes of dissonance reduction. *Journal of Personality and Social Psychology,* 1967, **7**, 211-216.

Zajonc, R. B. The concepts of balance, congruity, and dissonance. *Public Opinion Quarterly,* 1960, **24**, 280-286.

Zimbardo, P. G. Involvement and communication discrepancy as determinants of opinion conformity. *Journal of Abnormal and Social Psychology,* 1960, **60**, 86-94.

Zimbardo, P. G. A critical analysis of Smith's "grasshopper" experiment. Dept. Psychol., New York University. 13 pp., 1964. mimeo (a).

Zimbardo, P. G. A reply to Jordan's attack on dissonance theory. *Contemporary Psychology,* 1964, **9**, 332-333. (b).

Zimbardo, P. G. The effect of effort and improvisation on self-persuasion produced by role playing. *Journal of Experimental Social Psychology,* 1965, **1**, 103-120.

ATTITUDES AND ATTRACTION

Donn Byrne

DEPARTMENT OF PSYCHOLOGY
UNIVERSITY OF TEXAS
AUSTIN, TEXAS

When one attempts to describe even a relatively circumscribed area of psychological research, beliefs and biases operate in selecting and organizing the material to be presented. Because controversies centering on such beliefs and biases are common among personality and social psychologists at the present time, it will be useful to place this body of research in a somewhat broader context than is represented by the content itself. Specifically, the aim is to describe, in terms of historical antecedents and current developments, research on interpersonal attraction in relation to a philosophy of science.

The effect of the expression of attitude statements on subsequent affective responses directed toward the source of such statements constitutes both a problem of substantive research interest and, hopefully, a heuristic example of research in personality and social psychology.

I. The Antecedents of Current Research on Attitudes and Attraction

A. COMMON SENSE OBSERVATIONS

In describing the scientific commonalities which unite such areas as physics and psychology, Robert Oppenheimer (1956, p. 128) noted, "Both sciences, all sciences, arise as refinements, corrections, and adaptations of common sense." To say that science begins with common sense suggests that out of the complex and confusing swirl of events which make up everyday life, a regularity or lawfulness is observed and then generalized in a more abstract form. The survival of these generalizations is in part a function of their adequacy in increasing man's ability to predict and control his environment, although there are numerous examples of long-lived inaccuracies in folk wisdom. Nevertheless, if the same observation occurs in different cultures despite temporal, geographic, and linguistic variations, there is increased reason to suspect that a valid law may be involved.

The observation that an individual's stated attitudes influence the way in which others evaluate him, including the extent to which they like him, is an ancient and apparently obvious one. A few scattered examples should serve to underline this point.

In the fourth century before Christ, Aristotle (translated 1932, pp. 103-105) indicated a number of sources of friendship versus hatred, including similarity versus dissimilarity of attitudes:

> And they are friends who have come to regard the same things as good and the same things as evil, they who are friends of the same people, and they who are enemies of the same people . . .

> We like those who resemble us, and are engaged in the same pursuits . . . We like those who desire the same things as we, if the case is such that we and they can share the things together . . .

Approximately 2000 years later in seventeenth century Holland, Spinoza (translated 1951, p. 151), in describing the origin and nature of the emotions, proposed:

If we conceive that anyone loves, desires, or hates anything which we ourselves love, desire, or hate, we shall thereupon regard the thing in question with more steadfast love, etc. On the contrary, if we think that anyone shrinks from something that we love, we shall undergo vacillation of soul.

... it follows that everyone endeavors, as far as possible, to cause others to love what he himself loves, and to hate what he himself hates ...

Samuel Johnson (Boswell, 1791, p. 266) in eighteenth century England not only observed the same sort of relationship but also suggested an underlying reason for the accompanying affect:

... being angry with one who controverts an opinion which you value, is a necessary consequence of the uneasiness which you feel. Every man who attacks my belief, diminishes in some degree my confidence in it, and therefore makes me uneasy ...

In short, we are able to note the antiquity and the ubiquity of observations concerning attitudinal similarity and attraction. As suggested, however, objective verification procedures frequently serve to tarnish the shine of common sense observations and generalizations. That next step, the attempt to operationalize the variables and to conduct systematic observations, constitutes the beginning of a research interest in the phenomenon. For an example of that approach to the study of attraction, we turn to the end of the nineteenth and the beginning of the twentieth century.

B. VALIDATING AND QUANTIFYING THE OBSERVATIONS

In 1870, Sir Francis Galton touched on the problem of attraction and similarity in his investigation of "hereditary genius." He noted that at the time this work was first published, "... the human mind was popularly thought to act independently of natural laws ..." (p. vii), and his aim was to show that abilities were inherited in a lawful manner. Though he did not specifically discuss attitude variables, Galton (1870, p. 315) noted the marriage patterns of his group of eminent men and the 300 families which produced them:

... (the findings) establish the existence of a tendency of "like to like" among intellectual men and women, and make it most probable, that the marriages of illustrious men with (equivalent) women ... are very common. On the other hand, there is no evidence of a strongly marked antagonistic taste ...

Later quantification of these and other data by Karl Pearson led to a similar conclusion that the bulk of the observed resemblance between spouses "... is due to a direct, if quite unconscious, selection of like by like ..." (Pearson and Lee, 1903, p. 375).

The subsequent correlational studies of attraction and similarity of attitudes, opinions, beliefs, and values have essentially involved attempts to further determine the validity and to extend the generality of this formulation. With minor variations, these investigations have consisted of the identification of pairs of individuals who indicate mutual attraction (spouses, fiances, and sociometrically identified friends), an assessment of these individuals on one or more attitudinal measures, and a statistical determination of the pairs' similarity. Often, this similarity is evaluated not only in terms of departure from a theoretical base line of chance pairings but also by comparison with the similarity of random pairs or mutually antagonistic pairs from the same population. Over several decades in numerous samples on a wide variety of measures, the proposed relationship between attitude similarity and attraction has been consistently verified.

1. Husband—Wife Similarity

Initiating this kind of research, Schiller (1932) studied resemblances within 46 married couples on a series of measures including a public opinion questionnaire dealing with economic, racial, religious, industrial, and social matters. Husband—wife similarity was shown by a percentage of agreement of 72 and a correlation of .65. On a scale designed to measure religious attitudes, Kirkpatrick and Stone (1935) reported a husband—wife correlation of .56 among parents of University of Minnesota students. Similarly, Morgan and Remmers (1935) measured liberal—conservative attitudes in a small group of couples and found spouses' scores to correlate .38. Hunt (1935) constructed a scale to measure relative values with respect to characteristics such as cleanliness, courage, and obedience; subjects were asked to rank order these items in terms of importance. Individual husband—wife correlations were obtained for 62 married couples, and the median r was .48, while for 62 random pairs the median r was .25.

A somewhat more elaborate study was carried out by Schooley (1936). A sample of married couples in Pennsylvania responded to a series of tests including measures of intellectual ability, personality traits, and visual acuity. Of interest here is the use by Schooley of two Thurstone blanks measuring attitudes toward communism and birth control and also the Allport-Vernon Scale of Values. Table I shows the husband—wife correlations for these variables. The findings are consistent and

TABLE I
HUSBAND—WIFE CORRELATIONS
ON ATTITUDES AND VALUES[a]

Variable	r
Attitudes	
Communism	.60
Birth control	.58
Values	
Theoretical	.37
Economic	.25
Aesthetic	.23
Political	.45
Religious	.38

[a] After Schooley, (1936, p. 343).

clear (Schooley, 1936, p. 346): "Husbands and wives tend to marry persons similar to themselves in all of the characteristics measured by the present study."

In a study of intrafamily relationships in attitude, Newcomb and Svehla (1937) administered Thurstone scales dealing with attitudes toward church, war, and communism to members of over 500 families. The intraspouse similarities are shown by correlations of .76, .43, and .58 on the three topics. A smaller separate group of *young* husbands and wives yielded very similar coefficients ($r = .67, .53,$ and $.71$).

2. Similarity between Friends

The study of attitude similarity between pairs of friends has led to results parallel to those involving married couples. Winslow (1937, p. 433) suggested, "The bases for the establishment of the feeling of friendship between two persons are undoubtedly numerous. It may well be that an awareness of unanimity of opinion by two individuals fosters the establishment of friendship." To test this notion, he employed as attitude topics: the Negro, American foreign policy, current economic policy, religion, and the policies of the U.S. government. The items were combined in a questionnaire, and subjects responded to each on a 5-point scale ranging from strong agreement to strong opposition. The subjects were general psychology students at Brooklyn College; they responded to the questionnaire and also gave it to a friend of their own sex. When all of the items were scored in a liberal versus conservative direction, the opinions of the pairs were found to correlate .24. For specific topics, the coefficients ranged from .11 for economic issues to .44 on questions concerning Negroes. Winslow (1937, p. 441) concluded:

> The positive correlation found between friends' opinions, however, must indeed indicate that friends possess considerably more resemblance than could be expected by chance. But, of course, the question is not answered as to whether the similarity is produced by the influence of the opinion of one upon the other in the friendship pair, or is really the basis in the first place for the establishment of the friendship.

Richardson (1940) tested the similarity hypothesis by comparing the degree of resemblance between friends versus the similarity of random pairs of individuals on the Allport-Vernon scale. Richardson's subjects were drawn from a group of female students at the New Jersey College for Women and a separate group of adult women. The findings, shown in Table II, again tend to be positive.

The social visiting patterns and the political affiliations (Nazi, Socialist, Communist, etc.) of the residents of a German village were compared by Loomis (1946). To a significant extent, social visits tended to be among families of the same political persuasion.

The effect of similarity on a somewhat different type of relationship— subordinates and supervisors in an industrial setting—was reported by Triandis (1959). Subjects responded to questions about jobs and about people, and the similarity of the responses of subordinates and supervisors was determined. Similarity was significantly related to liking one's supervisor and to the effectiveness of communication within pairs.

In reviewing the husband—wife and friendship similarity studies conducted between 1928 and 1939, Richardson (1939) concluded that attitudinal traits yielded the most consistent positive results. That same

TABLE II

CORRELATION BETWEEN PAIRS OF FRIENDS
VERSUS RANDOM PAIRS ON VALUES[a]

Values	Undergraduate friends, 46 pairs	Adult friends, 22 pairs	Random undergraduates, 48 pairs	Random adults, 21 pairs
Theoretical	.21	.30	.06	−.33
Economic	.10	.36	−.06	−.13
Aesthetic	.26	.37	−.02	.02
Social	.15	.26	−.04	−.37
Political	.13	.01	−.18	−.09
Religious	.34	.45	−.08	−.21

[a] After Richardson (1940, p. 307).

conclusion still holds with only a scattering of negative results (Pintner, Forlano, and Freedman, 1937; Reilly, Commins, and Stefic, 1960; Vreeland and Corey, 1935). With respect to the types of topics which have been utilized in the various investigations, husbands and wives tend to resemble one another on a greater than chance basis, and pairs of friends show the same tendency toward similarity. When one considers that these investigators each employed only a small number of attitudinal measures and that attraction is undoubtedly multidetermined, the fact that positive results are reported with great frequency in these real-life studies is rather remarkable. It would appear that the basic notion of a relationship between attitude similarity and attraction was an accurate one. A frequently noted problem of interpretation, however, was the sequence of the similarity-attraction relationship. The answer to this question necessitated a longitudinal investigation in which attitudes were assessed prior to friendship formation.

C. THE SEQUENCE OF THE SIMILARITY-ATTRACTION RELATIONSHIP

The work of Newcomb (1961) represents the apex of the type of correlational study so far described and also perhaps a transition between an interest in "real-life" interaction and the controlled laboratory investigations.

For two different samples of male transfer students at the University of Michigan, Newcomb provided a rent-free semester in a cooperative housing unit in return for time spent each week serving as subjects. In each sample, the students were strangers to one another when they arrived on the campus, and Newcomb's interest centered on the intragroup relationships which subsequently formed.

Attraction was measured by means of a rank ordering of group members and by a 100-point rating scale concerning "favorableness of feeling" toward each of the other group members. Measures of attitudes dealt with a great many different issues in each sample, including attitude toward each of the other house members. Among the numerous findings were results indicating that attraction is associated with perceived agreement. In terms of actual agreement about other house members, the correlation within pairs changed from zero at the beginning of the semester to correlations of .50 and .56 for the two samples at the end of their respective semesters. With regard to nonperson attitudinal topics and also values, it was found that agreement *prior to* acquaintance was associated with attraction *after* acquaintance.[1] Agreement did not predict initial attraction

[1]Levinger and Breedlove (1966) point out that Newcomb's statistical evidence with respect to attitudes and values is much weaker than that dealing with other house members.

but, rather, attraction patterns formed later in the semester. Newcomb (1961, p. 85) concluded:

> This total set of findings, in support of our predictions, suggests (1) that agreement concerning attitudes which change very little during the acquaintance process becomes a significant determinant of attraction preferences; and (2) that high-attraction preferences ... change, from early to late acquaintance, in such manner that agreement concerning other House members also becomes a significant determinant of high pair attraction.

In a later reanalysis of the same data, Newcomb (1963, p. 385) added:

> As group members interact with one another, each of them selects and processes information—about objects of common interest, about one another as objects of attraction—in such ways that the inconsistencies and conflicts involved in imbalanced relationships tend to be avoided.

> ... the consequence of reciprocal adaptation is a mutual relationship that is in fact maximally satisfying to both or all of them—that is, maximally within the limits of what is possible.

D. EXTENDING THE SIMILARITY-ATTRACTION RELATIONSHIP

1. Similarity and the Success of the Relationship

Terman and Buttenwieser (1935a, 1935b) obtained data on happily married, unhappily married, and divorced couples with about 100 pairs in each category. The subjects were given a questionnaire dealing with various aspects of marriage along with the Strong Vocational Interest Blank and the Bernreuter Personality Inventory. On the marriage items with attitudinal components, the husband—wife correlations were substantial, for example, appraisal of the happiness of the marriage ($r = .65$) and desire for children ($r = .86$). Regardless of the happiness of the marriage, the interest scores of husbands and wives tended to be significantly related. The authors noted (Terman and Buttenwieser, 1935b, p. 268), "Despite the smallness of most of the correlations, the evidence points consistently to the conclusion that such selection as takes place in these traits is in the direction of 'like' rather than 'unlike' matings ..." There was also a determination of husband—wife correlations on each individual test item. This procedure yielded a large number of significant relationships, including many which differentiated the three groups of couples. A few selected examples are shown in Table III.

2. Assumed Similarity

To a group of married couples, Byrne and Blaylock (1963) administered Rokeach's Left Opinionation, Right Opinionation and Dogmatism

Scales (the latter scale may or may not be considered as an attitudinal measure). Each subject also filled out the scales as it was assumed that his or her spouse would do. In the findings shown in Table IV, the husband—wife similarity is significant for each of the three scales, but there is a significantly greater relationship between husband and wife in *assumed similarity* of political attitudes than in actual similarity. It was suggested (Byrne and Blaylock, 1963, p. 639):

> As predicted by Newcomb's model, distortion of the perceived attitudes of marital partners acts to bring about symmetrical relationships. For both sexes, there is a strong tendency to distort modest actual similarities in the direction of much greater congruence than is objectively present.

TABLE III
HUSBAND—WIFE CORRELATIONS ON SELECTED ITEMS OF THE STRONG VOCATIONAL INTEREST BLANK[a]

Item	Happily married	Unhappily married	Divorced
Playing bridge	.66	.53	.23
Amusement parks	.39	.19	.03
Picnics	.39	.20	.08
Musical comedy	.57	.52	.38
Symphony concerts	.45	.34	−.13
Teaching adults	.50	.08	−.23
Contributing to charity	.52	.16	.10
A collection of antique furniture	.44	−.02	.12
Conservative people	.38	.23	−.08
Teetotalers	.48	.41	−.17
Thomas A. Edison	.44	.03	.21
Book vs going to movies	.30	.19	−.08

[a] Data from Terman and Buttenwieser (1935b).

TABLE IV
ACTUAL SIMILARITY AND ASSUMED SIMILARITY OF POLITICAL ATTITUDES AMONG HUSBANDS AND WIVES[a]

Rokeach scale	Actual similarity	Assumed similarity by husbands	Assumed similarity by wives
Left opinionation	.30	.74	.79
Right opinionation	.44	.69	.89
Dogmatism	.31	.70	.85

[a] After Byrne and Blaylock (1963, p. 638).

In extending this work, Levinger and Breedlove (1966) corroborated the assumed similarity findings in a group of 60 married couples with respect to attitudes about family life. Again, although there was actual husband—wife similarity in attitudes, assumed similarity was significantly greater than actual similarity. In addition, the authors reported that the greater the assumed agreement, the greater the marital satisfaction.

II. Basic Research on the Attitude-Attraction Relationship

In attempting to communicate with others about experimental work on attraction, the author has slowly come to the realization that misunderstandings and confusions about research goals and research methods in personality and social psychology occur frequently. There are several issues involved when research interest moves from "real-life" studies closely tied to naturalistic observations (such as those just described) into laboratory research in which some variables are manipulated and others controlled. A brief digression here will hopefully serve to place attraction research in perspective.

A. PREPARADIGM VERSUS PARADIGM RESEARCH

In an incisive philosophical monograph, Thomas Kuhn (1962) stresses the contrast between normal science and scientific revolutions. Of relevance here is his description of normal science. He sees an essential step in science as the acquisition of a paradigm. By the term "paradigm" he means a specific body of research consisting of procedures, measuring devices, empirical laws, and a theoretical superstructure—all of which is accepted by a group of scientists.

For any field, there is a preparadigm period in which fact-gathering is a nearly random activity with diverse methodology, fragmentary theorizing, and a concern with available data which is close to everyday life observations. The outcome of such research is noncumulative; scientific knowledge simply does not progress by means of the collection of bits and pieces of stray data. The preparadigm period is ". . . a condition in which all members practice science but in which their gross product scarcely resembles science at all" (Kuhn, 1962, p. 100).

Upon the acquisition of a paradigm, however, a research area enters into the period of normal science. With agreements about procedures, operations, etc., scientific activity then is concentrated on attempts to increase the precision, reliability, and scope with which the facts are known, to test predictions from the paradigm theory within agreed-upon boundary conditions, and to conduct research designed to articulate and extend the paradigm theory. By delimiting and specifying the area of concentration, it becomes important to discover quantitative laws, determine physical constants, and to apply the paradigm to new areas.

Kuhn conceptualized paradigm research as analogous to fitting the bits of a puzzle together. Normal science does not aim for novel facts or novel theories. Novelty and surprises do arise, of course. In fact (Kuhn, 1962, p. 52):

> Without the special apparatus that is constructed mainly for anticipated functions, the results that lead ultimately to novelty could not occur. And even when the apparatus exists, novelty ordinarily emerges only for the man who, knowing *with precision* what he should expect, is able to recognize that something has gone wrong. Anomaly appears only against the background provided by the paradigm.

B. ACQUIRING A PARADIGM

Kuhn described psychology as a field in the preparadigm period. This characterization may be unfair to some areas such as learning, but it seems eminently correct with respect to areas such as personality and social. Not only have we not made much progress toward normal science, but also there clearly seem to be pressures against an interest in basic research. As Kantor noted in 1939, psychologists often seem to confuse societal goals with the way in which research should be conducted. There seem to be continual pronouncements that psychological research should concern itself with the real world, naturalistic settings, and application (e.g., Allport, 1966; Bordin, 1966; Katz, 1965; Sanford, 1965). In effect, we are asked to remain in the preparadigm stage, avoid basic research, and somehow achieve a viable technology in a manner unique in the history of science.

The work to be described in the following sections represents one attempt to conduct basic research on attitudes and attraction. It should be noted that the "paradigm" to be described falls far short of those paradigms which Kuhn discussed. From a historical viewpoint, he was examining primarily the clearly significant and highly successful paradigms which have characterized astronomy, physics, biology, and chemistry over the past few centuries. At the present time, we can only describe attempts to move beyond preparadigm research. For any given problem area, it is possible to point out a large number of possible candidates for paradigm. Though any given candidate may fail in a historical sense, it seems absolutely necessary for research activity to be conducted *as if* it represented an integral part of a well-established paradigm. "Without commitment to a paradigm, there could be no normal science" (Kuhn, 1962, p. 99).

With respect to the relationship between attitude similarity and attraction, what are the possible candidates?

1. Small-Group Research and Communication Theory

A familiar setting for research in social psychology is the small group. For example, Schachter (1951) used such a design to investigate the consequences of deviation by a group member from the attitudes or opinions of the remainder of the group. Basically, there were a series of small groups in which bogus members behaved in prearranged ways in order to create conditions of opinion similarity—dissimilarity. Attraction was measured by a sociometric rank ordering of group members. The general theoretical orientation was based on the work of Festinger and his colleagues (Festinger and Thibaut, 1951; Festinger, Gerard, Hymovitch, Kelley, and Raven, 1952). The results were generally as predicted. The stooge who was the opinion deviate was the most rejected across groups.

2. Pseudo-Groups and Affiliation Need

With a relatively similar approach to that of Schachter, Berkowitz and Howard (1959) utilized a group "discussion" in which messages were supposedly passed among members seated in separate cubicles. The messages received by each subject were fictitious, having been prepared by the experimenter in order to create bogus group members with opinions similar to and dissimilar from those of the subjects. Attraction was measured on a 9-point scale. Generally, depending in part on the level of the subject's affiliation need, the deviate was rated more negatively than other group members.

3. Tape-Recorded Strangers and Dissonance Theory

Worchel and McCormick (1963) introduced Festinger's cognitive dissonance concept to account for response to the threat of attitudinal discrepancy. It was proposed that self-ideal discrepancy was one of the determinants of mode of dissonance reduction. Subjects were each given a problem, asked to decide between two alternate solutions, and then listen to the solution chosen by another subject (a tape-recorded voice). Subjects rated the stranger on eight 5-point scales. It was found that a disagreeing stranger was rated more negatively than an agreeing one and that the low self-ideal discrepancy group showed the greatest reaction to agreement and disagreement.

4. Paper and Pencil Strangers and Balance Theory

A paper and pencil presentation of the stimulus person has been used by several investigators. Among the first was Smith (1957) who worked within Heider's theoretical framework. Subjects responded to the Allport-Vernon-Lindzey scale and later in the semester were given two partially completed scales attributed to other students. One scale was filled out exactly like the subject's and one contained dissimilar responses. The subjects were to complete the scales as the other students would have done and also were to respond in terms of a 5-point attraction scale. Both the attraction measure and the assumed similarity measure were different for the two strangers.

C. SELECTING AMONG POSSIBLE PARADIGMS

Perhaps it should be reemphasized that the ultimate utility of any paradigm cannot be determined on an *a priori* basis. There are a few considerations which might serve to influence one's choice — the uncontrolled stimulus variability inherent in the small group method, the measurement limitations of a rank order procedure, or the differential development of theory in various potential paradigms. Whatever the starting point, however, any program of basic research should lead to increased precision, improved measuring devices, and extended theory.

Another point, and one which is not terribly obvious, is the fact that whatever the general similarities among the experimental approaches just described, they are *not* part of the same paradigm. Even the Schachter and the Berkowitz-Howard research designs are only roughly parallel. They differ in terms of the nature of the stimulus presented to the subject, the amount of experimenter control over the stimulus, the topic about which opinions are elicited, and the way in which the dependent variable is measured. Because we have no agreed-upon paradigm and because the available data are limited, most of us pretend in writing journal articles that the findings of all such studies provide cumulative facts about the same problem. Thus, all reasonable-sounding measures of attraction are treated as interchangeable as are all reasonable-sounding operational definitions of similarity and dissimilarity. The fact is that the approaches cited above each represent *different* possible paradigms, both in theory and in method, and such differences will become manifest as the field progresses. A necessary, though hardly sufficient, condition for progress in research is consistency of operations across experiments. Different operations may or may not yield precisely the same results, but this is a matter for empirical determination.

In any event, we are able to conclude that the common sense observation about a relationship between attitudinal similarity and attraction is sufficiently accurate and sufficiently general and sufficiently powerful to hold across a variety of situations, both in everyday life and in the laboratory, and across a variety of operational definitions of the variables. Given a powerful and pervasive relationship, there is reasonable basis for suggesting that intensive research within a single paradigm could prove to be a valuable endeavor. It is to one such line of research that we now turn our attention.

III. A Possible Research Paradigm for the Study of Attitude Similarity – Dissimilarity and Attraction

The research to be described[2] represents the product of several years of work by the author, his students, and numerous colleagues. While the present form and scope of the research were by no means envisioned when the first studies were undertaken, at least three assumptions have remained unchanged from the beginning. First, a meaningful increase in knowledge is possible only if the same operations or empirically determined equivalents of those operations serve as connecting links across experiments. Second, theoretical constructs refer to the experimental variables and their extensions and derivatives rather than to the "real-life" variables from which these operational constructs originated. Third, as a matter of individual inclination, the initial theoretical model is broadly based on behavior theory and utilizes a stimulus – response language system. It is hoped that the seeming banality of the first two statements will be mitigated by the knowledge that such assumptions are not universally shared.

A. DEVISING A METHOD

The basic method was utilized first in an experimental investigation which initially represented simply a further demonstration of the effect of attitude similarity – dissimilarity on attraction (Byrne, 1961).

1. Procedure

It was decided to use a variant of the Smith (1957) approach. Subjects were told that they were taking part in a study of interpersonal judgment in which they would be given certain information about another individual and then asked to make several judgments concerning him. With minor modifications, the same instructions have been used in the subsequent studies.

---

[2]In the presentation to follow, there will necessarily be some alteration of the chronological order and of the description of specific investigations for the sake of clarity. Irrelevant portions of an experiment are often omitted entirely, and different aspects of the same investigation may be reported in separate sections.

College undergraduates were given a 26-item attitude scale early in the semester and then were assigned to one of two experimental groups. For each of the subjects in the Similar Attitude group, an attitude scale was filled out in such a way that the "stranger" responded to all 26 of the issues exactly as the subject had done. In the Dissimilar Attitude group, each subject received a scale which was a mirror image of his own. For example, if the subject were strongly against integration and mildly in favor of smoking, the stranger was strongly in favor of integration and mildly against smoking. These bogus scales were filled out in a variety of styles (left- and right-handed check marks, X's, large and small writing style, etc.) and in a variety of colors in several writing media (fountain pen, ball-point pen, pencil, etc.). The background information at the top of the first page was cut out with a pair of scissors, purportedly to preserve the anonymity of the student who had filled out the scale.

2. The Attitude Scale

On the basis of the numerous studies which had been carried out earlier, it was assumed that the specific content of the attitudes, beliefs, opinions, and values was not a crucial factor. In a pilot study, another group of undergraduates had been asked to list a number of issues about which they and their acquaintances ever engaged in discussions. Of the topics given, the 26 most frequently mentioned were converted into simple scales of the following type[3]:

5. Belief in God (check one)
   _____I strongly believe that there is a God.
   _____I believe that there is a God.
   _____I feel that perhaps there is a God.
   _____I feel that perhaps there is no God.
   _____I believe that there is no God.
   _____I strongly believe that there is no God.
23. Political Parties (check one)
   _____I am a strong supporter of the Democratic party.
   _____I prefer the Democratic party.
   _____I have a slight preference for the Democratic party.
   _____I have a slight preference for the Republican party.
   _____I prefer the Republican party.
   _____I am a strong supporter of the Republican party.

3. The Attraction Measure

The measure of attraction consisted of two simple rating scales which essentially asked the two rather straightforward questions most fre-

---

[3]In the initial study, these were 7-point scales, but in the subsequent work 6-point scales were used.

quently utilized in sociometric research. With respect to the stranger, each subject was asked to indicate whether he felt that he would like or dislike this person and whether he believed he would enjoy or dislike working with this person. These two variables are each measured on a 7-point scale. They are scored from 1 to 7 and then summed to constitute the measure of attraction which ranges from 2 (most negative) to 14 (most positive). Conceptualized as a 2-item response measure, this attraction score has been found to have a split-half reliability of .85 (Byrne and Nelson, 1965a).

In order to disguise to some degree the major purpose of the experiment and to lend credence to the instructions concerning interpersonal judgment, the two attraction scales were embedded as the last two items in a 6-point Interpersonal Judgment Scale (IJS) (Byrne, 1966, pp. 41–43). The first four items called for evaluations of the stranger's intelligence, knowledge of current events, morality, and adjustment.

4. Results

The mean attraction response of the Similar Attitude group was 13.00 while that of the Dissimilar Attitude group was 4.41. A t test indicates this difference to be a highly significant one ($p < .001$). In fact, the most negative response in the Similar Attitude group was more positive than the most positive response in the Dissimilar Attitude group; the stimulus variable was sufficiently potent that there was no response overlap between the two conditions. As a subsidiary finding, it might be noted that equally significant group differences were found on the four evaluative scales. Dissimilar strangers were rated as less intelligent, less knowledgable about current events, less moral, and less well adjusted than similar strangers.

The next research step was to attempt an analysis of the stimulus–response relationship thus established. One might say that the task was to specify more precisely the stimulus to which subjects are responding.

B. DEVIANCY VERSUS DISSIMILARITY

As is usually the case, even a seemingly clear-cut finding such as the foregoing may be seen to raise a number of questions.

1. Problem

In the previous investigation, one of the two stimulus conditions was labeled "dissimilar attitudes." Because of a methodological problem, however, this label remained open to question. It was found that the experimental subjects were relatively homogeneous with respect to a large proportion of the attitude items. For example, almost all of the subjects indicated that they believed in God, liked sports, and enjoyed science fiction. Since the majority of the items were answered with this type of uniformity, the resulting bogus stranger necessarily raised interpretational ambiguities. A similar stranger not only agreed with the subject but also appeared to be a normal, average, conforming member of this undergraduate culture. A dissimilar stranger not only disgreed with the subject but also could be seen as an abnormal individual whose viewpoint was extremely deviant in this culture. Thus, the stimulus for the attraction responses could have been similarity — dissimilarity, conformity — deviancy, or some combination of these variables.

In order to identify the stimulus more explicitly, another investigation (Byrne, 1962) was undertaken in which the attitudinal items elicited heterogeneous responses. On the basis of the responses of earlier subjects, the 7 items of the 26-item scale on which there was the greatest diversity of opinion were arranged in a 7-item attitude scale. Now, a stranger could be made to express attitudes similar to or dissimilar from those of the subject without at the same time expressing either conforming or deviant beliefs. The specific topics were undergraduates getting married, smoking, integration in public schools, drinking, money as a goal, the university grading system, and political parties.

Another purpose of this investigation was to explore for the first time the functional relationship between similarity — dissimilarity and attraction. In the various experimental investigations cited earlier, a factorial approach had been the rule. There is an attempt to create similarity (as in the 26 similar, 0 dissimilar condition) and dissimilarity (as in the 0 similar, 26 dissimilar condition). It is then assumed that these two conditions represent points along a stimulus continuum and that intermediate points would yield intermediate responses. With the 7-item attitude scale, it was feasible to present subjects with each possible variation in the similar and dissimilar attitudes expressed by a stranger.

2. Procedure

The over-all procedure followed that of the initial experiment. Each of 112 students was given the attitude scale and later presented with a scale supposedly filled out by a stranger to be evaluated on the IJS.

With respect to the bogus scales, the subjects were assigned to one of eight experimental groups. Those in the first were given a stranger who was similar to themselves on all seven issues (7 — 0). The next group received a stranger similar on six issues and dissimilar on one (6 — 1); the particular item which was dissimilar was varied randomly among the subjects in that condition. Each subsequent group, then, differed in the number of similar and dissimilar items on through the eighth group in which there was dissimilarity on all topics (0 — 7).

3. Results

The mean attraction responses of the eight experimental groups are shown in Table V. Once again the experimental treatment was found to have a significant ($p < .001$) effect on attraction. It is also clear that the stimulus to which subjects respond may reasonably be labeled "similarity — dissimilarity" and that a functional stimulus — response relationship may be described. Rather than simply affirming that similarity and dissimilarity elicit different attraction responses, it is now possible to conceptualize the relationship as a continuous one in which the specific response to the given set of attitudes may be predicted if the subject's own responses to these 7 items are known. Also, this sample yields a stimulus — response correlation of .64 ($p < .001$) which indicates that almost 41% of the variance of the attraction responses is attributable to attitude similarity — dissimilarity.

There are, nevertheless, still ambiguities concerning the stimulus.

C. PROPORTION OF SIMILAR ATTITUDES

1. Problem

In the investigation just described, the eight experimental conditions in which attitude similarity — dissimilarity was varied could be conceptualized as representing three different stimulus variables: number of similar attitudes, number of dissimilar attitudes, and the relationship between these two expressed as a ratio or a proportion. Each of these three stimuli varied across the experimental conditions, and the attraction responses could conceivably have been elicited by any one of them or any combination. This problem was resolved experimentally (Byrne and Nelson, 1965a).

TABLE V

FUNCTIONAL RELATIONSHIP BETWEEN
ATTITUDE SIMILARITY — DISSIMILARITY AND ATTRACTION

Experimental condition	Mean attraction response
7 Similar, 0 Dissimilar	12.15
6 Similar, 1 Dissimilar	11.15
5 Similar, 2 Dissimilar	11.43
4 Similar, 3 Dissimilar	9.07
3 Similar, 4 Dissimilar	8.69
2 Similar, 5 Dissimilar	8.47
1 Similar, 6 Dissimilar	7.71
0 Similar, 7 Dissimilar	7.00

TABLE VI

EXPERIMENTAL DESIGN: NUMBER OF ITEMS
ON WHICH THE STRANGER HELD SIMILAR–DISSIMILAR ATTITUDES[a]

Proportion of similar attitudes	Number of similar attitudes		
	4	8	16
1.00	4/0	8/0	16/0
.67	4/2	8/4	16/8
.50	4/4	8/8	16/16
.33	4/8	8/16	16/32

[a] After Byrne and Nelson (1965a, p. 660).

2. Procedure

It was necessary to provide an experimental design in which number of similar and dissimilar attitudes as well as the ratio between them could each vary independently. To do this, a series of attitude scales of different lengths was constructed. The 26 items already discussed plus additional items of similar format were scaled for importance (as will be described later). Then, eight scales of different length (4 to 48 items) were built and matched with respect to the importance of the topics and also the homogeneity–heterogeneity of response to them.

Each of 168 students filled out one of these attitude scales and went through the standard experimental procedure. Stranger similarity–dissimilarity was manipulated according to the scheme depicted in Table VI. It may be seen that if significant attraction differences were found across columns, they would be attributable to the number of similar attitudes. Significant row differences would be attributable to the proportion variable. If number of dissimilar attitudes were the crucial stimulus, there would be significant column differences, significant row differences, and most importantly a significant interaction.

3. Results

The means for these various conditions are shown in Table VII. Both an inspection of the data in Table VII and the analysis of variance indicate that the only significant effect ($p < .001$) is that of the proportion variable. Thus, we have a still clearer conception of the stimulus.

At this point in our research effort, it also became possible to describe the stimulus–response relationship with increased precision (Byrne and Nelson, 1965a). With the stimulus identified as proportion of similar attitudes, data from a variety of our investigations could be meaningfully combined even though attitude scales of various lengths had been

TABLE VII
MEANS OF ATTRACTION SCORES TOWARD STRANGERS
WITH VARYING NUMBERS AND VARYING PROPORTIONS
OF SIMILAR ATTITUDES[a]

Proportion of similar attitudes	Number of similar attitudes			
	4	8	16	Total
1.00	11.14	12.79	10.93	11.62
.67	10.79	9.36	9.50	9.88
.50	9.36	9.57	7.93	8.95
.33	8.14	6.64	6.57	7.12
Total	9.86	9.59	8.73	

[a] After Byrne and Nelson (1965a, p. 660).

used. A total of 790 subjects had each been exposed to 1 of 11 proportions of similar attitude attributed to a stranger and then had evaluated that stranger on the IJS. Plotting the relationship, as shown in Fig. 1, the mean attraction scores for the 11 stimulus values suggested linearity. A straight-line function was fitted to the data by the least-squares method, yielding the formula $Y = 5.44X + 6.62$. At this point, then, the relationship between attitudinal similarity — dissimilarity and attraction could be stated in terms of an empirical law, a law which enables us to predict specific attraction responses within this type of experimental situation.

D. RESPONSE DISCREPANCY ON THE ATTITUDE SCALE

1. Problem

With the attitudinal material utilized in this paradigm, the definition of "similar" and "dissimilar" responses by a stranger can be specified in more than one way. Each item consists of a 6-point scale with 3 points representing varying strengths of opinion in one direction (e.g., pro-Republican) and 3 points representing varying strengths of opinion in the other direction (e.g., pro-Democrat). Similarity has been defined as any response on the same side of the neutral point as the subject's response and dissimilarity as any response on the opposite side of the neutral point. In constructing a scale for a bogus stranger, several patterns of faking have been used. The differences can perhaps best be visualized by means of the information in Table VIII.

As shown in the table, the original faking pattern (Identity-Mirror) was one in which a stranger responded to each item exactly as the subject did or in exactly the opposite way. The major reasons for switching to the

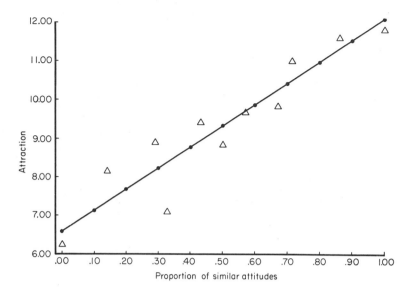

Fig. 1. Attraction toward a stranger as a linear function of proportion of similar attitudes; $Y = 5.44 X + 6.62$. (After Byrne and Nelson, 1965, p. 661.)

TABLE VIII
DIFFERENT FAKING PATTERNS FOR SIMILAR AND
DISSIMILAR ITEM RESPONSES BY BOGUS STRANGER

Subject's response	Identity-mirror		Moderate discrepancy		Constant discrepancy	
	Similar	Dissimilar	Similar	Dissimilar	Similar	Dissimilar
1	1	6	2	5	2	4
2	2	5	3	4	1 or 3	5
3	3	4	2	5	2	6
4	4	3	5	2	5	1
5	5	2	4	3	4 or 6	2
6	6	1	5	2	5	3

Moderate Discrepancy pattern in subsequent research were an attempt to
disguise further the relationship between the subject's own responses and
those of the stranger and also to avoid the possible effects of extreme responses by a stranger (the 1 and 6 points were never used). Nelson (1965)
pointed out that one result of using this pattern was that a dissimilar response varied from 2 to 4 scale points discrepancy from that of the subject
while a similar response was always 1 scale point away. With the Identity-
Mirror pattern, similarity equals 0 discrepancy while dissimilarity varies

from 1 to 5. Nelson investigated the possible effects of this differential discrepancy in his dissertation research.

2. Method

Nelson employed a 12-item attitude scale, and followed the standard procedures of the attraction studies. In the experiment, each subject was asked to respond to a stranger who was either similar (1.00 agreement) or dissimilar (.00 agreement) on all 12 items. Within each similarity group, there was a manipulation of response discrepancy (small or large).

3. Results

The means of the attraction scores are shown in Table IX. As may be seen, subjects apparently are responsive to discrepancy as well as to similarity — dissimilarity. Analysis of variance confirmed the significance of the effects of each variable. Thus, ". . . a simple agree-disagree dichotomy does not account for all the variance in attraction. . . " (Nelson, 1965, p. 35).

Methodologically, this finding has led to the adoption of the Constant Discrepancy faking pattern shown in Table VIII which eliminates discrepancy differences among similar items and among dissimilar items. Conceptually, it suggests that proportion of similar attitudes and discrepancy constitute two related but partially independent stimulus dimensions. Subsequent research (Byrne, Clore, and Griffitt, 1967) has confirmed this proposition. Subjects apparently respond to extremely small degrees of discrepancy between themselves and strangers *in addition to* the more gross variable of agreement versus disagreement.

IV. The Generality of the Similarity-Attraction Relationship

Before discussing in any detail the theoretical formulation which has been proposed to account for the relationship between similarity and at-

TABLE IX

MEANS OF ATTRACTION SCORES TOWARD
SIMILAR AND DISSIMILAR STRANGERS WITH LARGE
AND SMALL RESPONSE DISCREPANCY[a]

Similarity	Small discrepancy	Large discrepancy
1.00	11.50	10.10
.00	8.05	6.45

[a] Data from Nelson (1965).

traction, several different aspects of the generality of this function will be indicated briefly.

A. TOPIC IMPORTANCE

A frequently discussed parameter of the attitude-attraction literature has been the importance of the topic about which individuals agree and disagree. For example, Newcomb (1956, p. 578) proposed that "The discovery of agreement between oneself and a new acquaintance regarding some matter of only casual interest will probably be less rewarding than the discovery of agreement concerning one's own pet prejudices." As a consequence of this assumption, Newcomb's (1961) index of agreement between two individuals is limited to topics of importance to both.

In the present paradigm, attitude items were deliberately selected to represent varying degrees of importance, and the possible effects of this variable have been controlled via randomization. Two investigations (Byrne and Nelson, 1964, 1965b) were undertaken specifically to determine the effects of topic importance.

In a preliminary study, importance ratings were obtained for 56 attitude items. On the basis of these ratings, the items were divided into four 14-item scales varying from the 14 least important (e.g., gardening, modern art) to the 14 most important topics (e.g., God, American Way of Life). In the first study, each of 112 subjects responded to one of these scales and then later was asked to respond to a stranger who had filled out the same scale. There was either 1.00 or .00 similarity between subject and stranger on topics at one to four levels of importance. It was once again found that proportion of similar attitudes had a significant effect on attraction ($p < .001$), but neither topic importance nor the interaction between importance and similarity even approached significance.

It seemed possible that one reason for that finding was that subjects had not been exposed to the entire range of topic importance and hence were showing an adaptation level effect. The second investigation sought to eliminate this problem by having each of 40 undergraduates respond to all four 14-item scales and later evaluate four strangers. All four strangers were either 1.00 or .00 similar, but each stranger had responded to only one 14-item scale and thus agreed or disagreed on only one of the topic importance levels. Order of presentation was systematically varied across subjects. Again, however, only proportion of similar attitudes had a significant effect on attraction ($p < .001$) while no other variable approached significance.

In two recent experiments (Byrne, London, and Griffitt, 1968; Clore and Baldridge, 1968) it was found that *if* a stranger expresses opinions on items heterogeneous in importance and *if* the similarity level is at an intermediate point between .00 and 1.00, then items of differential importance affect attraction differentially. Thus, the importance of attitudinal topics is a relevant variable only under quite specific conditions.

B. STIMULUS MODES

The research described here has employed a very specific stimulus condition for the presentation of the attitudes attributed to a stranger. Nevertheless, if we have correctly identified the crucial aspects of the attitudinal stimuli, it should not matter whether the attitudes are expressed on a mimeographed scale, on a tape recording, on the sound tract of a movie, or in a face-to-face interaction.

This type of generality was tested by Byrne and Clore (1966). One hundred and twenty students were asked to fill out a 12-item attitude scale, and immediately afterward were exposed to a same-sex stranger. One-third of the subjects read the stranger's responses on an attitude scale, one-third listened to a recording of the stranger's responses, and one-third viewed an 8 mm color, sound movie of the stranger giving his or her opinions. In each condition there was a male and a female stranger, each of whom had responded with both a standard A and B pattern of responses. Each subject responded to only one stranger in one stimulus condition.

The similarity between any given subject and the stranger to whom he was exposed could vary from .00 to 1.00 similarity. Subjects were divided approximately evenly into four groups in terms of the similarity dimension. As usual, attitude similarity was found to affect attraction ($p < .001$), but the three stimulus modes did not differ nor was there an interaction effect.

Data for all 120 subjects were combined, and the attraction responses were plotted as a function of proportion of similar attitudes expressed by the stranger. The least-squares method yielded a straight-line function with the formula $Y = 6.74X + 5.06$, as shown in Fig. 2. The linear relationship between similarity of attitudes and attraction was found to hold across quite divergent stimulus conditions.

The possible effects of one other stimulus mode, face-to-face interaction with a stranger, were investigated by McWhirter and Jecker (1967) with a group of 48 undergraduates. Each subject first filled out a 7-item attitude scale. For half of the subjects, the experimenter prepared a bogus attitude scale on which the stranger agreed with the subject on 2, 4, or 6 of the items. For the other half, another student served as a stooge. The subject and stooge each read his attitude responses

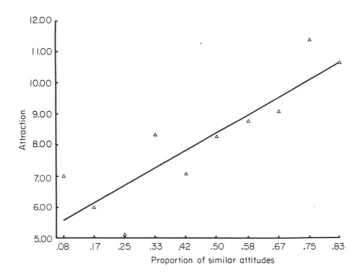

Fig. 2. Attraction toward a stranger as a linear function of proportion of similar attitudes with movie, tape recording, and mimeograph conditions combined; $Y = 6.74\,X + 5.06$. (After Byrne and Clore, 1966, p. 240.)

aloud; the subject responded first and the stooge then gave similar responses on 2, 4, or 6 of the items. Afterward, all subjects filled out a questionnaire which contained the two attraction items from the IJS. It was found that attraction was significantly influenced by number of agreements but not by the stimulus mode.

C. Populations

It is a truism that psychologists are building laws of behavior based on investigations of the college sophomore and the laboratory rat. With respect to the type of empirical law established in the attraction investigations, one could make a convincing argument that the findings are largely attributable to the nature of the subjects — relatively bright, well-educated, middle-class, late adolescents. If these findings were, in fact, limited to this rather special group, they would be of less interest than if they were applicable to a broader segment of the population.

1. Female Clerical Workers

As part of a larger study, Krauss (1966) administered a 20-item attitude scale to 160 female clerical employees of the Bell Telephone Laboratories. Shortly afterward, each subject received a scale supposedly filled out by a fellow worker. The bogus scales conformed to either a 17 — 3 or a

3 – 17 similar – dissimilar pattern. Utilizing the method described here, Krauss then asked each subject to evaluate the other individual on the IJS.

Though mean attraction responses were not reported, analysis of variance indicated attraction differences significant at well beyond the .001 level. It might be noted that these office workers also responded differentially to similar and dissimilar partners on the other items of the IJS.

2. Children

Another test of the generality of the attraction findings was provided by Byrne and Griffitt (1966a) with children who differed from college undergraduates in age, intelligence, educational level, and socioeconomic status.

The subjects were 272 primary and secondary public school children of both sexes in grades 4 through 12 inclusively. Their ages ranged from 9 to 20. Each subject filled out an 8-item attitude scale. For the fourth to ninth graders the topics included summer camp, trips with parents, and comic books. For the older subjects, the topics included strict rules, studying, and racial integration. Immediately afterward, the subjects were given the standard instructions and then asked to read the scale of someone "in the same grade and of the same sex" as themselves. The IJS was modified slightly for reasons of vocabulary. Half of the "strangers" had one random pattern of opinions, and half had the reverse of these opinions.

The subjects were divided into two levels on the basis of age and three levels on the basis of attitude similarity; the mean attraction respon-

TABLE X

MEANS OF ATTRACTION SCORES OF SUBJECTS
REPRESENTING TWO AGE LEVELS TOWARD STRANGERS
DIFFERING IN PROPORTION OF SIMILAR ATTITUDES[a]

Age level	Proportion of similar attitudes			
	Low .12 – .38	Medium .50	High .62 – .88	Total
Older:				
Grades 8 – 12	6.80	7.90	9.29	8.07
Younger:				
Grades 4 – 8	8.39	8.76	10.06	9.12
Total	7.60	8.33	9.68	

[a] After Byrne and Griffitt (1966a, p. 700).

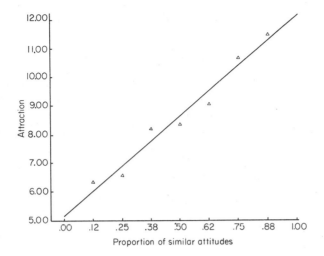

Fig. 3.   Attraction toward a stranger as a linear function of proportion of similar attitudes among elementary and secondary school students in grades 4 through 12; $Y = 7.03$
$X + 5.16$. (After Byrne and Griffitt, 1966a, p. 701.)

ses are shown in Table X. Analysis of variance indicated a highly significant effect for attitude similarity and also for age (the younger children
gave more positive responses). Nevertheless, both age groups responded
to the similarity variable in the same linear fashion.

In addition, two goodness of fit analyses were carried out, and the
responses of each age group were compared to the responses predicted by
the Byrne-Clore formula derived in a college population. In neither group
did the obtained responses differ significantly from the predicted responses. Also, as shown in Fig. 3, a straight-line function fitted to these data
yields constants very similar to those reported for college undergraduates.
Therefore, not only is the shape of the function the same, but the *specific
attraction responses made by the children* are predictable on the basis of a
formula derived in a sample of college students.

3.   Job Corpsmen

In a study recently completed, Byrne, Griffitt, Hudgins, and Reeves
(in press) were able to carry out the attitude-attraction procedure in a
population as yet relatively untapped by behavioral research. A total of
82 young men enrolled at the Gary Job Corps Training Center at San
Marcos, Texas, were asked to fill out a 12-item attitude scale and then
read the responses of a stranger and evaluate him on the IJS. The stranger
was described as a fellow job corpsman.

These subjects consisted of about equal numbers of Negroes and whites, ranging in age from 16 to 22, with an educational level ranging from the sixth to twelfth grade. They also represent a socioeconomic level considerably different from that of undergraduates.

It was found, nevertheless, that attraction was significantly ($p < .01$) related to the proportion of similar attitudes attributed to the stranger. A goodness of fit analysis between the predictions of the Byrne-Clore formula and these data indicated that the predicted and obtained responses did not differ significantly.

4. Hospital Patients

As part of the study just reported, attraction experiments were conducted with 42 hospitalized male schizophrenics at the Austin State Hospital, 13 surgical patients, and 29 hospitalized alcoholics.

Subjects filled out an 8-item attitude scale, a short delay was introduced while the experimenter prepared a faked stranger with either .00, .50, or 1.00 similarity to the subject, and then the subject evaluated this stranger on the IJS. These subjects were older and more poorly educated and represented a lower socioeconomic level than any of our undergraduate samples.

Table XI presents the mean attraction scores of these patients in response to the strangers with differing levels of attitude similarity. Once again, similarity was found to influence attraction significantly ($p < .001$), and once again the function was shown to be a linear one.

It may be seen that the empirical law relating attitude similarity to attraction appears to have quite impressive generality across extremely diverse subpopulations.

TABLE XI

MEAN ATTRACTION SCORES OF SURGICAL, ALCOHOLIC, AND SCHIZOPHRENIC PATIENTS RESPONDING TO STRANGERS WITH SIMILAR AND DISSIMILAR ATTITUDES[a]

Patients	Proportion of similar attitudes			
	.00	.50	1.00	Total
Surgical	5.00	7.60	10.75	7.77
Alcoholic	6.10	7.56	10.00	7.90
Schizophrenic	8.35	9.79	11.64	9.93
Total	7.07	8.68	10.93	

[a] After Byrne, Griffitt, Hudgins, and Reeves, in press.

D. Nonattitudinal Similarity — Dissimilarity

Based in part on Festinger's (1950, 1954) theory of social comparison processes and in part on Nelson's (1965) discrepancy findings, it has tentatively been proposed that any aspect of similarity — dissimilarity affects attraction in the same manner as does attitude similarity — dissimilarity (Byrne, Clore, and Worchel, 1966). A few relevant findings will be described.

1. Economic Similarity — Dissimilarity

Using the same general method as in the attitudinal studies, Byrne *et al.* (1966) manipulated the similarity between subject and stranger with respect to several indices of economic level. In the preliminary session, undergraduates responded to a 4-item attitude scale and a 4-item economic scale. The latter dealt with such things as expenditures on entertainment and clothes. In the experimental session, each subject was given both attitudinal and economic information about a stranger. All strangers were similar to the subject on half of the attitude items. With respect to economic level, subjects of relatively low economic level were asked to evaluate high economic level strangers, subjects of high economic level were asked to evaluate low economic level strangers, and both low and high level subjects were asked to evaluate strangers similar to themselves in economic level.

It was found that attraction responses were most positive toward strangers of similar economic status and least positive toward strangers of dissimilar economic status ($p < .001$). Another analysis involved the prediction of attraction responses. With each of the 4 economic items and the 4 attitude items treated as equal units of information, proportion of similar responses to the 8 items was determined for each condition. It was found that the obtained attraction responses did not differ significantly from those predicted by the Byrne-Nelson formula. It was suggested that in any type of social comparison with other human beings, similarity is preferable to dissimilarity.

2. Defense Mechanisms

In another investigation in this series, subject-stranger similarity with respect to a measure of repression — sensitization was manipulated (Byrne, Griffitt, and Stefaniak, 1967).

From a pool of over 450 undergraduates who had taken the 127-item Repression — Sensitization Scale (Byrne, 1964b), 48 sensitizers, 54 neutrals, and 49 repressers were selected for the experiment. Each subject was assigned to one of three similarity conditions (.20, .50, and .80) based on the relationship between himself and a stranger in responding to the 127 true—false items.

Attraction responses were found to be significantly influenced by this type of similarity ($p < .001$). A more surprising finding, however, was that attraction was also influenced by the discrepancy between the subject's repression—sensitization *score* and the score obtained by the bogus stranger. Within a given level of similarity, this discrepancy varied widely because the specific items of similarity—dissimilarity were chosen randomly for each subject. With either similarity—dissimilarity or discrepancy controlled, the other variable was still significantly related to attraction.

It appears, then, that the subjects were responding to two independent stimulus dimensions, each representing a different aspect of similarity. The multiple correlation between attraction and these two independent variables was .59 ($p < .001$). In this instance, the attraction formula is provided by a multiple regression equation in which $Y = -.04X_1 + 3.88X_2 + 7.16$. The mean difference between the obtained responses and those predicted with this equation was zero. Thus, subjects responded not only to specific response similarity but also to similarity at a more abstract or generalized level, that is, to the personality dimension itself.

3. Self-Concept

Griffitt (1966) utilized a method much like that of the repression—sensitization study in order to determine the relationship between similarity in self-concept and attraction. From a pool of over 250 students who had taken Worchel's (1957) Self-Activity Inventory (SAI), extreme scorers on the self-ideal discrepancy dimension were selected as subjects.

In the experiment, each subject was asked to evaluate a stranger on the basis of his or her responses to the SAI. The bogus self scales were either similar to the subject on 33% or 100% of the items. In the .33 group, for half of the subjects the discrepant responses were in the direction of more ineffectual adjustment and for the other half they were in a more effectual direction.

For both high and low self-ideal discrepancy subjects, attraction was significantly greater toward 1.00 similar strangers ($M = 11.61$) than toward .33 similar strangers ($M = 8.76$). Similarity to self was the only variable to yield a significant effect ($p < .001$); the direction of item discrepancy in terms of effectual—ineffectual did not affect attraction.

An additional finding was that the obtained attraction responses did not differ significantly from those predicted by the Byrne-Nelson formula for attitude similarity.

E. EFFECTS OF OTHER STIMULUS VARIABLES: RACE

1. Belief versus Race

Rokeach, Smith, and Evans (1960) made the novel proposal that what is commonly labeled as racial prejudice is actually reducible to prejudice concerning beliefs and attitudes. They hypothesized that ". . . *insofar as psychological processes are involved*, belief is more important than ethnic or racial membership as a determinant of social discrimination" (p. 135). Their initial investigation confirmed the hypothesis.

Subsequently, Triandis (1961) objected to the Rokeach *et al.* conclusions in that their dependent variable was limited to friendship choices while their conclusions dealt more broadly with prejudice. With a social distance measure, he found that race, philosophy, religion, and occupation each had an effect and that most of the variance was attributable to race. Rokeach (1961) pointed out that Triandis had not only used a different dependent variable but had altered the independent variable as well.

A number of investigations have since been conducted in an effort to resolve the controversy (e.g., Rokeach and Mezei, 1966; Smith, Williams, and Willis, 1967; Stein, 1966; Stein, Hardyck, and Smith, 1965; Triandis, Loh, and Levin, 1966). It seems clear that the relative influence of belief and race is a function of the specific operations used in defining race and belief, the specific way in which the dependent variable is measured, and the specific population from which subjects are drawn. One conclusion, then, is that both belief and race affect attraction and that the abstract question of the relative power of the two variables is a meaningless one.

2. Race as a Stimulus Variable

Within the present attraction paradigm, race is conceptualized as a stimulus variable which should influence attraction only to the extent that it arouses positive or negative expectancies concerning the consequents of interaction. Further, individual differences in racial prejudice as measured by a general questionnaire should lead us to make quite specific predictions about different subjects.

A series of investigations have now been conducted in which subjects are initially separated roughly into high and low prejudice subgroups. Such subgroups are found to differ in their expectancies about Negroes (Byrne and Andres, 1964), in attraction toward strangers identified on the basis of race (Wong, 1961), and in amount of attitude similarity assumed between themselves and a Negro stranger (Byrne and Wong, 1962).

When information about both race and attitudes is given to subjects (Byrne and McGraw, 1964; Byrne and Wong, 1962), low prejudice subjects tend to respond to a Negro stranger as they do to a white stranger. For them, race has essentially no effect. High prejudice subjects, on the other hand, tend to respond to race *and* to attitudes. One tentative formulation is that for high prejudice subjects only, the fact that the stranger is a Negro is equivalent to 10 dissimilar attitudes expressed by a white stranger. Thus, the relative effects of race and belief with respect to the attraction measure used in the present investigations are a function of the subject's initial prejudice and of the number of similar attitudes pitted against the race variable.

F. RESPONSE GENERALITY

The primary strategy of this research on attraction has been to utilize a single dependent variable while manipulating numerous independent variables. Though a question is sometimes raised concerning the "'validity" of the attraction measure, the question is not an appropriate one. The response to the IJS is not conceptualized as either an imperfect substitute for everyday life attraction or as an inadequate index of the subject's "real" though unobserved feelings of attraction. Rather, this attraction response constitutes the dependent variable which our research is designed to explicate. This may seem to be a niggling distinction, but psychologists seem able to generate a great deal of confusion around just such questions (see Byrne, 1964a; Lindzey and Byrne, in press).

It may nevertheless be said that any relationship or lack of relationship between the attraction measure and other response variables is of interest. The concern is not with validating the measure in a psychometric sense but with establishing its generality as a construct.

1. Social Distance

As part of his dissertation research, Schwartz (1966) obtained IJS attraction responses and responses to a social distance scale from 109 high school students. The social distance scale consisted of 10 items on which subjects responded with yes or no as to their willingness to invite the person home to dinner, go to a party with the person, live in the same apartment house, sit next to the person, etc. The correlation between the two sets of responses was .68 ($p < .001$).

2. Interpersonal Judgment Apparatus

For a series of planned investigations, it was deemed desirable to move away from the paper and pencil IJS and devise an apparatus which required the subject to indicate attraction by means of a simple physical manipulation.

In order to retain the same general magnitude of response as represented by the IJS, a 30-inch rectangular wooden box containing 13 holes was designed. The two end points and the center were labeled with printed statements based on the attraction items of the IJS. A subject indicated his response toward a stimulus person by inserting a small round wooden indicator into the appropriate slot. Responses were scored ordinally from 2 to 14.

In a pilot study, subjects who had taken a 12-item attitude scale were given the usual interpersonal judgment instructions except that there was no mention of intelligence, adjustment, etc. In addition, they were told how to use the Interpersonal Judgment Apparatus. The attitude scales of each stranger constituted .17, .50, or .83 similarity to the subject. The mean attraction responses as measured by this device were 5.57, 9.00, and 10.75. These responses conformed to a linear function, were significantly different from one another ($p < .01$), and gave promise of close comparability between the two response measures of attraction.

In summary, this series of investigations suggested that the attitude-attraction function was unafffected by the importance of the attitude topics in most conditions, was not influenced by the specific stimulus mode in which the stranger was presented, was relatively unchanged across a diverse array of populations, and was probably representative of a much more general relationship between subject-stranger similarity and attraction. Further, the specific measure of attraction used in this research was related to other measures of the same construct.

V. A Theory of Attraction: A Reinforcement Model

Beginning with the initial paper in this series (Byrne, 1961), the underlying assumption of all the research has been that attraction toward X is a function of the relative number of rewards and punishments associated with X. More recently (Byrne and Nelson, 1965a, p. 662), a tentative law of attraction was proposed as "$A_x = mPR_x + k$ or attraction toward X is a positive linear function of the proportion of positive reinforcements received from X." At a purely tactical level, the reinforcement formulation has two major advantages. First, a wide variety of seemingly different stimulus conditions can be conceptualized in terms of a single unifying construct rather than as an infinite array of unrelated conditions each requiring a new set of explanatory principles. Second, the concept of reinforcement obviously suggests the possibility of a relationship between the attraction paradigm and learning theory. As Clore (1966, p. 11) noted:

> When the words *reinforcement model* are used they imply that the attributes and general inference rules of the model come from the experimental literature on reinforcement. The concept of reinforcement used to explain attraction is a model rather than a theory for at least two reasons. First, reinforcement theory is a system with its own ideas and laws external to the attraction phenomenon. The attributes and meanings of this system are being transferred from their original realm, simple animal learning, to the previously unrelated data of interpersonal attraction. Secondly, a model rather than a theory is in use because we are not interested in altering learning theory with our data but rather in suggesting a theory of attraction. If our model does not fit we may certainly discard it, but we would not claim that learning theory had been shown to be in error. If the reinforcement model is worthwhile, one may expect it to play the role of midwife in the formulation of a genuine theory of attraction and in the generation of experimental situations that might not otherwise have been conceived.

Lott (1966), in a similar vein, indicates, "By defining attraction toward persons in S−R terms we are able to place this concept within a large nomological net in which other concepts have already been linked, theoretically and empirically, and which provides a basis for derivations specific to the investigation of social behavior."

In this final section of the article, a few implications of the reinforcement model will be outlined.

A. BACKGROUND

It might be well to note the obvious relationship between the present use of a reinforcement model in attraction research and the venerable doctrine that organisms are motivated to behave in such a way as to maximize pleasure and minimize pain. From hedonism to Hull-Spence theory, this general view of behavior is a familiar one.

The utilization of this principle in attempting to explain interpersonal attraction also has a long history. A brief return to Aristotle and Spinoza will serve to make the point.

In Aristotle's (translated 1932, pp. 103 − 106) words:

> Further, men love any one who has done good to them or to those for whom they are concerned . . . .

> Further, men like those who are able and inclined to benefit them in a pecuniary way, or to promote their personal safety . . . those who are pleasant to live with, and to spend the day with; such are the good-tempered − people who are not given to catching up one's mistakes, and are not pertinacious or crossgrained . . . . Further, we like those who praise our good qualities, and especially if we are afraid we do not possess them . . . . We like those who take us seriously − who

admire us, who show us respect, who take pleasure in our society . . . . We like those who do not frighten us, and in dealing with whom we do not lose our aplomb — for no one likes a person of whom he is afraid.

In more general terms, Spinoza (translated 1951, pp. 140 – 141) proposed:

Love is nothing else but *pleasure accompanied by the idea of an external cause*: Hate is nothing else but *pain accompanied by the idea of an external cause* . . . .

Simply from the fact that we have regarded a thing with the emotion of pleasure or pain, though that thing be not the efficient cause of the emotion, we can either love or hate it.

In the relatively recent research on attraction, reinforcement is frequently employed as an explanatory principle. Though his development of the A-B-X- model places Newcomb in the group of cognitive-consistency theorists, he has proposed (1956, p. 577), " . . . that we acquire favorable or unfavorable attitudes toward persons as we are rewarded or punished by them, and that the principles of contiguity, of reciprocal reward, and of complementarity have to do with the conditions under which rewards are most probable." In Pepitone's (1964, p. 222) need-satisfaction-frustration model, " . . . the attractiveness of another person is a function of the need satisfaction which that person brings about, whereas hostility toward another person is a function of the need frustration which this person imposes." Lott and Lott (1960, p. 298) have formalized the reinforcement notion in a series of assumptions:

1. Persons may be conceptualized as discriminable stiumli to which responses may be learned.

2. A person who experiences reinforcement or reward for some behavior will react to the reward, i.e., will perform some observable or covert goal response (R_g or r_g).

3. This response to reward will become conditioned, like any other response, to all discriminable stimuli present at the time of reinforcement.

4. A person . . . who is present at the time that Individual X, for example, is rewarded thus becomes able, in a later situation, to evoke R_g or, what is more likely, its fractional and anticipatory component, $r_g - s_g$.

In the present line of research on attitude similarity and attraction, such a reinforcement model has been employed along with speculations about some of the specific effects of attitude statements. First, the most general explanatory concept used to account for the effect of attitude similarity — dissimilarity on attraction is reward and punishment. When one individual receives positive reinforcement from another, positive affect is elicited and, through simple conditioning, becomes associated with the other individual. Subsequent evaluative responses directed toward that other individual will be positive. When one individual receives negative reinforcement from another, negative affect is elicited and becomes associated with the other individual. In this instance, subsequent evaluative responses directed toward that other individual will be negative. The relative number and relative strength of rewards and punishments associated with a given individual determine the strength and direction of attraction toward him.

Second, the empirically established effect of similar and dissimilar attitudes on attraction is interpreted as a special case of reward and punishment. Specifically, it is proposed that attitude statements are affect arousing; the motive involved is the learned drive to be logical and to interpret correctly one's stimulus world (Byrne, 1966, pp. 47 – 48):

> A child must learn the correct labels to apply to the stimulus events in his environment (for example, Mama, thirsty, little), the proper sequence of cause and effect relationships (for example, pulling down on the handle opens the refrigerator), and the distinction between reality and fantasy (last summer's vacation versus last night's dream). The learning which must take place is sometimes difficult, is spread over a long period of time, and continues throughout our lifetime. That is, we continually strive to make sense out of our physical and social world. Especially difficult is the social world of attitudes, beliefs, opinions, and values concerning politics, religion, race relations, and the like. About such topics there is simply no way to determine whether we are correct in making sense out of the stimulus data. When another person agrees with us and hence offers consensual validation concerning the correctness of our position, our "correctness" is supported. Frustration of this motive to be logical and correct takes place when others disagree with our views, when they offer consensual invalidation. Therefore, the finding that the expression of attitudes congruent with those of a subject elicits a positive response while discrepant attitudes elicit a negative response may be interpreted on a reward and punishment basis.

The remainder of this chapter will consist of a description of the research which has been conducted in an effort to test a series of hypotheses generated by this reinforcement model of attraction.

B. SIMILAR AND DISSIMILAR ATTITUDES: AFFECT AROUSAL

1. Positive and Negative Affect

In an attempt to obtain evidence concerning the affect arousal properties of attitude statements, Byrne and Clore utilized 6 of the evaluative scales of Osgood's Semantic Differential (Osgood, Suci, and Tannenbaum, 1957). The scales were comfortable – uncomfortable, bad – good, high – low, sad – happy, pleasant – unpleasant, and negative – positive. Sixteen subjects who had responded to a 12-item attitude scale earlier in the semester were seen individually in the experimental sessions. They were told:

> The purpose of this study is to explore a few of the dimensions of everyday feelings people have. We are asking a number of students to describe their feelings on a series of scales after exposure to several common stimuli.

The subject was seated facing a screen and the experimenter was behind him. A recording in which either 12 agreeing or 12 disagreeing attitudes were expressed was played, feelings were rated, a second recording (the opposite of the first) was played, and feelings were indicated.

Feelings on the 6 scales were summed, and as hypothesized, the difference in aroused affect (30.56 versus 20.88) was significant ($p < .05$).

2. Effectance Arousal by Attitudinal Material

As suggested earlier, a specific motivational state has been hypothesized to result from exposure to similar and dissimilar attitudes. Byrne and Clore (1967, p. 2) described this motive:

> It is proposed that the motive which is presumably activated by attitudinal material is not unique to that particular stimulus situation. Rather, the motivational properties of attitude statements represent a special instance of a more general phenomenon. At the risk of erring by "the inclusion in the same category of events which only superficially belong together . . . (Dember & Earl, 1957, p. 91), we suggest that the type of secondary motive described in the attraction studies has appeared under various labels and in various contexts. Examples are the need for cognition or the need to experience an integrated and meaningful world (Cohen, Stotland, & Wolfe, 1955), the need to be able to know and predict the environment (Kelly, 1955; Pervin, 1963), the desire for certainty which involves understanding the environment and making it predictable (Brim & Hoff, 1957), and the drive to evaluate one's own opinions and abilities (Festinger, 1954). It has previously been suggested (Byrne, Nelson, & Reeves, 1966) that these various concepts all fit within White's (1959) *effectance motive* in that each involves a process related to effective interaction with the environment.

It was further suggested (Byrne and Clore, 1967, pp. 3–4):

> . . . well adjusted adults in a relatively stable, civilized society should be protected against unpleasant levels of effectance arousal by effective social training in childhood, years of experience in which to build up coding capacity, and a stable environment with built-in predictability. There may be occasional minor jolts (momentary forgetting of the location of one's car after a football game, minor loss of orientation just after moving to a new house, seeing an unidentified

flying object) and at times major disruptions (economic depression, earthquake, war) which prevent in varying degrees the satisfaction of the effectance motive. For most of us most of the time, physical reality does not actually pose major problems related to effectance. Nevertheless, there remains what Festinger (1950) calls "social reality" in which there is a much greater degree of unpredictability, lack of necessary knowledge, and the occurrence of seemingly illogical events....

Included here are all of the major aspects of our world about which we hold attitudes, opinions, beliefs, and values. Is there a God? What are the consequences of assuming an aggressive military posture with respect to Communist China? Is it reasonable to enjoy television comedies? Has the Civil Rights movement gone too far or not far enough? How should one raise his children? Is op art just a passing fad? To what should the sexual practices of adolescents be limited? It is obvious that the list can be extended almost endlessly and that the resolution of such questions in terms of discovering the correct answer, mastering the problem, dealing effectively with the issue, or testing the empirical consequents of one's assumptions is not possible. Thus, the raising of such issues should arouse the effectance motive. Further, the only relevant evidence to bring about effectance reduction lies in consensual validation or invalidation. The former occurs when others agree with or share our outlook and hence provide satisfaction of the effectance motive. Consensual invalidation occurs when others disagree with us and hence frustrate the satisfaction of the effectance motive.

It is suggested, then, that the attitudes of others are important to us because human beings depend on one another as sources of information about countless aspects of the environment.

A self-rating scale was designed to measure this specific motive system. The five characteristics of high effectance arousal included in the scale were uneasiness, confusion, a sense of unreality, dreamlike feelings, and a desire for social comparison. Responses to these five items are summed, and in a series of validational studies, each item was found to correlate significantly with the combined score on the other four items.

In one of the investigations using this scale, 46 students took part in a standard interpersonal judgment experiment in which they evaluated a stranger on the basis of his responses to an attitude scale. They were also asked to fill out the Effectance Arousal Scale indicating their feelings while reading the stranger's attitudes.

Compared to effectance arousal in response to a neutral stimulus ($M = 7.82$), arousal following the attitudinal material ($M = 9.52$) was significantly greater ($p < .001$). It was also proposed that the larger the proportion of dissimilar attitude items, the greater should be the arousal. The subjects were divided into those who were given relatively similar strangers (.58 to 1.00) and those with relatively dissimilar strangers (.25 to .50). The mean effectance score of the latter ($M = 10.22$) was significantly greater than that of the former ($M = 8.83$) ($p < .05$). Not only does attitudinal material arouse the effectance motive, but arousal is a function of the proportion of similar and dissimilar attitudes.

3. Independent Arousal of the Effectance Motive

Another experimental approach to the proposed motivational system has been an attempt to arouse subjects differentially with respect to this motive and then to obtain responses to similar and dissimilar strangers. In one investigation (Byrne, Nelson, and Reeves, 1966) it was proposed that the degree of verifiability of the issues about which there was agreement or disagreement should be related to the amount of effectance arousal and that the greater the arousal, the steeper the similarity — attraction function. Specifically, unverifiable issues (e.g., whether one's church is the one true religion) should be more arousing than those verifiable in the future (e.g., whether Pope Paul will declare the Catholic Church to be the one true religion) or at present (e.g., whether the early Christians taught that their church was the one true religion). Each of 168 undergraduates responded to one of three 12-item scales containing one of these types of items. Later, each subject was exposed to the responses of a stranger who was similar on .33, .50, .67, or 1.00 of the items. As hypothesized, attraction was a function of proportion of similar attitudes ($p < .001$) and of the interaction between similarity and the verifiability of the items ($p < .05$). Trend analysis indicated that each of the three types of items yielded a linear relationship between similarity and attraction and that each was different from the others. The findings are depicted in Fig. 4.

A somewhat more elaborate attempt at effectance arousal was undertaken by Byrne and Clore (1967). It was proposed that any situation which provided evidence of one's predictive inaccuracy, inability to understand, incorrectness, illogicality, or lack of reality orientation would arouse and frustrate the effectance motive. The experimental operations designed to create these conditions were two 8 mm sound color movies, each of which contained scenes having no meaningful interrelationships and no logical sequence. In one movie, scenes include ceramic figures of cannibals cooking a missionary, an aerial view of a toy battleship, Mr. Ed the talking horse, a flushing toilet, a chess game played with cosmetic bottles, Negro children playing, a girl swimming, a dizzying ride through treetops, and a variety of animals. The sound tract is predominantly that of *Voodoo Suite* played by Perez Prado with occasional interpolations of other sounds. In the other, there were scenes of a wrecked building, faces on billboards, people crossing a busy street, a silent encounter between a boy and a girl in an open field, chairs marching around a maypole, a toy globe floating in a stream, and other unrelated episodes. The sound track

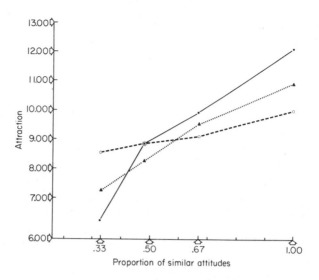

Fig. 4. Attraction toward a stranger as a linear function of proportion of similar attitudes on topics differing in verifiability: (●) not verifiable, (○) verifiable in future, and (▲)
verifiable at present. (After Byrne, Nelson, and Reeves, 1966, p. 103.)

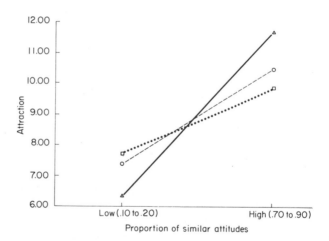

Fig. 5. Attraction toward a stranger as an interactive function of proportion of similar attitudes and level of effectance arousal: (△) experimental – moderate arousal, (○) control – low arousal, and (□) experimental – high arousal. (After Byrne and Clore, 1967.)

includes a Ravel string quartet, a musical ballad, a woodwind quintet by
Poulenc, and a harpsicord etude.

With respect to the Effectance Arousal Scale, each nonpredictable movie yielded higher scores ($M = 12.48$ and 13.17) than either a neutral predictable movie ($M = 7.20$) or a predictable but anxiety-arousing movie of a cataract operation ($M = 9.60$).

In a series of investigations in which subjects were exposed to one of the movies prior to exposure to the attitudes of a stranger, a somewhat complex relationship was found between level of effectance arousal and response to attitude similarity—dissimilarity. As shown in Fig. 5, the control group which represents low arousal yields the usual similarity—attraction function while experimental subjects who were moderately aroused (means of $9-12$) yielded a steeper function as hypothesized. An unexpected finding was that experimental subjects who indicated high levels of arousal yielded a function less steep than that of either the moderately aroused or the control group. This latter group, it appears, is less responsive to similarity—dissimilarity cues and expresses less affect, either positive or negative, toward the stranger.

It seems, then, that the intervening construct of affect arousal in the attitude-attraction relationship is a useful one, and there is some evidence that the magnitude of arousal is crucial in determining response to similar and dissimilar attitudes.

C. Positive and Negative Reinforcement as Determinants of Attraction

If similar and dissimilar attitude statements influence attraction because they function as positive and negative reinforcements, it follows that other types of reinforcing stimuli should influence attraction in the same linear fashion.

1. Positive and Negative Ratings

McDonald (1962) selected an achievement-related task in which each subject was asked to tell a series of seven stories in response to Thematic Apperception Test (TAT) pictures. Another subject (actually a stooge) was supposed to listen to each story and then rate it on a $1-10$ scale in terms of its creativity by pressing a button connected with a series of numbered lights. Actually, each subject received a prearranged series of positive and negative ratings. Eight different conditions were created ranging from seven high ratings to seven low ratings. Afterward, each subject was asked to evaluate the stooge on the IJS.

A highly significant relationship was found between proportion of high ratings and attraction toward the stooge. As shown in Fig. 6, this function was a linear one just as when the stimuli are similar and dissimilar attitudes.

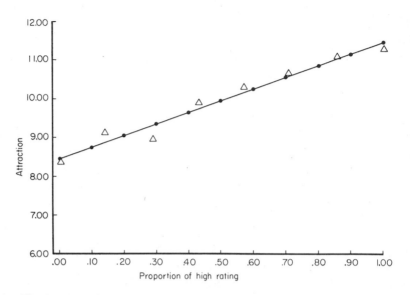

Fig. 6.   Attraction toward a stranger as a linear function of proportion of high creativity ratings; $Y = 2.98X + 8.47$. (After Byrne and Nelson, 1965a, p. 662.)

2. Positive and Negative Personal Evaluations

Byrne and Rhamey (1965) assumed that rewards and punishments of a relatively large magnitude are provided by positive and negative evaluations of one's self by another person. A situation was created whereby subjects received information concerning a stranger's attitudes on a 12-item scale (.00, .33, .67, or 1.00 similarity) and information concerning the stranger's evaluation of him. Supposedly, the stranger had read the subject's attitude scale and evaluated him on the IJS. Thus, subjects were informed of the stranger's positive evaluation of his intelligence, adjustment, etc., or of his negative evaluation on the 6 items of the IJS.

The mean attraction responses are shown in Table XII. Analysis of variance indicated highly significant effects for both attitude similarity and personal evaluations. In order to express the effects of both variables in the law of attraction, the formula was modified to include a weighting factor for differential magnitude,

$$A_x = m \left(\frac{\sum(PR_x \times M)}{\sum(PR_x \times M) + \sum(NR_x \times M)} \right) + k$$

or attraction toward X is a positive linear function of the sum of the weighted positive reinforcements (number × magnitude) received from X divided by the total number of weighted positive and negative reinforcements received from X.

In an exploratory fashion, differential weighting coefficients for the two types of stimulus information were tried out, and values of three for evaluation items and one for attitude items were found to be the most satisfactory. Thus, the weighted positive reinforcement received by a subject would be determined as shown in Table XIII. When attraction is plotted as a function of weighted positive reinforcements, as shown in Fig. 7, we once again see a linear relationship.

An extension of the Byrne and Rhamey findings was provided by Aronson and Worchel (1966). They proposed that in a face-to-face interaction between subject and stranger, attraction would be entirely a function of personal evaluations with attitude similarity having a negligible effect. Even with a relatively narrow range of attitudinal differences (2 out of 7 versus 5 out of 7 agreements) to pit against the evaluation variable, the effect of attitude similarity was almost significant ($p = .06$) along with the significant ($p < .01$) evaluation effect. When Byrne and Griffitt (1966) repeated this investigation with a slightly increased range of attitude similarity (0 out of 7 versus 7 out of 7 agreements), both the evaluation variable and the similarity variable were found to influence attraction at the .001 level. More surprising was the finding that the Byrne-Rhamey weighting coefficients were applicable in this face-to-face encounter. As shown in Fig. 8, the combined data of the two experiments again indicate a linear relationship between proportion of weighted positive reinforcements and attraction.

TABLE XII

MEAN ATTRACTION SCORES TOWARD STRANGERS WHO HAD
EVALUATED THE SUBJECT POSITIVELY OR NEGATIVELY
AND WHO DIFFERED IN PROPORTION OF SIMILAR ATTITUDES[a]

Proportion of similar attitudes	Evaluation conditions	
	Positive	Negative
1.00	13.13	8.40
.67	13.00	5.87
.33	10.73	4.87
.00	10.33	3.47

[a] After Byrne and Rhamey (1965, p. 886).

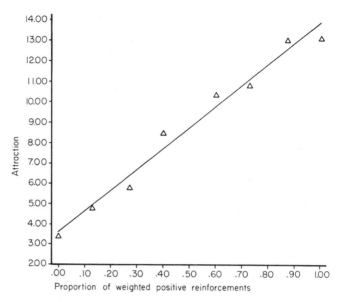

Fig. 7. Attraction toward a stranger as a linear function of proportion of positive reinforcements based on weighted combination of evaluation items and attitudinal items; $Y = 10.17X + 3.64$. (After Byrne and Rhamey, 1965, p. 888.)

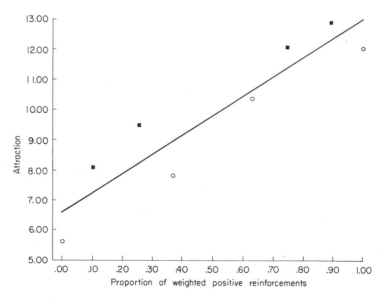

Fig. 8. Attraction toward stooge as a linear function of proportion of positive reinforcements based on weighted combination of evaluation statements and attitudinal items; $Y = 6.45X + 6.62$. (■) Aronson-Worchel data and (○) Byrne-Griffitt data. (After Byrne and Griffitt, 1966b, p. 296.)

TABLE XIII

PROPORTION OF POSITIVE REINFORCEMENTS
BASED ON WEIGHTED COMBINATIONS OF
EVALUATION ITEMS ($W = 3$) AND ATTITUDINAL ITEMS ($W = 1$)[a]

Proportion of similar attitudes	Evaluation conditions	
	Positive (18+, 0−)	Negative (0+, 18−)
1.00 (12+, 0−)	1.00	.40
.67 (8+, 4−)	.87	.27
.33 (4+, 8−)	.73	.13
.00 (0+, 12−)	.60	.00

[a]After Byrne and Rhamey (1965, p. 888).

D. THE REINFORCEMENT PROPERTIES OF SIMILAR AND DISSIMILAR ATTITUDES

One further area of research follows from the proposition that if attitude statements determine attraction because of their reinforcement properties, it should be possible to utilize such statements as reinforcing stimuli in a quite different context. Specifically, similar and dissimilar attitudes should function as positive and negative reinforcements in a learning task.

1. Combined Effects of Similar and Dissimilar Attitudes

Beginning with the first of these learning experiments (Golightly and Byrne, 1964) a simple discrimination learning task (adapted from Prentice, 1949) was employed using an apparatus developed by Dallenbach (1960). Subjects were placed in front of a large wooden apparatus which contained a window for the presentation of the stimulus cards. On each of 96 trials, a card containing a circle and a square was presented; one of the figures was black and one was white, one was large and one small. Each of the eight possible combinations of shape, size, color, and position appeared in random order in each block of eight trials. The 60 subjects were run individually and each was told that he was taking part in a learning experiment. Whenever a stimulus card was shown, the subject was to choose one of the two figures and say it aloud. Immediately afterward, a card would come out of a slit, and the subject was to read the card and then dispose of it in a discard box. The discrimination to be learned was small—large, with small correct for half of the subjects and large correct for the other half. The message on the card constituted the reinforcing stimulus.

For one-third of the subjects, a traditional reward — punishment feed-back was used in that each card contained the word "right" or "wrong." Another third of the subjects, the attitude similarity — dissimilarity group, received cards containing statements agreeing (for correct response) or disagreeing (for incorrect response) with the subject's attitudes indicated earlier in the semester on a 45-item scale. These statements were of the form "There is definitely a God" versus "There is no God." A control group constituted the final third, and these subjects received neutral state-ments (e.g., "Most modern religions are monotheistic") regardless of their response. Trials were continued until the subject gave eight consecutive correct responses or until 96 trials had been completed.

The findings are depicted in Fig. 9. While the traditional reward — punishment group showed the fastest learning and the highest perfor-mance levels, the crucial comparison was between the other two groups. Both in terms of over-all performance ($p < .001$) and the linear trend

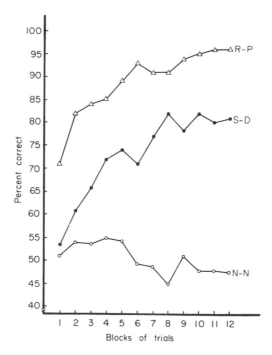

Fig. 9. Learning curves for the three groups of subjects showing percentage of cor-rect responses over eight trial blocks as a function of experimental conditions, where R — P indicates the reward — punishment group, N — N indicates neutral control group, and S — D indicates the attitudinal similarity — dissimilarity group. (After Golightly and Byrne, 1964, p. 798.)

$(p < .001)$, the attitude similarity—dissimilarity group was superior to the control group.

Since the presentation of similar and dissimilar attitude statements served to change response probability, the reinforcement interpretation of the attitude-attraction relationship was once again supported.

2. Separate Effects of Similar and Dissimilar Attitudes

The research design just described makes it impossible to determine whether it is necessary to use both similar and dissimilar statements to bring about learning or whether either type of statement alone is sufficient. Byrne, Young, and Griffitt (1966) conducted two experiments using the discrimination apparatus in order to clarify this problem.

The first investigation replicated the Golightly-Byrne design with the three experimental groups plus the addition of two other groups. One of these consisted of a similar-neutral group in which correct responses were followed by an agreeing attitude statement and incorrect responses by a neutral statement. The other was a neutral-dissimilar group in which neutral statements followed correct responses and disagreeing statements followed incorrect responses.

The findings for the three replication groups closely paralleled the Golightly-Byrne findings. Of the new groups, the neutral-dissimilar group clearly learned the task while the performance of the similar-neutral group was indistinguishable from the control group. These relationships are depicted in Fig. 10.

One possible explanation for these unexpected findings was that they were a consequence of the reinforcing value of neutral statements. Since the "neutral" statements actually were factual in content, they also could be conceptualized as constituting instances of consensual validation and hence should be reinforcing. To test this possibility, a second experiment was undertaken in which statements were contrasted with blank cards. Subjects were assigned to either a similar-blank, neutral-blank, or blank-dissimilar condition. As may be seen in Fig. 11, all three experimental groups learned the discrimination. Analysis of variance indicated a significant over-all trials effect, and trend analysis indicated that these curves fit a linear function. Thus, it appears that both similar attitude statements and neutral statements act as positive reinforcement while dissimilar attitude statements act as negative reinforcers.

Alternative explanations were considered by Byrne, Young, and Griffitt (1966, pp. 271–272):

A possible alternative explanation is that the attitude statements serve as discriminating stimuli . . . This argument is a specious one on several counts. First,

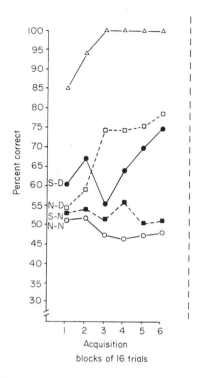

Fig. 10. Acquisition curves for the five groups in the first experiment showing percentage of correct responses over 16 trial blocks as a function of experimental conditions, where, R – P indicates reward – punishment, S – D indicates similar – dissimilar attitudes, N – D indicates neutral-dissimilar attitudes, S – N indicates similar attitudes – neutral, and N – N indicates neutral control group. (After Byrne, Young, and Griffitt, 1966, p. 268.)

the presence of discriminating stimuli would inform the subject of the experimenter's definition of the relevant dimensions, but performance would remain unaffected. To verify this rather obvious proposition, another group of 15 subjects was run on the discrimination apparatus with discriminable but nonreinforcing stimuli presented after each response. Correct responses were followed by a card containing a nonsense syllable beginning with the letter b, and incorrect responses were followed by a nonsense syllable beginning with d. The two sets of syllables were matched for association value. After each set of 24 trials, subjects were asked to verbalize their thoughts about the experiment. By the end of the 96 acquisition trials, the majority of the subjects indicated awareness that b and d syllables were associated with the large and small stimulus figures. Performance remained at the chance level, nevertheless, for both aware and unaware subjects. There was no reason to suspect that either type of nonsense syllable would be reinforcing, that b and d have differential incentive value, that subjects would have any reason to prefer one over the other. Simple discrimination does not lead to performance changes.

Once the discrimination is made, then, performance is affected only if differential reinforcement is provided. This may take the form of "RIGHT" versus "WRONG," similar versus dissimilar statements, neutral versus dissimilar statements, or as in Prentice's (1949) experiment a light versus a buzzer. It is possible that in all of these instances the reinforcing stimuli are simply interpreted by the subjects to mean "correct" and "incorrect." Even if this were the case, the designation "reinforcement" is still not an inaccurate one in that response probability is altered in the predicted direction by such material; this is the usual definitional criterion of secondary reinforcement (e.g., Hull, 1943; Skinner, 1938; Spence, 1951).

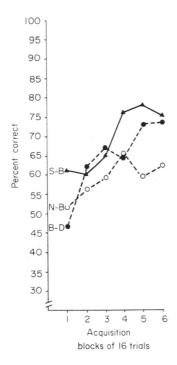

Fig. 11.   Acquisition curves for the three groups in the second experiment showing percentage of correct responses over 16 trial blocks as a function of experimental conditions, where S − B indicates similar attitudes − blank, N − B indicates neutral − blank, and B − D indicates blank-dissimilar attitudes. (After Byrne, Young, and Griffitt, 1966, p. 270.)

3. *Magnitude of Attitudinal Reinforcement*

Given evidence that attitudinal statements may be used as reinforcers in a learning task, a number of possible correspondences are suggested between variables operative in learning research and various attributes of attitudinal material. Clore (1966) attempted to manipulate magnitude of reinforcement by means of differential wording of the attitude statements. In one of his conditions, subjects were again told that they were taking part in a learning task. Three different conditions were created. The high magnitude group received feedback statements paralleling those in the Byrne-Rhamey (1965) investigation in that personal evaluation statements (supposedly written about the subject by another student) were presented after each response; e.g., "I believe that this person is above average in intelligence." The medium magnitude group received statements dealing with attitudes held by the subject and characterizing those who held such beliefs in a positive or negative way; e.g., "People who favor socialized medicine are poorly informed." The low magnitude group received the same similar and dissimilar attitude statements used in the previous studies; e.g., "American medicine should be socialized."

The high magnitude group shows superior performance, especially in the first half of the trials, but all three groups eventually reach approximately the same asymptote. The "low" and "medium" magnitude groups are reversed in their expected relationship.

Clore also ran a separate group of subjects on the same task with nonlearning instructions. Specifically, they were told: "There is no right or wrong response in this experiment. Since no choice is correct or incorrect, just choose whatever figure gives you the kind of statement you would rather get." Though there was a lower level of performance for these subjects than for those given learning instructions, significant performance changes over trials were also found for these subjects. As Clore (1966, p. 69) noted: "That subjects learned, in the absence of instructions to do so, was interpreted as a stringent test of the reinforcement hypothesis."

E. COMPARISON OF REINFORCEMENT AND COGNITIVE THEORIES

The question sometimes arises as to the relative efficacy of the two theoretical approaches to the study of attraction.

It should be noted that there are a great many similarities. The same predictions are made concerning the effects of similar and dissimilar attitudes on attraction. And an intervening state (imbalance or the effectance motive) is postulated by both systems. There is a different motivational emphasis in that cognitive theorists stress a homeostatic mechanism whereas reinforcement theorists stress the positive and negative consequents of external stimulation. Is there any way in which the differences in theorizing lead to differences in research beyond linguistic disparities?

The primary distinction would seem to lie in the direction in which the research moves beyond the attitude-attraction relationship. The cognitive systems seem to be more limited to the person-person-object interconnections and seem to remain closer to naturalistic situations. Thus, there are studies of the development of A-B-X relationships, attempts to discover whether balanced relationships actually occur more often than unbalanced ones in real life, and demonstrations that subjects prefer balanced to unbalanced configurations. The primary advance beyond such studies has been the formulation of the responses evoked by A-B-X imbalance in addition to attraction. That is, imbalance also may lead to A's attempts to reinstate balance by misperceptions of B's attitude, by attempts to induce change in B's attitude toward X, or by changes in A's own attitude toward X. Though such findings present no interpretational difficulties to reinforcement theorists, it seems unlikely that a reinforcement model would have led directly to this sort of research.

By way of comparison, a reinforcement interpretation has led to the manipulation of attitudinal stimuli in laboratory experiments and hence to the discovery of a linear relationship between similarity and attraction which seems to some extent alien to the closed A-B-X systems. More importantly, the generality of the phenomenon is enhanced by the reinforcement concept. Thus, studies of the effect of nonattitudinal stimuli on attraction and of the effects of attitudinal stimuli on performance in a learning task suggest that the attitude-attraction function is only a starting point. The general relationship between reinforcing stimuli (of whatever kind) and evaluative responses (of whatever kind) involves a broad sphere of behavior and a host of research possibilities.

The final test of relative theoretical merit, if there ever is such a thing, lies in the generality and the precision with which the alternative approaches can be utilized in accounting for behavior. Whether the particular paradigm presented in the foregoing pages will prove to be of such general utility is an open question. The necessity for paradigmatic research in personality and social psychology, whatever the initial orienting theory, should be self-evident.

ACKNOWLEDGMENTS

The author wishes to express his appreciation to George Levinger, Leonard Berkowitz, and Louis J. Moran for their comments and suggestions in response to the first draft of this paper.

REFERENCES

Allport, G. W. Traits revisited. *American Psychologist*, 1966, 21, 1-10.

Aristotle. *The rhetoric*. New York: Appleton-Century, 1932.

Aronson, E., and Worchel, P. Similarity versus liking as determinants of interpersonal attractiveness. *Psychonomic Science*, 1966, 5, 157-158.

Berkowitz, L., and Howard, R. C. Reactions to opinion deviates as affected by affiliation need (*n*) and group member interdependence. *Sociometry*, 1959, 22, 81-91.

Bordin, E. S. Curiosity, compassion, and doubt: the dilemma of the psychologist. *American Psychologist*, 1966, 21, 116-121.

Boswell, J. *The life of Samuel Johnson L.L.D.* (1791) Vol. 2. New York: Heritage, 1963.

Brim, O. G., Jr., and Hoff, D. B. Individual and situational differences in desire for certainty. *Journal of Abnormal and Social Psychology*, 1957, 54, 225-229.

Byrne, D. Interpersonal attraction and attitude similarity. *Journal of Abnormal and Social Psychology*, 1961, 62, 713-715.

Byrne, D. Response to attitude similarity-dissimilarity as a function of affiliation need. *Journal of Personality*, 1962, 30, 164-177.

Byrne, D. Assessing personality variables and their alteration. In P. Worchel and D. Byrne (Eds.), *Personality change*. New York: Wiley, 1964. Pp. 38-68. (a)

Byrne, D. Repression-sensitization as a dimension of personality. In B. A. Maher (Ed.), *Progress in experimental personality research*. Vol. I. New York: Academic Press, 1964. Pp. 169-220. (b)

Byrne, D. *An introduction to personality: A research approach*. Englewood Cliffs, New Jersey: Prentice-Hall, 1966.

Byrne, D., and Andres, D. Prejudice and interpersonal expectancies. *Journal of Negro Education*, 1964, 33, 441-445.

Byrne, D., and Blaylock, Barbara. Similarity and assumed similarity of attitudes between husbands and wives. *Journal of Abnormal and Social Psychology*, 1963, 67, 636-640.

Byrne, D., and Clore, G. L., Jr. Predicting interpersonal attraction toward strangers presented in three different stimulus modes. *Psychonomic Science*, 1966, 4, 239-240.

Byrne, D., and Clore, G. L. Jr. Effectance arousal and attraction. *Journal of Personality and Social Psychology*, 1967, 6, No. 4 (whole No. 638).

Byrne, D., Clore, G. L., Jr., and Griffitt, W. Response discrepancy versus attitude similarity-dissimilarity as determinants of attraction. *Psychonomic Science*, 1967, 7, 397-398.

Byrne, D., Clore, G. L., Jr., and Worchel, P. The effect of economic similarity-dissimilarity on interpersonal attraction. *Journal of Personality and Social Psychology*, 1966, 4, 220-224.

Byrne, D., and Griffitt, W. A developmental investigation of the law of attraction. *Journal of Personality and Social Psychology*, 1966, 4, 699-702. (a)

Byrne, D., and Griffitt, W. Similarity versus liking: A clarification. *Psychonomic Science*, 1966, 6, 295-296. (b)

Byrne, D., Griffitt, W., Hudgins, W., and Reeves, K. Attitude similarity-dissimilarity and attraction: generality beyond the college sophomore. *Journal of Social Psychology*, in press.

Byrne, D., Griffitt, W., and Stefaniak, D. Attraction and similarity of personality characteristics. *Journal of Personality and Social Psychology*, 1967, 5, 82-90.

Byrne, D., London, O., and Griffitt, W. The effect of topic importance and attitude similarity-dissimilarity on attraction in an intrastranger design. *Psychonomic Science*, 1968, 11, 303-304.

Byrne, D., and McGraw, C. Interpersonal attraction toward Negroes. *Human Relations*, 1964, 17, 201-213.

Byrne, D., and Nelson, D. Attraction as a function of attitude similarity-dissimilarity: the effect of topic importance. *Psychonomic Science*, 1964, 1, 93-94.

Byrne, D., and Nelson, D. Attraction as a linear function of proportion of positive reinforcements. *Journal of Personality and Social Psychology*, 1965, 1, 659-663. (a)

Byrne, D., and Nelson, D. The effect of topic importance and attitude similarity-dissimilarity on attraction in a multistranger design. *Psychonomic Science*, 1965, 3, 449-450. (b)

Byrne, D., Nelson, D., and Reeves, K. Effects of consensual validation and invalidation on attraction as a function of verifiability. *Journal of Experimental Social Psychology*, 1966, 2, 98-107.

Byrne, D., and Rhamey, R. Magnitude of positive and negative reinforcements as a determinant of attraction. *Journal of Personality and Social Psychology*, 1965, 2, 884-889.

Byrne, D., and Wong, T. J. Racial prejudice, interpersonal attraction, and assumed dissimilarity of attitudes. *Journal of Abnormal and Social Psychology*, 1962, 65, 246-253.

Byrne, D., Young, R. K., and Griffitt, W. The reinforcement properties of attitude statements. *Journal of Experimental Research in Personality*, 1966, 1, 266-276.

Clore, G. L., Jr. Discrimination learning as a function of awareness and magnitude of attitudinal reinforcement. Unpublished doctoral dissertation, University of Texas, 1966.

Clore, G. L., and Baldridge, B. Interpersonal attraction: the role of agreement and topic interest. *Journal of Personality and Social Psychology*, 1968, 9, 340-346.

Cohen, A., Stotland, E., and Wolfe, D. M. An experimental investigation of need for cognition. *Journal of Abnormal and Social Psychology*, 1955, 51, 291-297.

Dallenbach, K. M. A simple and inexpensive card-changer. *American Journal of Psychology*, 1960, 73, 139-141.

Dember, W. N., and Earl, R. W. Analysis of exploratory, manipulatory and curiosity behaviors. *Psychological Review*, 1957, 64, 91-96.

Festinger, L. Informal social communication. *Psychological Review*, 1950, 57, 271-282.

Festinger, L. A theory of social comparison processes. *Human Relations*, 1954, 7, 117-140.

Festinger, L., Gerard, H., Hymovitch, B., Kelley, H., and Raven, B. The influence process in the presence of extreme deviates. *Human Relations*, 1952, 5, 327-346.

Festinger, L., and Thibaut, J. Interpersonal communication in small groups. *Journal of Abnormal and Social Psychology*, 1951, 46, 92-99.

Galton, F. *Hereditary genius: an inquiry into its laws and consequences.* (1870) New York: Horizon, 1952.

Golightly, Carole, and Byrne, D. Attitude statements as positive and negative reinforcements. *Science*, 1964, 146, 798-799.

Griffitt, W. B. Interpersonal attraction as a function of self-concept and personality similarity-dissimilarity. *Journal of Personality and Social Psychology*, 1966, 4, 581-584.

Hull, C. L. *Principles of behavior.* New York: Appleton-Century, 1943.

Hunt, Alice McC. A study of the relative value of certain ideals. *Journal of Abnormal and Social Psychology*, 1935, 30, 222-228.

Kantor, J. R. The current situation in social psychology. *Psychological Bulletin*, 1939, 36, 307-360.

Katz, D. Editorial. *Journal of Personality and Social Psychology*, 1965, 1, 1-2.

Kelly, G. A. *The psychology of personal constructs.* New York: Norton, 1955.

Kirkpatrick, C., and Stone, Sarah. Attitude measurement and the comparison of generations. *Journal of Applied Psychology*, 1935, 19, 564-582.

Krauss, R. M. Structural and attitudinal factors in interpersonal bargaining. *Journal of Experimental Social Psychology*, 1966, 2, 42-55.

Kuhn, T. S. *The structure of scientific revolutions*. Chicago: University of Chicago Press, 1962.

Levinger, G., and Breedlove, J. Interpersonal attraction and agreement: a study of marriage partners. *Journal of Personality and Social Psychology*, 1966, 3, 367-372.

Lindzey, G., and Byrne, D. Measurement of social choice and interpersonal attractiveness. In G. Lindzey and E. Aronson (Eds.), *Handbook of social psychology*. Cambridge, Mass.: Addison-Wesley, in press.

Loomis, C. P. Political and occupational cleavages in a Hanoverian village, Germany, a sociometric study. *Sociometry*, 1946, 9, 316-333.

Lott, A. J. Learning and liking. Paper read at meeting of Southwestern Psychological Association, Arlington, Texas, 1966.

Lott, Bernice E., and Lott, A. J. The formation of positive attitudes toward group members. *Journal of Abnormal and Social Psychology*, 1960, 61, 297-300.

McDonald, R. D. The effect of reward-punishment and affiliation need on interpersonal attraction. Unpublished doctoral dissertation, University of Texas, 1962.

McWhirter, R. M., and Jecker, J. D. Attitude similarity and inferred attraction. *Psychonomic Science*, 1967, 7, 225-226.

Morgan, C. L., and Remmers, H. H. Liberalism and conservatism of college students as affected by the depression. *School and Society*, 1935, 41, 780-784.

Nelson, D. A. The effect of differential magnitude of reinforcement on interpersonal attraction. Unpublished doctoral dissertation, University of Texas, 1965.

Newcomb, T. M. The prediction of interpersonal attraction. *American Psychologist*, 1956, 11, 575-586.

Newcomb, T. M. *The acquaintance process*. New York: Holt, Rinehart, and Winston, 1961.

Newcomb, T. M. Stabilities underlying changes in interpersonal attraction. *Journal of Abnormal and Social Psychology*, 1963, 66, 376-386.

Newcomb, T., and Svehla, G. Intra-family relationships in attitudes. *Sociometry*, 1937, 1, 180-205.

Oppenheimer, R. Analogy in science. *American Psychologist*, 1956, 11, 127-136.

Osgood, C. E., Suci, G. J., and Tannenbaum, P. H. *The measurement of meaning*. Urbana, Illinois: University of Illinois Press, 1957.

Pearson, K., and Lee, Alice. On the laws of inheritance in man. I. Inheritance of physical characters. *Biometrika*, 1903, 2, 357-462.

Pepitone, A. *Attraction & hostility*. New York: Atherton, 1964.

Pervin, L. A. The need to predict and control under conditions of threat. *Journal of Personality*, 1963, 31, 570-587.

Pintner, R., Forlano, G., and Freedman, H. Personality and attitudinal similarity among classroom friends. *Journal of Applied Psychology*, 1937, 21, 48-65.

Prentice, W. C. H. Continuity in human learning. *Journal of Experimental Psychology*, 1949, 39, 187-194.

Reilly, Mary S. A., Commins, W. D., and Stefic, E. C. The complementarity of personality needs in friendship choice. *Journal of Abnormal and Social Psychology*, 1960, 61, 292-294.

Richardson, Helen M. Studies of mental resemblance between husbands and wives and between friends. *Psychological Bulletin*, 1939, 36, 104-120.

Richardson, Helen M. Community of values as a factor in friendships of college and adult women. *Journal of Social Psychology*, 1940, 11, 303-312.

Rokeach, M. Belief versus race as determinants of social distance: comments on Triandis' paper. *Journal of Abnormal and Social Psychology*, 1961, 62, 187-188.

Rokeach, M., and Mezei, L. Race and shared belief as factors in social choice. *Science*, 1966, **151**, 167-172.

Rokeach, M., Smith, P. W., and Evans, R. I. Two kinds of prejudice or one? In M. Rokeach, *The open and closed mind*. New York: Basic Books, 1960. Pp. 132-168.

Sanford, N. Will psychologists study human problems? *American Psychologist*, 1965, **20**, 192-202.

Schachter, S. Deviation, rejection, and communication. *Journal of Abnormal and Social Psychology*, 1951, **46**, 190-207.

Schiller, Belle. A quantitative analysis of marriage selection in a small group. *Journal of Social Psychology*, 1932, **3**, 297-319.

Schooley, Mary. Personality resemblances among married couples. *Journal of Abnormal and Social Psychology*, 1936, **31**, 340-347.

Schwartz, M. S. Effectance motivation and interpersonal attraction: individual differences and personality correlates. Unpublished doctoral dissertation, University of Texas, 1966.

Skinner, B. F. *The behavior of organisms*. New York: Appleton-Century, 1938.

Smith A. J. Similarity of values and its relation to acceptance and the projection of similarity. *Journal of Psychology*, 1957, **43**, 251-260.

Smith, C. R., Williams, L., and Willis, R. H. Race, sex, and belief as determinants of friendship acceptance. *Journal of Personality and Social Psychology*, 1967, **5**, 127-137.

Spence, K. W. Theoretical interpretations of learning. In S. S. Stevens (Ed.), *Handbook of experimental psychology*. New York: Wiley, 1951. Pp. 690-729.

Spinoza, B. de. *The ethics*. New York: Dover, 1951.

Stein, D. D. The influence of belief systems on interpersonal preference: a validation study of Rokeach's theory of prejudice. *Psychological Monographs*, 1966, **80** (8, Whole No. 616).

Stein, D. D., Hardyck, J. A., and Smith, M. B. Race *and* belief: an open and shut case. *Journal of Abnormal and Social Psychology*, 1965, **1**, 281-290.

Terman, L. M., and Buttenwieser, P. Personality factors in marital compatibility. *Journal of Social Psychology*, 1935, **6**, 143-171. (a)

Terman, L. M., and Buttenwieser, P. Personality factors in marital compatibility: II. *Journal of Social Psychology*, 1935, **6**, 267-289. (b)

Triandis, H. C. Cognitive similarity and interpersonal communication in industry. *Journal of Applied Psychology*, 1959, **43**, 321-326.

Triandis, H.C. A note on Rokeach's theory of prejudice. *Journal of Abnormal and Social Psychology*, 1961, **62**, 184-186.

Triandis, H. C., Loh, W. D., and Levin, L. A. Race, status, quality of spoken English, and opinions about civil rights as determinants of interpersonal attitudes. *Journal of Personality and Social Psychology*, 1966, **3**, 468-472.

Vreeland, F. M., and Corey, S. M. A study of college friendships. *Journal of Abnormal and Social Psychology*, 1935, **30**, 229-236.

White, R. W. Motivation reconsidered: the concept of competence. *Psychological Review*, 1959, **66**, 297-333.

Winslow, C. N. A study of the extent of agreement between friends' opinions and their ability to estimate the opinions of each other. *Journal of Social Psychology*, 1937, **8**, 433-442.

Wong, T. J. The effect of attitude similarity and prejudice on interpersonal evaluation and attraction. Unpublished master's thesis, University of Texas, 1961.

Worchel, P. Adaptability screening of flying personnel: development of a self-concept inventory for predicting maladjustment. *USAF School of Aviation Medicine Report*, 1957, No. 56-62.

Worchel, P., and McCormick, Betty L. Self-concept and dissonance reduction. *Journal of Personality*, 1963, **31**, 588-599.

SOCIOLINGUISTICS

Susan M. Ervin-Tripp

SPEECH DEPARTMENT
UNIVERSITY OF CALIFORNIA
BERKELEY, CALIFORNIA

I. Introduction

Group therapy session:
  Joe: Ken face it, you're a poor little rich kid.
  Ken: Yes, Mommy. Thank you.
                               Class notes No. 11 of Harvey Sacks
Classroom scene:
  Mrs. Tripp: Miss Hayashijima?
  Student: Yes, sir.

The possibility of insult and of humor based on linguistic choices means that members agree on the underlying rules of speech and on the social meaning of linguistic features. Linguistic selection is deeply enmeshed in the structure of society; members can readily recognize and interpret socially codified deviations from the norms.

During the past few years, the systematic study of the relation of linguistic forms and social meaning has greatly accelerated. The formal recognition of a field of sociolinguistics has been marked in the United States by courses, programs, seminars, and textbooks (Bright, 1966; Fishman, 1968; Hymes, 1964b; Gumperz and Hymes, 1964, in press; Lieberson, 1966). In two respects, the recent history of the field seems different from that of psycholinguistics. Psychologists were largely consumers in the interaction between the fields of psychology and linguistics. Out of concerns that arose from theoretical questions indigenous to psychology, they found that linguistic methods and concepts could provide entirely new ways of accounting for phenomena they had already observed and raise new questions of great interest to them as psychologists. In contrast, many of the central figures in the development of sociolinguistics are regarded as linguists and have developed their sociolinguistic concepts because they found social features continually central to linguistic descriptions. A second difference lies in the disciplinary diversity of social scientists; it is not clear just what the "socio-" implies in the new field. It will be obvious in this article that anthropologists, sociologists, social psychologists, and psychotherapists all have trodden on the terrain we shall define as sociolinguistic, without being much aware of each other.

This article is confined to micro-sociolinguistics, though some references to larger social phenomena are unavoidable. Sociolinguistics in this context will include studies of the components of face-to-face interaction as they bear on, or are affected by, the formal structure of speech. These components may include the personnel, the situation, the function of the interaction, the topic and message, and the channel. As Fishman has pointed out, sociolinguistics is thus distinct from "communication." "It is concerned with *characteristics of the code* and their relationship to characteristics of the communicators or the communication situation, rather than with message or communication functions and processes alone" 1967, p. 590.

During the past decade, psycholinguistics has been profoundly affected by the impact of structural linguistics. Psychologists have come to recognize that verbal output and comprehension are guided by "rules,"[1] so that unique sentences can be produced and understood by speakers in the same speech community. Currently, performance models are begin-

---

[1]"Rules" in this article are not prescriptive but descriptive. They may not be in conscious awareness. Unlike habits, they may include complex structures inferred from the occurrence of interpretable and appropriate novel behavior.

ning to be developed which can account for speech, imitation, comprehension, and other forms of performance, and studies are being made of the development of these abilities in children and of the interpretation of deviant utterances (Chapman, 1967; Ervin-Tripp and Slobin, 1966; Slobin and Welsh, 1967).

In this article, evidence will be assembled to show that the rules of verbal output and comprehension must be organized to specify social features. We can assume that the next step will be the development of sociolinguistic performance models, studies of socialization and the development of sociolinguistic competence (Slama-Cazacu, 1960; Slobin, 1967), and research on the interpretation of sociolinguistically deviant behavior.

This article has three main sections. The first will provide some detailed examples of what kinds of sociolinguistic rules we can expect to find, the second will define specific features which may be the components of sociolinguistic rules, and the third will examine examples of research on differences in rules between different speech communities.

II. Sociolinguistic Rules

A. ALTERNATION RULES

1. *American Rules of Address*

A scene on a public street in contemporary U.S.:
>   "What's your name, boy?" the policeman asked . . . .
>   "Dr. Poussaint. I'm a physician . . . ."
>   "What's your first name, boy? . . ."
>   "Alvin."
>   Poussaint (1967, p. 53)

Anybody familiar with American address rules (see footnote 1) can tell us the feelings reported by Dr. Poussaint: "As my heart palpitated, I muttered in profound humiliation . . . . For the moment, my manhood had been ripped from me . . . . No amount of self-love could have salvaged my pride or preserved my integrity . . . [I felt] self-hate." It is possible to specify quite precisely the rule employed by the policeman. Dr. Poussaint's overt, though coerced, acquiescence in a public insult through widely recognized rules of address is the source of his extreme emotion.

Brown and Ford (Hymes, 1964b) have done pioneering and ingenious research on forms of address in American English, using as corpora American plays, observed usage in a Boston business firm, and reported usage of business executives. They found primarily first name (FN) reciprocation or title plus last name (TLN) reciprocation. However, asymmetrical exchanges were found where there was age difference or occupational rank difference. Intimacy was related to the use of multiple names.

Expanding their analysis from my own rules of address, I have found the structure expressed in the diagram in Fig. 1. The advantage of formal diagraming is that it offers precision greater than that of discursive description (Hymes, 1967). The type of diagram presented here, following Geoghegan (in press), is to be read like a computer flow chart. The entrance point is on the left, and from left to right there is a series of selectors, usually binary. Each path through the diagram leads to a possible outcome, that is, one of the possible alternative forms of address.

Note that the set of paths, or the rule, is like a formal grammar in that it is a way of representing a logical model. The diagram is not intended as a model of a process of the actual decision sequence by which a speaker chooses a form of address or a listener interprets one. The two structures may or may not correspond. In any case, the task of determining the structure implicit in people's knowledge of what forms of address are possible and appropriate is clearly distinct from the task of studying how people, in real situations and in real time, make choices. The criteria and methods of the two kinds of study are quite different. Just as two individuals who share the same grammar might not share the same performance rules, so two individuals might have different decision or interpretation procedures for sociolinguistic alternatives, but still might have an identical logical structure to their behavior.

The person whose knowledge of address is represented in Fig. 1 is assumed to be a competent adult member of a western American academic community. The address forms which are the "outcomes" to be accounted for might fit in frames like "Look, — — — —, it's time to leave." The outcomes themselves are formal sets, with alternative realizations. For example, first names may alternate with nicknames, as will be indicated in a later section. One possible outcome is no-naming, indicated in Fig. 1 by the linguistic symbol for zero [Ø].

The diamonds indicate selectors. They are points where the social categories allow different paths. At first glance, some selectors look like simple external features, but the social determinants vary according to the system, and the specific nature of the categories must be discovered by ethnographic means. For example, "older" implies knowledge of the range of age defined as contemporary. In some southeast Asian systems, even one day makes a person socially older.

The first selector checks whether the addressee is a child or not. In face-to-face address, if the addressee is a child, all of the other distinctions can be ignored. What is the dividing line between adult and child? In my own system, it seems to be school-leaving age, at around age 18. An employed 16-year-old might be classified as an adult.

Status-marked situations are settings such as the courtroom, the

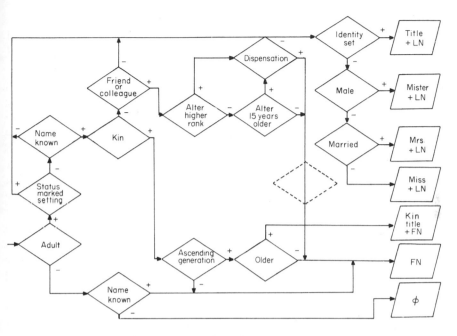

Fig. 1. An American address system.

large faculty meeting, or Congress, where status is clearly specified, speech style is rigidly prescribed, and the form of address of each person is derived from his social identity, for example, "Your honor," "Mr. Chairman." The test for establishing the list of such settings is whether personal friendships are apparent in the address forms or whether they are neutralized (or masked) by the formal requirements of the setting. There are, of course, other channels by which personal relations might be revealed, but here we are concerned only with address alternations, not with tone of voice, connotations of lexicon, and so on.

Among nonkin, the dominant selector of first-naming is whether alter is classified as having the status of a colleague or social acquaintance. When introducing social acquaintances or new work colleagues, it is necessary to employ first names so that the new acquaintances can first-name each other immediately. Familiarity is not a factor within dyads of the same age and rank, and there are no options. For an American assistant professor to call a new colleague of the same rank and age "Professor Watkins" or "Mr. Watkins" would be considered strange, at least on the West Coast.

Rank here refers to a hierarchy within a working group, or to ranked statuses like teacher — pupil. In the American system, no distinction in address is made to equals or subordinates since both receive FN. The distinction may be made elsewhere in the linguistic system, for example, in the style of requests used. We have found that subordinates outside the family receive direct commands in the form of imperatives more often than equals, to whom requests are phrased in other ways at least in some settings (see below).

A senior alter has the option of dispensing the speaker from offering TLN by suggesting that he use a first name or by tacitly accepting first name. Brown and Ford (Hymes, 1964a) have discussed the ambiguity that arises because it is not clear whether the superior, for instance, a professor addressing a doctoral candidate or younger instructor, wishes to receive back the FN he gives. This problem is mentioned by Emily Post: "It is also effrontery for a younger person to call an older by her or his first name, without being asked to do so. Only a very underbred, thick-skinned person would attempt it" (Post, 1922, p.54). In the American system described in Fig. 1, age difference is not significant until it is nearly the size of a generation, which suggests its origin in the family. The presence of options, or dispensation, creates a locus for the expression of individual and situational nuances. The form of address can reveal dispensation, and therefore be a matter for display or concealment of third parties. No-naming or Ø is an outcome of uncertainty among these options.[2]

The *identity* set refers to a list of occupational titles or courtesy titles accorded people in certain statuses. Examples are Judge, Doctor, and Professor. A priest, physician, dentist, or judge may be addressed by title alone, but a plain citizen or an academic person may not. In the latter cases, if the name is unknown, there is no address form (or zero, Ø) available and we simply no-name the addressee. The parentheses below refer to optional elements, the bracketed elements to social selectional categories.

[Cardinal]:	Your excellency
[U.S. President]:	Mr. President
[Priest]:	Father (+ LN)
[Nun]:	Sister (+ religious name)
[Physician]:	Doctor (+ LN)
[Ph.D., Ed.D.], etc.:	(Doctor + LN)
[Professor]:	(Professor + LN)
[Adult], etc.:	(Mister + LN)
	(Mrs. + LN)
	(Miss + LN)

[2]In the system in Fig. 1, it is possible to create asymmetrical address by using FN to a familiar addressee who cannot reciprocate because of rank or age difference, and his unwillingness or lack of dispensation, e.g., a domestic servant. E. Hughes has noted a shift from TLN to FN by physicians whose patients move from private fees to Medicare. This usage does not fit into the rule in Fig. 1.

Wherever the parenthetical items cannot be fully realized, as when last name (LN) is unknown, and there is no lone title, the addressee is no-named by a set of rules of the form as follows: Father $+ \emptyset \rightarrow$ Father, Professor $+ \emptyset \rightarrow \emptyset$, Mister $+ \emptyset \rightarrow \emptyset$, etc. An older male addressee may be called "sir" if deference is intended, as an optional extra marking.

These are my rules, and seem to apply fairly narrowly within the academic circle I know. Nonacademic university personnel can be heard saying "Professor" or "Doctor" without LN, as can school teachers. These delicate differences in sociolinguistic rules are sensitive indicators of the communication net.

The zero forms imply that often no address form is available to follow routines like "yes," "no," "pardon me," and "thank you." Speakers of languages or dialects where all such routines must contain an address form are likely in English either to use full name or to adopt forms like "sir" and "ma'am," which are either not used or used only to elderly addressees in this system.

One might expect to be able to collapse the rule system by treating kin terms as a form of title, but it appears that the selectors are not identical for kin and nonkin. A rule which specifies that *ascending generation* only receives title implies that a first cousin would not be called "cousin" but merely FN, whereas an aunt of the same age would receive a kin title, as would a parent's cousin. If a title is normally used in direct address and there are several members of the kin category, a first name may also be given (e.g., Aunt Louise). Frequently there are additional features marked within a given family such as patrilineal vs. matrilineal, and near vs. distant. Whenever the address forms for an individual person's relatives are studied, this proves to be the case, in my experience.

Presumably, the individual set of rules or the regional dialect of a reader of this article may differ in some details from that reported in Fig. 1. Perhaps sociolinguists will begin to use a favorite frame of linguists: "In my dialect we say . . ." to illustrate such differences in sociolinguistic rules. For example, I have been told that in some American communities there may be a specific status of familiarity beyond first-naming, where a variant of the middle name is optional among intimates. This form then becomes the normal or unmarked address form to the addressee.

"What's your name, boy?"
"Dr. Poussaint. I'm a physician."
"What's your first name, boy?"
"Alvin."

The policeman insulted Dr. Poussaint three times. First, he employed a social selector for race in addressing him as "boy," which neutralizes identity set, rank, and even adult status. If addressed to a white, "boy" presumably would be used only for a child, youth, or menial regarded as a nonperson.

Dr. Poussaint's reply supplied only TLN and its justification. He made clear that he wanted the officer to suppress the race selector, yielding a rule like that in Fig. 1. This is clearly a nondeferential reply, since it does not contain the FN required by the policemen's address rule. The officer next treated TLN as failure to answer his demand, as a non-name, and demanded FN; third, he repeated the term "boy" which would be appropriate to unknown addressees.

According to Fig. 1, under no circumstances should a stranger address a physician by his first name. Indeed, the prestige of physicians even exempts them from first-naming (but not from "Doc") by used-car salesmen, and physicians' wives can be heard so identifying themselves in public in order to claim more deference than "Mrs." brings. Thus the policeman's message is quite precise: "Blacks are wrong to claim adult status or occupational rank. You are children." Dr. Poussaint was stripped of all deference due his age and rank.

Communication has been perfect in this interchange. Both were familiar with an address system which contained a selector for race available to both black and white for insult, condescension, or deference, as needed. Only because they shared these norms could the policeman's act have its unequivocal impact.

2. Comparative Rule Studies

The formulation of rules in this fashion can allow us to contrast one sociolinguistic system with another in a systematic way. A shared language does not necessarily mean a shared set of sociolinguistic rules. For instance, rules in educated circles in England vary. In upper class boarding schools, boys and some girls address each other by LN instead of FN. In some universities and other milieux affected by the public school usage, solidary address between male acquaintances and colleagues is LN rather than FN. To women it may be Mrs. or Miss + LN by men (not title + LN) or FN. Women usually do not use LN. Thus sex of both speaker and addressee is important.

In other university circles, the difference from the American rule is less; prior to dispensation by seniors with whom one is acquainted, one may use Mister or Mrs. rather than occupational title as an acceptably solidary but deferential form. Note that this is the solidary usage to women by some male addressees in the other system. The two English systems contrast with the American one in allowing basically three, rather than two classes of alternatives for nonkin: occupational title + LN, M + LN, and FN/LN. The intermediate class is used for the familiar person who must be deferred to or treated with courtesy.

Two Asian systems of address have been described recently. The pioneering work of William Geohegan (in press) described the naming system of a speaker of Bisayan, a Philippine language. Geohegan's formal presentation of the system in a talk some years ago was the model for the rules used in the figures in this article. As in most systems, children routinely receive the familiar address form. The Bisayan system, like the American and English, chooses on the basis of relative rank, relative age, and friendship. But there are important differences. In the United States, all adult strangers are treated with deference; in the Bisayan system, social inferiors do not receive titled address. In the American system for nonkin, added age, like higher rank, merely increases distance or delays familiar address; in the Bisayan system, inferiors or friends who are older receive a special term of address uniting informality and deference.

The Korean system is even less like the American (Howell, 1967). In Korea, relative rank must first be assessed. If rank is equal, relative age within two years is assessed, and if that is equal, solidarity (e.g., classmates) will differentiate familiar from polite speech. This system differs both in its components and its order from the American and Bisayan rules. Both inferiors and superiors are addressed differently from equals. Many kinds of dyads differ in authority — husband-wife, customer-tradesman, teacher-pupil, employer-employee — and in each case, asymmetrical address is used. Addressees more than two years older or younger than the speaker are differentially addressed, so that close friendship is rigidly age-graded. Solidary relations arise from status, just as they do between equal colleagues in the American system, regardless of personal ties. There are more familiar address forms yet to signal intimacy within solidary dyads. If the English system has three levels, there are even more in the Korean system. Since the criteria were multiple in the Howell study, instead of a single frame, the comparison is not quite exact.

As Howell pointed out, the Korean system illustrates that the dimension of approach that Brown and Gilman (1960) called solidarity may in fact have several forms in one society. In the Korean system intimacy is separable from solidarity. This separation may also exist in the American system but in a different way. One is required to first-name colleagues even though they are disliked. On the other hand, as Brown and Ford (Hymes, 1964b) showed, nicknames may indicate friendship more intimate than the solidarity requiring FN. They found that various criteria of intimacy, such as self-disclosure, were related to the *number* of FN alternates, such as nicknames and sometimes LN, which were used to an addressee, and they suggested that intimacy creates more complex and varied dyadic relations which speakers may signal by address variants. Thus, in the American system two points of major option for speakers exist: the ambiguous address relation between solidary speakers of unequal age or status and intimacy. Systems can be expected to vary in the points where address is prescribed or where options exist; Brown and Ford suggested a universal feature, on the other hand, in saying that in all systems frequent and intimate interaction should be related to address variation.[3] This, they suggest is related to a semantic principle of greater differentiation of important domains.

3. Two-Choice Systems

The brilliant work of Brown and Gilman (1960) which initiated the recent wave of studies of address systems was based on a study of T and V, the second person verbs and pronouns in European languages. In English, the same alternation existed before "thou" was lost.

One might expect two-choice systems to be somewhat simpler than a system like Bisayan, which in Geohegan's description gives 19 output categories. But the number of outcomes can be few although the number of selectors is many or the kinds of rules relating them complex. Figure 2 gives a description of the nineteenth century rules of the Russian gentry, as I derive them from the excellent analysis by Friedrich (1966), which gives sufficiently full detail to permit resolution of priorities. *Special statuses* refers to the tsar and God, who seem not to fit on any status continuum. *Status marked settings* mentioned by Friedrich were the court, parliament, public occasions, duels, and examinations. *Rank* inferiors might be lower in social class, army rank, or ethnic group, or be servants. *Familiarity* applied to classmates, fellow students, fellow revolutionaries, lovers, and intimate friends. There does not seem to be the prescription in the Korean and American solidary relation. A feature of the system which Friedrich's literary examples illustrate vividly is its sensitivity to situational features. Thus T means "the right to use Ty," but not the obligation to do so. Within the kin group, household is of considerable importance because of the large households separated by distance in traditional Russia.

A slightly later Eastern European system described by Slobin (1963) is given in Fig. 3. The Yiddish system is somewhat more like the American than like the Russian system in that deference is always given adult strangers regardless of rank. However, an older person receives defer-

---

[3] William Geohegan has privately suggested that in his Philippine studies the extremely high intimacy in families resulted in use of paralinguistic rather than lexical alternatives for "address variation" of the type Brown and Ford discuss.

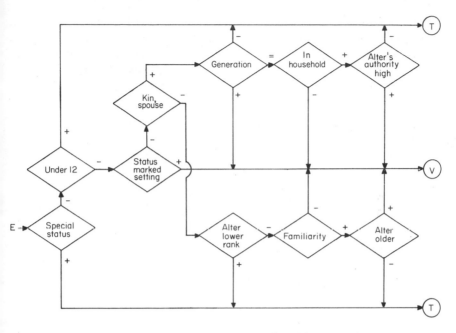

Fig. 2. Nineteenth century Russian address.

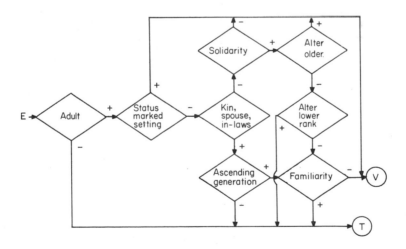

Fig. 3. Yiddish address system.

ence, despite familiarity, unless he is a member of the kin group. In the American system, familiarity can neutralize age.

How have these systems changed? We have some evidence from the

Soviet Union. The Russian revolutionaries, unlike the French, decreed V, implying that they wanted respect more than solidarity. The current system is identical to the old with one exception: Within the family, asymmetry has given way to reciprocal T, as it has in most of western Europe, at least in urbanized groups. For nonkin in ranked systems like factories, superiors receive Vy and give Ty:

> When a new employee is addressed as Ty, she says: "Why do I call you *'vy'* while you call me *'ty'*?"
> Kormilitzyn gleefully shoots back a ready answer: "If I were to call everyone *'vy'* I'd never get my plan fulfilled. You don't fulfill plans by using *'vy'*" (Kantorovich, 1966, p. 30).

Evidently the upperclass habit of using *"vy"* until familiarity was established (a system reflecting the fact that the T/V contrast itself came in from above as a borrowing from French) has seeped downward. "A half-century ago even upon first meeting two workers of the same generation would immediately use *'ty'*. Today things are different. Middle-aged workers maintain *'vy'* for a long time, or else adopt the intermediate form which is very widespread among people within a given profession: *'ty'* combined with first name and patronymic" (Kantorovich, 1966, p. 81).

Kantorovich, true to the 1917 decree, complains about three features of the current system: *ty* to inferiors regardless of age, *ty* to older kin, and first names alone among young acquaintances. Thus he favors the more deferential alternative in each case. Social change in Russia has been relatively slow in sociolinguistic rules, has affected family life more than public life, and has spread the practices of the gentry among the workers.

The Puerto Rican two-choice system in Fig. 4 is quite simple since it is a system of children. The data were generously supplied by Wallace

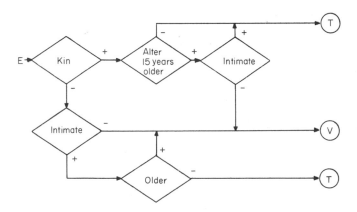

Fig. 4. Puerto Rican address system (children).

Lambert and his collaborators from a large-scale study of comparative address systems in several cultures. Elementary and high school students filled in questionnaires about the forms of address given and received. In this chart, interlocale and intersubject differences have been suppressed. The striking feature of this system is that it requires only three discriminations. It is likely, of course, that adult informants would elaborate further details. Intimacy, in this system, refers to close ties of friendship, which can occur with others of widely varying age, e.g., with godparents, and is quite distinct from solidarity, which arises from status alone. Adolescent girls, for example, do not give "tu" to a classmate unless she is a friend.

Lambert and his collaborators have collected slightly less detailed data from samples of schoolchildren in Montreal, from a small town in Quebec, from Mayenne, France, and from St. Pierre et Michelon, an island colony with close ties to France, much closer than to nearby Canada.

The system of kin address varies considerably. In both Mayenne and St. Pierre, all kin and godparents receive "tu." In Quebec, the urban middle class is moving in this direction, but the lower class and the rural regions from which it derives retain an address system like Puerto Rico's in which distance (including age) within the family is important. In some families, even older siblings receive "vous." If changes in kin address arise during social change, one would expect between-family differences to be greater than in nonkin address, since sanctions are intrafamily. Generally, "intimate" means parents, then aunts, uncles, and godparents, then grandparents. Some interfamily differences might be accounted for by finding which family members live in the household, which nearby, and which far away.

Lambert and Tucker (in press) have referred to a study of the social connotations of this changing system for urban school children in Montreal. Children were asked to judge taped family interaction varying in "tu" or "vous" to parents, and in the outcome of the interaction — giving or not giving the child a requested bicycle. In addition to the class differences (*tu* users richer, more educated families), the judges drew from the pronoun usage a set of expectations about family values, resulting in favorable judgments when the interaction outcome was congruent. For instance, *tu*-using families sound modern and tolerant, the mothers more active, the fathers more tolerant than *vous*-using families, if they prove child-centered. However, it is *vous*-using families that sound religious, with a good family spirit, an active mother and tolerant father when the decision goes against the child.

Sex of addressee appears to be a feature of adult systems, or may influence the probabilities of intimacy where there is a selector. In Quebec, adults generally give "tu" to children and young men, regardless of familiarity. In St. Pierre, except to upper class girls, who are less likely to receive "tu" under any conditions, acquaintance legitimizes "tu" and is necessary even in addressing children. In Mayenne, middle class little boys said they received "tu" from everyone (and reported often reciprocating to strangers), but otherwise familiarity seems to be required, as in Puerto Rico, in the Mayenne system. Boys generally receive T from employers, and in the country and the urban lower class they receive T from service personnel. It should be noted that the analysis from the children's standpoint of what they think they receive is an interesting reflection of the fact that people know what they should say themselves, and they also expect some standard form from others. In analyzing the adult rule systems, however, the children's data are not the best; the adults of rural or lower class background may have different rules (e.g., service personnel, perhaps) than others.

The compressed presentation here of Lambert's work has indicated several directions for research on social criteria of address selection. Lambert has shown that these rules are sensitive indicators of differences between social groups and of social change. One must look beyond the address system for independent social features correlated with address systems of a defined type. In order to do such studies, a clear-cut formal system for typing properties of address systems (like language typologies) is necessary.

Lambert (1967b) has discussed the development of address rules with age. There are several interesting problems in the learning of these systems, one being the visibility of the various social selectors. One can assume that rank graduations in an adult system might be learned late (at least in terms of generalizability to new addressees), as would generation differentiations not highly related to age. A second problem emphasized by Lambert is the system of alternation itself. Children in most language communities learn fairly early to employ the asymmetry of first and second person (for a case study see McNeill, 1963). Thus if they always received T and gave V, there might be less difficulty; however, they see others exchanging reciprocal V and T as well as asymmetrical address, and they give T to some alters. These problems could be studied in natural language communities where the language structure provides different category systems and social selectors (Slobin, 1967).

4. Socialization

Adults entering a new system because of geographical or occupational mobility may have to learn new sociolinguistic rules. A contrastive analysis of formal rules, in combination with a theory of social learning, would allow specification of what will happen.

First, we can predict what the speaker will do. We can expect, on the basis of research on bilinguals (Ervin-Tripp, in press; Haugen, 1956), that the linguistic alternatives will at first be assimilated to familiar forms, to "diamorphs." Thus a Frenchman in the United States might start out by assuming that Monsieur = Mister, Madame = Mrs., and so on.

However, the rules for occurrence of these forms are different in France. In the polite discourse of many speakers, routines like "merci," "au revoir," "bonjour," "pardon" do not occur without an address form in France, although they may in the United States. One always says "Au revoir, Madame" or some alternative address form. "Madame" differs from "Mrs." in at least two ways. Unknown female addressees of a certain age are normally called "Madame" regardless of marital status. Further, Mrs. $+ \emptyset = \emptyset$; Madame $+ \emptyset =$ Madame. As a matter of fact, the rule requiring address with routines implies that when LN is not known, there cannot be a "zero alternate" — some form of address must be used anyway, like the English "sir." As a result of these differences in rules, we can expect to hear elderly spinsters addressed as "Pardon me, Mrs."

How do listeners account for errors? I suggested earlier that shifting at certain points in sociolinguistic rules is regularly available as an option. Normally, it is interpreted as changing the listener's perceived identity or his relation to the speaker. The result may be complementary, as "sir" to an unknown working class male, or insulting, as "Mommy" to an adolescent male. If the learner of a sociolinguistic system makes an error that falls within this range of interpretable shifts, he may constantly convey predictably faulty social meanings. Suppose the speaker, but not the listener, has a system in which familiarity, not merely solidarity, is required for use of a first name. He will use TLN in the United States to his new colleagues and be regarded as aloof or excessively formal. He will feel that first-name usage from his colleagues is brash and intrusive. In the same way, encounters across social groups may lead to misunderstandings within the United States. Suppose a used-car salesman regards his relation to his customers as solidary, or a physician so regards his relation to old patients. The American using the rule in Fig. 1 might regard such speakers as intrusive, having made a false claim to a solidary status. In this way, one can pinpoint abrasive features of interaction across groups.

Another possible outcome is that the alternative selected is completely outside the system. This would be the case with "Excuse me, Mrs." which cannot be used under any circumstances by rule 1. This behavior is then interpreted with the help of any additional cues available, such as the face, dress, or accent of a foreigner. In such cases, if sociolinguistic rules are imperfectly learned, there may be social utility in retaining an accent wherever the attitude toward the group of foreigners is sufficiently benign; it is better to be designated a foreigner than to risk insulting or offending addressees.

5. Integrated Sociolinguistic Rules

The rules given above are fractional. They are selective regarding the linguistic alternations accounted for. They define only specific linguistic entries as the universe of outcomes to be predicted. If one starts from social variables, a different set of rules might emerge. This is the outlook of William Geohegan (in press) and Ward Goodenough (1965), as well as Dell Hymes (1964a), who suggested taking "a specific or universal function, such as the distinguishing of the status or role of man and woman, derogation, respect, or the like, and . . . investigating the diverse means so organized within the language habits of the community, . . . [rather than] looking for function as a correlative of structure already established" (p. 44).

Using such an approach, Goodenough examined behavior toward a range of statuses, and found that it was possible to rank both the statuses and the forms of behavior into Guttman scales and equivalent classes, grouped at the same scale point (1965). In this way, various kinds of verbal and nonverbal behavior can be shown to be outcomes of the same social selectors.

Deference, the feature studied by Goodenough, may be indicated by pronoun alternations, names or titles, tone of voice, grammatical forms, vocabulary, and so on (Capell, 1966, pp. 104ff; Martin, in Hymes, 1964b). Deferential behavior in some systems may be realized only in special situations such as in introductions or in making requests. If one compares an isolated segment of two sociolinguistic systems, he cannot legitimately conclude that a given social variable is more important in one system than in the other. It may simply be realized through a different form of behavior.

It is not clear how the different realizations of social selectors might be important. Address, pronominal selection, or consistent verb suffixing (as in Japanese) can be consciously controlled more readily, perhaps, than intonation contours or syntactic complexity. Frenchmen report "trying to use 'tu'" with friends. Such forms can be taught by rule specification to children or newcomers. Forms which allow specific exceptions, or which have options so that too great or too little frequency might be conspicuous, cannot be taught so easily. Such rules can be acquired by newcomers only by long and intense exposure rather than by formal teaching.

Some alternations are common and required, others can be avoided. Howell reported that in Knoxville, Tennessee, Negroes uncertain of whether or not to reciprocate FN simply avoided address forms to colleagues (Howell, 1967, pp. 81 – 83), an approach that Brown and Ford also observed in the academic rank system. In a pronominal rank system like French or Russian such avoidance is impossible. Among bilinguals, language switching may be employed to avoid rank signaling (Howell, 1967; Tanner, 1967). The avoidable selector can be considered a special case of the presence of options in the system. Tyler (1965) has noticed that morphological deference features (like the Japanese) are more common in societies of particular kinship types, such as lineage organization.

This description was primarily drawn from the standpoint of predicting a speaker's choice of alternatives in some frame. It is also possible to examine these rules from the standpoint of comprehension or interpretation, as have Blom and Gumperz (in press) in their discussion of *social meaning*. Just as one can comprehend a language without speaking it, as actors we can interpret the social meaning of the acts of others without necessarily using rules identical to our own. The relation between production and comprehension rules remains to be studied.

B. Sequencing Rules

1. Leave-Taking

After an introduction, when you have talked for some time to a stranger whom you have found agreeable, and you then take leave, you say, "Good-by, I am very glad to have met you," or "Good-by, I hope I shall see you again soon' – or 'some time." The other person answers, "Thank you," or perhaps adds, "I hope so, too."

Emily Post (1922, p. 9)

The sequential events mentioned in this description are Introduction + Conversation + Leave-taking. Leaving aside the components of the first two, elsewhere specified, leave-taking (LT) has two parts, for the two actors.

$$
\begin{aligned}
\text{Leave-taking} &\longrightarrow \text{LT } 1 + \text{LT } 2 \\
\text{LT } 1 &\longrightarrow \text{Goodbye} + \text{CP} \\
\text{CP} &\longrightarrow \begin{cases} \text{I am very glad to have met you} \\ \text{I hope I shall see you again} \begin{cases} \text{soon} \\ \text{some time} \end{cases} \end{cases} \\
\text{LT } 2 &\longrightarrow \text{Thank you } (\text{+I hope so, too}).
\end{aligned}
$$

This is a notation, borrowed from grammars, illustrating a phrase structure rule. The plus marks indicate sequential events, the arrows expansions or replacements in the "derivation tree" to be read as "rewrite leave-taking as LT 1 + LT 2," the braces alternatives, and the parentheses optional elements. The more general rule states that introduction always precedes the other two events. Presumably the rules will indicate that while introduction and leave-taking are relatively fixed routines, conversation can be expanded to hours. We can regard these routines as transition markers between speech events.

2. Summons Sequence

A phone rings in Jim's home:
Jim: Hello.
George: Hi, how are you?
Jim: O.K., but listen, I'm in a phone booth and this is my last dime. Barbara's phone is busy and I won't be able to meet her at seven. Could you keep trying to get her for me and tell her?
George: What the hell are you talking about?

Adapted from Schegloff (in press)

Jim was a sociology student who was trying to violate rules of telephone conversation. The rules derived by Schegloff from a large sample of phone conversations can be characterized as follows:

Summons Sequence $\longrightarrow$ Summons + Answer + Continuation + Response

Summons $\longrightarrow$ $\begin{cases} \text{Courtesy Phrase [to stranger]} \\ \text{Attention-call [nonstranger]} \\ \text{Telephone bell} \ldots \end{cases}$

Answer [phone] $\longrightarrow$ Greeting 1 (+ Identification [office])

Continuation $\longrightarrow$ (Greeting 2) + (Identification) + Message

Response $\longrightarrow$ (Deferral +) Reply to message

Following every summons, there are three phases to complete the cycle. The omission of any part, if a second party is present, is unusual and must be accounted for. The summons can be realized in a variety of ways, depending on whether alter is physically present, known, and so on. To a stranger one might say "pardon me!" or "hey!" Attention-calls include "waiter!" "Dr. Conant!" "Joe!" Their selection rules would be close to Fig. 1.

Alter must answer a summons. Lecturers may find it hard to ignore waving hands in the audience. If there is nonresponse, the summons is repeated. On the phone: "Hello ... Hello ... Hello? .... Hello!" There are definite limits (longer for children) for such repetitions of summonses.

The next major step is that following the limited routines of exchanging greetings, the caller gives a message, explaining his reason for calling.

In the example, Jim tried to play the role of caller rather than called. He did this by not giving George a chance to give a message and by giving a message itself semantically deviant and appropriate only to George's status as caller.

If the caller did not intend a summons, or if his need has vanished, he fills the continuation position with an account: "Never mind." "I was just saying hello." "I was just checking the phone." If he states a request, alter must respond.

We have not stated the rule in its full detail. The realizations of Greeting 1 vary, according to circumstance. Thus the alternatives might be "Yes," on an intercom, "Good morning, Macy's," for a receptionist on an institutional telephone, "Hello," on other outside phones. Greeting 2 has different alternation sets than Greeting 1, for example "Hi," to a friend, "How are you," to a friend, "Hello," to others. Thus the realizations of particular units in the sequencing rules may involve alternations which are dependent on social features. Also, some of the optional positions may be selected or omitted by social criteria.

The selection of certain alternates may entail an expansion at that position in the sequence. For example, if "How are you?" occurs as the Greeting 2 realization, the addressee must reply. The result may be an embedded interchange about his health. The called person at this point, like anyone asked this question, has two options. He can either give a routine response to nonintimate alters, such as "Okay," or "Fine," or, if the alter is a friend, he has the option of describing the real state of his health. Indeed, he may be obligated to do so since a close friend might be insulted at not being informed of his broken leg at the time of the conversation rather than later. Sacks has described the routine response as an obligation to lie, but formally it is a neutralization of the semantic selection feature — simply a briefer route.

If Greeting 2 establishes that the caller is a friend, the addressee has the option of providing a new greeting which is for a friend, as Greeting 1 was not:

"Hello."

"Hi, Joe. How are you?"

"Oh, hi. I'm okay . . ."

Note that by this system, "hi" is more intimate than "hello." Not so in 1922, when Emily Post said that "hello" is "never used except between intimate friends who call each other by the first name" (1922, p. 19).

In the conversation just cited, *identification* is through the channel of voice recognition. Between strangers, identification is required, according to Sacks' evidence (in press). Sacks has pointed out that self-identifications, introductions, and third-party categorizations are important social devices. Since everyone has many statuses, the selection in each case where a status (other than a proper name) is given follows certain fixed rules, among them consistency with other choices. In a series of such events in the same situation, the categories tend to be members of the same contrast set, e.g., occupations.

3. Invitation Sets

Slots in sequences such as the summons sequence are not necessarily recognized by the speakers or labeled by them. Sacks, for example, has cited in lectures the observation that many encounters include an optional sequence at a time when a newcomer enters a group or a dyad begins conversation. These he called "pre-invitation," "pre-invitation/rejection," "invitation," and "rejection."

a. *Pre-invitation.*
"Hello? Hello. What are you doing?"
"Nothing."

The person called interprets the question as a preliminary to an invitation. If the reply is "nothing" the caller might suggest coming over, might launch into a long conversation, and so on. The person called does not talk about the things he is doing that are irrelevant to the supposed invitation.

b. *Pre-invitation/rejection.*
"Can I see you for a moment?"
"What do you want?"

The question is designed to gather information suitable for deciding about offering an invitation or a rejection. So too, according to Sacks' analysis, the sequence in Pittenger, Hockett, and Danehy's *The First Five Minutes*:

Therapist: What brings you here . . . ?
Patient: I don't feel like talking.

Sacks observes that the patient knows that her acceptability for therapy depends on her answer, also that she must reveal her private concerns to someone who is not yet defined as her regular physician, appropriate to such disclosures. Here the open-ended question underlines the ambiguity of the new relationship.

c. *Rejection.* When a wife greets her husband by announcing that her visiting friends are discussing nursery schools or the sewing circle, she implies his absence would be welcome. In this act, the wife asserts that the activity of the group is bound to a category of which he is not a member.

d. Invitation. Sacks cited the late arrival of a member to a group therapy session:

"Hi. We were having an automobile discussion."
". . . discussing the psychological motives for . . ."
"drag racing in the streets."

Here the latecomer was invited into the conversation by three members in one sentence.

Emily Post referred to such practices as "including someone in conversation," and suggested that it can be done without an introduction, for example, by saying to a friend who arrives during a conversation with a gardener, "[Hello, Gladys,] Mr. Smith is suggesting that I dig up these cannas and put in delphiniums." This is evidently a semi-introduction, since it allows the superior to address the inferior, but without the implication of equality lying in a full introduction.

These four slots are not recognized by speakers as such. They enter into complex sequencing rules which have not yet been analyzed sufficiently; it is clear, for example, that the first two occupy different positions, one being uttered by the summoner, the other by the respondent. Rejection/invitation are alternatives in the same rule. The function of and sequence rules for these speech acts can be checked not only from natural conversations but by experimental omission or alteration of the temporal location in the sequence of acts.

4. Narratives

Labov and Waletzky (1967) recently presented a framework for the analysis of informal narratives or oral versions of personal experience. Narratives, whether formal or casual, involve problems of sequencing *par excellence*, since it is inherent in the problem of narration that the hearer must understand the sequence in the *referent* events. The article defined a series of clause types in terms of their permutation properties. The preservation of causal relations implied by narrative sequence is evident as early as age 6, according to Brent and Katz, in very simple tasks (1967). A basic contrast in the analysis of Labov and Waletzky is between free clauses, which could occur anywhere in the narration (e.g., descriptions of character of hero), and clauses which must occur before, after, or between certain others, which define their displacement range.

By utilizing the units of this formal analysis to characterize the whole narrative sequence, Labov and Waletzky were able to identify five portions in the maximally expanded narrative, which they call orientation, complication, evaluation, resolution, and coda. The minimum possible narrative has only complication. While they noted that the amount of narrative structure used beyond the minimum was related to the verbal skill of the speaker, it was also apparent that differences of group styles, age, and so on could be profitably examined through such formal means.

5. Tying Rules

In his class lectures, Sacks has discussed many details of sequencing within conversations. One problem has to do with the sequence of speakers. In a dyadic conversation, he has found that the rule is alternation of adequate complete utterances between the two speakers. But in larger groups, more complex patterns obtain. The next speaker may be indicated by asking a question. Then the addressee has the right to the floor whenever he chooses to talk, and the asker has the right after the responder. The rule is such that other material can intervene between question and response. "When I've asked a question, then the pause between my talk and yours is your silence," according to Sacks. Thus a question is a "first speaker form," since it implies that a second speaker is called on. So, in the groups he has studied, is an insult.

Second speaker forms include pronouns tying back to earlier utterances, and pro-verbs. Some forms are even more complex, such as "I still say, though . . ." which implies a third activity of which some prior one was done by the same person.

The result of using the sequence features Sacks has discussed is that a great deal of information can be obtained from single utterances. In the example, "Ken, face it, you're a poor little rich kid," he points out that we know that Ken is the addressee, that Ken now has the right to speak, that he has the right to give an insult to the speaker, and that some categorization device (e.g., Mommy) in a contrast set with "kid" is likely.

6. Speech Event Analysis

Sequence rules are appropriate for the description of what may be called "speech events," which, in turn, may be parts of or coterminous with *focused interaction* (Goffman, 1963). Traditionally, anthropologists were aware of such organized units only in the case of ceremonies and tales, where preservation of the same thematic sequences, or even the same wording, was highly valued. These repeated routines were, of course, obvious even to the most casual observer. *The Book of Common Prayer,* for example, clearly labels each speech event, its components, and the alternatives at each point.

Even so simple a sequence as a short telephone conversation, as Schegloff has shown, has underlying structural rules. These rules refer to abstract categories not evident on the surface of behavior. Since multi-party interactions must be even more complex, we can assume that the rules for such encounters will not be simple. At least, one cannot expect that the rules of speech events are any simpler than the grammar of sentences.

Frake (1964) identified segments of the speech event as *discourse stages*. Components of the stages or coterminous with them are *exchanges,* which Frake defined as "sets of utterances with a common topic focus," probably similar to Watson and Potter's (1962) *episodes. Speech acts* are utterances or utterance sets with an interpretable function. Examples might be the routines that can mark the boundaries of episodes such as "That reminds me . . ." promises, jokes, apologies, greetings, requests, or insults. Speech acts, unlike functions, are cultural units, and must be discovered by ethnological methods.

Some of the features of order between these units have been considered in the context of narration by Labov and Waletzky (1967) and others. The displacement sets and other categories they have defined for clauses can also apply to other units such as speech acts. Where displacement occurs, of self-identification, for instance, it may be marked by special routines, "By the way, my name is — — — —" which would not be used except for the deviation.

The categories which Schegloff and Sacks discussed are sufficiently general in many cases so that one can expect them to be found universally. The summons sequence is a good candidate. Schegloff showed, with respect to telephone conversations, that the basic rules he gave, with called answering first, caller providing initial topic, and so on, are required by the distribution of information at the start. On the other hand, the specific selections available within each formal category in this case are likely to be highly culture- or group-specific. The strategy for the discovery of alternations and of sequencing rules is similar. In the latter case, one tests the response of members to omissions or permutations, rather than to substitutions.

C. CO-OCCURRENCE RULES

1. Types of Rules

"How's it going, Your Eminence? Centrifuging okay? Also, have you been analyzin' whatch'unnertook t'achieve?"

The bizarreness of this hypothetical episode arises from the oscillations between different varieties of speech. It violates the co-occurrence rules that we assume English to have.

In the preceding section, we were concerned with the selection of lexical items, pronouns, or inflectional alternatives. We conceived of each instance as involving social selectors. Once a selection has been made, however, later occurrences within the same utterance, conversation, or even between the same dyad may be predictable. Whenever there is predictability between two linguistic forms, we can speak of co-occurrence rules.

Co-occurrence rules could be of two kinds. Predictability through time might be called horizontal, since it specifies relations between items sequentially in the discourse. Another type might be called vertical, specifying the realization of an item at each of the levels of structure of a language. For instance, given a syntactical form, only certain lexicon may normally be employed, and a particular set of phonetic values may realize the lexicon. If one learned political terms in New York and gardening terms in Virginia, the phonetic coloring of the lexicon might reflect their provenance in the individual's history. The most striking case lies in the well-practiced bilingual who uses French syntax and pronunciation for French vocabulary and English syntax and pronunciation for English vocabulary.

In the example, the following are violations of vertical co-occurrence:

(1) "How's it going" is a phrase from casual speech, but the suffix "-ing" is used, rather than "-in" which is normal for casual speech.

(2) An elliptical construction is used in the second utterance, which contains only a participle, but the formal "-ing" appears again.

(3) A technical word, "centrifuge" is used in the elliptical construction.

(4) The "-in" suffix is used with the formal "analyze."

(5) Rapid informal articulation is used for the pedantic phrase "undertook to achieve."

Horizontal co-occurrence rules refer to the same level of structure, and might be lexical or structural. The vocabulary in the example oscillates between slang and technical terms, the syntax between ellipsis and parallel nonellipsis. In bilingual speech, one may find structural predictability independent of lexicon, as in an example of Pennsylvania German:

Di kau ist over di fens jumpt.

Here the syntax and grammatical morphemes are German, the lexicon English. Horizontal co-occurrence rules governing selection of morphemes are common with lexical switching and phrase switching allowed. Diebold (1963) also gave examples in which Greek-Americans who can speak both languages with "perfect" co-occurrence rules, if they employ English loanwords in the Greek discourse, realize them in the Greek phonological system. This would suggest that for these speakers, horizontal phonological rules override vertical realization rules.

One of the startling aberrations in the example is the use of slang to a cardinal. We would expect to find that deferential address forms would be co-occurrent with formal style. One pictures a cardinal in a microbiology laboratory addressed by a janitor who knows technical terms but cannot fully control formal syntax and phonology. Like ungrammatical sentences, sociolinguistically deviant utterances become normal if one can define setting and personnel to locate them. This is of course the point. Wherever there are regular co-occurrences, deviant behavior is marked and may carry social meaning.

The most extreme forms of co-occurrence restrictions are likely to be found in ritualized religious speech in traditional societies. Here it would be blasphemous to utter the wrong speech. Indeed, Gumperz has suggested that linguistics first began with the Sanskrit scholars' efforts to identify the formal features of religious texts and transmit them unchanged. It is co-occurrence restrictions which allow the recognition of language in multilingual societies.

At the opposite extreme are the conditions in American college lecturing, where technical terms, slang, and informal and formal syntax may alternate to some extent. Friedrich also gives examples (1966) of delicate communication of changing relationships by shifts within conversations.

2. Style

a. Formal style. Style is the term normally used to refer to the co-occurrent changes at various levels of linguistic structure within one language. Hymes (1964) has commented that probably every society has at least three style levels: formal or polite, colloquial, and slang or vulgar.

If Hymes is right about a polite style which contrasts with the unmarked (or "normal") colloquial, it might be proposed that this is the style preferred in public, serious, ceremonial occasions. Co-occurrence restrictions are particularly likely because of the seriousness of such situations. The style becomes a formal marker for occasions of societal importance where the personal relationship is minimized. We would expect that the distant or superior form of address and pronoun is universally employed in public high style. In Figs. 1 and 2 "status-marked situations" which call for titles and V may also call for polite style. Thus speakers who exchange colloquial style normally might change to this style in certain public occasions such as funerals or graduation ceremonies.

It might generally be the case in English that in otherwise identical situations, an alter addressed with TLN receives polite style more than one addressed with FN. Howell (1967, p. 99) reported such correlations in Korean. Formal lexicon and "-ing" should be related. Fischer (Hymes, 1964b) found that "criticizing, visiting, interesting, reading, correcting" and "flubbin, punchin, swimmin, chewin, hittin" occurred in a single speaker's usage. It is not clear here whether it is lexical style or topic that is at issue, since there were no examples of denotative synonyms with different vocabulary. Examples of the sort given in Newman (Hymes, 1964b), and found plentifully in English lexicon for body functions (e.g., urinate vs. weewee), provide clearer evidence for co-occurrence restrictions between lexicon and structure.

Labov (1966) did include "-ing" vs. "-in" in his study of style contrasts in different social strata, and he found that it worked precisely as the phonological variables did. Polite style in a speaker might require a certain higher frequency of [r], of [ð] rather than [d] in, e.g., "this," and of "-ing" (see Figs. 5 and 6). While the variables differentiating polite from casual style tended to be the same in different classes, the precise frequency reached for each variable varied (Labov, 1966). Thus his evidence suggests co-occurrence rules for grammatical morphemes and phonology. Labov (1966) and Klima (1964) considered the formal description of phonological and syntactic style features, respectively.

b. Informal style. In trying to sample different styles while interviewing, Labov made the assumption that speakers would use a more formal style during the interview questioning than at other times. He used several devices for locating such shifts contextually: speech outside the interview situation; speech to others, usually in the family; rambling asides;

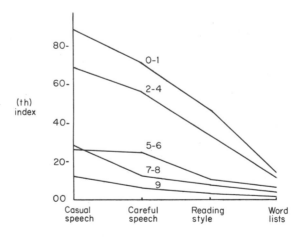

Fig. 5. Class and style stratification of [th] in thing, three, etc., for adult native New York City speakers (Labov, 1966).

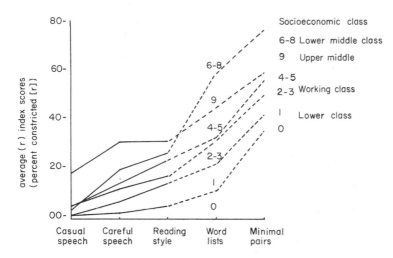

Fig. 6. Class stratification of [r] in guard, car, beer, beard, etc., for native New York City adults (Labov, 1966).

role-playing (specifically, getting adults to recite childhood rhymes); and answers to a question about a dangerous experience. He found that when "channel cues" (changes in tempo, pitch range, volume, or rate of breathing) indicated a change to casual or spontaneous speech within a speech episode, the phonological features changed. In the examples illustrating the shifts, lexicon and syntax changed too.

It is commonly the case that as one moves from the least deferent speech to the most, from the informal to the ceremonial, there is more elaboration and less abbreviation. Probably this difference is a universal, for two reasons. One is that elaboration is a cost, and is therefore most likely to occur in culturally valued situations or relationships (Homans, 1958). The other is that a high degree of abbreviation is only possible in in-group communication. While ceremonials may be confined to a sacred few, wherever they have a public function and must communicate content, we can assume that this principle of elaboration holds. Elaboration could be defined with respect to a surface structure, or to the complexity of embedded forms in the syntax, or some such criteria. A very brief poem might be, in fact, more complex in terms of rules and "effort" of compression more complex than a discursive report of the "same" content. Some forms are unambiguous: suffixed vs. unsuffixed forms, as in Japanese honorifics or polite verb suffixes, titles vs. nontitles, and so on.

From a formal grammatical standpoint, ellipsis is more complex than nonellipsis, since the grammar must contain an additional rule. It is not clear how ellipsis might be handled in a performance model. However, ellipsis in the syntactical sense is clearly more common in informal speech. Some examples can be given from questions and answers:

"Do (you(want(more cake?"
"I would like more cake."
"I'd like more cake."
"I would."
"Me."

From Soskin and John's text of (1963) of a married couple; we find the following:

Bet you didn't learn it there. . . .
Your name? (from attendant) . . .
Want me to take it . . .
Wanna take your shoes off? . . .
Getting seasick, dear? . . .
Think I can catch up with them? . . .
Not that way! . . .
Directly into it. . . .

The formal rules for sentence contractions and ellipsis are readily written.

Another form of ellipsis is that used in conversational episodes in second-speaker forms or to complete one's own earlier utterances. From Soskin and John (1963):

That fish, Honey. . . .
But I have a handicap. . . .
Like this? . . .
Which? This? Down here? . . .
You should be able to. . . .
Undulating! . . .
Yeah, if you want to. . . .
Rowed! . . .
With both of them! . . .
Well, you wanted to. . . .
You sure are. . . .
Well, I could. . . .

These forms of ellipsis are learned. Brent and Katz (1967) found that pronominalization is rare in young children; it is obligatory in second speaker rules. Bellugi (1967) found also that contractions occur later than uncontracted forms in the speech of children.

Semantic compression is also available in casual speech among intimates as will be evident later.

Phonetically, a form which occurs in casual speech more than in polite styles is rapid speech, which entails horizontal restrictions.

"What are you doing?"
"Whaddya doin?"
"Whach doon?"

There are regular phonetic alternations related to rate, e.g.:

(1) Retention of syllable of major stress and peak pitch.
(2) As degree of speeding increases, loss of segments with weakest stress.
(3) Loss or assimilation of semivowels.

[r] in postvocalic position lost.
[d] + [y] → [j], e.g., "Whadja do?"
[t] + [y] → [č], e.g., "Whacha doin?"[4]

(4) Marginal phonological distinctions like /hw/ vs. /w/ may be lost, perhaps part of casual speech style.
(5) Unstressed vowels centralized.

There is a *reverse* set of rules available to speakers used to the above alternations. The extra-slow style may be employed in sounding-out for a dictionary or over the telephone.Thus normal "school" may become slow [sɨkuwɨl].

3. Registers and Occupational Argots

Husband: Whaddya say you just *quit* ...
    Wife: I can't simply *quit* the airlines because *notice must* be *given,* but I'll certainly take what you *say* into *consideration,* and *report* it to my *superiors* ...
Husband: I don't *know* you. I don't feel *close* to you.
    Wife: Well, I'm *awfully sorry.* There's *nothing* I can do right now because I *am* preparing a *meal,* but *if* you'll *wait* until *after* I've made the *beverage,* perhaps —
Husband: I can't *stand* it. I want *out,* I want a *divorce!*
    Wife: Well, all I can *say* is, it's been nice having you *aboard* —

Nichols and May (1959)

[4] Alert readers will note these "rules" will not account for non-voicing of [č] in ellipsis of underlying "what are" but not of "what did," suggesting the rules cannot use merely surface phonetic segments.

The register of airlines or tourist businesses is revealed here in lexical choices like meal, beverage, and aboard, and "preparing a meal" rather than "getting breakfast." Register is reflected primarily in lexicon, since different topics are required in different milieux. However, in this case the paralinguistic features also change, including stress on words like "must," "am." "if." "after," "do." "about." "will." "back." which would usually not be stressed. In the register of psychologists are both professional lexicon like "interaction" and syntactic structures like the passive "It was felt that."

Slang is similar to register variation in that the alternates are primarily lexical. As Newman (Hymes, 1964b) has pointed out, the actual forms used are not necessarily different, but in sacred or slang contexts they take on a different meaning, so that in speaking of slang vocabulary one must include both form and semantic features. Since slang is highly transitory by definition, it will be understood in a given sense only within the group or network where it developed or to which it has moved at a given time. Thus one might predict that the selection rules for slang should restrict it to addressees to whom one claims a solidary relation. By this interpretation, a college lecture laced with slang is a claim on the identification of the audience. The nature of co-occurrence restrictions with slang needs investigation.

4. Linguistic Repertoire

Co-occurrence restrictions refer to the selection of alternates within the repertoire of a speaker in terms of previous or concomitant selections. The range of alternates should be known in a study of restriction. In an American monolingual, the range is likely to include informal style, slang, perhaps an occupational register, and some formal style. Labov (1964) has pointed out, however, that it is rare to control a very wide stylistic range unless one is a speech specialist, and that upwardly mobile persons usually lose the "ability to switch 'downwards' to their original vernacular" (p. 92).

In many parts of the world, a code that is relatively distinct from the casual vernacular is used in formal situations. This condition, called "diglossia" in Ferguson's (Hymes, 1964b) classic article, may, because of the greater code difference, be accompanied by more co-occurrence restriction than is style shifting, where the common features of the styles may outweigh their differences. Examples where the codes are related are Greece, German Switzerland, Haiti, and Arab countries. Standard languages coexisting with local dialects are somewhat less distinguished, and historically the dialect does not usually maintain itself except phonetically, though there may be ideological resistance to borrowing from the standard (Blom and Gumperz, in press).

Where diglossia takes the form of bilingualism (Fishman, 1967), one might at first assume that the co-occurrence restrictions would primarily govern the high form. Such a condition exists in many American bilingual communities with English as the high form. However, these are not usually pure cases, since English is the vernacular if there are casual contacts outside the immigrant community. Under these conditions, there can be considerable interpenetration (Gumperz, 1967; Ervin-Tripp, in press).

Co-occurrence restrictions in common-sense terms refer to "language-mixing." Some bilingual communities have strong attitudinal opposition to switching (usually they mean lexical co-occurrence). Blom and Gumperz (in press) found that in a Norwegian village, speakers were unconscious of the use of standard forms and were very upset to hear tapes showing lack of co-occurrence restrictions in behavior. In practice, the maintenance of coordinate or segregated systems depends upon social factors. Coordinate bilingualism is possible if there is a complete range of equivalent lexicon in both systems, and social support for the bilingualism. If this is not the case, some topics cannot be discussed, some emotions cannot be conveyed, and borrowing, perhaps surrounded by a routine disclaimer frame, will occur. The other social conditions permitting such segregation in diglossia are the closed network circumstances reported by Blom and Gumperz (in press), where certain topics and transactional types simply would not occur in casual discourse. Thus American researchers can find rich grounds for the study of behavioral support or loss of co-occurrence rules, in either English style, registers, or multilingualism.

III. Switching

If a given speaker is observed during his daily round, all the features of his speech may show some systematic changes. The total repertoire of some speakers is far greater than others. Some are bilinguals, and some are community leaders with a wide range of styles reflecting their varying relationships and activities. In this section, we shall bring together evidence on some of the major classes of variables affecting variation within individual speakers.

A. PERSONNEL

In any act of communication, there is a "sender" and one or more "receivers" who together may be called "interlocutors" (Hymes, 1962). In addition, there may be present an audience which is not the primary addressee of the message. The distribution of these roles has been discussed elsewhere (Ervin-Tripp, 1964). The role of sender, or speaker, is rarely distributed in equal time to all participants. There appear to be four factors which affect the amount of talking each participant may do. One factor is the situation. In informal small-group conversation, the roles of sender and receiver may alternate. In a sermon, the sender role is available to only one participant; in choral responses in a ritual, or in a question period following a lecture, the role of sender is allocated at specific times. The allocation of the role of sender is specified by sequencing rules for each type of speech event, and a sender may select his successor by a question or a gaze. A second, related, determinant of the amount of talking is the role the participant has in the group and his social and physical centrality. He may be a therapy patient, chairman, teacher, or switchboard operator, so that his formal status requires communication with great frequency; he may informally select such a role, as in the case of a raconteur or expert on the topic at hand. Third there is a personal constant carried from group to group. The net effect of the second and third factors is that the sending frequency of participants in a group is almost always unequal, and it has been shown to have regular mathematical properties in ad hoc discussion groups (Stephan and Mishler, 1952; Bales and Borgatta, 1955). Because relative frequency of speaking is steeply graded, not evenly distributed, in a large group the least frequent speaker may get almost no chance to speak. Knutson (1960) was able to produce radical alterations in participation rates by forming homogeneous groups on the basis of participation frequency. He found that talkative persons were generally regarded as better contributors, so there was great surprise when the homogeneously quiet group produced better work, by objective outside ratings.

The receiver role is also unequally distributed, even in face-to-face groups, being allocated in work talk to the most central, the most powerful, those with highest status, the most frequent speakers, and in highly valued groups, to the most deviant. In social conversation, proximity may be important (Hare, 1962, p. 289; Schachter, 1951).

In addition to their roles within the interaction situation, the personnel bring with them other statuses. These are, according to Goodenough (1965), "rights, duties, privileges, powers, liabilities, and immunities." I have mentioned that one of the functions of identity marking in speech is to indicate precisely what is required in the relationship. In any particular interaction, of course, not all the statuses of all participants are relevant.

Obviously, the specific relations tying participants are most salient, e.g., a husband and his wife or an employer and his employee.

In addition to determining the forms that interaction might take, the identity of alter, and his relation to ego, will establish whether interaction is possible or obligatory. For example, following a death in the family, there is a specific sequence of persons who must be informed (Sacks' example).

Personnel include the audience as well as the receiver. The presence of others can, wherever there are options, weigh the selectors differently, according to whether one wants to conceal or display them to others. Thus, in a medical laboratory, technicians employ more formal and deferential speech to doctors when the supervisor or patients are present. In public the relation doctor-technician takes precedence over familiarity, so that, "Hey, Len, shoot the chart to me, will ya?" becomes, "Do you want the chart, Doctor?" Note the co-occurrence of formal structure and formal address.

I indicated in Section II that there are formal constraints on address. The rules for reference to third parties are more complex, for they are related both to the third party and to the addressee. In the American system, where the adult personnel present exchange FN they may regularly omit T in reference to third parties whom they normally address with TFN or TLN. If an addressee is lower in age or rank, e.g., a child or employee, and uses T to the referent, then T is used by both parties in reference. Thus "Daddy" might be used in addressing a child. Emily Post recommended that women refer to their husbands as TLN to inferiors in rank or age, "my husband" to strangers, and FN to friends "on the dinner list " (1922, p. 54). The friend, however, could not necessarily address the husband by FN (presumably some familiarity criterion was in use). "It is bad form to go about saying 'Edith Worldly' or 'Ethel Norman' to those who do not call them Edith or Ethel, and to speak thus familiarly of one whom you do not call by her first name, is unforgivable."

When the addressee is equal or slightly superior in rank, and thus eligible for receiving confidences (Slobin *et al.,* in press), when they share statuses which exclude the referent party, emotion toward the referent may be revealed. These constraints apply in particular to pejorative or affectionate nicknames toward persons addressed with TLN.

To the extent that the referent and addressee are alike, there is an implication of deference to the addressee in the form of reference selected. In the Japanese system of honorifics and "stylemes" (Martin, in Hymes, 1964b) both the terms for the referent and the verb suffixes are altered by deference, i.e., by selectors of relative rank, age, sex, and solidarity. In the most polite style, dialect forms are absent and the suffixes are employed. Children of ages 8 or 9 first learn control over reference, but still employ dialect forms freely and do not differentiate age of addressees by the "stylemes" (i.e., linguistic markers) of polite speech (Horikawa *et al.,* 1956). Possibly there is in Japanese, as in English, a rule by which reference employs honorifics when a child is addressed; thus it becomes the normal name for the referent.

Deference is undoubtedly a social feature present in all sociolinguistic systems to some degree. The most elaborate structural forms are evidently those found in the Far East. Geertz' description of the Javanese system is of general importance; he contrasted "stylemes," including affixes and function morphemes governed by co-occurrence restrictions, as in our formal style, with honorific vocabulary which is more sporadic. It seems, like the American "sir," to be governed by a rule of frequency (Martin, in Hymes, 1964b), rather than required presence or absence (Geertz, 1960).

Language choice itself, rather than stylistic alternatives, may be governed by addressee features of rank, age, and solidarity. Rubin's (1962) characterization of the alternation between Spanish and Guarani in Paraguay, according to addressee, nearly matches Fig. 2, with V = Spanish, and T = Guarani.

Familiarity entered into several of the address rules in Section II. Familiarity increases the probability that an addressee will be talked to, and for this reason familiar interaction is likely to be marked by many forms of ellipsis at all levels, unless some setting or deference constraints interfere. Omissions of subject and modal follow this pattern in English, as a form of syntactic ellipsis. In-group slang frequently is situationally selected by familiarity of addressee.

When a friend is addressed in the Two Person Communication game, in which separated parties communicate solely by verbal messages, the selections among nonsense forms or colors are coded more efficiently, even though there is no feedback. In studies of sorority girls, comparison of speech to friend and nonfriend addressees repeatedly revealed a contrast in the *time* to describe objects when the speaker saw one and the hearer an array. The friends were both more succinct and more successful. Only in part was this difference because of reference to obviously private experience; e.g., "It's the color of Jan's new sweater." Most conspicuous was the contrast between technical descriptions to nonfriends and metaphorical description to friends; e.g., "It's an elephant doing the push-ups." The striking feature of these metaphorical descriptions is that they are very successful even when a nonfriend encounters them; thus, the question arises, Why not use metaphor to strangers? Two explanations need testing: possibly the use of metaphor seems self-revealing; our formal educational system clearly downgrades metaphorical forms of description. The contrast between Brent and Katz' (1967) college students and Job Corps Negroes illustrates the latter fact; given geometrical forms, descriptions much like college students' familiar speech were given by the less educated subjects.

How does the similarity of speech between friends arise? It is a common feature of interaction between two persons that if the parameters of speech are different they become more similar during the interaction. Thus, a given person's speech may vary depending on the speech features of the addressee. This phenomenon has been noted in the production features of rate, durations, and silence (e.g., Matarazzo *et al.* 1965), and is clearly the case for such features as lexical selection and syntax in addressing children. Ramanujan has commented that Brahmins adopt stereotyped non-Brahmin speech when addressing non-Brahmins; the same comparison needs to be made across social classes in this country. Address to children, i.e., baby talk, is also likely to be stereotyped. If in fact the similarity is an effect of the speech of alter, it should increase during the course of a long interaction; if it arises purely from stereotypes, it may remain unchanged.

In multilingual communities there must be some regularities in the control over the code to be used if both are to speak in the same code (Barker, 1947; Herman, 1961). Perhaps the more powerful controls the code choice, if setting and topic permit an option. Deference might be realized either by the adaptation of the lower ranked person to the preference of the higher, or by respectful avoidance of imitation—"keeping one's place." Cross-cultural research is needed to locate systematic features of social systems which may predict which party in a dyad changes more, and in which linguistic features. Further speculations are given in Grimshaw's survey paper (in press).

The most dramatic example of language shift affected by addressee is baby talk. This is a speech style occurring in many societies (Ferguson, 1964) for address to infants, and often to pets and lovers. In English, baby talk affects all levels of structure.

Most speakers are likely to be conscious of baby-talk lexicon, as they often are of the lexical features of styles. Baby-talk lexicon includes words like "potty," "weewee," "bunny," "night-night," "mommy," and "daddy." Many other words in adult speech become appropriate for speaking to infants when the suffix "-ie" is added. Work in progress by Kerry Drach and Ben Kobashigawa suggests that speech to children may be dramatically different in syntax, being simpler, and containing fewer errors, fewer subordinate clauses, more repetitions, and more imperatives and questions requiring feedback.

Phonological effects and paralinguistic features are especially conspicuous. Samples of talk to infants show certain general phonetic changes such as palatalization. Most striking is the use of a higher pitch and a sing-song, wide-ranging intonation. The younger the infant, the higher the pitch. Observations of the social distribution of this style show it to be more common in addressing other people's children than one's own. For instance, nurses use the paralinguistic features, at least, in persuading children, and in cooperative nurseries comparison of own-child and other-child addressees shows a distinct shift to more age attribution to own child.

Children themselves use many of the features of adult baby talk very early. In addressing younger siblings they may adopt lexical and paralinguistic features of the adult baby talk as early as age 2. In role-play, they use phrases and address terms from baby talk, e.g.; "Goo-goo, little baby," and freely employ the sing-song intonation in addressing "babies." In other respects, their role play is stereotyped rather than strictly imitative, for example, in the frequent use of role-names. It may be that the intonational and lexical features of baby talk may function simply as role markers in their play.

B. SITUATION

A situation refers to any constellation of statuses and setting which constrains the interaction that should or may occur—what Barker and Wright (1954) called the "standing behavior patterns." A situation, like a status, is a cultural unit, so that ethnological study is necessary to determine classes of situations.

At the university, a class is a situation. From the standpoint of the authorities, the criteria include the presence of an authorized instructor, students, and an approved time and place. From the standpoint of the instructor and students, there are strong constraints on function and on topical relevance.

Recently a student and faculty strike at the University of California brought these criteria to light. Instructors varied in which features of the definition they suspended in their effort to meet their obligations to the students but not to the university administration. Some met at a different time, others at a different place. Some used the same setting but discussed strike issues or public affairs. When the administration threatened to fire instructors who "failed to meet their obligations," it was not at all clear whether they used a minimal or maximal set of criteria.

Situation is most clearly defined when there are jointly dependent statuses and locales: church and priest, school and teacher, store and salesgirl, bus and driver, restaurant and waitress, plane and stewardess,

clinic and physician. If the same personnel encounter each other elsewhere, for instance, at a baseball game, address terms (as distinct from
attention-getting terms) may remain the same, but everything else about
the interaction is likely to change.

If we examine these clear cases, we see that there are constraints on
expected activities, rights, and obligations, and that there are, in several
cases, clearly defined speech events such as the church service, the classroom lecture, the order to the waitress, the welcome, oxygen lecture of
the stewardess, and the medical history in the clinic. Both the activities
and the speech events are likely to be specific to the locale, though we
might conceive of asking some information questions of the teacher or
physician when he is off duty.

Because the activities and speech events have sequencing rules, they
may be demarcated into discourse stages. The boundaries may be marked
by routines or by code changes. After a church service, priest and pari-
shioner may exchange personal greetings as friends, the priest using a radically different style than in his sermon. After a formal lecture, the opening of the floor to questions in cases of diglossia is signaled by a switch to
the "lower" code, e.g. colloquial Arabic or Guarani (Ferguson, in Hymes
1964b; Rubin, in press). These are predictable discourse stages, and in
this respect they differ from shifts which are at the option of the participants. Blom and Gumperz (in press) mentioned that local residents of
Hemnisberget might use standard Norwegian when enacting their roles as
buyer and seller, but if one wished to initiate a private conversation on
personal matters, he would shift to the local dialect.

Analogous style switches occur here between colloquial speech and
occupational argots, according to personnel present or situation. In some
academic communities, it is considered a breach of etiquette to use occupational argot or discuss occupational topics at a dinner party or other
"social situation"; others define these rules solely by personnel. Thus, the
topic and register may change when wives are listening or when there is
occupational diversity among the participants.

One strategy in identifying situations is to look for folk terminology
for them, such as church service, party, interview, picnic, lunch break,
conversation, chat, class, and discussion. The status-oriented interaction
between customers and sales personnel or waitresses has no name, and
the interaction arising from statuses in work organizations has no folk
name in English. If there is some independent and reliable way of identifying situational categories, then the difference between the named and the
unnamed is important, for it suggests that the named situations enter into
members' accounts.

Restricted languages illustrate situational constraints vividly. In hamburger stands and short-order cafes in the United States, abbreviated forms of speech appear. In these settings, there is a premium on speed in transmission of orders from the waitress to the cook. The number of alternatives is semantically limited, with certain high probabilities. In the ordering, one can see evidence that the code has been reduced almost to the minimum required for efficiency, within the structure of English syntax, by radical ellipsis. In studies by Brian Stross (1964) and by Marion Williams (1964), corpora were collected in a range of local settings:

one	one hamburger
two sweets	two sweet rolls
barbeef	barbecued beef sandwich
boil five	5-minute boiled egg
burger without	one hamburger without onions
beeny up	bacon and eggs, sunny side up
bacon and	bacon and eggs (differs with locale)
one M. O.	one hamburger, mustard only
L. T. plain	lettuce and tomato salad
ham and over rye	ham and eggs over, on rye
five squirt three	five coffees, three with cream

Stross pointed out that the underlying rule for all of these instances, except the last, is (number) + (name) + (describer). This kind of syntax appears in normal English in phrases like "five hamburgers without onions." The odd appearance of the restricted syntax arises from the optional omission of *any* of these elements, and from the appearance in the describer class of items like "and" and "without" which normally do not appear alone. It is hard to think of any way of omitting the function word rather than the noun in "without onions," but in the case of "ham and eggs" it seems possible that the form could be "ham eggs." This would violate the general rule that the last item be a describer and obviously subordinate. Note that when there is an adjective-noun phrase in the gloss, the two can be compressed into one word by making the adjective a prefix, as in "barbeef."

The abbreviation devices summarized by Stross include loss of segments (burger), use of initials (especially to replace conjoined nouns), loss of name (of most probable item), container for contents (cup for spaghetti), and preparation unique to an item (boil for egg).

The last item on the list does not follow the structural rule. It comes from a trucker's cafe, in which the corpus was kitchen talk rather than waitress ordering. This corpus was distinguished by a lot of colorful slang, much of it from vintage army usage and pejorative in tone. The efficiency pressure did not take priority here, and the structural rules were therefore different. Single word examples are "wop" for spaghetti, "pig" for hot dogs, "rabbit" for salad, and "grease" for fries. Longer units of the slang type are "burn a cow" for two well-done hamburgers, "bowl a slop" for a bowl of the soup of the day, "cap'ns galley" for pancakes topped by egg. That abbreviation did not dominate is suggested in cases which the other rule would reduce: "one order grease," "one wop with balls." In the last case humor wins out over brevity, which would yield "one wop with" or even "wop with." "One green bitch with T.I." for green goddess salad with thousand island dressing could have been reduced to "green T.I." or "bitch T.I."

Restaurants in Switzerland and London were observed, and similar forms of restricted language were found only in London's "Wimpy bars." Here the forms are so similar to American hamburger stands that one can guess that some of the language traveled with the product. In the interchanges in other restaurants, no evidence of radical ellipsis was found. One reason may be that observations were made within kitchens and, as we have seen in regard to the trucker's cafe, kitchen talk evidently is not constrained by the same brevity pressures as orders to the kitchen.

The mere cataloging of cultural units is not likely to bear much fruit unless the features of the situations which effect sociolinguistic rules can be identified. Moscovici (1967) has cleverly manipulated situational features in the Two Person Communication game. It is common to speak of "formal" situations, but it is not clear what makes a situation formal. Labov has suggested that degree of self-monitoring constitutes a dimension permitting alignment of situations on a continuum. Work- or status-oriented situations vs. person-oriented situations provides another contrast. In the first case, there is likely to be some criterion of achievement in an activity; in the second, the focus of attention can be turned to selves and to expressions of personal emotions. Watson (1958) distinguished work, family, and sociable interaction. But these differences are essentially differences in function.

C. Speech Acts, Topic, and Message

"What are you talking about?" "We were just saying hello." "We were telling jokes." "I was introducing Joe." Subordinate to organized exchanges like parties and work situations are classes we have called "speech acts." In the above examples, their identity is suggested by the folk classification. Here the informants can label segments of interaction.

There also must be unlabeled interaction. "Hello. Where is the post office?" addressed to a passerby, or, "My name is George Landers. What time is it?" to a stranger, violate, according to Labov, sequencing rules. If this is the case, the conjoined segments must have identifiable properties by which the rules can be characterized abstractly. In bilingual interaction, the segments may entail language shift.

There is no reason to assume that speech acts are the same everywhere. Certain special forms of discourse like poetry and speech-making may have components known only to specialists. Whether and why there are labels used in the teaching of these performances is itself a sociolinguistic problem.

Speech acts in English include greetings, self-identification, invitations, rejections, apologies, and so on. The ones identified so far tend to be routines, but we can expect to find other more abstract units as research proceeds.

When conversations have an explicit message with informational content, they can be said to have a *topic*. "What are you talking about?" "Nothing." "Gossip." "Shop talk." "The weather." "The war." "We were having an automobile discussion about the psychological motives for drag-racing in the streets." In everyday discourse, the question of topic is most likely to occur in invitations or rejections so that the answers serve either to exclude a new arrival or to give him enough information to participate. Besides selecting personnel for participation, topics may be governed by a continuity rule. In a formal lecture in a university, there is a constraint on continuity and relevance, just as there is in technical writing, where editing can enforce the constraint. Evidences of constraint are apologies for deviation: "That reminds me ... " "Oh, by the way ... " "To get back to the question ... " "To change the subject ... " Cultural rules regarding speech events may include constraints as to the grounds for relevance.

Kjolseth (1967) has found in analysis of some group interaction that topical episodes are key factors in speakers' tactics:

> A performer's tactic may be to direct his episode as a probe into the preceding episode. In contrast, in another situation his tactic may be to extend and elaborate some antecedent episode. On still another occasion his tactic may be to close off and limit a previous episode .... These tactical types are based on, or defined in terms of, two qualities abstracted from the performances: a) the episodic locus of relevances drawn from the existent conversation resource, and b) the purpose of the episode with respect to surrounding episodes."

Lennard and Bernstein (in press) have examined topical continuity in therapeutic sessions, and found the amount of continuity to be related to satisfaction. The three examples given by Kjolseth would involve topical continuation, recycling, or change, respectively. These general features of speech events require that members be able to identify relevance but not necessarily label topics.

There is yet a third form of evidence that topic may be a cultural unit.

Bilinguals can frequently give reliable accounts of topical code-switching, and their behavior often corresponds, in general, to their accounts (Ervin-Tripp, 1964).

We can thus argue that *topic* must be a basic variable in interaction, on the grounds that speakers can identify topical change as generating code-shift, that speakers can sometimes report what they are talking about, and that topical continuity, recycling, and change may be normative features of speech events, or at least relevant to values regarding good conversations.

The analysis of *messages* refers to two-term relationships, whereas *topic* is a single term allowing for simple taxonomies. Here I intend to refer only to the manifest or explicit message. The reason for the distinction is that latent content categories typically refer to intent (e.g., Dollard and Auld, 1959; Katz, 1966; Leary, 1957; Marsden, 1965). My position here is that intent or function is part of the constellation of social features out of which interaction is generated. It can be realized in a variety of ways, of which verbal interaction is only one. We seek regular rules by which one can relate underlying categories with their formal realizations or the formal features of interaction with their social meanings. Failure to discover such rules has led to considerable discouragement with the evident arbitrariness of content classifications in studies of natural discourse.

The manifest message, on the other hand, is the product of the social features of the situation as well as of intent, and is therefore inseparable from the interaction product. All the selections made in realization of the functions of communication can carry some kind of information, whether about the speaker, the situation, the hearer, or the topic. In detail, given alternations cannot do all at once, though they may be ambiguous as to which is intended. In this case, the *message* is intended to refer only to what is said or implied about the topic. There have been numerous summaries of ways of classifying messages (e.g., Pool, 1959). A recent innovation is logical analysis (Véron *et al.*, 1965). The underlying structure of logical linkages between terms in utterances is analyzed, and semantic relations are then described in terms of logical relations between pairs of units (e.g., equivalence, inference, conjunction, specification of conditions, sequential relations, explanation, and opposition, causes). A Markov semantic analysis revealed very large and consistent differences between subject groups, which were, in the study reported, clinical categories.

The same speaker information potentially can be realized through different means, for example, through explicit message content and through paralinguistic features. The conflict between these messages creates an interesting question about which is dominant. According to Mehrabian and Wiener (1967), who used controlled stimulus materials, regardless of the instructions to the listeners, the tone of voice is the dominant signal for judging affect. What is called the "double bind" must be a consequence of more than conflicting messages; for instance, it could be a requirement of overt response to the overt message on one occasion and to the paralinguistic cue on another, with no signal as to which is required.

The definition of appropriate units for analysis is important in comparing results of different studies. Watson and Potter (1962) discussed a macro-unit, the episode, which is defined by the stability of component features: the role system of the participants, the major participants, the focus of attention, and the relationship toward the focus of attention. The unit thus may be less than an utterance in length or may include the contributions of many speakers. In Lennard's research, one might say that satisfaction is related to the length of episodes. Watson and Potter chose the term "focus of attention" in order to differentiate cases where the topic is a person's experience, an on-going activity, or an abstract referential category as in a "discussion."

In thematic analyses, it is common to use either episodic (Katz, 1966) or sentence units (Auld and White, 1956). However, the sentence is not, strictly speaking, a unit in oral discourse. One can see texts in which long sequences of clauses linked by "and then . . . " occur. Are these separate sentences or one sentence? There have been four criteria used separately with different results: message criteria, structural or linguistic units (e.g., any segment containing a verb or naming phrases in isolation; John and Berney, 1967); pauses, and intonational contours (Dittman and Llewellyn, 1967).

D. FUNCTIONS OF INTERACTION

1. Criteria

Firth (Hymes, 1964b) was one among many who sought to identify the functions of speech. He included phatic communion (solidarity); pragmatic efficiency (accompanying work); planning and guidance; address; greetings, farewells, adjustment of relations, and so on; and speech as a commitment (courts, promises). Primarily, his view of function was the social value of the act.

To a psychologist, function is likely to be viewed from the standpoint of the interacting parties, either the sender or the receiver. Soskin has played tapes to listeners and asked them to report what they would *say* and what they would *think*. This method assumes that function is effect. It is close to Blom and Gumperz' (in press) criterion of social meaning.

A second method is to analyze actual instances of acts and to infer whether the receiver's response satisfied the speaker, either from his overt behavior or by questioning him. This method includes action, response, and reaction. It is derived from Skinner's (1957) theory that speech is operant behavior which affects the speaker through the media-tion of a hearer. Feedback and audience consistency presumably "shape" effective speech in the normal person. In this method, function is identi-fied by classes of satisfactory listener responses.

If intent, conscious or unconscious, is imputed to a speaker on the basis of some features of the content or form of his speech, a third form of functional analysis appears. This, of course, is the method of latent con-tent analysis (e.g., Katz, 1966; Watson, 1958).

A set of function categories was devised to account for the initiation of dyadic interaction on the basis of a corpus of instances of action, re-sponse, and reaction (Ervin-Tripp, 1964): The list includes explicit re-quests for goods, services, and information; implicit requests for social responses; offering of information or interpretations; expressive mono-logues; routines; and speech to avoid alternative activities.

Soskin and John (1963) devised a category system based on a combi-nation of structural and semantic features. We can use their system to subclassify each of the above functional categories. For example, the fol-lowing might all be requests for the loan of a coat:

"It's cold today." (structone)

"Lend me your coat." (regnone)

"I'm cold." (signone)

"That looks like a warm coat you have." (metrone)

"Br-r-r." (expressive)

"I wonder if I brought a coat."(excogitative)

One simple way to examine requests is to compare regnones, in which the request function is explicit, with all other categories, in terms of social distribution. In a term paper, Bessie Dikeman and Patricia Parker (1964) found that within families indirect request forms dominated be-tween equals, almost half were regnones when seniors addressed juniors, and from juniors, regnones dominated. Examples from their paper are these:

> "Where's the coffee, Dremsel?" (it is visible).
>   (to wife) [gloss: bring me the coffee]
> "Is that enough bacon for you and Thelma?" (to husband)
>   [gloss: save some for Thelma]
> "It's 7:15" (to daughter)
>   [gloss: hurry up]
>   "Mother, you know I don't have a robe. Well, we're
> having a slumber party tomorrow night."
> "Oh, dear I wish I were taller." (to adult brother)
>   [gloss: get down the dishes]

In factory settings, by contrast, requests to subordinates were more often regnones and often direct imperatives.

In a sample of requests offered during 80 hours of observation in a university office, Carol Pfuderer (1968) found that the major selector was familiarity and rank.

(1) Whatever their status, familiar peers used direct imperatives.

(2) When the peer was farther away, the imperative was followed by tag questions, "please," address forms, with rising pitch, e.g., "ask Marcy, why don't you?"

(3) Requests within the addressee's territory were deferential, even to familiar peers.

(4) Requests to addressees of either higher or lower rank took the form of modal questions ("Would you get me some coffee, Jeanie?"), pragmatic neutralizations, or displacement of addressee. Neutralization refers to cases where two different functions could be realized by identical speech acts, which are therefore ambiguous, in intent.

(5) Pragmatic neutralizations included information questions ("Has anyone gone to Accounting this week?" "Whose turn is it to make coffee this week, Ruby?") and structones ("It's stuffy in here"; "Someone has to see Dean Smith").

(6) Where there was a large rank difference upward, the request might be displaced to an addressee nearer in rank. For example, a request for a stapler by a seated secretary was given not to the senior professor standing next to it but to a peer standing equidistant from it, and the deferential form was used: "Joan, would you please get the stapler for me?"

Request and persuasion require action on the part of alter so that the obligations and privileges inherent in the social relations of the personnel are likely to be realized in differences in linguistic expression. We might expect pragmatic neutralization when the requestor is deferent or reluctant to ask at all, or in situations where requests are highly frequent and familiarity produces high mutual nurturance and assurance of interpretability. In the restaurant studies, "please" was used for requested acts extraneous to the addressee's duties, perhaps a version of the territoriality feature in Miss Pfuderer's findings.

We can expect that where variant address forms exist, they might alternate in request situations. Milla Ayoub (1962), in a discussion of bipolar kin terms in Arabic, pointed out that in addition to proper names, a mother could call her son by either of two terms that can also mean "my mother." When a parent wishes to cajole or placate a child, but not command him, he uses these bipolar terms. This is particularly the case with sons. These terms are never heard in direct commands.

In discussing current address practices in the Soviet Union, Kantorovich (1966) mentioned that friends might switch from "ty" to "vy" with first name and patronymic when help was asked.

2. Approval-Seeking

In human communication, as among lower primates (Diebold, 1967), many of the signals for what we have called "requests for social responses" are gestural or paralinguistic. Rosenfeld (1966) found that among American males, liking was related to the following factors in the speaker's behavior: long sentences, few self-words, and high reinforcement of the speech of alter through head nods and verbal routines; among women, frequent initiation of utterances, many sentences per speech, many speech disturbances and false starts, many questions and many words referring to alter, and reinforcement by nods produced greater liking by strangers. Rosenfeld also found which of these features were subject to conscious manipulation under instructions and role-playing: volubility, frequency of speaking and length of sentences, and more speech disturbances, as well as verbal reinforcing routines. The major omission is the semantic component (the kind Dale Carnegie discusses) of orienting the *content* of the interaction to alter rather than self. Probably address forms change also, among friends, when affiliative functions are primary. Tyler (1965), for example, suggested that certain address alternatives in the Koya kin system are employed when cross-cousins engage in the joking relationship which is their privilege. It was noted earlier that such alternates might even be used in deferential address with familiar addressees, for example, "Dr. S." rather than "Dr. Smith" from technician to physician when outsiders were absent.

There may prove to be classes of functionally equivalent responses by alter, such as head nods and brief verbal routines both occurring as options in response to the same stimuli. The identification of these response classes in turn can provide a criterion for recognizing the speech variables which elicit them from alter, and thus provide grounds for classifying "approval-seeking behavior," more objective than the intuition of judges. Of course whether or not there is any empirical value in these categories depends on whether or not they enter into speech rules consistently.

3. Effects of Function Shifts

Functions can enter into rules for the selection of settings by participants, the selection of addressees, and formal changes within the interaction.

"Oh my back, it's killing me today. I can hardly move."

"Yeah, it must be the weather. My leg's been aching all day."

"I was supposed to get a shot of cortisone today, but my husband couldn't take me to the doctor's."

"I hurt my leg in the army . . ." (long description).

"Oh. Well, I must get back to work."

Something went wrong in this interaction. The woman did not, in effect, respond to the man's story of woe and terminated the conversation.

The collection of large corpora of natural sequences might not yield enough such instances for analysis by classification; a role-playing method might be one approximation. We might find that responses to statements of physical distress take the form of inquiries of cause, routine sympathy expressions, or offers of help. In this case, none of these happened. Instead, the addressee himself made a statement of physical distress and preempted the floor. Watson and Potter (1962) stated that when the focus of attention of conversation is tied to self, "interaction is governed by rules of tact." Presumably these include certain obligations of response and limitations on inquiry topics. Only a method which allows gathering data on appropriate responses and testing the consequences of inappropriate responses can identify what these rules might be.

In the course of any given discourse segment, we can expect to find changes in the functions, which, in turn, affect form. These episodes arise from:

(1) Sequencing rules within the speech event.

(2) Changes in the activity, if any, accompanying the interaction (e.g., a ball game, dinner preparation).

(3) Disruptive events such as the arrival of new personnel, accidents like bumps, sneezes, and phone calls, which require routines to correct the situation.

(4) Shifts arising from unexpected responses of alter, leading to changes in tactics or a change in function.

(5) Function satiation. Functions presumably oscillate in patterned ways in stable groups.

(6) Topic-evoked shifts in functions. Under the impact of instructions or of associative dynamics, the topic may change in the course of the conversation. These changes can alter the available resources for the participants and thereby change their intent. If the topic shifts from child-rearing to economics, for example, a bachelor may find he has greater resources for displaying knowledge and receiving recognition. He may speak more and use more technical vocabulary, perhaps even to the point that listeners do not understand. Many such instances have been observed in the speech of bilinguals when topic and language were controlled by instructions (Ervin, 1964; Ervin-Tripp, 1964, 1967).

Blom and Gumperz (in press) found that among university-trained villagers, many features of standard Norwegian appeared when topics shifted from local to nonlocal. But they found that the change depended on the message. In the offering of information, speakers with a large repertoire of speech alternatives can maximize credibility by adopting the most suitable role. Thus, discussion of university structure might elicit use of more standard Norwegian forms than would gossip about instructors, where student speech features would be adopted, especially those shared with addressees.

Gumperz has noted that among Puerto Ricans in Jersey City, in situations where Spanish is spoken, English is an attention getter. In Trukese and Ponapean (Fischer, 1965), a phonotactic feature of the other language is a marker for function shifting of specific kinds that fit the stereotypes of the groups, just as a dialect feature might be here.

As functions change, address too may change through a conversation. David Day has described changes when an argument occurred in a class regarding an instructor's views of the student's beliefs. Address progressed from FN to Dr. LN to Professor LN. In comments with other students as addressee, LN was used in reference to the instructor in front of him. Concurrently, slang decreased.

When there is agreement about the normal, unmarked address form to alters of specified statuses, then any shift is a message. Friedrich (Hymes, 1964b) gave convincing cases of momentary shifts at times of personal crises. He pointed out that in a public setting, friends would mask their intimacy with V; in talking of personal topics they could invoke their friendship with "ty" and remove it for impersonal topics with "vy."

Kantorovich (1966, p. 43) gave similar examples in current practice: "I say 'ty' to my subordinates, but I certainly don't do this in order to belittle them. I know that they'll answer me with 'vy,' but this isn't grovelling — it's a mark of respect . . . . Somebody I call 'ty' is somehow closer to me than someone I have to call 'vy' . . . . If I get mad at one of my workers, and he needs a bawling out, I frequently switch to 'vy' . . . ."

" . . . When cursing, many people who customarily use 'ty' suddenly switch to 'vy,' and many who are on a mutual 'vy' basis switch to 'ty'" (Kostomarov, 1967).

In systems with age or rank asymmetries of address, the use of the more deferential form to an equal or subordinate can mean either that they are receiving respect or are being put off at a distance. Brown and Gilman (1960) found that conservatives use V more than radicals. To account fully for the interpretation of such actions by the receivers, we need to know the other signals, such as tone of voice and other address features, and the available ambiguities of the relationship. In the case of courtship, for example, the important dimension is closeness or distance, and address changes would be so interpreted.

E.   RULES FOR SWITCHING

I have emphasized throughout this article that linguistic interaction is a system of behavior in which underlying functions are realized through an organized set of output rules within a social situation. If the function requires conveying an explicit message with informational content, some semantic information is presented in the alternatives selected. Other alternatives require the representation of social information.

In addressee-dominated rules like those in Section II, the effects of function switching can be represented as transformations upon the outputs of the addressee rules. They may take the form of simple replacements, e.g., if familiarity exists, different names may be employed as a direct representation of varied functions. Thus a mode or selector for familiarity and for function is added to the branching rules. Similarly, Tyler (1966) has formal rules for selection of kin reference according to situation, after other semantic selectors.

Blom and Gumperz (in press) have suggested that metaphorical switching simply consists of treating the addressee as though his social features were different. In this case, the rule acts upon the selection points. In the case of Dr. Poussaint, hostile intent was represented in the selection of Adult— rather than Adult + at the first selection point. Presumably this possibility suggested itself by the existence of a traditional southern system of address to Negroes in which all but the very old (aunty) were addressed as children. When Sacks asked his students to play the role of boarders with their families during vacation, their silence, politeness of address and request, and withdrawal from gossip and semantic ellipsis in conversation were interpreted by their families as evidence of sickness or hostility.

The Russian example implies that a simple transformation upon the output forms can express hostility; on the other hand, the inversion may be a consequence of transformation of selection features, making the friend a nonfriend and the formal associate an inferior. Such general rules are a necessity if familiarity is absent, since they permit the interpretation of new instances on the basis of the hearer's general knowledge of the system of sociolinguistic rules.

"Rules" could refer to structures for generating or interpreting speech, to reports of beliefs about practices, or to standards of correctness. We have given examples of all three kinds of rules, not always clearly distinguishing them. Labov's Index of Linguistic Insecurity (1966) compared the last two.

Behavioral rules and reports about behavior are likely to be systematically different. If the norms contain a probability or frequency factor, a speaker's beliefs are, instead, categorical (Labov, 1966). Beliefs about the social selectors in sociolinguistic rules are more likely to include features of personnel (since categorization devices realize these features) than to note functional variation. Syntactical variables are not remembered (Sachs, 1967) beyond the time needed for decoding, unless they are markers that help us classify the speaker.

In multilingual communities, phonological, syntactic, and semantic shifting is not observed (Gumperz, 1964, 1967). Even borrowed vocabulary is unnoticed by members if values oppose borrowing (Blom and Gumperz, in press). Some speakers cannot remember the language in which they just spoke, let alone report it to an interviewer. These phenomena are not merely grounds for distrusting members' reports. Just as reference to a relative (Tyler, 1966) is affected by more than the semantic dimensions of reference, so the act of describing even to one's self, is a product which could realize a variety of functions. Members' reports are likely to be as sensitive to social variation as any speech act mentioned in this article, and therefore prove as amenable to study.

IV. Linguistic Diversity

A. THE FUNDAMENTALS OF COMMUNICATION

The fundamental fact about language is its obvious diversity. Moving from country to country, region to region, class to class, and caste to caste, we find changes in language. Linguistic diversity apparently is related to social interaction.

Linguistic similarity must be explained, for it is clear that separated sets of speakers will develop different languages. Two quite different bases for similarity can be examined: the fundamental requirement of mutual intelligibility among people who belong to the same social community, and the consequences of variability in overt behavior in terms of social values.

A test for mutual intelligibility might be the Two Person Communication game. First used by Carroll (1958) several decades ago, it has recently been revived (Maclay, 1962; Krauss and Weinheimer, 1964; Brent and Katz, 1967). A hearer out of sight of a speaker selects, constructs, or in some way responds to instructions from a speaker regarding a set of materials. Feedback may or may not be allowed. The advantage of this method is that one can examine the relation between success in the objective task and various speech features, and that the social relation of speaker and hearer can be controlled. For our question about the degree of similarity required for intelligibility, we shall assume optimal social attitudes (Wolff, in Hymes, 1964b) and simply concern ourselves with features of linguistic structure. No feedback is allowed, and we shall ask what the bare minimum of linguistic similarity might be that would allow successful transmission of messages about referents.

(1) There must be shared categories of meaning so that speakers will attend to the same features of the referent materials.

(2) There must be shared lexicon identifying the significant referents, attributes, relationships, and actions, and shared central meanings for this lexicon. Languages which are related and have many cognates are instances.

(3) The shared lexicon must be recognizable. Thus its morphophonemic realizations must be similar, and the phonological and phonetic systems must be sufficiently alike to allow recognition of the similar items. Precisely what these limitations entail is not clear. Wurm and Laycock (1961) have shown that both phonetic and phonemic differences can lead to asymmetrical intelligibility of cognates among related dialects. They have found instances where A understood B but not vice versa. They suggested use of a phonetic hierarchy of rank to account for such cases. For instance, they found that the speaker using a stop could understand a speaker using a homologous fricative, but not the reverse. This suggestion is important and needs further testing. I would have predicted the reverse, on the grounds that a speaker's repertoire in comprehension includes child variants, which tend to be of "higher rank" phonetically than their adult models.

A second point they make is that the phonological system relationships, i.e., those found in contrastive analysis, may allow predictions. We can suppose that one-to-one high frequency substitutions might be easy to recognize where the phonetic realization, but not the phonological system, is affected. Comprehension of foreign accents is easiest in such cases. O'Neil (in press) found that Faroese could understand Icelanders, but not vice versa, because of many-to-one conversion rules.

Further, there must be some similarities in phonotactic rules so that the lexical forms can be related. In instances of children's renditions of adult words, we often find that adults cannot comprehend because of the radical alteration in the word formation. Thus [mana] and [ŋən] are unlikely to be recognized as "banana" and "gun," and [me] and [ni] in another child are even less likely to recognized as "blanket" and "candy." although each arises from regular replacement rules (Ervin-Tripp, 1966).

In each case, the initial consonant is nasal if a nasal occurs anyplace in the adult word, and it is homologous with the initial consonant of the model word. Other word length and syllable-forming canons differ for two children.

(4) There must be shared order rules for the basic grammatical relations. By basic relations (McNeill, 1966), we mean subject-verb, verb-object, and modifier-head. Unless these minimal structures can be identified, the communication of messages is not possible, although topics or labels could be listed. Of course, these order constraints do not apply where the lexical items could only express one of these relations, as often is the case.

There has been, to my knowledge, no research raising precisely the above structural questions and using the Two Person Communication game. Esper (1966) studied the transmission of linguistic forms through a series of speakers experimentally, employing referents and artificial languages, but in a different procedure. He found surprisingly rapid morphological regularization, which suggests that this is the "natural" tendency historically, within socially isolated groups.

Stewart (1967) has commented on two natural instances of cross-language communication where precisely these factors might impair intelligibility. He cited two examples in which the dialect might impair intelligibility: "Ah 'own know wey 'ey lib," he argued, contains sufficient changes in phonetic realizations, word-formation rules, and so on, to seriously impair recognition of "I don't know where they live." "Dey ain't like dat" is likely to be misunderstood as "They aren't like that" rather than "They didn't like that." The dialect translation of the first would be "Dey not like dat" or "Dey don't be like dat," depending on a semantic contrast, not realized in standard English, between momentary and repeated conditions. This second example indicates that the basic grammatical relations may be the same, but misunderstanding still remains possible. Of course, Stewart was not discussing the highly restricted referential situation of our experiment.

The fascinating permutations on this experimental procedure would permit testing many analogs of natural language change and language contact. We have predicted that when speaker A addresses listener B, under optimal social conditions, the success of the initial communication depends on structural relations between languages a and b. If B has had earlier experience with other speakers of a, we might expect him to have learned to translate features of a into b, to some extent. It must take some frequency of instances to recognize structural similarities. We already know that A will provide better instructions, even without any feedback, with time (if he is old enough) (Krauss and Weinheimer, 1964). Where exchange is always unidirectional, B learns to understand language a to some degree, and becomes a "passive bilingual." Note that B is not just listening but is required by the task to perform actions; thus, he is not like a television watcher.

If give-and-take can occur, it is conceivable that a third language, c, might develop, with shared properties drawn from a and b. Such a development would be like the growth of a pidgin between two monolinguals under the press of trade or other limited encounters (Reinecke, in Hymes, 1964b). One test of the degree to which c is actually intermediate between the other two, or a composite, is to test whether when c is the code, A can communicate more successfully with B than he first did with B. That is, we assume that if c is closer to b than was a, it should be a more efficient means of communication, even to a neophyte listener.

The encounter of speakers from different language communities has had a variety of outcomes in natural conditions, including mutual bilingualism, the evolution of a pidgin, and one-way bilingualism (Reinecke, in Hymes, 1964b; Weinreich, 1953). It might be possible to explore the social conditions yielding these varied results by controlled manipulation of conditions.

An important feature of this procedure is that it can allow separate assessment of *comprehension* and *speech similarity*. If system a is understood or perhaps translated into b by the listener, there is no implication that B necessarily can speak language a. It is quite a separate issue whether features of a enter into the speech of B; under some social conditions, features could perhaps be transmitted without comprehension.

Several recent studies of intergroup "comprehension" make the issue of objective measurement of intelligibility important. Peisach (1965) has studied replacement of omitted items (the Cloze procedure) in passages of children's speech. She found that middle class children do better than lower class children in replacing every nth word verbatim in the middle class samples of speech, and on the lower class speech they do as well as the lower class children. When similarity of grammatical category alone is considered, she found Negro speech replaceable equally by all, but white speech easier for the middle class children (and for white children). The Cloze procedure requires actual emission of the appropriate response. It can be considered a form of comprehension test only if one believes in the "analysis-by-synthesis" theory of comprehension; it is not, on its face, a comprehension measure. Another way of stating the results is that middle class children can predict and imitate lower class and Negro speech, but lower class and Negro children are unwilling (or unable) to produce middle class and white speech by the fifth grade. Harms (1961) found the opposite among adults, who "understood" speakers of high social rank best, or of their own level when using Cloze.

Labov and Cohen (1967) have some striking evidence suggesting that many Negro children, also in New York, can comprehend but not produce standard English. Many of the children highly motivated to imitate sentences gave back "I asked Alvin if he knows how to play basketball" as "I aks Alvin do he know how to play basketball." These translations are regarded by the children as accurate imitations. Likewise "Nobody ever saw that game" would become "Nobody never saw that game." For the deep grammatical differences not arising by deletion rules out of the standard grammar, the children frequently *understood* but were not able to produce the standard forms. Nor did they notice the difference, going directly to the meaning (Jacqueline Sacks, 1967).

Two groups can communicate extremely well, indeed perfectly, though they speak different languages. Multilingual conversations are an everyday occurrence in many social milieux. There may be interspersed lexical borrowings in both languages, but if there is a common semantic core, mutual communication can survive very different realization rules.

If it is the case that the social life of a community could be carried on without speech similarity, then we cannot explain language similarity solely by the demands of basic communication. A more profound account is needed.

B. COMMUNICATIVE FREQUENCY

A common explanation for the evidence of linguistic similarity and its distribution is the frequency of communication between speakers. The most obvious determinants of frequency are proximity, work, power, and liking. If one undertakes to write a rule predicting who will speak to whom, with a given intent, proximity always enters into the rule. Thus in housing projects, people at positions near high-traffic points are talked with more; in classrooms, neighbors become acquainted; and in small groups, seating controls interchange frequency (Hare and Bales, 1963).

Some selection factors may make proximity secondary, except as a cost component, so that we find people commuting hours to a place of work or flying six thousand miles to a conference. In small groups, resources or status, assigned or assumed, may increase frequency of interchange (Bales *et al.*, 1951). Considerable research suggests that people select "similar" addressees for social interaction, which, in turn, increases their liking. Homans, in fact, pointed out that the interaction arising from sheer proximity could create "sentiments" (1950) and thereby increase liking. All of these features which measurably increase interaction in studies of face-to-face groups have cumulative effects that are visible sociologically.

These features of face-to-face interaction compounded over many individuals should be evident in the geographical distribution of linguistic features. One of the oldest forms of sociolinguistics is dialect geography. The distribution of particular speech features is mapped, the boundaries being isoglosses. Normally these are not identical for different speech features. Extensive studies have been made of such distributions in Europe and in the United States—for instance, of bag vs. sack, grea/s/y vs. grea/z/y. In general, linguistic features reveal the patterns of migration, intermarriage, and transportation routes. If there are natural barriers or social barriers to marriage or friendship, isoglosses may appear. Thus, McDavid (1951) noted that the rise of the large northern ghettoes in the past 40 years has led to an increase in the linguistic distance between northern whites and Negroes. Individual lexical items may follow the salesman: "tonic" is used in the Boston marketing area for soft drinks, and "chesterfield" for couch or sofa in the San Francisco wholesale region.

The political boundaries between communities are sharp but may not seriously effect interaction frequency over time. This we can infer from the fact that isoglosses do not match political boundaries. Isoglosses often do not even correspond with each other; that is, individual features may not diffuse at the same time or in the same way. Changes, as one would expect on a frequency model, are gradual. Gumperz (1958), in a study of phonemic isoglosses, found that changes were gradual even within the isoglosses. The functional load or practical importance of the contrast gradually decreased until it disappeared, and the phonetic distinctiveness also decreased.

The most extreme test of the argument that frequency of communication reduces speech diversity occurs in bilingual contacts. Gumperz (1967) located a border region between Indo-Aryan and Dravidian speaking sectors of India in which speakers were bilingual, using Marathi and Kannada in different settings. These border dialects have become increasingly similar in centuries of bilingualism. They have the same semantic features, syntax, and phonology, and differ only in the phonemic shape of morphemes, what we might call the vocabulary and function words. Each dialect is essentially a morpheme-by-morpheme translation of the other. However, other speakers of Kannada still identify this dialect as a form of Kannada because they recognize its morphemes—it is simply a deviant form, as Jamaican Creole is a deviant form of English.

This example illustrates both convergence of speech with high interaction frequency, and the maintenance of contrast. The convergence occurs at those levels of language we believe are least conscious and least criterial for the identification of the language. Speakers tend to identify languages by the shape of the morphemes, by the vocabulary, but even more by its function words and inflectional and derivational morphemes. The Kannada-Marathi example demonstrates that in spite of high contact frequency, speakers may insist on maintaining linguistic diversity, and that they may, in fact, believe it to be greater than it is.

There are many instances, to be discussed later, where frequency is high but speech distinctiveness is maintained. Castes in India interact with high frequency; Negro servants in the United States interact with employers; lower class pupils interact with teachers; and monolingual Spanish-speaking grandmothers interact with monolingual English-speaking grandsons — yet diversity persists.

High frequency of communication is a necessary but not a sufficient condition for increased linguistic similarity. High frequency of communication must result, at a minimum, in passive bilingualism of both parties, active bilingualism of one party, or a lingua franca. The only necessity is that each understand the speech of the other.

We do not yet know what the consequences of passive control of two systems must be. Active control typically leads to convergence at certain levels, starting with semantic boundaries and frequency of syntactic options, (Earle, 1967; Ervin, 1961; McNeill, 1966; Ervin-Tripp, in press). We have argued that there are cognitive reasons for such fusions and that they tend to take place when social conditions, such as contact with monolinguals, reading, and strong values about co-occurrence restrictions, do not provide strong support for system separation. Presumably, passive control of a second language has less impact.

Only one study has directly related the communication frequency of individual persons who all communicate to speech similarity. Hammer *et al.*, (1965) measured the observed centrality of individuals, and also the person-to-person frequency for every pair in a New York coffee shop with a regular clientele. They obtained speech samples and used the Cloze procedure. Central persons were most predictable, and each person most successfully predicted the omitted items from the speech of persons with whom he interacted most.

It is not quite clear what is measured in Cloze. All phonological features are missing. What is included are semantic factors that influence collocations, vocabulary, and perhaps some aspects of grammar. This study at first seems to support frequency as a critical variable in similarity, but it may not actually meet the critical limitations. The study was done in a social setting, interaction was social, and the members were parts of friendship networks. That is, some third variables may have determined both interaction frequency and similarity on Cloze. The hidden variable seems to be cohesiveness.

C. COHESIVENESS AND LINGUISTIC DIVERSITY

It seems that people talk like those with whom they have the closest social ties. We do not know precisely why this is the case; it may be that the features of social relationships which bring about this result are not the same for all types of speech similarity. In social networks and groups, there is a high frequency of interaction. The high attraction of others in the group or network means that they not only serve as models but can also act as reinforcing agents in their responses to speech, affecting attitudes toward features in the community repertoire. In addition, there might be secondary reinforcement in sounding like a valued person.

All levels of speech appear to be affected. With respect to the phonetic realization of phonemes, age may constrain changes in the system. Even under optimal conditions, many persons over 12 years old seem to have difficulty changing their phonetic realization rules except under careful monitoring.

Labov (1966) has argued that the everyday vernacular is stabilized by puberty on the basis of the peer model. Cultures where peer ties are weaker (if any exist) would provide a valuable comparison.

The *functions* of communication in cohesive networks necessarily include a high frequency of requests for social reinforcement, and of expressive speech. The social group may or may not be concerned with information and opinion exchange for its own sake. Davis (1961), in a study of the maintenance or dissolution of "great books" discussion groups, found that if there were many members of a social network in such a group, its durability was enhanced for college-educated members and decreased for noncollege-educated. He suggested that for the latter there might be a conflict between interaction practices in the network and the constraints of the discussion group. Bossard (1945) commented on large differences between families in the extent of information-exchange in dinner table conversation.

The most ingenious work on interfamily differences in communication has been conducted by Basil Bernstein. He has pointed out (in press a,b) that communicative patterns and socialization methods within families are related to occupational roles and to the character of a family's social network. Empirical support was found in mothers' reports of use of appeals to children, emphasis on different functions of language, and encouragement of interaction. In turn, London five-year-olds differed by social class (and by mothers' reports) in the variety of nouns and adjectives, use of relative clauses, use of pronouns with extraverbal referents, and in ability to switch style with task. That some of these differences may reflect performance customs rather than capacity is suggested by the report of Cowan (1967) that American working class children, though less successful than middle class children on the Two Person Communication game, learned fast when paired with middle class partners.

Hess and Shipman (1965), who observed actual mother—child interaction in Negro preschool families, found considerable social class variation and between-family variation in the extent to which mothers used the situation to elicit labeling and informational communication from the children. The measures correlated two years later with oral comprehension. Schatzmann and Strauss (1955) found social class differences in oral narratives that may be related to Bernstein's distinction. See also Lawton (1964).

There has been too little study of natural interaction *within* social groups to extricate what the important differences are—whether they lie in the amount of interaction of children with adults vs. peers and siblings, whether there are differences in encounters with strangers and training of children in competence with outsiders, or whether there are differences in emphasis in intragroup speech functions.

Because evidence about the verbal skills of lower class Negroes came from formal testing situations and classrooms, there have been widespread misconceptions about "verbal deprivation" in American society, with expensive educational consequences. Recent investigators such as Labov and Cohen (1967) in Harlem and Eddington and Claudia Mitchell in San Francisco and Oakland have recorded natural interaction. All have found that Negro lower class speakers are highly verbal in terms of speech frequency. Both adolescents and children engage with great skill in verbal games for which they have complex traditions. "Controlled situations" may, in fact, obscure the very skills which have been most developed within a particular group.

"General verbal deprivation" could conceivably exist. It most probably would be found in unusual social isolation, or in cases of social marginality, particularly where a language has been lost but there has not been full access to a range of functions in a second language. For further detailed discussion of research on this point and some new data, see Cazden (1966,1967).

Topics of discourse are likely to be different in cohesive networks as a result of differing values and interests. This produces considerable impact on the semantic structure and lexicon.

One way of studying differences in messages arising from communication is to examine content shifts, under acculturation, where there may be radical changes in social allegiances. A study of this phenomenon in Japanese women married to Americans showed that there was considerable difference between women who gave messages typical of their agemates in Tokyo and those who were more like American women, even when speaking Japanese (Ervin-Tripp, 1967). Word associations, sentence completions, TATs, story completions, and semantic differentials were all used in both languages. In general, the women who remained more Japanese in response content would rather be Japanese than American, preserve more Japanese customs, and keep up strong ties to Japan. The chief characteristics of the women who shifted to American responses were that they identified with American women, had close American friends, read American magazines, and met somewhat less opposition to their marriage from Japanese friends and family. The last point implies that in Japan they may have been less conservative. Though both sets of women would seem, on the surface, to have had a cohesive tie to an American partner, the interviews revealed striking differences. Marriages in Japan involve far more social separation of husband and wife than here; for example, there is little joint socializing with nonkin. Many of the Japanese women in this country do not regard their husbands as confidants in trouble, and may, indeed, seldom see them. When either the husband or an American friend was regarded as a close confidant, the messages were more American. It is, in fact, not easy to give "typically American" responses on many of these tests, so their ability to do so represents a considerable degree of subtle learning.

Semantic innovation is one of the striking features of cohesive groups. There may be new activities requiring new names; there may be finer discriminations required along continua; and there may be new conceptual categories. These are realized by lexical innovations which spread within the network. Examples are "she's in high drag" in the homosexual network, referring to a male homosexual in women's clothing (Cory, 1952); "prat," "breech," "insider," "tail pit," and "fob," pickpocket jargon for pockets (Conwell, 1937); "cooling the mark out" by the confidence man (Goffman, 1952); and "trivial," "motivated," and reflexive," terms used among transformationalists and ethnomethodologists, respectively, with special meanings. Many examples can be found in Mauer (1962).

A glimpse of the workings of this process can be seen in the Two Person Communication game.

Krauss and Weinheimer (1964) found that reference phrases became abbreviated with practice. Given the limitation on necessary referential distinctions, abbreviated coding is efficient. The result is not merely a change in the external shape of the form but a semantic shift, since the simplest term comes to have the specific meaning of the highly qualified phrase. The authors mention analogies like "hypo" among photographers and "comps" among graduate students.

Brent and Katz (1967) made comparisons of types of coding of drawings by middle class whites and by Negro Job Corps teen-agers. Unfortunately, they used geometric shapes, which gives a distinct advantage to subjects who are formally educated. They found that the Negro subjects were relatively successful although they used nontechnical names like "sharp-pointed piece," "a square wiggling," and "the funny looking piece." It would be an advantage to use materials equally strange or equally familiar to both groups and to control network features of the speaker and listener. We have strong evidence that members of the same social group prefer nontechnical communication. Where materials are neutral (e.g., nonsense forms), nontechnical, highly metaphorical communication is most efficient in terms of both brevity and success in a nonfeedback condition.

Even though the semantic distinctions made are not new, group *jargon* or new morphophonemic realizations for lexical categories are common in cohesive groups. Occasionally, such terminology arises to allow secrecy before outsiders (though Conwell and Mauer commented that secrecy is better served by semantic shift employing conventional morphemes). New morphemes are the most apparent mark of an in-group, whether or not they realize novel semantic distinctions. In fact, the best test for the symbolic value of the marker is whether it has referential meaning and, if so, whether it is translatable. Conwell (1937) pointed out that the pickpocket's terminology is not used before outsiders, but it is used to test the trustworthiness of a member of the network and to find how much he knows. In simple terms, the use of such terms can symbolize membership if the group is large or boundary maintenance is important; if the group is small, like a family, and its members known, the terms are used to indicate solidarity. Bossard (1945) cited examples of family words; many baby words or nicknames survive with such social meanings.

Where the incidence of social or regional dialect difference coincides with density of friendship network, the *structural* dialect features, including syntax and phonology, may come to be markers of cohesiveness. Blom and Gumperz (in press) found that the local dialect of Hemnisberget, Norway, had this significance to its residents.

Labov (1963) observed that the rate of dialect change was different in Martha's Vineyard among young men, depending upon their social loyalties. There was a change in progress very markedly differentiating young men from their grandparents. The men who went along in this direction were those who had the strongest local ties and did not want to move off-island. It is not clear whether or not interaction frequencies were also affected by the different values. The effect showed up in articulation.

Strong social ties affect all aspects of linguistic systems; our evidence suggests that the most quickly affected are the semantic system and lexicon — in short, the vocabulary. The structural morphemes evidently are not as sensitive to the forces of cohesion as are other morphemes.

D. IDENTITY MARKING

Every society is differentiated by age and sex; in addition, rank, occupational identities, and other categories will be found. Since the rights and duties of its members are a function of these identities, it is of great social importance to establish high visibility for them. Sometimes this has been done by legislation controlling permissible clothing, house type, and so on. Everywhere it seems to be the case that information about social identity is contained in speech variables. In urban societies, the social function of such marking is greater, since it may be the only information available; on the other hand, the social sanctions for violation may be reduced. McCormack (1960) has noted the spread of upper caste dialect features in urban lower caste speakers in India.

In some cases, there may be more frequent communication within, rather than between, categories. Clearly, this is not always the case: within the western family, communication occurs with high frequency across both sex and age categories. Therefore, something other than frequency of communication or group cohesion must account for the preservation of speech diversity which marks social identity.

It is not precisely clear what features of speech mark *sex* in the United States. In some languages (Haas, in Hymes, 1964b; Martin, in Hymes, 1964b) lexicon, function words, and phonological rules are different for males and females. The study of the training of boys by women in such societies would be enlightening. There are clearly topical differences arising from occupational and family status and, therefore, possibly semantic differences and differences in lexical repertoire. Masculinity — femininity tests have leaned heavily on differences in lexicon, particularly in the meanings realized, or in collocations. Sociolinguistic rules are probably not the same; e.g., speech etiquette concerning taboo words. Men and women do not use terms of address in quite the same way, and young women, at least, use more deferential request forms than young men. In fact, it is commonly the case in many languages that women employ more deferential speech, but one can expect that such differences are related to other indicators of relative rank. For example, in jury deliberations (Strodtbeck *et al.*, 1957), women are several steps lower in social class, in terms of their speech frequency and evaluation by fellow jurors. Labov (1966) and Levine and Crockett (1966) found more situational style shifting by women; Fischer (Hymes, 1964b) recorded the formal "-ing" suffix relatively more often from girls than boys.

Age differences in speech arise both through language change and age-grading. Though grandparent and grandchild may communicate, they are unlikely to have the same system. Labov (1963, 1966) related several such changes to current distributions. For instance, he points out the spread of "r" in New York City. In the top social class, in casual speech, "r" was used by only 43% of the respondents over 40 years old but by twice as many of the younger respondents. Changes like ice box-refriger-ator (for the latter object), and victrola-phonograph-record player-stereo are apparent to all of us.

In addition, certain lexicon or structures may be considered inappro-priate at a particular age. Newman (Hymes, 1964b) remarked that slang is for the young Zunis. Children over a certain age are expected to stop us-ing nursery terms like "bunny," "piggy," "potty," and "horsie," except in addressing infants. Pig Latin and other playful transforms (Conklin, in Hymes, 1964b) may be age-restricted. Stewart has claimed that a form he calls "basilect" is learned among Washington, D.C. Negroes from their peers in early childhood and begins to disappear, under negative sanc-tions, around age 7 or 8. Adolescents studied in New York (Labov and Cohen, 1967) had forms similar to the adolescent speech of some Wash-ington D.C. speakers, including two features absent in standard English: a completive or intensive-perfective "I done seen it" or "I done forgot it" (semantically contrasted with the simple past or perfect); and a distinction with *be* analogous to the distinction between habitual use and momentary or ongoing action (a distinction made in the standard language only for other action verbs): "He be with us all the time," vs. "He with us right now." (He walks every day vs. He's walking right now).

Many statuses entail the learning of specialized languages or super-posed varieties. The Brahmin, for example, is likely to have studied En-glish and to have many more borrowings in his speech than the non-Brah-min. Brahmins can sometimes be identified by such borrowed forms or by literary vocabulary (McCormack, 1960), just as psychologists' occupa-tional register can identify them. In addition, the functions and topics imposed by occupations can alter the speech of parents in the home, and in "anticipatory socialization" the children from different occupational milieux may be affected.

One way to differentiate similarity arising from cohesion from difference arising from identity marking is the presence of negative sanc-tions. Ramanujan pointed out (1967) that Brahmin parents specifically reject non-Brahmin items or use them with pejorative connotations. The Brahmins show, in several respects, that they value the preservation of markers of their identity. They consciously borrow more foreign forms and preserve their phonological deviance so that their phonological repertoire is very large. They have maintained more morphological irregularities (like our strong verbs) in their development of various inflectional paradigms, even though the evidence suggests that the earlier language (now written) was more regular. The evidence from the Esper experiment (1966) and the evolution of the non-Brahmin dialects is that regularization is the more normal destiny unless some factor interferes. In cases of phonological difference from the non-Brahmin dialects, in the realization of cognates, they have, in morphemes where the realizations fall together in the two dialects and would thus be indistinguishable, innovated a distinction. The semantic space is far more differentiated, as is the lexicon. The learning of a language full of irregularities is obviously more difficult — every child spontaneously regularizes. Like the Mandarin learning Chinese characters, the Brahmin puts additional effort into the maintenance of an elite dialect because the reward is its distinctive marking of his identity.

One might assume that lower castes would adopt prestige speech, and there is, as cited earlier, some evidence of such tendencies in urban milieux. One way of preventing such spread is the use of a non-Brahmin style when addressing non-Brahmins which, of course, reduces frequency of exposure. In addition, there are sanctions against such emulation.

American Negro speech may provide an example of identity marking although the evidence is ambiguous. Stewart has argued (1967) that Negro speech is based on creoles used in the early slave period, and that this history accounts for some of the basic semantic and syntactical differences Labov and Cohen (1967) have recently cited, which appear in various black communities all over the country. Labov has suggested that working class casual speech features connote solidarity, reducing the impact of standard English heard in school on casual style.

Certainly the clearest evidence of the identity-marking function of language is language maintenance during contact. Fishman (1967) has extensively discussed various features of language maintenance programs. Although the dominant groups in the United States have strongly favored language shift by immigrants, to the point of legislating against vernacular education, some groups continued to resist the loss of their language. Those who succeeded best, according to Kloss (in Fishman, 1967), did so either by total isolation (like the Canadian Dukhobors) or by living in sufficiently dense concentrations to allow a high frequency of in-group communication and the use of their language for the widest range of social functions. In particular, many maintained their own educational facilities, e.g., Chinese, Japanese, and Russians, promoting in-group cohesion among the children. A critical turning point lies in the speech practices of teen-agers. Where they are forced to mix with outsiders in large urban schools or consolidated rural school districts, the group language tends to disappear.

In parts of the world where there is a stabilized condition of great language diversity, as in Africa and Asia, it is quite normal to retain the group vernacular as a home language but to be bilingual for wider communication. Probably the degree of language distance in these cases is relatively small, as Gumperz has pointed out (1967). In these instances, the shape of morphemes is an important identity marker; shifting between co-occurrent sets of morphemes by such bilinguals is merely a more extreme instance of the small group vocabulary of the family, stabilized through time by endogamy and by the high value placed on group identity markers.

An extreme case in the opposite direction occurs in initial invention of pidgins. Here values of identity may be unimportant, and the practical need to communicate dominates. In fact, pidgins tend to develop when the norms which sustain co-occurrence rules are missing. Thus they appear in the transitory encounters of traders away from home, in the fortuitous combination of diverse speakers in the setting of work—in plantations, mines, and harbor cities. In this respect, African urbanization and slavery shared a feature, and we may guess that earlier circumstances of urbanization in Europe also gave rise to pidgins. Pidgins are characterized structurally by morphological simplification and regularization, and by use of material from more than one language. At first, they are spoken with the phonetic features of the respective mother tongues. Of course, with time the pidgin can come to symbolize the subordinate—employer relation. Temporary communication systems much like pidgins occur widely in contact conditions in the United States. These situations have never been given the serious study they deserve.

When a pidgin becomes the mother tongue of its speakers (and thereby technically a creole), it may acquire all the values of group identity of other vernaculars. Meredith (1964) quoted a speaker of Hawaiian Pidgin (a creole language) who was subjected to a university requirement of mastery of standard English: "Why you try change me? I no want to speak like damn haole!" Meredith reported "hostility, disinterest, and resistance to change" in the remedial class.

E. ATTITUDES TOWARD SPEECH DIVERSITY

In studying phonological diversity in New York City speech, Labov (1966) identified three different categories of social phenomena arising from diversity. These he called "indicators," "markers," and "stereotypes."

Indicators are features which are noted only by the trained observer. For example, few people are aware that "cot" and "caught" are distinguished in some areas and not in others. Indicators are features which are functions of social indices like class or region but neither vary with style in a given speaker nor enter into beliefs about language.

Markers, in Labov's system, vary with both group membership and style of the speaker, and can be used in role-switching. In the New York City system, he found that "r," "oh," and "eh" were very powerful markers, in that they changed radically according to the self-monitoring of the speaker. In Fig. 5, the use of less [t] and more [th] with increased self-monitoring is shown by the slopes. A speaker who in rapid excited speech might say, "It wasn't a good day but a bid one," or "Ian saw tree cahs goin by," might in reading say "bad," and "Ann saw three cars going by."

Stereotypes, like their social counterparts, may or may not conform to social reality, and tend to be categorical. Thus, although a working class man might use [t] or [d] only 40% to 50% of the time, he will be heard as always saying "dis," "dat," and "ting." Evidence suggests that children as young as 2 or 3 years old may notice and remember differences like "bath" vs. "baf," and "window" vs. "winda," though they may ignore simple phonetic shifts.

Hypercorrection involves the spread of a speech feature from a higher prestige group to another, with overgeneralization of the feature based on a categorical stereotype. In Fig. 6, the upper middle class used "r" considerably less in self-conscious speech than did the lower middle class, who believed it to be characteristic of the best speech. A more common example can be seen in the contrast between standard English "He and I came" and nonstandard "Him and me came." Hypercorrect versions can be found which yield "She wrote to him and I" or "She wrote to he and I." Lexical examples were given by Ian Ross (1956) and even by Emily Post (1922); usually these are instances of the extension of formal, literary, or commercial vocabulary into casual speech. Labov (1966) has shown that hypercorrection is greatest among speakers who score high on a Linguistic Insecurity Index, derived from comparison of what they report they say and what they select as correct in pairs which, in fact, are not markers. Levine and Crockett (1966) also found that the second highest group shifted most with style.

Blau (1956) has observed a very similar phenomenon among upwardly mobile persons in quite different measures of insecurity: These people report more nervousness, are more likely to discriminate against Negro neighbors than any other types, and in these respects the members of high and low social classes are more alike than the intermediate people, provided they are mobile.

Labov (1966) has suggested that there may be "unconscious" stereotypes which account for borrowings which are not from prestige groups. He suggested that the masculinity connotation of working class casual speech might be such an instance. His measure of subjective reaction to speech samples required subjects to rank the speaker occupationally, thus, clearly asking for social class indicators rather than features imply-ing some other social meaning.

The richest variety of work along this line is that of Lambert (1963, 1967) and his collaborators, who have had the same speaker use "guises" to produce samples. These then are rated for a great range of features like personality, intelligence, and physical traits. French Canadians, he found, rated a "French guise" as less intelligent and less a leader than the En-glish-Canadian guise. In a study in Israel (Lambert et al., 1965), on the other hand, it was found that Arabic-speaking and Hebrew-speaking sub-jects had mutually hostile stereotypes when judging the guises. Tucker and Lambert (in press) found that evaluation by northern white and south-ern Negro college students differed in that Mississippi Negro college speech was least favored by the whites, and southern educated white speech least favored by the Negroes. Top-valued forms were the same for both groups.

Harms (1961) recorded speech from different social classes and found that 10 — 15 second samples could be differentiated by listeners. Regardless of their own class, they rated high-ranked speakers as more credible. This method, like that of Lambert's, does not allow isolation of the critical linguistic features. Lambert, on the other hand, has been able to identify a far wider range of social meanings in the speech variations than did the single scales of Labov and of Harms.

Triandis et al. (1966) tried to balance various sources of judgment by counterbalancing race, messages (on discrimination legislation), and stan-dard vs. nonstandard grammar. Slides were shown while a tape was played. College students who were uninfluenced by race as "liberals" were still much influenced by grammar, even more than by the message, in their judgment of the man's character, ideas, value, and social accept-ability. Three-fourths of the variance on admiration and evaluation is car-ried by the linguistic contrast. A new test for liberals might be this: "Would you want your daughter to marry a man who says ain't?"

Some consequences of these stereotypes about language can be seen in Rosenthal and Jackson's (1965) finding that IQ rose 15 points when teachers were told arbitrary children were "fast gainers." Linguistic vari-ables may convey the same message.

F. RULES FOR DIVERSITY

William Labov has begun to use his large collection of material on speech of different New York City groups to discover rules accounting both for stylistic and intergroup diversity quantitatively. He has been able to use quantitative functions because he has been measuring articulation ranges and frequencies of occurrence as speech variables, as well as using quantitative measures of social variables. Thus the rules he can find are not categorical in structure like those in Section II.

Figure 5 shows that a phonetic feature is a linear function both of social class and of style. Because of the apparently regular change with style, Labov hypothesized that there is a single dimension he called "self-monitoring" underlying the style differences. Obviously, the relationship can be expressed by a linear equation in which the phonetic variable $= a$ (class) $+ b$ (style) $+ c$.

In the case of hypercorrection of the kind shown in Fig. 6, the measure of linguistic insecurity can be used as a function of style, increasing its slope. For such phonetic variables, the function is a (class) $+ b$ (style) (Linguistic Insecurity Index) $+ c$. Some adjustments are made for age as well, since there is an interaction of age, class, and norms.

These rules are important innovations. They treat linguistic phenomena as continuous variables. Whether the use of continuous measures is possible except at the phonetic and semantic edge of linguistics is not clear; frequencies certainly are quantifiable for discrete categories too. The rules, like those in Section II, introduce social features as integral components. Normally, social features are mentioned in linguistic descriptions as a last resort, such as in a few style variations like those in Japanese where morphological rules must consider addressee. Finally, they include, in a single formal description, the differences *between* speakers and the differences *within* speakers. The fact that this is possible is impressive evidence of the existence of an over-all sociolinguistic system larger than the cognitive structure of members individually. As Labov has pointed out, a single member sees the system only along the coordinates of his own position in it; he only witnesses the full style variation of his own social peers. In fact, the possibility of writing rules which transcend class suggests a new criterion for a speech community.

What do sociolinguistic rules, the major emphasis of this article, imply for the social psychologist? Most narrowly, they provide him with new and far more sensitive indices of class or group identification, socialization, and role-shifting than interviewing alone can supply. The great precision with which linguistic features can be specified makes them technically ripe both for measurement and for deeper and richer study of the process of interaction. Linguistic interaction is deeply embedded in nearly all our social processes, in socialization in the family, into new occupations, and into a new community. Sociolinguistic rules are central to, even if they do not totally compose the organized structure which generates our social acts and through which we interpret others. Just as the study of linguistic structure is seen by many as a penetrating route to cognitive structure in the individual, so may sociolinguistic rules lead to rules for social action.

APPENDIX. TAPE RECORDING

Several social psychologists have had severe disappointments when they found that the taped material they had made at great expense was useless because of poor recording method or storage. For details of method see Samarin (1967) and Slobin (1967).

1. Equipment

First, make sure that the recording machine itself has a wide enough frequency range for good voice recordings by testing *at the speed needed*. If a battery machine is required, the Nagra, the Sony, or the Uher are available, with new products appearing monthly. Videotapes may require better quality sound receiving equipment as a supplement.

An additional investment in microphones and earphones other than those supplied with the machine usually is worthwhile. Lavalier (neck) microphones are desirable if a separate channel is available for each person, and if scraping of clothing or handling of the microphone can be avoided. In groups, stereo arrangements can both provide a wider range of close recording and give binaural cues for identifying speakers while minimizing background noise. Wireless microphones for children's groups, or figure-eight microphones for lined-up speakers and the filtering out of noise at the sides may be appropriate. If several microphones are used simultaneously, it is necessary to provide occasional synchronizing cues by voice or other device except on stereo.

2. Tape

Tape print-through can create blurred recordings by the transfer of magnetic patterns from one layer of tape to another. It can be minimized by the use of "low print-through" tape. Reducing the recording level will also decrease print-through, which is usually not serious if the original recording is very clear.

At the time of purchase, leaders should be spliced to tapes lacking them. A leader spliced at both ends of a tape allows one to label it *before* it is used, minimizing accidental erasures. Box labeling or reel labeling is untrustworthy. Tape labeling is related to a log or index file.

3. Recording Techniques

Reverberation and other background noise is the chief enemy. If there is one wall, face the microphone away from it to deaden its input. If there is more than one, or metal cabinet, or floor reverberations, use curtains, coats, or any means of deadening the sound reflection. Open the windows if the outside is quiet. The microphone should be removed from the noisy machine, and placed equidistant from speakers — if possible, about a foot from them. Point the tail of the microphone at noise sources or too noisy personnel, to deaden their input.

Take the time to learn to record well, to train field workers under realistic conditions, and to test with as much care as one checks a team of coders. Good recordings should allow discrimination of Ruth and roof, boot and boots, mutts and much, sin and sing.

4. Storage

If recordings are made in a hot climate, mail them out and have them copied on a high-quality machine immediately for storage on low print-through tape. While Mylar tapes last relatively well, temperatures should be constant around $60° - 70°C$, and humidity kept low, if necessary with silica gel. Store on edge, far from sources of magnetism such as electric outlets and appliances. Language laboratories in large universities often have suitable storage room. Rewind tapes annually to reduce print-through and warping.

ACKNOWLEDGMENTS

I am deeply indebted to John Gumperz and to William Labov for detailed commentary on a draft of this article, and to Dell Hymes and other members of the Sociolinguistics Committee of the Social Science Research Council, as well as to our work group in Berkeley, for discussions which have radically altered my view of this field. This article was written with the support of the Institute of Human Development and some aid from the Laboratory for Language Behavior Research of the University of California. Elizabeth Closs-Traugott provided some address data. Student work contributing to generalizations in the text included studies by Renée Ackerman, Lou Bilter, Camille Chamberlain, Judith Horner, Andrea Kaciff, Terrence Keeney, Jane Logan, Dana Meyer, Paula Palmquist, Elaine Rogers, Joan von Schlegell, Elisabeth Selkirk, and Billi Wooley. Papers cited more fully can be obtained from the linguistic ERIC system at the Center for Applied Linguistics, 1717 Massachusetts Avenue, N. W., Washington, D.C. Soviet material was provided by Dan Slobin.

REFERENCES

Auld, F., Jr., and White, Alice M. Rules for dividing interviews into sentences. *Journal of Psychology*, 1956, **42**, 273-281.

Ayoub, Milla. Bi-polarity in Arabic kinship terms. In H. G. Lunt (Ed.), *Proceedings of the ninth international congress of linguists*. The Hague: Mouton, 1962. Pp. 1100-1106.

Bales, R. F., and Borgatta, E. F. Size of groups as a factor in the interaction profile. In *Small groups*. A. Hare, E. F. Borgatta, and R. F. Bales, (Eds.), New York: Wiley, 1955. Pp. 396-413.

Bales, R. F., Strodtbeck, F., Mills, T., and Roseborough, Mary E. Channels of communication in small groups. *American Sociological Review*, 1951, **6**, 461-468.

Barker, G. C. Social functions of language in a Mexican-American community. *Acta Americana*, 1947, **5**, 185-202.

Barker, R., and Wright, H. F. *Midwest and its children*. Evanston, Illinois: Row, Peterson, 1954.

Bellugi, Ursula. The acquisition of negation. Ph. D. dissertation, Harvard Graduate School of Education, 1967.

Bernstein, B. (Ed.) *Language, primary socialisation and education*. London: Routledge and Kegan Paul, in press. (a)

Bernstein, B. A socio-linguistic approach to socialisation: with some references to educability. In J. J. Gumperz and D. Hymes (Eds.), *Directions in sociolinguistics*. New York: Holt, Rinehart and Winston, in press. (b)

Blau, P. Social mobility and interpersonal relations. *American Sociological Review*, 1956, **21**, 290-295.

Blom, J. P., and Gumperz, J. J. Some social determinants of verbal behavior. In J. J. Gumperz and D. Hymes (Eds.), *Directions in sociolinguistics*. New York: Holt, Rinehart, and Winston, in press.

Boomer, D. S., and Dittman, A. T. Hesitation pauses and juncture pauses in speech. *Language and Speech*, 1965, **8**, 215-220.

Bossard, J. H. S. Family modes of expression. *American Sociological Review*, 1945, **10**, 226-237.

Brent, S. B., and Katz, Evelyn W. A study of language deviations and cognitive processes. OEO-Job Corps Project 1209, Progress Report No. 3, Wayne State University, 1967.

Bright, W. (Ed.) *Sociolinguistics*. The Hague: Mouton, 1966.

Brown, R. W., and Gilman, A. The pronouns of power and solidarity. In T. Sebeok (Ed.), Style in language, Cambridge, Massachusetts: M. I. T. Press, 1960. Pp. 253-276.

Capell, A. *Studies in socio-linguistics*. The Hague: Mouton, 1966.

Carroll, J. B. Process and content in psycholinguistics. In R. Glaser (Ed.), *Current trends in the description and analysis of behavior*. Pittsburg , Pennsylvania: University of Pittsburgh Press, 1958. Pp. 175-200.

Cazden, Courtney B. Subcultural differences in child language: An inter-disciplinary review. *Merrill-Palmer Quarterly*, 1966, **12**, 185-219.

Cazden, Courtney B. On individual differences in language competence and performance. *Journal of Special Education*, 1967, **1**, 135-150.

Chapman, Robin S. The interpretation of deviant sentences. Ph.D. Dissertation, University of California, Berkeley, 1967.

Conwell, C. *The professional thief*. Chicago, Illinois: University of Chicago Press, 1937.

Cory, D. W. *The homosexual in America*. New York: Greenberg, 1952.

Cowan, P. The link between cognitive structure and social structure in two-child verbal interaction. Symposium presented at the Society for Research on Child Development meeting, 1967.

Davis, J. A. Compositional effects, systems, and the survival of small discussion groups. *Public Opinion Quarterly*, 1961, 25, 574-584.

Diebold, A. R. Code-switching in Greek-English bilingual speech. *Georgetown University Monograph*, 15, 1963.

Diebold, A. R. Anthropology and the comparative psychology of communicative behavior. In T. Sebeok, (Ed.), *Animal communication: techniques of study and results of research.* Bloomington, Indiana: Indiana University Press, 1967.

Dikeman, Bessie and Parker, Patricia. Request forms. Term paper for Speech 160B, University of California, Berkeley, 1964.

Dittman, A., and Llewellyn, Lynn G. The phonemic clause as a unit of speech decoding. *J. of Personality and Social Psychology*, 1967, 6, 341-348.

Dollard, J., and Auld, F., Jr. *Scoring human motives: a manual.* New Haven, Connecticut: Yale University Press, 1959.

Drach, K., Kobashigawa, B., Pfuderer, C., and Slobin, D. The structure of linguistic input to children. Language Behavior Research Laboratory Working Paper No. 14, Berkeley, California, 1968.

Earle, Margaret J. Bilingual semantic merging and an aspect of acculturation. *Journal of Personality and Social Psychology*, 1967, 6, 304-312.

Ervin, Susan M. Semantic shift in bilingualism. *American Journal of Psychology*, 1961, 74, 233-241.

Ervin, Susan M. Language and TAT content in bilinguals. *J. of Abnormal and Social Psychology*, 1964, 68, 500-507.

Ervin-Tripp, Susan M. An analysis of the interaction of language, topic, and listener. *American Anthropologist*, 1964, 66, No. 6, Part 2, 86-102.

Ervin-Tripp, Susan M. Language development. In Lois and Martin Hoffman (Eds.), *Review of child development research*, Vol. 2, New York: Russell Sage Foundation, 1966. Pp. 55-106.

Ervin-Tripp, Susan M. An Issei learns English. *Journal of Social Issues*, 1967, 23, No. 2, 78-90.

Ervin-Tripp, Susan M. Becoming a bilingual. *In* "Proceedings of the 1967 UNESCO Conference on the Description and Measurement of Bilingualism," in press.

Ervin-Tripp, Susan M., and Slobin, D. I. Psycholinguistics. *Annual Review of Psychology*, 1966, 18, 435-474.

Esper, E. A. Social transmission of an artificial language. *Language*, 1966, 42, 575-580.

Ferguson, D. A. Baby talk in six languages. *American Anthropologist*, 1964, 66, No. 6, Part 2, 103-114.

Fischer, J. L. The stylistic significance of consonantal sandhi in Trukese and Ponapean. *American Anthropologist*, 1965, 67, 1495-1502.

Fishman, J. A. *Language loyalty in the United States.* The Hague: Mouton, 1966.

Fishman, J. A. Bilingualism with and without diglossia; diglossia with and without bilingualism. *Journal of Social Issues*, 1967, 23, No. 2, 29-38.

Fishman, J. A. Review of J. Hertzler: "A sociology of language." *Language,* 1967, 43, 586-604.

Fishman, J. A. *Readings in the sociology of language.* The Hague: Mouton, 1968.

Frake, C. O. How to ask for a drink in Subanun. *American Anthropologist*, 1964, 66, No. 6, Part 2, 127-132.

Friedrich, P. Structural implications of Russian pronominal usage. In W. Bright (Ed.), *Sociolinguistics.* The Hague: Mouton, Pp. 214-253, 1966.

Geertz, C. *The religion of Java*. Glencoe, Illinois: Free Press, 1960.

Geohegan, W. Information processing systems in culture. In P. Kay (Ed.), *Explorations in mathematical anthropology*. Cambridge, Massachusetts: M.I.T. Press, in press.

Goffman, E. Cooling the mark out. *Psychiatry*, 1952, 15, 451-463.

Goffman, E. Alienation from interaction. *Human Relations*, 1957, 10, 47-60.

Goffman, E. *Behavior in public places*. Glencoe, Illinois: Free Press, 1963.

Goodenough, W. H. Rethinking 'status' and 'role': toward a general model of the cultural organization of social relationships. In M. Banton (Ed.), *The relevance of models for social anthropology*. London: Tavistock, 1965. Pp. 1-24.

Grimshaw, A. D. Sociolinguistics. In N. Maccoby (Ed.), *Handbook of communication*, in press.

Gumperz, J. J. Phonological differences in three Hindi dialects. *Language*, 1958, 34, 212-224.

Gumperz, J. J. Hindi-Punjabi code-switching in Delhi. In H. G. Lunt (Ed.), *Proceedings of the Ninth International Congress of Linguists*. The Hague: Mouton, 1964. Pp. 1115-1124.

Gumperz, J. J. On the linguistic markers of bilingual communication. *Journal of Social Issues*, 1967, 23, No. 2, 48-57.

Gumperz, J. J., and Hymes, D. (Eds.) *The ethnology of communication. American Anthropologist*, 1964, 66, No. 6.

Gumperz, J. J., and Hymes, D. (Eds.) *Directions in sociolinguistics*. New York: Holt, Rinehart, and Winston, in press.

Hammel, E. A. (Ed.) *Formal semantic analysis. American Anthropologist*, 1965, 67, No. 5, Part 2.

Hammer, Muriel, Polgar, Sylvia, and Salzinger, K. Comparison of data-sources in a sociolinguistic study. Paper presented at American Anthropological Association meeting, Denver, Colorado, 1965.

Hare, A. P. *Handbook of small group research*. Glencoe, Illinois: Free Press, 1962.

Hare, A. P., and Bales, R. F. Seating position and small group interaction. *Sociometry*, 1963, 26, 480-486.

Harms, L. S. Listener comprehension of speakers of three status groups. *Language and Speech*, 1961, 4, 109-112.

Haugen, E. (1956). Bilingualism in the Americas: A bibliography and research guide. *American Dialect Society*, 1956, 26.

Herman, S. Explorations in the social psychology of language choice. *Human Relations*, 1961, 14, 149-164.

Hess, R. D., and Shipman, Virginia. Early experience and the socialization of cognitive modes in children. *Child Development*, 1965, 36, 869-886.

Homans, G. C. *The human group*. New York: Harcourt, Brace, and World, 1950.

Homans, G. C. Social behavior as exchange. *American Journal of Sociology*, 1958, 62, 597-606.

Horikawa, K., Ohwaki, Y., and Watanabe, T. Variation of verbal activity through different psychological situations. *Tohoku Psychologica Folia*, 1956, 15, 65-90.

Howell, R. W. Linguistic choice as an index to social change. Ph. D. dissertation, University of California, Berkeley, 1967.

Hymes, D. The ethnography of speaking. In T. Gladwin and W. C. Sturtevant (Eds.), *Anthropology and human behavior*. Washington, D. C.: Anthropological Soc. Washington, 1962. Pp. 13-53.

Hymes, D. Directions in (ethno-) linguistic theory. *American Anthropologist*, 1964, 66, No. 3, Part 2, 6-56. (a)

Hymes, D. *Language in culture and society.* New York: Harper and Row, 1964. (b)

Hymes, D. Toward ethnographies of communication. *American Anthropologist*, 1964, **66**, No. 6, Part 2, 1-34. (c)

Hymes, D. Models of the interaction of language and social setting. *Journal of Social Issues*, 1967, **23**, No. 2, 8-28.

Jakobson, R. (1960). Linguistics and poetics. In T. Sebeok (Ed.), *Style in language.* Cambridge, Massachusetts: M.I.T. Press, 1960. Pp. 350-377.

John, Vera and Berney, Tomi D. Analysis of story retelling as a measure of the effects of ethnic content in stories. OEO Project No. 577, Yeshiva University, New York, 1967.

Joos, M. The five clocks. *International Journal of American Linguistics*, 1962, **28**, Part 5.

Kantorovich, V. *Ty i vy: Zametki pisatelya* (*Ty* and *vy*: a writer's notes). Moscow: Izd-vo pol. lit., 1966.

Katz, Evelyn. A content-analytic method for studying themes of interpersonal behavior. *Psychological Bulletin*, 1966, **66**, 419-422.

Kjolseth, J. R. Structure and process in conversation. Paper at American Sociological Society meetings, San Francisco, 1967.

Klima, E. S. Relatedness between grammatical systems. *Language*, 1964, **40**, 1-20.

Knutson, A. L. Quiet and vocal groups. *Sociometry*, 1960, **23**, 36-49.

Kostomarov, V. G. Russkiy rechevoy stiket (Russian speech etiquette). *Russkiy yazyk za rubezhom*, 1967, **1**, 56-62.

Krauss, R. M., and Weinheimer, S. Changes in reference phrases as a function of frequency of usage in social interaction; a preliminary study. *Psychonomic Science*, 1964, **1**, 113-114.

Labov, W. The social motivation of a sound change. *Word*, 1963, **19**, 273-309.

Labov, W. Phonological correlates of social stratification. *American Anthropologist*, 1964, **66**, No. 6, 164-176.

Labov, W. *The social stratification of English in New York City.* Washington, D.C.: Center for Applied Linguistics, 1966.

Labov, W., and Cohen, P. Systematic relations of standard and nonstandard rules in the grammars of Negro speakers. *Project Literacy Reports*, 1967, No. 8, Cornell University, Ithaca, New York.

Labov, W., and Waletzky, J. Narrative analysis: Oral versions of personal experience. In June Helm (Ed.), *Essays on the verbal and visual arts.* Seattle: University Washington Press, 1967. Pp. 12-44.

Lambert, W. E. Psychological approaches to the study of language. II. On second-language learning and bilingualism. *Modern Language Journal*, 1963, **47**, 114-121.

Lambert, W. E. A social psychology of bilingualism. *Journal of social Issues*, 1967, **23**, No. 2, 91-109. (a)

Lambert, W. E. The use of *Tu* and *Vous* as forms of address in French Canada: A pilot study. *Journal of Verbal Learning and Verbal Behavior*, 1967, **6**, 614-617. (b)

Lambert, W. E., Anisfeld, M., and Yeni-Komshian, Grace. Evaluational reactions of Jewish and Arab adolescents to dialect and language variations. *Journal of Personality and Social Psychology*, 1965, **2**, 84-90.

Lambert, W. E., and Tucker, G. R. A social-psychological study of interpersonal modes of address: I. A French-Canadian illustration, In press.

Lawton, D. Social class language differences in group discussions. *Language and speech*, 1964, **7**, 183-204.

Leary, T. *Interpersonal diagnosis of personality.* New York: Ronald Press, 1957.

Lennard, H. L., and Bernstein, A. *Patterns in interaction.* San Francisco: Jossey-Bass Press, in press.

Levine, L., and Crockett, H. J., Jr. Speech variation in a Piedmont community: Postvocalic r. *Sociological Inquiry*, 1966, 36, No. 2, 204-226.

Lieberson, S. (Ed.) "Explorations in sociolinguistics." *Sociological Inquiry*, 1966, 36, No. 2.

McCormack, W. Social dialects in Dharwar Kannada. *International Journal of American Linguistics*, 1960, 26, No. 3, 79-91.

McDavid, R. I. Dialect differences and inter-group tensions. *Studies in Linguistics*, 1951, 9, 27-33.

Maclay, H., and Newman, S. Two variables affecting the message in communication. In Dorothy K. Wilner (Ed.), *Decisions, Values, and Groups*. New York: Pergamon Press, 1960. Pp. 218-219.

McNeill, D. The psychology of *you* and *I*: A case history of a small language system. Paper presented at American Psychological Association meeting, 1963.

McNeill, D. Developmental psycholinguistics. In F. Smith and G. A. Miller (Eds.), *The genesis of language*. Cambridge, Massachusetts: M. I. T. Press, 1966. Pp. 15-84.

Markel, N. N. The reliability of coding paralanguage: pitch, loudness, and tempo. *Journal of Verbal Learning and Verbal Behavior*, 1965, 4, 306-308.

Marsden, G. Content-analysis studies of therapeutic interviews: 1954-1964. *Psychological Bulletin* 1965, 63, 298-321.

Matarazzo, J. D., Wiens, A. N., and Saslow, G. Studies in interview speech behavior. In L. Krasner and P. Ullman (Eds.), *Research in behavior modification: New developments and their clinical implications.* New York: Holt, Rinehart, and Winston, 1965. Pp. 179-210.

Mauer, D. W. *The big con*. New York: New American Library, 1962.

Mehrabian, A., and Wiener, M. Decoding of inconsistent communications. *Journal of Personality and Social Psychology*, 1967, 6, 109-114.

Meredith, G. M. Personality correlates of pidgin English usage among Japanese-American college students in Hawaii. *Japanese Psychological Research*, 1964, 6, 176-183.

Moscovici, S. Communication processes and the properties of language. In L. Berkowitz (Ed.), *Advances in Experimental Social Psychology*, Vol. 3, New York: Academic Press, 1967. Pp. 226-271.

Nichols, M., and May, Elaine. Conversation at breakfast. *Echo Magazine*, 1959, 1, No. 1.

O'Neil, W. A. Transformational dialectology. *Proceedings of the Second International Congress of Dialectologists*, Marburg. (in press).

Peisach, Estelle C. Children's comprehension of teacher and peer speech. *Child Development*, 1965, 36, 467-480.

Pfuderer, Carol (1968). A scale of politeness of request forms in English. Term paper for Speech 164A, University of California, Berkeley, 1968.

Piaget, J., and Inhelder, B. *The child's conception of space*. London: Routledge and Kegan Paul, 1956.

Pittenger, R. E., Hockett, C. F., and Danehy, J. J. *The first five minutes*. Ithaca, New York: Martineau, 1960.

Pool, I. *Trends in content analysis*. Urbana, Illinois: University of Illinois Press, 1959.

Post, Emily. *Etiquette*. New York: Funk and Wagnalls, 1922.

Poussaint, A. F. A Negro psychiatrist explains the Negro psyche. *New York Times Magazine*, 1967, August 20. 52 ff.

Ramanujan, A. K. The structure of variation: A study in caste dialects. In B. Cohn and M. Singer (Eds.), *Social structure and social change in India*. New York: Aldine, 1967. Pp. 461-474.

Romney, A. K., and D'Andrade, F. G. (Eds.) "Transcultural Studies in Cognition." *American Anthropologist*, 1964, 66, No. 3, Part 2.

Rosenfeld, H. M. Approval seeking and approval-inducing functions of verbal and nonverbal responses in the dyad. *Journal of Abnormal and Social Psychology*, 1966, 4, 597-605.

Rosenthal, R., and Jackson, Lenore. Teacher's expectancies: Determinants of pupil's I.Q. gains. *Psychological Reports*, 1966, 19, 115-118.

Ross, I. U and non-U: An essay in sociological linguistics. In Nancy Mitford (Ed.), *Noblesse oblige*. New York: Harpers, 1956. Pp. 55-92.

Rubin, Joan. Bilingualism in Paraguay. *Anthropological Linguistics*, 1962, 4, 52-58.

Rubin, Joan. *National bilingualism in Paraguay*. The Hague: Mouton, in press.

Sachs, Jacqueline S. Recognition memory for syntactic and semantic aspects of connected discourse. *Perception and Psychophysics*, 1967, 2, 437-442.

Sacks, H. On some features of a method used in selecting identifications: An exercise in the formal study of natural social activities. ms. in press.

Samarin, W. J. *Field linguistics: A guide to linguistic field work*. New York: Holt, Rinehart and Winston, 1967.

Schachter, S. Deviation, rejection, and communication. *Journal of Abnormal and Social Psychology*, 1951, 46, 190-207.

Schatzman, L., and Strauss, A. Social class and modes of communication. *American Journal of Sociology*, 1955, 6, 329-338.

Schegloff, E. Sequencing in conversational openings. In J. J. Gumperz and D. Hymes (Eds.), *Directions in sociolinguistics*. New York: Holt, Rinehart, and Winston, in press.

Skinner, B. F. *Verbal behavior*. New York: Appleton-Century-Crofts, 1957.

Slama-Cazacu, Tatiana. Some features of the dialogue of small children. *Problems of Psychology*, 1960, 4, 377-387.

Slobin, D. I. Some aspects of the use of pronouns of address in Yiddish. *Word*, 1963, 19, 193-202.

Slobin, D. I. (Ed.) *A field manual for cross-cultural study of the acquisition of communicative competence*. University of California, Berkeley, A.S.U.C. Bookstore, 1967.

Slobin, D. I., Miller, S. H., and Porter, L. W. Forms of address and social relations in a business organization. *Journal of Personality and Social Psychology*, 1968, 8, 289-293.

Slobin, D. I., and Welsh, C. A. Elicited imitation as a research tool in developmental psycholinguistics. Language Behavior Research Laboratory Working Paper No. 10, Berkeley, California, 1967.

Soskin, W. F., and John, Vera. The study of spontaneous talk. In R. G. Barker (Ed.), *The stream of behavior*. New York: Appleton-Century-Crofts, '963.

Stephan, F. F., and Mishler, E. G. The distribution of participation in small groups: An exponential approximation. *American Sociological Review*, 1952, 22, 713-719.

Stewart, W. A. Urban Negro speech: sociolinguistic factors affecting English teaching. In R. Shuy (Ed.), *Social dialects and language learning*. Champaign, Illinois: Nat'l Council of Teachers of English, 1964. Pp. 10-18.

Stewart, W. A. Sociolinguistic factors in the history of American Negro dialects. *The Florida FL Reporter*, 1967, 5, No. 2, 1-4.

Strodtbeck, F. L., James, Rita, and Hawkins, C. Social status and jury deliberations. *American Sociological Review*, 1957, 22, 713-719.

Stross, B. Waiter-to-cook speech in restaurants. Term paper, Speech 160B, University of California, Berkeley, 1964.

Tanner, Nancy. Speech and society among the Indonesian elite: A case study of a multilingual community. *Anthropological Linguistics*, 1967, 9, Part 3, 15-40.

Triandis, H. C., Loh, W. D., and Levin, Leslie. Race, status, quality of spoken English, and opinions about civil rights as determinants of interpersonal attitudes. *Journal of Personality and Social Psychology*, 1966, 3, 468-472.

Tucker, G. R., and Lambert, W. White and Negro listeners' reactions to various American-English dialects, paper presented at Eastern Psychological Association meeting, 1967. In press.

Tyler, S. Koya language morphology and patterns of kinship behavior. *American Anthropologist*, 1965, 67, 1428-1440.

Tyler, S. Context and variation in Koya kinship terminology. *American Anthropologist*, 1966, 68, 693-707.

Véron, E., Sluzki, C. E., Korn, F., Kornblit, A., and Malfe, R. *Communication and neurosis*, University of Buenos Aires Inst. Sociologia. (mimeo.), 1965.

Watson, Jeanne. A formal analysis of sociable interaction. *Sociometry*, 1958, 21, 269-281.

Watson, Jeanne, and Potter, R. J. An analytic unit for the study of interaction. *Human Relations*, 1962, 15, 245-263.

Weinreich, U. *Languages in contact*. Linguistic Circle of New York, 1953.

Williams, Marion. Restaurant syntax. Term paper, Speech 160B, University of California, Berkeley, 1964.

Wurm, S. A., and Laycock, D. C. The question of language and dialect in New Guinea. *Oceania*, 1961, 32, 128-143.

RECOGNITION OF EMOTION

Nico H. Frijda

DEPARTMENT OF PSYCHOLOGY
AMSTERDAM UNIVERSITY
AMSTERDAM, HOLLAND

I. Introduction

Recognizing emotion in others is, of course, an important aspect of social interaction. The fact that much of this recognition is based upon nonverbal cues—expressive movements, gestures, extralingual vocal phenomena—offers some intriguing problems concerning the utilization of these cues.

The problem of recognition of emotion has wider implications and is placed in a wider context than that of social perception only. Historically, the problem has philosophical origins in the question concerning the existence of other minds or, at least, the knowing of another's inner feelings. In this connection, Bain (1895) brought forward his theory of reasoning by analogy and Lipps (1905) his notion of empathy (*Einfüh-lung*). In addition to this, recognition of emotion is related to "physiognomic perception" in general. Any theory for explaining recognition of emotion in others should be compatible with this wider range of phenomena.

II. Definition of Recognition of Emotion

What, in fact, is recognition of emotion? One should distinguish between two components of this recognition. First, we have the production of an identifying response to behavioral stimuli. Recognition refers here to a psychophysical problem. Second, this identifying response may have a certain accuracy, and recognition of emotion therefore also involves a validity problem. This second component is obviously not relevant for physiognomic perception in general which is only concerned with certain rules of impression formation. In the study of emotional behavior, the psychophysical problem is also important in its own right. Even if judgments of emotion were generally erroneous (as personality impressions based upon morphological characteristics frequently are), their origin is of interest and they may have considerable social importance. If sensuality is ascribed to thick-lipped people, this may determine attitudes toward them.

The identifying response, obviously, is made to the meaning of the observed event and not to the event as such; classifying a certain stimulus pattern as a frown is not recognition of *emotion*. The observer must be responding to what is usually referred to as "emotion." Although we, too, will refer to it by that term, we have in mind a broader class of events, best indicated by a concept such as "motivational state," in which we may include nonemotional states such as sleepiness, attention, or liveliness, as well as anger or fear.

Both concepts, that of emotion and that of motivational state, are abstract ones. When using them for problems of recognition of emotion, one should ask how they are defined for a person observing another person. One should ask what *he* means by anger, fear, or interest when these are recognized in someone else.

We can distinguish three kinds of events meant by "emotion" and, at the same time, three systems of identifying responses constituting its recognition. These are situational reference, action anticipation, and emotional experience.

A. SITUATIONAL REFERENCE

The standard procedure in classical psychological experiments on recognition of expression consists of having the subject label the expressions with a word denoting some emotional state. This procedure, obviously, is quite unlike what happens in daily social interaction. Occasionally, people wonder about other people's inner experience or they verbalize their impressions by using categories like "anger" or "fear" or "being in love." Far more commonly, however, all that happens is that the observed person's behavior presents the world to the observer in a new perspective. The objects of discussion, or features of the actual situation, appear endowed with new or other qualities for the observed person, for the observer, or for both. When we see someone become terrified, we expect also to see something with startling properties in the observed person's line of sight. This manner of recognition of expression is the rule rather than the exception, even under laboratory conditions. When asked for free interpretations of photographed or filmed expressions, the large majority of responses consist of emotionally colored situational descriptions rather than of emotion-labeling adjectives (Frijda, 1953). "She looks as if she is looking at a small child playing," or "She looks as if she sees two cars rushing toward each other, nearly colliding and just missing each other," are examples of responses obtained. It seems that the experimental subjects have a preference for giving their interpretations in this way, that it is their natural way of going about it, particularly when the emotions concerned are not of the simplest, easily labeled kind. Situational reference is the "meaning" of most expressive behavior; or rather, expressive behavior is usually categorized under this meaning system.

B. ACTION ANTICIPATION

A different meaning system consists of anticipations of the stimulus person's behavior. Much expressive behavior is the starting point, initial phase, or general preparation of goal-directed emotional behavior. The "identifying response" may therefore consist of the corresponding anticipation or expectation. Understanding a given reaction as "anger" may consist of readying one's self to receive attack. Understanding friendliness may simply mean the sensing of the other person's likely receptivity to approach, or the increase in one's own readiness for affiliating activities. The "meaning response" may, on occasion, be nothing more than the shifting of the probabilities with which the observed person may imminently manifest his various responses and one's own emotional answer.

Actually, both situational reference and action anticipation constitute recognition of emotion among animals, to judge from the observations of Köhler (1921) and the experiments of Miller *et al.* (1959, 1962, 1963, 1967) on communication of affect among primates. They also constitute the only meaningful ways of talking about recognition of emotion of such animals, as Hebb (1946) has clearly indicated.

C. EMOTIONAL EXPERIENCE

Finally, the meaning of expressive behavior may refer to an emotional experience or attitude in the observed person. The observer may produce an inner imaginary representation of the other person's feeling; or he may instead evoke a verbal label or put one in readiness; or the inner empathic representation may be replaced by incipient or actual motor imitation of the preceived movements. All these seem to occur on occasion, to judge from descriptions in the literature and from introspections of experimental subjects. Empathy, in its different guises, should be considered a form of meaning response, a way of coding behavioral meaning rather than being the source of its emergence.[1] Empathy and verbal labeling have to be considered as only two possible meaning responses among several. Empathy and labeling, it is true, are common in psychological experiments on recognition of emotion. They — empathy, in particular — also seem to be frequent in other situations of "disinterested" observations, as in the theater or the circus. Such disinterested observation may well constitute the very special condition for their occurrence. However, they are uncommon in real interaction situations.

Recognition of emotion can be viewed as the emergence of a media-

[1]Contrary to classical theorizing by Lipps (1905) and Langfeld (1920), among others, observation of involuntary imitative movement made to expressive behavior shows that often a movement is made which is different from the perceived one but which is similar in meaning: grasping one's pipe in response to the stimulus person's tightening lips, for example (Frijda, 1953). When asking subjects to imitate facial expressions, they first start interpreting and only then move their faces. Also, it appears that if their subsequent verbal interpretations differ from the intended meaning of the model expression, their imitation resembles their own interpretation rather than the intended meaning (Frijda, 1956). Empathy may assist in interpreting emotion, but not because it would objectively copy the stimulus movement.

tional process which, in turn, is the starting point for an array of different identifying responses. This has consequences for experimentation. Questions concerning accuracy of recognition can and should be phrased in various ways. They should not be answered with respect to only one response system, the third, explicit one of the uninvolved spectator.

III. Survey of Experiments on Recognition of Emotion

A.   METHODS

Research on recognition of emotion has used facial or expression as material in addition to vocal expression. In this article, we will be concerned only with facial and bodily expression, although we expect basically the same regularities to hold for vocal expression as well. Research on vocal expression has been reviewed by Davitz (1964).

The general run of experiments on recognition of emotion requires the subject to label verbally the emotion expressed. More recently, rating scales have come into use with from 2 to 28 scales per stimulus.

There are other possibilities belonging less exclusively to our third response category. Dashiell (1927) asked children to match expression photographs to passages in a story; he found evidence of more subtle recognition than is usual with more traditional methods. Spitz and Wolff (1946) studied the stimulus aspects of the human face which are effective for infants by using their smiling response, as did Kaila (1932) before him. Action anticipation may be involved in an interesting task devised by Stringer (1968b), that of ordering expression photographs in a plausible temporal sequence. The outstanding experiments by Miller *et al.* (1959, 1962, 1963, 1967) demonstrate recognition of emotion among rhesus monkeys in a way which distinctly belongs in our first category. Their monkeys could, and did, switch off an electric current which shocked another monkey whose face was visible only on a television screen.

None of these methods has yet been used extensively for our problems. The same holds for another group of methods which has been developed for the study of individual differences but which could fruitfully be adapted to general recognition problems. Vandenberg and Mattson (1961) had their subjects select from a set of facial expression photographs that one which was similar in meaning to a given key expression. O'Sullivan, Guilford, and de Mille (1965) and Davitz (1964) used sets of alternatives which were different in kind from the key expression; O'Sullivan *et al.* used facial expressions versus manual gestures and body postures, and Davitz used vocal expressions versus stick figure drawings.

The tasks mentioned are probably all quite different in their factorial composition in terms of the factors isolated by O'Sullivan *et al.* (1965; see also Guilford, 1967). They would seem to entail mixtures of different activites and, thus, different psychological processes; they also would seem to entail activities foreign to recognition of emotion proper.

The traditional labeling task, for instance, is most likely to be composed not only of cognition of behavioral units (CBU) but also of convergent production of semantic units (NMU) or, where the checking of adjectives in a list is required, of cognition of semantic units (CMU). Even the relatively simple task of selecting the matching expression from a set of alternatives is not always free from such admixtures. Davitz (1964) reported correlations of his "emotional sensitivity instrument" of +.37 with a Thorndike Vocabulary Test. The "expressions" test of O'Sullivan *et al.* correlates +.40 with a verbal comprehension test. Vandenberg and Mattson found a correlation of over +.50 between their task and the Wechsler Verbal Scale.

In free description tasks, situational reference and action anticipation do, as mentioned, occur. To that extent cognition of behavioral implications (CBI) may be involved, together with semantic abilities. Different factors, again, should operate in tasks based upon similarity judgment. Rating degree of similarity between facial expressions as in the studies by Royal and Hays (1959), Abelson and Sermat (1962), and Gladstones (1962) may involve cognition of behavioral relations (CBR); convergent production of behavioral classes (NBC) should certainly be present in free grouping as used by Hulin and Katz (1935) and recently by Stringer (1967). More importantly, extraneous factors such as figural abilities — cognition of figural classes (CFC) and cognition of figural relations (CFR) — almost certainly play a role in tasks of this kind.

B. THE PROBLEM OF RECOGNITION ACCURACY

The presumably different factorial compositions may reflect factors which also operate outside the laboratory. Recognition of emotion is probably always a complex process. It resembles in no way the kind of simple, straightforward perceptual process suggested by theorists like the Gestaltists (Köhler, 1929; Arnheim, 1949) or Klages (1935). Moreover, the differences in the activities involved in the various experimental tasks may well account for the large differences in experimental results, particularly those on accuracy of recognition.

The problem of recognition accuracy was the subject of much experimental work in the twenties and thirties. It has recently attracted renewed attention because of the possible cue value of expressive behavior in clinical situations (Dittmann, 1962; Ekman, 1965a; Ekman and Friesen, 1967c; Exline and Winters, 1965; Knapp, 1963; Mahl *et al.*, 1959; Scheflen, 1965).

There are a number of factors which may have caused the estimates of recognition accuracy to vary widely and made it impossible to compare the obtained recognition scores or even to give them a meaningful interpretation. Experiments on recognition of expression differ in at least five important respects: (1) the task of the subjects, (2) the selection of permitted responses, (3) the nature of the stimuli, (4) the sampling of those stimuli, and (5) the computation of accuracy scores.

Variations in task have been discussed already. Within the tasks, experiments differ in the kind and number of responses that the subjects can use. Of course, results will diverge according to whether a list of 2 adjectives (Ekman, 1964, 1965a,b), of 8 or 9 (Coleman, 1949; Tomkins and McCarter, 1964), or of 100 (Féléky, 1914) should be checked. They will also differ depending on whether a check list is given or subjects are allowed free selections of terms (Kanner, 1933), free selection of 3 adjectives per stimulus (Frijda and Van de Geer, 1961), or free description (Frijda, 1953). It will also make quite a difference whether response should be in terms of emotion (either labeled or rated) or in terms of emotion-eliciting situations (Landis, 1929; Sherman, 1927; Coleman, 1949; Ekman, 1964, 1965a,b). There is no reason to prefer one approach over another as long as a rationale for the method chosen is given. Usually, however, this is nothing but sheer experimental or computational convenience. At any rate, not much can be said concerning general recognition performance when we find that photographs can be identified as happy or unhappy significantly better than by chance.

There is also quite a variety in the kind and quality of the pictorial materials used. Posed photographs are encountered most frequently and, occasionally, posed live expressions (Osgood, 1955) or fully acted live expressions (Thompson and Meltzer, 1964). They are nearly useless for recognition accuracy studies. Posed expressions are considerably more "typical" and pronounced than spontaneous expressions. Gottschaldt (1961) reports that whereas recordings of spontaneous reactions to startling noises showed 2.6% of what he called "fruitful expressive moments," there were 52.4% of those in sequences acted by the same subjects. Recognition of posed expressions is accordingly more accurate (Coleman, 1949; Gottschaldt, 1961; Kalina, 1960). Posed expressions are useful, however, in studies of the recognition process such as those to be reviewed in the following sections. Experiments using them also indicate that at least some conditions can be found under which certain emotions can be discriminated (Tomkins and McCarter, 1964; Ekman and Friesen, 1967a), which indicates the possibility of the existence of corresponding expression types.

Schematic drawings, too, have been used and can be profitable for studying the relationship between stimulus attributes and impressions (Brunswik and Reiter, 1938; Harrison, 1964; Kühnel, 1954; Frijda, 1956), the influence of contextual factors (Eistel, 1953; Cline 1956), or the development of physiognomic responses in children (Ahrens, 1954; Honkavaara, 1961). To make inferences concerning dimensions of expression on this basis however (Kühnel, 1954; Harrison, 1964) would seem to be of very limited value. As with posed expressions, research with schematic drawings may confirm the possibility of identifying emotion on the basis of certain cues such as body posture (Hardyck, in Sarbin, 1954; Rosenberg and Langer, 1965).

The deficiencies in the sampling of expressions in experiments on recognition of emotion have been discussed by Bruner and Tagiuri (1954) and Davitz (1964). Representative sampling, as Brunswik emphasized (1956), is absolutely essential for any meaningful statement on recognition accuracy. No study using spontaneous expressions in any way approaches this requirement. Small series of laboratory-produced reactions (Coleman, 1949), haphazard magazine selections (Munn, 1940), or reactions from very special situations such as stress and nonstress inverviews (Ekman, 1965a) are illustrative of what stimulus series are used. As a matter of fact, systematic studies on the ecology of expression, whether for recognition purposes or not, are absent. Some authors mention systematic registration of expressive reactions under specific conditions (Gottschaldt, 1958, 1961; Benesch 1960), but the only ones presenting data are Thompson (1941) on expressions of blind children and Krout (1935) on "autistic gestures" during interviews, with some extensions by Sainsbury (1955).

In view of all this, statements concerning absolute measures of recognition accuracy cannot be made. What *can* be said is that all recognition studies which used spontaneous expressions in adults (Coleman, 1949; Dittmann, 1962; Ekman, 1965a; Frijda, 1953; Gottschaldt, 1961; Munn, 1940), with the exception of a well-criticized study by Landis [(1929); the criticism comes from Davis (1934)], conclude that recognition of emotion performance is better than chance. This conclusion is supported by the experiments of Miller *et al.* (1959,1962,1963,1967) with rhesus monkeys. It agrees, of course, with most studies on posed facial or vocal expressions (Davitz, 1964). Some communication of affect by expressive behavior is obviously present. However, it is difficult to give meaning to that "some."

To give an impression of what it may mean, we will present some data from our own study (Frijda, 1953), since it is among the few using films of spontaneous expressions and since it used a fair number of them.

In a conversation situation, emotions were elicited and filmed, and unprovoked states were also recorded. A total of 68 film sequences of 2—15 seconds were obtained by using two different women and containing practically all more or less interesting moments of the 9 hours of recording sessions. This method of obtaining the expressions is of interest because of the tendency toward representative sampling of the expressive behavior. The film sequences, and still photographs taken from them, were presented to 40 Ss, who were asked for free interpretative descriptions. Interpretations were scored on a 5-point scale according to their judged correspondence with the description of the "true" emotion. The latter was based upon the stimulus person's introspection plus the experimenter's knowledge of the emotional situation and subsequent interpretation. Scoring was performed by the experimenter.

Under these conditions, the subjects obtained an average score of 1.73 out of a maximum possible score of 4, or 43.2% of the possible maximum. Twelve percent of the responses received the maximum rating, and an additional 20% the next best score (3). Score averages ranged over expressions from 3.82 (95.5%) to 0.70 (17.5%). Although the absolute level of these figures does not prove much and chance levels are unknown, it does indicate that recognition of expression is by no means impossible, even with spontaneous and fairly unselected expressions.

The scoring system used allowed subjects' responses to be erroneous in varying degree. The importance of this condition has been stressed by Woodworth (1938). Examination of results of older experiments using adjective check lists led him to establish a 6-point linear scale consisting of the following categories: (1) love, mirth, happiness; (2) surprise; (3) fear, suffering; (4) anger, determination; (5) disgust; and (6) contempt. (Points in order given.) Response distributions from several older experiments appeared to be far from random. Responses rarely fell outside three adjacent categories. Conclusions as to recognition accuracy on this basis were considerably more positive than on that of the original analyses.

Further inspection of the data led to a circular scale (Schlosberg, 1941; Woodworth and Schlosberg, 1955). Schlosberg (1952) then reasoned that since any circular surface can be represented by two dimensions, recognition of expression might be a two-dimensional judgment process.

Experiment proved this idea to be useful. Judgment on two 9-point scales labeled "pleasantness—unpleasantness" (P—U) and "attention—rejection" (A—R) gave meaningful and consistent results. Reasonable accuracy of judgment in such terms was suggested by high correlations with the Woodworth circular scale values, which in turn were in reasonable agreement with the actors' intentions for the photographs concerned. Later, Schlosberg added a third dimension, "level of activation" or "sleep–tension" $(S-T)$, based upon theoretical considerations and having some prima facie evidence (Schlosberg, 1954; Engen, Levy, and Schlosberg, 1957). The method of scale rating proved valuable on crosscultural replication, and ratings appeared more reliable than those obtained by sorting into Woodworth categories (Triandis and Lambert, 1958), let alone traditional labeling. Rating reliability may be extremely high and produce test–retest correlations of over .90 (Engen, Levy, and Schlosberg, 1958; Hastorf, Osgood, and Ono, 1966). Levy, Orr, and Rosenzweig (1960) demonstrated that average scale ratings, at least on the $P-U$ dimension, were reliable over wide ranges of intellectual ability of raters.

IV. The Dimensionality of Judged Emotion

A. The Dimensional Conception

With these last studies, the investigation of accuracy of recognition has led to questions of dimensionality and judgmental process. The hypothesis has emerged that recognition errors follow similarities between emotions, similarities that may be conceived as proximities in a multidimensional space. Recognition of emotion can be conceived of as a process of multidimensional placement rather than as placement in one of a number of unrelated categories. Moreover, the multitude of emotions as distinguished in the language appears to be reducible to combinations of a far smaller number of dimensions.

This conception has led to a search for the most adequate set of dimensions, or of other ways of reducing the space of emotions. The search for adequate dimensions emanated from the fact that Schlosberg's dimensions were not satisfactory in all respects. They were more or less imposed upon the material, instead of somehow imposing themselves. Whereas the pleasantness–unpleasantness and activation dimensions have generally been found in other studies (Abelson and Sermat, 1962; Shepard, 1963; Gladstones, 1962; Osgood, 1955; Royal and Hays, 1959), discussion has centered around the dimension of attention–rejection. Numenmaa and Kauranne (1958) found it, but others considered it superfluous, since the correlation between Schlosberg's $A-R$ and $S-T$ dimensions appeared to be considerable. Gladstones (1962) reported these correlations, which for some strange reason do not agree with, and are higher than, our computations: $r_{P-U/A-R} = .347$, $r_{P-U/S-T} = .091$, and $r_{A-R/S-T} = .829$. Perhaps his correlations apply only to the 10 photographs used by him, which would have distorted the results of his study, where he found a factor correlating .53 with A — R that he called "expressionless — mobile."

The investigation of expressive meaning space, as we may call it, has used two rather different approaches, judgment of expressive meaning by means of adjective check lists or rating scales, and similarity judgment by means of paired comparisons, triads, or grouping procedures. The rationale of this second approach is that the subjects are in no way forced to use the experimenter's preconceived dimensions; they are to invent and use their own judgmental points of view.

Judgment of expressive meaning has been the basis for dimensional studies by Hofstätter, Osgood, and the present writer. Hofstätter's (1956) quite early study is merely suggestive, since only eight stimuli were used; factor analysis of judgments in twelve bipolar scales yielded two orthogonal factors labeled "positive contact" (love, friendliness, etc.) and "negative contact" (hate, anger, etc.). Osgood (1955) asked his Ss to select one from a list of 40 emotional state labels to characterize a live but motionless expression produced by a student actor; the actor portrayed one of the 40 labels. Three-dimensional plotting of distances derived from the frequencies of usage of each label for each expression led to dimensions labeled "pleasantness-unpleasantness," "intensity" (running from "complacency" to "joy," "rage," and "horror"), and one called "control." By "control" is meant that aspect of emotion which distinguishes stances taken and initiated by the subject from those elicited by the environment ("contempt" versus "fear," for instance). The first two factors clearly resemble Schlosberg's P — U and S — T dimensions; the third may or may not be identical to A — R.

B.   REANALYSIS OF OUR PREVIOUS RESULTS

In our own studies, we employed bipolar 7-point scales. In the first study, we constructed a set of 27 scales meant to be somewhat representative of approximately 400 terms used by 30 subjects in a free labeling experiment. Twelve subjects rated each of 30 photographs selected from a set of over 200 expressions posed by a young actress. We will refer to these photographs as the "Nelly series." The 30 photographs were selected to cover all varieties of expressive traits. Stringer (1967) presented evidence that this effort was not entirely successful, however, and that anger, particularly, was under represented. A centroid factor analysis of 22 scales was performed, and four factors were extracted (Frijda and Philipszoon, 1963).

Recently, the responses on all 27 scales were subjected to exhaustive principal components analysis. This resulted in six factors accounting for

92% of the variance. Scales, and loadings over .30 on the factors after Varimax rotation are given in the left half of Table I.

Two of the factors are familar: I is pleasant — unpleasant, amounting to 31.2% of the variance; III is level of activation (18%), although with some special overtones, considering the highest loading variable, "controlled — uncontrolled." For this reason we called it "intensity of emotional expression." The low end of this factor is formed not by a sleepy

TABLE I
ROTATED FACTOR LOADINGS OF THE STUDIES
USING NELLY AND MARJORIE LIGHTFOOT PHOTOGRAPHS

Scales	Nelly (N = 50)						Marjorie Lightfoot (N = 48)					
	I	II	III	IV	V	VI	I	II	III	IV	V	VI
1. Controlled–uncontrolled	+.44		−.81						−.82	−.39		
2. Indifferent–involved		−.56	−.74					−.89				
3. Friendly–angry	−.78		−.40				−.85				−.36	
4. Sleep–tension	+.37			−.88			+.42			−.79		
5. Abandonment–reserve	+.41	+.40	+.67				+.63	+.55				
6. Authoritarian–submissive		−.42	−.62	+.59								+.94
7. Startled–relieved	+.79				−.36		+.88		−.30			
8. Artificial–natural		−.91						−.89				
9. Unpleasant–pleasant	+.98						+.95					
10. Closed–open			−.79	−.36		−.33						−.33
11. Active–passive				+.89						+.73	−.48	
12. Derisive–mild			−.80				−.38	−.71			−.44	
13. Attention–rejection	+.51	+.43		+.57	+.38		+.41			+.57		−.44
14. Cool–warm	−.50		−.76				−.72	−.45			−.36	
15. Admiring–despising	+.38	+.66	+.49				+.71	+.30			+.53	
16. Quiet–anxious	−.76		+.45	+.38			−.76		+.42	+.35		
17. Hesitant–determined			+.69		+.45							+.91
18. Sad–happy	+.90						+.90			+.34		
19. Directed–undirected				+.93			—	—	—	—	—	—
20. Eagerness–distaste	−.95						−.89					
21. Deep–shallow	−.71	+.53				−.36	—	—	—	—	—	—
22. Amazed–understanding				+.43	+.77		−.62		+.56			
23. Dull–clear	−.55			−.69			−.55				−.75	
24. Moved–unmoved	−.51	+.41		+.67			—	—	—	—	—	—
25. Oppressed–free	+.81			+.36		+.31	+.92					
26. Complicated–simple	+.31			+.35		+.83	—	—	—	—	—	—
27. Withdrawing–approaching	+.85						+.80	+.39		+.35		
28. Relaxed–tense	—	—	—	—	—	—	−.78	−.36		+.36		
29. Interested–uninterested	—	—	—	—	—	—					−.94	
30. Excited–calm	—	—	—	—	—	—	+.34		−.58	−.65		
31. Gross–subtle	—	—	—	—	—	—	−.34		+.84			
32. Soft–hard	—	—	—	—	—	—	+.33				+.32	+.78
Percent variance:	31.2	12.8	18.0	19.5	5.0	5.8	36.4	10.8	10.5	19.7	10.8	4.5

face, which should be the lowest level of activation, but by an expression-less one, bland but somewhat tightlipped.

Factor IV (19.5% of the variance) resembles Schlosberg's attention — rejection; the scale itself has a loading of .57 on this factor. The opposite of attention seems to be disinterest rather than rejection, however. An "interest" factor is a quite plausible candidate, which may have been present in Osgood's (1955) analysis, as noted above, and emerged more clearly in his reanalysis (Osgood, 1966). We will call it "attentional activity." Interestingly, both "active — passive" and tension — sleep, as well as attention — rejection, have high loadings on this factor.

Factor II is a peculiar one. It is defined by the two scales "natural — artificial" and "mild — derisive." It was originally interpreted as social acceptability versus social rejection. This may well be adequate, but with a special emphasis. Most probably it represents a social evaluation factor, embodying the impact upon the observer rather than an aspect of the subject's inner life. This interpretation is suggested by the results of a study, similar to the present one, in which 10 pieces of classical music were rated on the present 27 scales *plus* the traditional semantic differential (Van Wijk, 1964). In that analysis, an evaluation factor emerged having "ugly — beautiful" as its highest loading scale. The loadings of our 27 scales on that factor correlated + .57 with their loadings in the present factor II.

A different interpretation was suggested by Stringer (1967), and connects with the loading of the scale "natural — artificial." The factor may represent the reactive versus active opposition — attitudes elicited by the environment versus those initiated by the subject. As a matter of fact, the most "artificial" expression was labeled "skeptical" or "cheeky" by Stringer's subjects, and those expressions labeled "pain" were rated as more natural than those labeled "disgust." In this case, the factor is indeed similar to Osgood's "control."

Two small meaningful factors remain. Factor V represents "surprise"; "understanding — amazed" is the highest loading scale. The factor may turn out to have broader meaning, however, and be more akin to Osgood's potency factor, since "determined — hesitating" has a sizable loading. Finally, factor VI is defined only by "simple — complicated" and, as a small loading, "shallow — deep."

A few remarks about the relationships between the dimensions are in order. Factors III and IV would seem to resemble each other since both have to do with activity. It is not surprising that so much discussion has centered around their distinction and that they were confused in Schlosberg's analysis. His nonorthogonal components are here redistributed into orthogonal ones. Their difference in meaning is perfectly clear, however. Factor III represents emotional intensity — emotional activation in the sense in which Duffy (1962) used the concept or in which Woodworth and Schlosberg (1955, Chapter 5) uses it. It has to do with "energy mobilization" without any reference to alertness. Factor IV, on the contrary, represents arousal in the sense of attentional arousal and the construct behind the orientation reflex. The facial features involved constitute, in fact, part of that reflex.

Factor III constitutes the intensity component of factors I and V. A graphic representation of factor scores on factors I and III produces a triangular plot, with the apex at the low degree of intensity (aloofness, pensiveness), just as suggested by Schlosberg (1954) and found by Osgood (1966). As a matter of fact, the photographs are neatly arranged along the somewhat concave sides of the triangle with, at base center, all those stimuli high on factors IV and V. Correlating factors' scores on factor III with absolute deviations from the mean on factor I (thus, with degree of either pleasantness or unpleasantness) gives a correlation of +.60.

Factor V is rather unipolar; it has a group of surprised photographs toward its high end and all the rest lumped toward the other. The meaningful tail forms a neat sloping line in the plot with factor III.

Factor IV also gives a somewhat triangular plot with factor I, indicating that disinterest does not occur with both high and low pleasantness. Implied in the above is that the most surprised photographs (factor V), and both the most disinterested ones and the most interested ones (of factor IV), tend to be neutral with respect to the pleasantness — unpleasantness dimension.

C. REPLICATION WITH THE LIGHTFOOT PHOTOGRAPHS

Confirmation of the factors was sought by replicating the study using Schlosberg's Marjorie Lightfoot photographs (Karsten, 1965). Some of the scales were replaced by others which looked useful; the number of scales was 28. Principal components analysis was again performed, and the eight factors submitted to Varimax rotation. Rotated loadings on the six largest factors are given next to those of the preceding study in Table I.

Both analyses correspond very closely. There are minor differences in individual scales, but the major factors appear again, with comparable magnitudes. In both analyses, the six factors account for about 90% of the variance, of which the first four take 82.5% and 77.4%, respectively. Factor III, control, or intensity of expression, has become somewhat smaller. Factor V looks similar to factor V of the preceding analysis; both have distinct determined — hesitating loadings. It has increased in importance because the "soft — hard" scale has been added. "Surprise" has disappeared from this factor, whereby its character as a "potency" or strength factor has increased. Factor VI is new. It seems to be a social factor different from number II, and best characterized as positive versus negative social attitude.

Correlations have been computed between Schlosberg's data (Engen, Levy, and Schlosberg, 1958) and our own. His A — R and S — T scale both correlate highest with our own scales "indifferent—involved" (+.81 and +.78), "uninterested—interested" (+.84 and +.74), and "passive—active" (+.71 and +.79). Attention—rejection correlates only moderately with our (unanchored) attention—rejection scale (+.56). Included in a special principal components analysis together with our scales, their high and only important loadings were in the factor here called "attentional activity" (factor IV, loadings of +.78 and +.81, respectively).

D. CORRELATIONS WITH FACIAL FEATURES

The two studies both suggest the importance of not less than five independent aspects of expression, at least two to three more than in the usual analysis. One may wonder whether the dimensions found reflect the meaning space of expression or, rather, the semantic space of the words defining the scales. Our evidence is that at least four of them reflect the space of expressive meaning. This evidence comes from the correlations between the dimensions of expressive meaning and the facial features.

Factor scores for the first five rotated factors of both studies were computed by using a complete regression method so that the multiple correlations between original scores and factor scores exactly reproduce the factor loadings (Elshout, 1967). Facial feature measures are derived from ratings or rankings of the photographs by three to five judges on a large number of different facial traits (see Frijda and Philipszoon, 1963, and Karsten, 1965). For most of the less obvious measures such as upturned upper lip or corners of the mouth drawn downward, inter-rater agreement was quite low. Correlations with the two sets of composite measures are given in Table II.

The two patterns of correlations are in substantial agreement. The kind of correlations found is not very surprising and corresponds well with those found for schematic drawings of faces by Harrison (1964).

More important than what features go with what meanings is the general result. Each of the expressive meaning factors correlates significantly with one or more of the facial feature measures. On the whole, those which correlate in the Nelly analysis correlate similarly in the Marjorie Lightfoot one, although the correlations tend to be lower in the latter analysis.

Moreover, those facial features which correlate with one factor tend to be uncorrelated with any of the others. As a matter of fact, when factor analyses were performed on the 11 facial feature measures, four factors emerged in both studies which, after Varimax rotation, reflected the correlation patterns of Table II. The two factors matrices were rather similar. Factor loadings in corresponding factors (in terms of Table II) correlated .91, .94, .70, and .76, respectively. The four factors accounted for 79.5% of the variance in the Nelly analysis and 56.1% in the Marjorie Lightfoot one.

The extent to which expressive meaning scores can be predicted from the facial features can be estimated from the multiple correlations; R's corrected for shrinkage are given in the top half of Table III. They are, on the whole, sizable and significant, and explain, with one exception, over 40% of the variance. Of course, the large number of variables may boost the correlations. However, use of only six of the measures reduces the correlations only slightly, as can be seen from the bottom half of Table III.

The present findings underscore the reality of at least four of the expressive meaning factors. They also indicate that much of expressive meaning, in terms of these factors, remains unpredictable on the basis of the facial features. The beta coefficients from both analyses differ to such

TABLE II

CORRELATIONS OF FACIAL FEATURES WITH DIMENSIONS OF EXPRESSIVE MEANING[a]

	Nelly ($N = 30$)[b]					Marjorie Lightfoot ($N = 48$)[b]				
	I	II	III	IV	V	I	II	III	IV	V
1. Defensive mouth postures	+.72		−.44							−.34
2. Approach-avoidance score	−.42				−.41				−.33	+.32
3. Smiling, laughter	−.81		−.33			−.50				
4. Frowning	+.63		−.33	+.34		+.30				
5. Tenseness		+.60		−.31	+.45	+.37	+.33			
6. Subtle traits score		+.51	−.36		+.33				−.35	
7. Expressiveness	+.35		−.71	−.31				−.52	−.33	
8. Muscular activity score			−.62	−.45			+.30	−.44	−.51	
9. Mouth open − closed			+.69			+.51		+.52	+.36	
10. Eyes open − closed		+.32		+.40	+.52			−.38		+.54
11. Attentional activity				+.58	+.29			−.38		+.51

[a]Only correlations over .30 are given.
[b]Critical values of r: for $N = 30$, $p = .05$ at .355, $p = .01$ at .456; for $N = 48$, $p = .05$ at .288, $p = .01$ at .372.

TABLE III
MULTIPLE CORRELATIONS BETWEEN FACTOR SCORES
AND FACIAL FEATURE MEASURES (CORRECTED)[a]

Factor	I	II	III	IV	V
Nelly	.97	.67	.85	.70	.73
Marjorie Lightfoot	.80	.72	.47	.64	.53

MULTIPLE CORRELATIONS BASED UPON SIX FACIAL
FEATURE MEASURES (NOS. 1,3,4,5,7,10)

Nelly	.95	.67	.75	.69	.70
Marjorie Lightfoot	.69	.55	.35	.62	.42

[a]Critical values for R: ($p = .05$): for $N = 30$, $m = 11$: .66; for $N = 48$, $m = 11$: .56; for $N = 30$, $m = 6$: .55; and for $N = 48$, $m = 6$: .46.

an extent that averaging into one regression formula would be meaningless. The reason for these differences in beta coefficients lies in some differences between the two sets of expressions. The expressiveness of the Nelly photographs is higher than that of the Marjorie Lightfoot ones; the average number of facial feature checks per photograph is 5.04 and 4.00, respectively. This may account for the generally lower correlations with expressive meaning scores in the second analysis. Indications making up the tenseness and subtlety scores, in particular, were less frequent, which made for slight differences in factorial composition. The communalities of the Marjorie Lightfoot facial feature analysis were considerably lower than those of Nelly.

E. THE NUMBER OF DIMENSIONS OF EMOTION

The number of factors found in our analyses is comparable only to those isolated by Osgood (1966). Rotation of his entire factor matrix did not result in the three dimensions of his original plotting, but in 12 unipolar factors, nine of which appeared interpretable. They correspond rather closely with his cluster analysis of the same data. The factors can be interpreted as: (1) anger; (2) amazement; (3) boredom; (4) quiet pleasure; (5) disgust; (6) anxiety, sorrow; (7) interest, expectancy; (8) joy; and (9) fear. For the most part, these factors can be matched with our factors without strain. The place of anger in our dimensions is unclear; the most angry photographs occur at the not-surprised end of factor V. Anxiety and disgust crowd together at the unpleasant end of factor I. Fear has no separate place in our analysis either. Frightened expressions are, in our studies, a combination of high attention and unpleasantness. Intensity, our factor III, is the intensifier for all factors. Boredom and quiet pleasure either constitute its low end or represent low interest (IV) and mildness (II), respectively.

As for the number of dimensions, the studies by Osgood and ourselves stand in sharp contrast to the results of similarity measuring experiments.

Two dimensions (Numenmaa and Kauranne, 1958; Abelson and Sermat, 1962; Shepard, 1963) or at most three (Royal and Hays, 1959; Gladstones, 1962; Stringer, 1968a) seem appropriate there.

Most of these experiments suffer from the fact that only very few expressions — 8 to 15 — have been used. This criticism does not apply to a study by Stringer (1967), who used the same 30 photographs of the Nelly series as those in our first study. His subjects were asked to perform free grouping and subsequently to label each photograph. The distance matrix derived from the free grouping results was submitted to a cluster analysis from which five clusters emerged. These were identified, on the basis of label frequencies, as worry and doubt, disgust and pain, surprise, thoughtfulness, and happiness. Anger, incidentally, was infrequent among the labels, indicating a lack in our set of photographs.

Stringer (1968a) also submitted his distance matrix to a Kruskal multidimensional scaling analysis. Three dimensions appeared; a four-dimensional solution did not result in an appreciable decrease of stress. After Varimax rotation, these dimensions neatly ordered the clusters at their poles. Dimension I represented one kind of pleasantness dimension: happiness — worry; II was thoughtfulness — surprise; III was another bipolar unpleasantness dimension: thoughtfulness — disgust and pain. All but one of the "worry" photographs fell toward the extreme of our factor of attentional activity.

The value of Stringer's distance analysis was further strengthened by asking subjects to order the expressions in a plausible temporal sequence (1968b). The resulting distance matrix showed a significant relationship to that of the free grouping task.

Finally, Stringer (1968a) submitted the correlation matrix from Frijda and Philipszoon (1963) to a Kruskal analysis. Again, three dimensions appeared; a four-dimensional solution decreased stress only from .078 to .058. After Varimax rotation, these three dimensions can be unambiguously interpreted on the basis of the scale "loadings" as: (1) attentional activity (our factor IV), (2) control versus intensity (our factor III), and (3) a mixture of pleasantness and artificiality (our factors I and II).

On the whole, the meaning of these studies is reasonably clear. There is a distinct difference in task between labeling or scale rating on the one hand, and similarity estimation on the other, as Stringer (1967) himself pointed out. In the first, the subject is asked to discriminate aspects; in the second, to overlook differences and search for similarities. What the studies do indicate, not too surprisingly, is that pleasantness and interest are more dominant principles of grouping, or of similarity estimation, than intensity or artificiality. They suggest, moreover, that what defines "emotions" as separate entities are those same two components, with, possibly, subdivisions within them (such as between "worry," which turns out to be a kind of attention, and "surprise").

Within those "emotions," different degrees of intensity, or artificiality, or possibly other components, may be distinguished; the photographs within the clusters do, in fact, differ in those aspects.

This interpretation does not, of course, explain Stringer's results with reanalysis of our own correlation matrix. He correctly pointed out that we treated nonmetric information of our rank order correlations metrically. Since this would not apply to our own reanalysis as presented here, we will leave this problem until further information is available.

Besides the different number of dimensions, some other discrepancies are worth noting. The ordering of polar opposites is, on the whole, quite different. Two of the three dimensions have a distinct unipolar flavor. It will be remembered that Osgood's analysis, too, led to unipolar factors. The bipolar pattern of our analyses, on the basis of these findings, may well partly result from our method of using bipolar rating scales.

If we keep formulating the independent aspects of the meaning of expression in terms of bipolar dimensions, four of them, at least, must necessarily be assumed. The strongest argument for this assertion comes from our factor analyses of the facial feature ratings. As we mentioned, four independent factors emerged, roughly identifiable as smiling or frowning, opening of the eyes, general expressiveness and opening of the mouth, and tenseness. Not even all of the variance of our facial feature measures was taken up by the expressive meaning factors. Moreover, the facial feature measures used were, for the most part, crude combinations of a large number of quite unreliably rated separate expression components. If larger numbers of photographs and more reliable measurements could be used, chances are fair that more independent dimensions would be identified.

When we go beyond frozen expressions as they appear on a photograph, the existence of more independent aspects of expressive movement is quite obvious, and the existence of corresponding aspects of emotional meaning is plausible. At least three groups of expressive components are of importance in addition to what is manifest in facial photographs. They are movements of other parts of the body, the temporal structure of expressive movement, and the dynamics of the gaze and of locomotion.

A few experiments (Kline and Johannsen, 1935; Carmichael, Roberts, and Wessel, 1937; Ekman, 1965c; Ekman and Friesen, 1967a; Dittman *et al.*, 1965) have demonstrated that movements or postures of other parts of the body and of hands and feet contribute to recognition of emotion. Inclusion of more parts in a picture increases accuracy of recognition (Blake, 1933). Expressive movement of parts of the body other than the face may contain cues of particular importance for the intensity aspect of emotion (Ekman, 1965b; Ekman and Friesen, 1967a); at least, more interobserver agreement was found for body judgments on that dimension than for face judgments. Not very surprisingly, these authors found body cues to be less informative for the P−U dimension or for discrimination of Woodworth classes. Ekman (1965b) found, oddly enough, no correlation between sleep−tension ratings for face and body of the same reactions. His findings also suggest that in case of disagreement in this respect between both body parts, body cues dominate the final judgment. Generally, it seems from our own data that discrepancies among expressive movements of different parts of body and face may be major cues for the dimension of spontaneity and naturalness versus inhibition and artificiality.

The importance of the temporal structure of expressive behavior is evident. In our recognition study (Frijda, 1953), judgment of the filmed expressions was compared to 10-second exposures of still photographs representing the culmination point (if present) of the expressions. An increase in accuracy of nearly 50% was found (mean scores of 1.73 and 1.22, respectively, or 43.2% and 30.6% of the possible maximum). Our study also offers some cues of what aspects of expressive meaning are contributed by the temporal components. By comparing expression for expression the dominant responses to films and still photographs, and by describing the form of the temporal development, some impressions were obtained. The dynamic aspects of single expressive movements seemed reducible to the rate of change at onset and at decline and to the duration at a relatively unchanging level. Rapid onset always seemed to suggest a breach in the behavioral continuity, either because of a sudden stimulus change (as in startle), because of a voluntary change in behavioral direction (as in a polite smile), or because of an impulse disrupting an effort for control (as in nervous movements). Gradual onset gives the impression of integrated emotional response, spontaneously emerging; and very slow onset appears as lack of energy or the presence of inhibiting forces. Similarly, rapid decline is felt as a disruption of continuity, either by an effort of will or the withdrawal of a voluntary impulse (it is difficult not to betray an only-polite smile by its brusque disappearance), while gradual fading translates the natural course of a spontaneous emotional impulse. In all this, the dimension of voluntariness versus spontaneous emotionality seems dominant, or more generally, something like behavioral integration or self-initiation versus discontinuity or reactivity.

We will be very brief on the topic of the dynamics of the gaze since some aspects of it have recently received considerable attention in the work of Exline (1963; Exline and Winters, 1965) and of Argyle and Kendon (see Argyle and Kendon, 1967). By the dynamics of the gaze, we mean the varied play of establishing, holding, and breaking visual contact as it occurs particularly with other human beings, and especially its manifestation as eye contact, when the mutual glance is the modulated event. The facts of looking or not looking, looking away, avoiding or seeking eye contact are seldom or never visible in photographs. They are typically expressive of social sentiments such as timidity, shame, and embarrassment (Exline, Gray, and Schuette, 1965), or of social attitudes such as intimacy, dependence, sincerity, or desire for contact. The temporal properties of the gaze and of eye contact probably specify much in the meaning of these activities by their aspects of relative and absolute duration of looking and looking away or looking elsewhere.

Closely related to the gaze's contribution to recognition of emotion is the structure of relational tendencies, evident in the subject's path of locomotion relative to the objects in his field. Lewin (1927) in particular has described children's "field actions" and Tagiuri (1960) has shown that judgment of emotion depends upon the subject's path.

Locomotion and, to some extent, the dynamics of the gaze are cues to emotion which cannot be seen in photographs; quite apart from their speed and duration characteristics, their form is only present in the temporal development. The same holds for the majority of manual, pedal, and bodily expressions, which Ekman and Friesen (1967b) called "body acts," in contradistinction to postures or body positions.

In addition to all those more or less general expressive aspects, there exists a whole array of specific indices which may be particular to a given culture, subculture, or individual. We mean the category of facial or manual gestures such as winking and nodding, those movements which Ekman and Friesen (1967b) call "regulators." We mean also the idiosyncratic "autistic gestures" which Krout (1935), who named them, demonstrated to be indicative of emotional perturbations, and which Sainsbury (1955) and others have further explored. These may serve, to those who know the culture or the individual, as further cues to emotional states.

V. The Meaning of the Dimensionality Studies

A. CONCEPTIONS OF THE SYSTEM OF EMOTIONAL EXPRESSION

How, on the basis of the research discussed so far, should emotional expression and recognition of emotion be conceptualized? How adequate is the view that recognition of emotion is a matter of multidimensional placement? Consider the three different possibilities: (1) the category conception, (2) the dimensional conception, and (3) a hierarchical conception.

First, the category conception. There may exist, as far as expression is concerned, a number of distinct, unrelated basic emotions, or, what amounts to the same thing, unipolar emotional dimensions. Judging emotion would then consist of mapping the observed behavior into one of a set of discrete, unrelated classes, or in more than one if the emotion represents a mixture. The number of classes may be large or small. Tomkins and McCarter (1964) recently made a case for distinguishing nine: (1) enjoyment, (2) interest, (3) surprise, (4) fear, (5) anger, (6) disgust, (7) shame, (8) distress, and (9) neutrality. Posed expressions for these nine categories could be reliably discriminated among. There is no indication that these categories are more adequate than any other set, however.

The main feature of this conception is that the classes are to be unrelated and unordered. In fact, Boucher and Ekman (1965) and Thompson and Meltzer (1964) presented evidence that the Woodworth classes are not as ordered as Woodworth (1938) and Schlosberg (1941) suggested. Their evidence is not too convincing, though, nor are the Woodworth classes necessarily the most adequate. Another argument for this conception would be the occurrence of few stimuli at one end of the dimensions in a dimensional analysis, and the majority at the other end. We found one such plot in the case of our "surprise" factor (factor V), of the Nelly analysis.

The second conception is Schlosberg's dimensional model, which was first proposed actually by Wundt. Emotions are considered to be essentially made up by a bit of this and a bit of that—a bit of pleasantness, attention, and activation. Emotions, as distinguished by the common verbal labels, should be distributed evenly throughout this n-dimensional space. The model is no doubt useful and highly adequate. It accounts for similarities between obviously different emotions such as horror and fascination, or disgust and contempt in the Woodworth studies; it accounts for the existence of differences between emotions having certain similarities and of the numerous shades of feeling within a given class, and for the obvious tendency to place emotions along the pleasantness—unpleasantness continuum, which is particularly evident in similarity rating experiments.

The model becomes clumsy, however, if the number of dimensions increases and, in particular, if the dimensions themselves obtain a specific flavor such as "surprise" or "anger." More of these seem fairly likely if more stimuli were to be used in the experiments. In the sensory field, expressions of disgust, foulness, sourness, and bitterness are almost certainly different, and so, perhaps, are even their emotional counterparts. Different clusters for disgust, fear, and pain are already indicated.

A hierarchical conception combines the two previous ones. It could be that at a given region of the n-dimensional space, points are differentiated in terms of dimensions meaningful only in that region. Disgust versus pain could be an example. Stated differently, emotions within, as well as across, categories could well be comparable in terms of a number of dimensional properties such as pleasantness, intensity, attentional activity involved, complexity, and integration into the stream of experience, while each category may still have something specific of its own such as the kind of attentional activity or the kind of unpleasantness. This, indeed, seems to be Tomkins and McCarter's viewpoint. Thus, the categories themselves could represent nonorthogonal dimensions and resemble each other in varying degrees. Such a conception probably comes closest to accounting for the various findings reviewed so far.

B. EMOTION AND EXPRESSION

However this may be, one important question has remained untouched: Does the system of dimensions, or clusters, define emotion? Is every emotion defined by its value on each of the dimensions? If not, we should try to define what aspects of emotion are covered by the dimensional system, and what aspects are not.

It should not be forgotten that both the dimensional system and the clusters, or classes, have a highly abstract character. "Pleasant states" comprise a large variety of quite different feelings, and this would seem to hold even when the states are defined multidimensionally. It would seem that different emotions, as distinguished in the language, cannot be distinguished on the basis of their corresponding expressive behavior, and are therefore confused by observers. This confusion, indeed, was what prompted Woodworth to form his categories, and Schlosberg (1952) arrived at the same conclusion.

The extent to which such confusion exists becomes particularly clear if judgments of expression are compared with their "true" meaning — true, of course, to the extent that it can be inferred from introspection and knowledge of the entire situation. Such comparisons may point to phenomena which may remain obscure when only judgments are compared among each other. Some enlightening comparisons can be obtained from the experiment with filmed spontaneous expressions referred to in Section III, B (Frijda, 1953).

Not only did the Ss employ a large number of different labels to describe one given expression, but also sometimes the majority of interpretations was quite dissimilar to the true state of affairs. The filmed reaction to smelling sulfuric acid was usually mistaken for the reaction to a morally repulsive story. Although both are named "disgust," the difference between the experiences is considerable. Or again, a startled reaction to a sudden explosion was usually interpreted as suppression of a sudden disagreeable thought, as a reaction to a pinprick or as irritation because of a nasty remark.

Sometimes the expressions manifested were quite different from what one would expect, given the emotion actually present; or at least they would not be considered typical expressions of that state. One filmed sequence showed the stimulus person, an artist, discussing her work with the experimenter. Her feelings were, as she said afterward, strong and vivid. The film showed her gazing out the window with a slightly vacant face and somewhat drooping mouth. Subjects interpreted the expression mostly as one of sadness. Or, again, more trivially, timidity was manifested by a somewhat awkward smile, usually judged to be amusement or restrained amusement.

These examples suffice to illustrate our point that quite different emotions can give rise to one and the same expression, and, consequently, to one location in our n-dimensional space. But they point, at the same time, to the fact that emotion is more than the aggregate of aspects defined by the dimensions. Sadness and intense "creative" feeling have something in common, at least sometimes; but they also have something specific which enables both subject and experimenter to discriminate between them. They must be defined by something in addition to the expressive behavior. The differentiation of emotion is finer than that of its behavioral counterparts. This opinion is current among workers in the physiology of emotion and has received additional emphasis in the work of Schachter (1964). According to Schachter, "Cognitions arising from the immediate situation, as interpreted by past experience, provide the framework within which one understands and labels his feelings. It is the cognition which determines whether the state of physiological arousal will be labeled 'anger,' 'joy,' or whatever" (Schachter, 1964, p. 51).

Schachter probably underestimates the specificity of emotional reactivity; at least, if observers manage to discriminate between more than just the level of arousal, the subject himself will most certainly be able to do so. There is skeletal reactivity as well as visceral, and in many cases this is demonstrably as primitive as visceral response [e.g., the startle pattern (Landis and Hunt, 1939); weeping in infants]. However, Schachter's general point seems to be adequate and important, and it fits well with the data on overt emotional expression and its recognition. Emotion is constituted by behavioral as well as situational, or, more generally, cognitive, factors. To return to our experimental illustrations: The difference between moral and olfactory disgust resides, obviously, in the cognitive reference, to events with wide value implications, and to sensory stimulation, respectively. The difference between fatigue and regret or sadness is one of reference to causes or concomitants. Both are, or can be, states of low general activity and low attentional arousal but, in the one case, stemming from previous physical exertions and, in the other, from the consciousness of some loss or missed occasion. Similar analyses hold for the other examples given.

The consequences for the recognition of emotion are obvious. To the extent that emotion is defined by cognitive aspects, it cannot be correctly identified on the basis of overt expressive behavior. Many emotions, particularly the "higher" ones, are so defined: pity, shame, remorse, and admiration for instance. They will be confused with other emotions defined by different cognitive referents but by similar behavioral components. They will occupy the same places in the n-dimensional space discussed before.

The cognitive aspects entering into the definition of emotion can be summarized as situational referents, specific causes of reaction, and values or valences involved. The definition of startle contains reference to a sudden event. Those aspects of emotion which do find their way into expression can also be brought under a general heading. Those aspects of emotion which are expressed in behavior constitute what may be called the person's "positionality" of the given moment (Frijda, 1953, 1965a). By this concept is meant, first, the structure of the person's approach and withdrawal tendencies, and his attentional propensities of that given moment. Expression realizes a given structure of relations with the outer world, real or imaginary. Second, it comprises the structure of activity with which this relational structure is realized; that is, the activation level, the degree of control exerted over one's own activity, the integration of this current activity in the activity stream. All of the meaning of expression which is caught by our dimensions can be framed in these concepts, and fruitfully so. The difference between "attention" (factor IV) and "surprise" (Nelly, factor V), for instance, can be formulated as active directed versus reactive diffuse, or uncontrolled attentional behavior; in fact, factor IV is characterized by wide eyes with knitted eyebrows, and factor V with wide eyes and raised eyebrows.

These two aspects — positional tendencies as such and activity structure — together form one part of the emotion as experienced. They constitute a richer, more varied experience than either James-Lange's visceral emotion or Schachter's arousal. Usually they combine into one experience with cognitive determinants. Sometimes they form all of emotion, as in the unnamed emotions expressed in dancing or suggested by music. As a matter of fact, recognition of expression seems first and foremost to be recognition of this positional activity, and only secondarily recognition of emotion. If no need for categorizing or situational extrapolation exists, as in the theater, all the observer does is to follow the play of varying opening and closure, approach and withdrawal, activity and relaxation patterns. In those terms, discrimination of expression may well be quite acute, as acute as discrimination of the line of regard appears to be (Gibson and Pick, 1963).

When it comes to recognition of emotion, there are several complicating matters. It appears that the positional structure may be of quite variable importance in that complex entity called emotion. According to Schachter, the large share, by far, in determining emotional specificity falls to the cognitive determinants. This may well be the case under some circumstances. When behavioral components are elaborate and complete, as in startle or crying, cognitive determinants will be relatively unimportant, for the subject himself as well as for an observer. An animal whose limbic system is being stimulated is angry, not amused. When behavioral components are undifferentiated, however, cognitive components increase in importance. Why behavioral components should sometimes be differentiated and sometimes not is not clear. That differences exist is evident. One can be happy inwardly or outwardly; this seems to be more than just a matter of self-control. In some cases, the nature of the emotion itself seems to preclude strong and specific outward realizations. Strong and vivid feelings of professional interest and satisfaction, as in the example given earlier, do not often find expression in smiling and shouting. It is somehow more plausible that the person should withdraw into himself, focused upon inner experiences. This relaxed absent-mindedness was interpreted by the observers as sadness.

The varying place of the expressive, or positional, component within emotion has another consequence. Emotions are, to a large extent, defined by only very gross aspects of that positional component, in addition to the cognitive one. "Anger" is any reaction to somebody else's negative actions in which some kind of a stand is taken, to any degree. The number of different stand-taking reactions is countless and, hence, the number of ways to be angry. Hence also the fact that many different expressions exist for any given emotion, and that no expression is typical for any emotion, as Landis (1924) stressed. Confusion in recognition of expression, in terms of emotions, has two roots: the fact that many motivational states share one and the same pattern of expressive behavior, and the fact that many expressions may realize the positional aspect of what is categorized as one and the same emotion.

Incidentally, if "positionality" as here defined constitutes the "true" meaning expression, the fact of its correct recognition is hardly surprising. In that case, the meaning of expression and expression itself are nearly identical. That is, if expressive activity is perceived in a functional sense as activity of approach, sensory readiness or closure, generalized tenseness and the like, this perception is perception of the expressive meaning. There is nothing "behind" the expressive activity which is expressed; rather, emotional experience is, in part, the consciousness of this positional activity or its intention. This agrees with theorizing on the nature of expression as such (Frijda, 1965a, 1968).

The only conditions for such perception are, it would seem, an understanding that eyes are for looking (that is, for acts preparatory to further, later acts in connection with the objects), that lips are for intake and physical contact, that approach indicates probable further interaction, and the like. The only expressions which cannot be subsumed under these functional principles, it would seem, are weeping and laughter. Acquisition of the general perceptual principles does not pose difficult problems for theory, while understanding of some of its aspects might possibly be innate (such as response to movement of the eyes or to weeping).

VI. Expression and Situational Cues

A. THE INFLUENCE OF CONTEXTUAL CUES

If, indeed, emotion consists of behavioral and cognitive determinants, recognition of emotion will rest upon cues of both kinds. As a matter of fact, expressive behavior is always perceived in context. Expressive behavior constitutes relational activity and derives most of its meaning from the fact that the reference point of movement, particularly of the glance, is given or assumed. But the context goes further than that and is made up of a large number or relevant information sources. Kirchhoff (1962) discussed some of these: the context provided by body type and facial characteristics, the purposive action at hand, the objective situation with its events, and the behavioral constants of the person concerned. To these we may add knowledge of the person's personality, of characteristics of his sex, cultural and age group, and the like. All these serve to define the probable cognitive determinants or aspects of the observed emotional reaction. The process of recognition of emotion can be conceived as a two stage process: assessment of the general positional activity pattern on the basis of expression, and subsequent specification of this pattern on the basis of situational and other contextual cues.

To put this specification hypotheses to a test, an experiment was performed (Frijda, 1958) in which four photographs of expressions were each paired with two different situations. Free interpretations were obtained and categorized into certain general ("positional") and specific ("emotional," feeling) components. Whereas the general components were equally frequent with a given photograph whatever the situational cue, the specific components differed significantly between situational cue conditions. Also, general components were significantly more frequent than under control conditions where no expressions but only situational cues were given; for the specifics, this was not the case (Rump, 1960; Frijda; 1961). Similar results were obtained by Cline (1956), who manipulated context by varying pairs of schematic drawings. A "glum" face was seen as angry, jealous, unhappy, or dismayed when paired with a smiling face, and aloof, independent, domineering, unafraid, or cool when paired with a frowning one. Although different, both groups of interpretations correspond in containing no happy states and no forms of open personal contact.

That situational cues drastically modify interpretation of expression is evident from these experiments, as well as from several others (Goldberg, 1951; Turhan, 1960). A study by Munn (1940) demonstrated an increase in recognition scores when situational cues are present. Such findings have sometimes been taken to mean that recognition of emotions is based primarily upon inference from situational cues. This opinion has been widespread in the older literature (e.g., Landis, 1929). There is by now sufficient evidence that expression does provide important cues for the recognition of emotion (cf. Section III,B).

Still, the contribution of expression might be weak and inconsequential when contextual cues are also available. This is suggested by a study by Giedt (1955) in which, for instance, judgments on personality traits such as anxiety or impulsivity of four mental patients, based upon silent films, tended to be less accurate than those based upon a transcription of the interview. This study itself is rather unconvincing from the present point of view, since the variables studied may not have been relevant for momentary expressive behavior. However, it indicates the possibility that the pattern of positional activity may not be very informative, relative to the contextual specifications.

If this is true, it should be particularly evident when contextual and expressive cues point in different directions and contradict each other. The possibility can be tested by pitting expression and situational cues against each other. Flores d'Arcais (1961) has done so by showing motion pictures with the original sound track, and with a sound track containing contrasting verbal utterances. We performed some experiments of a somewhat different design, more similar to one employed by Goodenough and Tinker (1931).

B. Conflict of Cues: Preliminary Experiment

In a preliminary experiment, four photographs from the Nelly series were each paired with two different situation descriptions. Six descriptions in all were used. Pairs of photographs and situation descriptions were composed in such a way that for each photograph one more or less concordant pair and one discordant pair were obtained, with respect to the suggested emotion.

The general procedure of this and the following experiments was as follows: The photographs were projected on a screen, one at a time. Subjects were asked to write down their free interpretations and to rate each photograph on ten 7-point bipolar scales. Next, the situation descriptions were presented in test booklets. The subjects were asked to imagine the emotion a person like the girl in the photographs could have experienced under each given condition, to write down this interpretation, and to rate this, too, on the 10 scales. During a second session, one week after the first, Ss were provided with a new booklet with one of the situation descriptions on each page. There were two different forms. The photographs were shown again, the subjects told that each photograph was taken in the situation with the corresponding number, and again interpretations and ratings were requested. Sixteen Ss were used.

Let us call the ratings of photograph and situation alone the "preratings" and the rating at the second session the "combination rating." By dividing the difference between the combination rating and the photograph prerating by the difference between the combination rating and the situation prerating, a measure for cue dominance can be obtained, the relative shift measure. If the quotient is larger than unity, situational cues dominate; if smaller, expressive cues dominate. No prediction was made for concordant combinations, but in the discordant combinations, expression was expected to win out. "Discordant" combinations are those in which the preratings on at least 6 of the 10 scales were in different scale halves.

Results supported the prediction. They are summarized in Table IV in which shifts are averaged over scales, combinations, and subjects. The shift away from the situation preratings is twice as large as that away from the expression preratings. For the discordant combinations it is nearly three times as large. There is, thus, clear-cut expression dominance, which was also what Flores d'Arcais (1961) reported. It is important to note, as Flores d'Arcais did, that all subjects accepted the task, appar-

TABLE IV
AVERAGE SHIFTS AND AVERAGE RELATIVE SHIFT — PRELIMINARY
EXPERIMENT

	N	$\overline{C} - \overline{E}^a$	$\overline{C} - \overline{S}^a$	$\overline{C} - \overline{E}/\overline{C} - \overline{S}$
Concordant pairs	640	.38	.65	.585
Discordant pairs	640	.52	1.43	.364
Total	1280	.47	1.06	.474

[a]Here, $C - E$ stands for absolute difference between combination rating and expression prerating, and $C - S$ is the same for situation prerating.

ently without much difficulty. Every expression used seemed reconcilable with every situation, a finding which both supports and explains the influence of "suggestion" on judgment of expression, reported in the older literature (e.g., Langfeld, 1918; Jarden and Fernberger, 1926; Fernberger, 1928). At the same time, the results refute their conclusion that this indicates lack of information in expression.

The experiment, though illustrative, is crude because the discordance is global and its nature therefore unclear. For that reason, the experiment was repeated with expressions and situations differing on only one dimension and as similar as possible on the other ones.

C. THE WARRIES EXPERIMENT

Warries (1963) chose discordance on the pleasantness dimension as his variable. Three photographs were used, one pleasant, one unpleasant, and one meant to be neutral but which turned out slightly unpleasant. There were nine situation descriptions, five pleasant and four unpleasant. These are given in Table V, together with their average preratings on the critical scale. Each subject received nine combinations, three for each expression. Every combination, and every separate cue in the first session, had to be interpreted verbally and rated on 9 scales in addition to happy — sad; five of those are given in Table XVII.

Three different relative shift measures were computed, which are differently illustrative but of course highly correlated. Data and results for the critical happy — sad scale are given in Table VI. The discordant combinations again manifest a clear-cut expression dominance. The average relative shift ($\overline{C} - \overline{E}/\overline{C} - \overline{S}$) is significantly smaller than 1.00 in the 14 discordant combinations. The combination rating shifts, on the average, 86% of the distance between both preratings away from the situation preratings. The correlation between expression prerating and combination rating is +.67; that between situation prerating and combination −.49. ($p < .01$ and nearly .05, respectively).

To judge from these data, if someone behaves happily or sadly when circumstances make us expect otherwise, we believe his behavior rather than our expectations. It should be noted that sometimes the combination rating is even more extreme than either the situation or the expression preratings. This happened with 7 out of the 14 discordant combination averages. Apparently the discordance sometimes enhances the suggested emotion.

In several of the combinations, the average combination rating is near the scale midpoint. It may be thought that in those cases expression dominance is more apparent than real and is suggested only because of the lower polarity of the expressions used. The general trend of the results does not make this interpretation the most plausible one, however. We will presently examine data which contradict it. Moreover, the proportion of ratings at the scale midpoint among the combination ratings is equal to that among the expression preratings (38%).

With respect to concordant combinations, we can be brief. The situations seemed to dominate in the sense of drawing the combination rating more toward their position than toward the average of situation as expression; this is not significant, however. Moreover, since in the concordant combination the situations had higher polarities, this might be caused by some sort of congruity principle in Osgood's sense.

D.   THE JAANUS EXPERIMENT

To replicate the above findings, and to see whether expression dominance holds also for other expressive dimensions, Jaanus (1966) repeated

TABLE V

SITUATIONS USED IN THE WARRIES EXPERIMENT[a]

1. All men at the party admire her dress and think it goes well on her. (5.88)
2. Her boyfriend says unkind and unjust things to her. (2.40)
3. Her boyfriend speaks sweet words to her. (4.80)
4. She talks with a man who says sweet things to her. (4.80)
5. A man says sweet things to her. (5.40)
6. She is told that her sister, with whom she has been together since early childhood, is incurably ill. (1.33)
7. Her boyfriend invites her to the opera *Don Carlos*, which is one of her favorites. (5.88)
8. She got a big grease spot on her evening dress, while the cab is at the door. (2.23)
9. She had saved a long time to buy this dress for the annual ball. Now the cab is at the door and she got a big grease spot on this dress. She will have to stay at home because the dress is spoiled. (1.67)

[a]Average score on 7-point sad-happy scale given in parentheses, where sad = 0, happy = 7. $N = 27$.

TABLE VI

AVERAGE SCORES AND SHIFT MEASURES ON THE HAPPY-SAD
SCALE FOR DIFFERENT EXPRESSION-SITUATION COMBINATIONS[a]
WARRIES EXPERIMENT

Expression	Situation	N	n situation	$\bar{E}$	$\bar{S}$	$\bar{C}$	$\frac{1}{2}(\bar{E}-\bar{S})/\bar{C}^b$	$\dfrac{\bar{C}-\bar{E}^c}{\bar{C}-\bar{S}}$	$\dfrac{\bar{C}-\bar{S}^c}{\bar{E}-\bar{S}}$
Happy	Sad	27	4	+1.33	−2.16	+0.38	+0.76	0.32	0.76
Neutral	Happy	33	5	−0.65	+1.55	+0.07	+0.39	0.58	0.64
Sad	Happy	33	5	−0.97	+1.35	−1.27	+1.47	0.02	1.13
Discordant		93	14				+0.88	0.22	0.86
Happy	Happy	33	5	+1.07	+1.35	+1.59	+0.43	2.45	0.37
Neutral	Sad	27	4	−0.69	−2.08	−1.27	+0.07	0.70	0.71
Sad	Sad	27	4	−1.09	−2.08	−2.01	−0.43	1.48	0.06
Concordant		87	13				−0.11	2.55	0.40
Total		180	2/				+0.40	0.45	0.75
Base line							0	1.00	0.50

[a] $+3.0$ = most happy; $−3.0$ = most sad. Situation scores represent averages over four or five different situations.

[b] Significance of expression dominance: on measure $\frac{1}{2}(\bar{E}-\bar{S})/\bar{C}$, t test for deviation of mean from zero: discordance $p < .005$, concordance not significant. On measure $\bar{C}-\bar{E}/\bar{C}-\bar{S}$ (and $\bar{C}-\bar{S}/\bar{E}-\bar{S}$): discordance 13 out of 14 averages < 1 (or > 0.50), $p < .001$ by binomial test; concordance 4 out of 13, not significant.

[c] Relative shift $(\bar{C}-\bar{E})/(\bar{C}-\bar{S})$ is taken to be zero if $C-E$ becomes negative, that is, when combination score is on the same side, but more extreme (or, as the case may be, more neutral) than E. If expression shift equals situation shift, $C-S/E-S$ is 0.50; it becomes larger than one if the combination score is more extreme than the expression score and negative if the combination score exceeds the situation score.

the above experiment with attentional activity as the critical dimension. Again, three photographs from the Nelly series were used, and nine situation descriptions, all varying primarily on the scale "actively attending—passive." The situation descriptions, together with their average scale values, are reproduced in Table VII. Results of the experiment are given in Table VIII.

The results are very similar to those of the preceding experiment. Discordant combinations are rated significantly more according to the expressive than to the situational cues. The combination rating shifts 78% of the distance between the preratings away from the situation prerating. Correlations in the discordant combinations between expression prerating and combination and between situation prerating and combination are $+.87$ and $−.36$, respectively ($p < .01$ and $> .05$).

Dominance of expressive cues in the recognition of emotion, under conditions of conflict of cues, appears once more to be the rule. Again, in 6 out of the 15 discordant combinations, the average combination rating was even more extreme than the expression prerating.

The concordant combinations present the same picture as before: no significant dominance of either cue. There are not infrequent instances of summation effects.

With this emphasis in dominance of behavioral cues, one should not overlook an equally distinct outcome of both experiments. That situational cues do influence the recognition of emotion, and that they do so rather strongly, is clear from the data given in Table IX, in which the results of both experiments are summarized. Taking the expression prerating as a base line, the situations do, for the most part, modify this rating. The influences are different for different discordant combinations, as can be seen more clearly from Table X. For some reason, the happy and passive expressions are much more drastically influenced than the others.

It might be expected that expressive and situational cues, taken together, make recognition of emotion more definite. As a matter of fact, this follows from our considerations given earlier, although the increase in consensus need not manifest itself in dimensional ratings. The relevant data can be found in Table XI. In both experiments, concordant combinations have somewhat smaller variances than discordant ones. The differences are not significant, however. Variances of discordant combinations tend to be higher than those of the expressions alone, but the differences again are not significant. The differences in variance are reflected, to some

TABLE VII
SITUATIONS USED IN THE JAANUS EXPERIMENT[a]

1. After a long working day she is home, sitting in a chair. (1.75)
2. She sits in a train for quite a while. (3.13)
3. She sits at the window; it rains outside. (3.13)
4. She has waited for some time in the waiting room to have her passport picture taken; it will not be her turn for quite a while. (3.87)
5. She is at home, sitting in a chair, with a magazine before her. (4.33)
6. She sits opposite a woman friend who chats about this and that. (3.78)
7. Her friend is on the point of sitting down on her new phonograph record without noticing it. (6.22)
8. She is at home; at the same time the telephone rings in the adjoining room someone rings the doorbell. (5.77)
9. Any moment she may be notified by telephone of the result of her examination. Now the telephone rings. (5.77)

[a]Average score on 7-point active–passive scale given in parentheses, where passive = 1, active = 7. $N = 27$.

TABLE VIII

AVERAGE SCORES AND SHIFT MEASURES ON THE ACTIVE – PASSIVE SCALE
FOR DIFFERENT EXPRESSION-SITUATION COMBINATIONS[a]
JAANUS EXPERIMENT

Expression	Situation	N	n situation	$\overline{E}$	$\overline{S}$	$\overline{C}$	$\frac{1}{2}(\overline{E}-\overline{S})/\overline{C}$[b]	$\overline{C}-\overline{E}/\overline{C}-\overline{S}^c$	$\overline{C}-\overline{S}/\overline{F}-\overline{S}^c$
Active	Passive	24	3	+2.04	−1.33	+1.83	+1.44	0.07	0.86
Active	Neutral	27	3	+2.29	−0.04	+1.70	+0.57	0.34	0.84
Neutral	Active	27	3	−0.81	+2.11	+0.04	+0.61	0.43	0.69
Passive	Neutral	27	3	−1.62	−0.04	−2.07	+1.27	0.22	1.10
Passive	Active	27	3	−1.44	+2.11	−0.62	+0.79	0.47	0.60
Discordant		132	15				+0.94	0.29	0.78
Active	Active	26	3	+2.35	+2.07	+2.52	+0.31	0.93	1.85
Neutral	Neutral	26	3	−1.13	−0.05	−0.64	+0.05	1.63	0.38
Neutral	Passive	24	3	−0.58	−1.33	−1.04	+0.42	1.91	0.81
Passive	Passive	23	3	−1.38	−1.29	−1.56	+0.18	2.67	0.82
Concordant		99	12				+0.24	1.02	0.74
Total		231	27				+0.59	0.40	0.78
Base line							0	0.50	1.00

[a] +3.0 = most active; −3.0 = most passive. Situation scores represent averages over three different situations.

[b] Significance of expression dominance: on measure $\frac{1}{2}(E-S)/C$, t test for deviation of mean from zero: discordance $p < .005$; concordance not significant. On measure $(\overline{C}-\overline{E})/(\overline{C}-\overline{S})$: discordance 13 out of 15 smaller than 1, $p < .004$ by binomial test. On measure $(\overline{C}-\overline{S})/(\overline{F}-\overline{S})$: discordance 14 out of 15 smaller than 0.50, p<.004 by binomial test; concordance not significant.

[c] For explanation of measures see Footnote c in Table VI.

extent, in the differences in polarity. Polarity and variance are, on the whole, negatively correlated (see Table XI); low average polarities mostly mean that widely different individual combination ratings are averaged out.

There are some differences between the two studies. In the Warries study, there is a clear-cut relationship between degree of discordance and combination variance: $r=+.76$. Both expression variance and situation polarity correlate with combination variance: $+.50$ and $+.58$, respectively. In the Jaanus study, the corresponding correlations are, for some reason, near zero.

In the concordant combinations, the relationships are understandably reversed: The more polarized the cues, the smaller the combination

TABLE IX
COMBINATION RATINGS COMPARED TO AVERAGE PRERATINGS[a]
Warries Experiment

Stimuli			Situations	
			Happy	Sad
		Preratings	+1.48	−1.79
Expressions	Happy	+1.10	+1.59	+0.05
	Neutral	−0.65	−0.04	−1.27
	Sad	−1.10	−1.27	−2.02

Jaanus Experiment

Stimuli			Situations		
			Active	Neutral	Passive
		Preratings	+2.11	−0.04	−1.33
Expressions	Active	+2.23	+2.35	+1.85	+1.93
	Neutral	−0.84	+0.50	−0.43	−1.00
	Passive	−1.63	−0.17	−2.05	−1.63

[a] Top and left margin of each part of the table represent average situation and expression preratings, respectively. Body of each part of the table represents average combination ratings.

TABLE X
RELATIVE SHIFT INDICES FOR DISCORDANT COMBINATIONS

Warries Experiment

Expression	Situation	Rel. shift index[a]
Happy	Sad	62.5
Neutral	Happy	50.8
Sad	Happy	33.4

Jaanus Experiment

Expression	Situation	Rel. shift index[a]
Passive	Active	58.3
Neutral	Active	81.7
Active	Neutral	38.3
Active	Passive	11.7

[a] $\overline{C}-\overline{E}/\overline{C}-\overline{S}$.

TABLE XI

VARIANCES AND POLARITIES IN THE WARRIES AND JAANUS EXPERIMENTS

	Average Variances				
Experiment	$\overline{s_E^2}$	$\overline{s_S^2}$	$\overline{s_C^2}_{\,disc}$	$\overline{s_C^2}_{\,conc}$	$\overline{s_C^2}$
Warries	.86	1.10	1.08	.83	1.00
df	19	59	92	86	179
Jaanus	1.78	2.05	2.27	2.18	2.23
df	26	74	131	98	230

	Average Polarities				
	E	S	C_{disc}	C_{conc}	C
Warries	.95	1.67	.61	1.62	1.15
Jaanus	1.60	1.21	1.35	1.44	1.40

	Correlations between Variance and Polarity				
Warries	+.84	−.55	−.13	−.51	−.27
Jaanus	−.92	−.66	−.75	−.79	−.76

variance tends to be (correlations are −.54 and −.63 in the Warries study and −.63 and −.02 in the Jaanus study). Contrary to expectations, the concordant combinations do not all lead to stronger polarity or to higher subjective certainty. Subjects in the Jaanus study were asked to indicate their rating certainty on a 5-point scale; the ratings do not differ among conditions. The concordant combination ratings are closely determined by the separate cue values: The correlations with the expression and the situation preratings are +.96 and .97, respectively, in the first experiment and +.97 and +.93 in the second. Other influences such as congruity effects are not visible.

E. CONDITIONS OF EXPRESSION DOMINANCE IN CUE CONFLICT

The generality of our finding of expression dominance is open to question. Our sample of photographs is very small, and the situation descriptions are limited to momentary events without explicit links to the individual's history.

There are at least four factors which might influence the fact or the degree of expression dominance: (1) polarity of expressive and situational cues, (2) cue ambiguity, (3) the degree of specification of the situational cues, and (4) the nature of the expressive cues.

We have no information concerning the third variable. It is probable that reference to personal history would make quite a difference. It may be expected that the situational cue dominates when we see someone laugh upon hearing that his beloved sister died — the laughter will probably be interpreted as dissimulation or nervous disturbance.

The nature of the expressive cues, and their degree of completeness, may also be a variable. Since more detailed expressive cues seem to lead to better recognition (see Section VI,A), increase in expression dominance may ensue. Moreover, facial and bodily expression may differ among themselves as regards dominance, at least for happy emotions (Dittman *et al.*, 1965). Some other qualitative aspects will be mentioned in a later section.

Concerning the other two variables, our experiments provide some information, although little insight. Effect of relative polarity is to be expected on the basis of Osgood's congruity principle. Relative shift and relative polarity should be negatively correlated. In fact, they are not. In both the Warries and Jaanus experiments, correlations with the various relative shift measures are in the neighborhood of $+.15$. Some indications that polarity may play a role are present though. In Table X, the neutral photographs of both experiments tend to show relatively low expression dominance; in the Jaanus experiment this is very strongly so. In combinations with the neutral photographs, two of the three instances of situation dominance occur.

Correlations between situation polarity and relative shift are inconsistent: $-.31$ in the first experiment and $+.33$ in the second. In fact, Tables V and VI indicate that the more extreme situations may go with strong expression dominance.

More important than sheer polarity is what we termed "cue ambiguity." A given situation or expression may suggest not one, but a number of emotional reactions. It may also, *post hoc,* seem compatible with a number of different emotions. This number may be characteristically different for different situations or expressions.

This cue ambiguity can be operationalized in various ways. We tried three of those: variance, subjective certainty, and "fixity," a measure which reflects to what extent different emotions seem compatible with a given situational cue.

Variance was used as an indicator because high rating variance of a given cue might reflect its lack of one definite meaning. Results resemble those on polarity; as said before, variance and polarity are strongly negatively correlated. Yet relative variance, σ_E^2/σ_S^2, may indeed be related to relative shift. Correlations are $-.21$ in the Warries experiment, but $+.53$ ($<.05$) in the Jaanus experiment; high relative expression variance goes with large relative expression shift, thus with lower expression dominance. The two cases of situation dominance in the Jaanus experiment occur in combinations with the situation which has the lowest variance and highest polarity (No. 7, +2.22).

Subjective certainty in the Jaanus experiment was rated on a 4-point scale. No correlations of any size were found; the ratings showed little variance, however.

"Fixity" of situation cues was measured in the Warries experiment. Subjects were asked to indicate, for every situation, the proportion of people they expected to agree or disagree with in each of 10 different interpretations (such as happy and disappointed). The sum of the deviations from a 50−50 judgment was taken as the fixity-of-meaning index. It turned out to be a meaningful index, since it correlated +.86 with polarity. It did not correlate with variance (.20), and, unfortunately, it did not correlate with relative shift.

In fine, we do not feel we pinned down the variables determining or influencing the degree of expression dominance. Polarity and ambiguity as measured by variance may be influential, but at least within the values those parameters took in these experiments, they do not seem to be major factors. Other indices of cue ambiguity may do better. In fact, such ambiguity can be surprisingly high. For situation description No. 6 (Table V), the seriously ill sister, subjects in the discordant condition find plausible happy implications: the sister always was a pest or she was a competitor since infancy, and the stimulus person is glad to get rid of her. Requests to list compatible emotions might have resulted in better predictions of relative shift.

F.   The Process of Judgment Formation in Cue Conflict

1.   Types of Interpretation

It might seem from the preceding pages that the judgment of conflicting expressive and situational cues is some sort of compromise between the impressions evoked by each of the cues alone. The final judgment seems to be some sort of weighted average of both cues with the highest weight going to expression.

However, there are a number of indications in the data which suggest a different description of the judgment process. The first indication is formed by the distribution of combination scores and of corresponding shifts. Table XII presents the distribution of expression shifts as computed from individual scores. As can be seen, only 39% of the ratings in the one experiment, and 44% in the other, takes the form of a compromise and shifts toward the situation. One-third to one-half of the ratings just

TABLE XII
DISTRIBUTION OF EXPRESSION SHIFTS (C − E), DISCORDANT COMBINATIONS[a]

Experiment	N	< 0	0	+1	> +1
Warries	93	17	39	21	16
(%)		18	43	22	17
Jaanus	132	30	45	22	35
(%)		22	34	17	27

[a] Scores were positive when shift was toward situation.

sticks to the expression preratings, and about 20% are more extreme than the expression rated alone. Of course, rating instability constitutes at least part of these shifts.

The combination ratings which shift toward the situation seem not to be randomly distributed over combinations. Table XIII presents a *post hoc* split of combinations, suggesting that in some combinations subjects tend simply to follow the expressive cues, while in others they either do likewise or they follow the situational cue. That is, what appears on the surface like an averaging of impressions of different strength may well be, in fact, a matter of lumping together of the results of various different hypothesis-forming activities.

This suggestion is considerably strengthened by inspection of the subjects' interpretations. From these, it appears that the subjects make use of conflict-reducing mechanisms of much the same kind as described, for instance, by Abelson (1959).

It will be remembered that the subjects in both experiments were asked first to describe the suggested emotional state and only then to rate this state on the 7-point scales. The resulting descriptions of emotional states can be grouped into different categories, which are defined in Table XIV. The types of interpretation which could be distinguished are quite similar to those found useful by Flores d'Arcais (1961). He distinguished between "concordance," in which the situational cues are adapted or just overlooked; inner conflict of the subject; or insincerity and the like. Examples of interpretations grouped into our categories make clear what is meant and illustrate the dynamics of impression formation and discordance resolution.

Category I. Warries experiment, happy photograph; situation: "She is told that her sister is incurably ill." Subject 9, photograph alone: "She is happy; probably she thinks of a pleasant memory." Situation alone: "She is aghast, crushed or powerless." Combination: "After having got over the first shock, she remembers some events from their childhood and smiles with a mixture of tenderness and melancholy."

TABLE XIII
DISTRIBUTION OF COMBINATION RATINGS, DISCORDANT[a]

	−3	−2	−1	0	+1	+2	+3	$\overline{C}-\overline{E}/\overline{C}-\overline{S}$
Warries experiment	−	1	8	3	2	⊥	4	.63
Combination happy 6, neutral 1								
Others	6	17	12	32	7	1	−	.45
Jaanus experiment								
Combination neutral 7,8, passive	10	7	6	1	5	9	7	.93
7,8, active 6								
Others	17	23	9	6	3	1	1	.16

[a]Scores are reversed for combinations with expression happy or active.

TABLE XIV
CATEGORIES FOR ANALYSIS OF FREE INTERPRETATIONS

Category   I. The emotion is a reaction to an event not mentioned in the situation description, or to an aspect of that situation which is invented and introduced by S
Category II. The person is stated to be not emotionally involved in the situation; she is considered aloof, withdrawn into herself, or indifferent
Category III. The person's outward behavior is different from the inner experience; she puts on a mask or controls herself
Category IV. Description of emotional state without any of the qualifications mentioned in the other categories

Jaanus experiment, active photograph; situation: "Waiting to have her passport picture taken." Subject 11, photograph alone: "Afraid, startled." Situation alone: "She sits there pondering." Combination: "She is mad at someone in that waiting room."

Category II. Warries experiment, "neutral" photograph (slightly sad); situation: "All men at the party admire her dress." Subject 6, photograph alone: "Thinks things which should not be thought." Situation alone: "Proud happiness, which happiness is threatened by each newly arriving girl." Combination: "Afraid of all the attention. Thinks they fool her."

Jaanus experiment, passive photograph; situation: "Chatting with a woman friend." Subject 16, photograph alone: "Looking at something, with her thoughts elsewhere." Situation alone: "Takes part in the conversation, but wants to get rid of her friend." Combination: "Hardly listening, thinking of something else."

Category III. Warries experiment, happy photograph; situation: "Her boyfriend invites her to the opera *Don Carlos*." Subject 17, photograph alone: "She laughs as if she sees someone in a train stumble over a briefcase." Situation alone: "She behaves as if it is as it ought to be." Combination: "She is very happy but does not want to show it."

Jaanus experiment, neutral photograph; situation: "Her friend is on the point of sitting down upon her new phonograph record." Subject 5, photograph alone: "Quite indifferent; I don't care at all anymore." Situation alone: "She cries out: hey, look out!" Combination: "She does not say anything, but hopes the record will not break."

Category IV. Warries experiment, sad photograph; situation: "Her boyfriend speaks sweet words to her." Subject 2, photograph alone: "Sad, worried mood." Situation alone: "Feels satisfied, content, thankful, happy, and ready for a reward." Combination: "Irritated, not in the mood for sweet words. Tired."

Jaanus experiment, active photograph; situation: "She sits at the window; it rains outside." Subject 25, photograph alone: "Angry, emotionally upset by something." Situation alone: "Somewhat sad, everything is so dreary." Combination: "Angry, a bit overdoing it."

2. *Differences between Interpretation Types*

The results of this categorizing are tentative, since grouping has so far been performed only by the present author. Yet the meaningfulness of the categories is reflected by the differences in number of words used per interpretation. Data are given in Tables XV and XVI. There are significant differences between the categories; the more complex interpretations (categories I, II, and III) consist of more words.

Discordant and concordant combinations differ in the relative frequencies with which the categories occur. The interpretations involving "mechanisms" (I, II, and III) are much more frequent in the discordant combinations in both experiments. They are also more frequent among the interpretations of cue combinations than among those of the situational cues alone, where integration of cues is not required. Evidently, subjects do resolve the conflict of cues by hypostatizing other events occurring at the same time and assuming the presence of meanings not mentioned in the situation description. They interpose sources of emotion between the situation as given and the facial expression. They sometimes divorce the person's reaction from the situation in a different way by supposing her to be aloof, indifferent, not touched, not involved; or else they accept the situational suggestion and interpret the nonmatching behavior as a mask, a show she puts on. Other "mechanisms" still seem to be hidden in the category IV interpretations. Occasionally the situational suggestion is simply disregarded, as in the second example of this category in the preceding section. Sometimes the conflict can be resolved by

TABLE XV

FREQUENCY OF OCCURRENCE, AVERAGE NUMBER OF WORDS PER INTERPRETATION, AND RELATIVE SHIFT (C−E/C−S) FOR CATEGORIES (WARRIES EXPERIMENT)

Category	Frequency in percent[a]				Average no. of words[a]				Relative shift[a]		
	Total	Discordant	Concordant	Situation	Total	Discordant	Concordant	Situation	Total	Discordant	Concordant
I	22.4	39.2	5.8	3.3	15.7	15.6	16.0	9.0	38.0	33.3	72.6
II	19.0	25.7	11.4	6.7	11.6	12.2	10.3	8.5	45.8	39.2	62.0
III	2.8	3.2	2.2	3.3	14.2	14.0	14.5	14.0	100.0	120.0	50.0
IV	55.4	31.4	80.6	86.7	7.5	7.8	6.7	8.5	98.4	61.8	130.8
Total	99.6	99.5	100.0	100.0	12.0	13.0	11.2	8.6	63.5	44.0	108.4
N	179	92	87	60							

[a]Significances: frequency: I + II + III versus IV, discordant versus concordant: $\chi^2 = 41.3$, $p < .001$. Average No. of words: I + II + III versus IV, totals: $t = 3.31$, $p < .01$. Relative shift: I + II versus IV, discordant: $t = 3.37$, $p < .01$.

TABLE XVI

FREQUENCY OF OCCURRENCE, AVERAGE NUMBER OF WORDS PER INTERPRETATION, AND
RELATIVE SHIFT (C−E/C−S) FOR CATEGORIES
(JAANUS EXPERIMENT)

Category	Frequency in percent[a]				Average No. of words[a]				Relative shift[a]		
	Total	Discordant	Concordant	Situation	Total	Discordant	Concordant	Situation	Total	Discordant	Concordant
I	23.2	30.3	13.7	6.6	14.4	15.9	11.1	9.2	34.1	24.4	76.7
II	15.8	22.0	7.9	6.6	8.1	8.1	8.2	8.2	49.9	51.8	35.2
III	3.0	4.5	1.0	1.2	16.4	15.7	21.0	7.0	173.0	150.0	300.0
IV	57.6	43.2	76.4	85.6	4.9	5.5	4.4	7.6	77.0	75.4	79.3
Total	99.6	100.0	100.0	100.0	7.7	9.9	5.8	7.3	60.3	53.6	77.0
N	234	132	102	234							

[a] Significances: Frequency: I + II + III versus IV, discordant versus concordant: $\chi^2 = 19.13$, $p < .001$. Average No. of words: I + II + III versus IV, totals: $t = 4.77$, $p < .001$. Relative shift: I + II + III versus IV, discordant: $t = 3.27$, $p < .01$.

ascribing an emotion which is different from the one originally intended for the situation but which may be equally plausible. An example is: Warries experiment, situation: "All men at the party admire her dress," slightly sad photograph; "Their attention makes her even more insecure than she already was;" or situation "A man says sweet things to her," sad photograph: "She disapproves and is shocked."

These notions about "mechanisms" or types of gap-filling hypotheses are further supported by the average relative shift indices of the interpretations in the different categories. Only the discordant combinations are relevant here. In both experiments, expression dominance is very outspoken in type I and II responses where, as it were, Ss stick to the emotion suggested by the face, albeit as a reaction to something other than the situation given. Expression dominance is considerably weaker in responses of category IV, where the gap-filling hypotheses are absent or unidentified, whereas the few instances of self-control and making a show (category III) manifest situation dominance in both studies.

3. Shift in General Rating Patterns

There is some further evidence for the present description. It will be remembered that the subjects in both experiments made ratings not only to the "critical" 7-point scale but also on a number of other scales. Among these there were several which should show a shift in the discordant combination if the above mentioned mechanisms operate with sufficient frequency. For the Warries study, data on ratings on these scales are given in Table XVII, and for the Jaanus study in Table XVIII. Shifts are computed over individual scores, excluding those where either the expression prerating or the situation prerating was at the scale midpoint.

The results from the first experiment are clear. In the discordant combinations, 16 out of 20 shifts are in the expected direction, and 10 of these are significantly so. In the concordant combinations, 3 shift indices are significant and, as it happens, all in the opposite direction. It may be objected that these shifts are only further results of discordance; as a matter of fact, the average distance between expression and situation preratings on these scales is .78 scale units, as opposed to .43 in the concordant combinations. However, in all but one case the shift for both expression and situation is in the same direction. The combination rating is more polarized than either of the preratings.

The Jaanus experiment gives no such results. The higher incidence of significant shifts in the discordant than in the concordant combinations is a consequence of the larger degree of discordance on the noncritical scales also (1.30 scale units as against .37). The data clearly do not support our thesis. Why they do not is not clear. It may be that our concep-

TABLE XVII
SHIFTS ON OTHER SCALES FOR VARIOUS CRITICAL SCALE COMBINATIONS
(WARRIES EXPERIMENT)

		Both happy	Both sad	Expression happy Situation sad	Expression sad Situation happy
	N	22	33	19	29
Uncontrolled −	C − E	− .45[a]	− .33	+ .53[b]	− .58[c]
controlled	C − S	+ .36	− .12	+ 1.95[c]	−1.35[c]
Natural −	C − E	+ .64	+ .45	+ 1.05[b]	+ 1.38
artificial	C − S	− .05	− .24	+ .53	+ .41
Spontaneous −	C − E	+ .09	+ .30	+ 1.26[c]	+ .52
reserved	C − S	− .14	− .33[b]	+ .26	+ 1.21[c]
Involved −	C − E	− .50[c]	+ .27	+ .53	+ 1.17[c]
indifferent	C − S	− .23	+ .24	+ 1.84[c]	+ .10
Simple −	C − E	− .41	− .48	+ 1.32[c]	+ .41
complicated	C − S	+ .09	− .97[c]	− .37	+ 1.14[c]

[a]Positive scores are in the direction of hypothesis.
[b]$p < .05$ two-tailed.
[c]$p < .01$ two-tailed.

tions are in error. It may also be that there is a real difference between the two experiments because of the difference in critical dimension. It could be that a contrast in suggested activity engenders less of a conflict than contrast in suggested mood.

There is, however, one other aspect of the data which deserves mention and, to our feeling, emphasis.

The data on shifts on noncritical scales show, in both experiments, an interesting asymmetry. In both experiments, one of the fully discordant conditions shows significant shifts on the scale "controlled − uncontrolled" in the expected direction, while the other fully discordant combination shows just the opposite, namely, a significant shift toward less control, less restraint. As a matter of fact, the shift in controlled − uncontrolled ratings was the only significant exception in the right half of Table XVII. The same asymmetry is present in the relative shift indices of the critical dimensions, as can be seen from Table X.

Expression dominance appears to be different for different kinds of combinations; perhaps extent of conflict, but, at any rate, *kinds* of conflict-resolving hypothesis are also different for different kinds of combinations. It is fairly obvious why this is the case in the present experiments. When someone is behaving happily when he should be sad, it may be

TABLE XVIII

SHIFTS ON OTHER SCALES FOR VARIOUS CRITICAL SCALE COMBINATIONS

(JAANUS EXPERIMENT)

		Both active	Both passive	Expression active Situation passive	Expression passive Situation active	Expression neutral Situation active	Expression active Situation neutral
N		17	16	16	17	17	19
Uncontrolled–controlled	C–E	.00	− .18[a]	− .95	+ .63[b]	+ .43[b]	− .51
	C–S	− .35	+ .25	− 1.78[c]	+ 2.13[c]	+ 2.06[c]	− 1.54[c]
Natural–artificial	C–E	− .43	− .50	+ .29	− .18	− .25	+ .38
	C–S	− .33	− .41	+ .29	+ .60	+ 1.91[b]	− .54
Direct–indirect	C–E	+ .11	+ .03	+ .40	− .30	− .37	+ .26
	C–S	− .31	− .09	− 2.28[c]	+ 2.24[c]	+ 1.80[b]	− 1.13[b]
Involved–not involved	C–E	− .06	− .16	+ .21	− .15	− .52	+ .34
	C–S	− .04	− .55	− 2.48[c]	+ 2.51	+ 1.70[c]	− 1.58[c]
Simple–complicated	C–E	+ .13	− .40	+ .58	− .69	+ .22	+ .29
	C–S	+ .08	− .17	+ .12	− .22	+ .15	+ .13
Moved–indifferent	C–E	− .05	+ .40	− .63	+ .04	+ .33	− 1.34
	C–S	− .72	− 1.08[b]	− 2.58[c]	+ 1.36[b]	+ 1.84[c]	− 2.91[c]

[a] Positive scores are in the direction of the hypothesis.
[b] $p < .05$ two-tailed.
[c] $p < .01$ two-tailed.

make-believe. When he is behaving sadly, make-believe is unlikely. One rarely hides ones feelings in that way. Moreover, the sad feeling must be very strong if it is uncontrollable even in the face of pleasurable events. Or again, a passive face may hide feelings, but activity without the situation's giving sufficient reason for it may well indicate exceptionally uninhibited impulses.

What these conclusions point to is a manipulation of very specific transitional probabilities between situational meanings, emotions, and emotional regulation. The resolution of cue conflict apparently makes use of an elaborate system of specific experiential couplings.

VII. Recognition of Emotion

One thing, we think, is clear from the results of the summarized experiments. Recognition of emotion is not a simple process permitting an explantion with the simplicity of the classical theories. The diversity of phenomena as well as of factors contributing to recognition is much too large.

Moreover, it would seem that recognition of emotion not only rests upon the integration of a large number of cues of different kinds. The manner of integration depends upon quite specific knowledge, upon a store of hypotheses concerning what goes usually with what in human life. Cues are combined by means of different kinds of hypotheses depending upon differences in the nature of those cues.

In other words, recognition of emotion seems to be an example of complex information processing. A number of information-processing steps proceed in sequence, wherein the selection of steps to be undertaken depends in part upon the results of the preceding ones. It is possible to describe the entire process, as here conceived, in some detail. We will couch the description in terms of the functioning of a mechanical system having as its task the recognition of emotion. This will allow us to formulate several assumptions implied in the conception in a way which may make clear what their consequences are.

The description is summarized by the flow diagram given in Table XIX. The sequence in which the subprocesses actually occur need not be exactly as presented. Some variations are immaterial to the conception and may in fact depending upon circumstances; for instance, we may know what situations a person is in before we perceive his reaction. Also, subprocesses may not be as independent as presented here.

In our description, we will follow the flow diagram.

1. The system, of course, must be able to understand a situation as such, and to know its implications. A given blotch must be recognized as a

TABLE XIX
THE PROCESS OF RECOGNITION OF EMOTION
AT A GIVEN MOMENT OF TIME

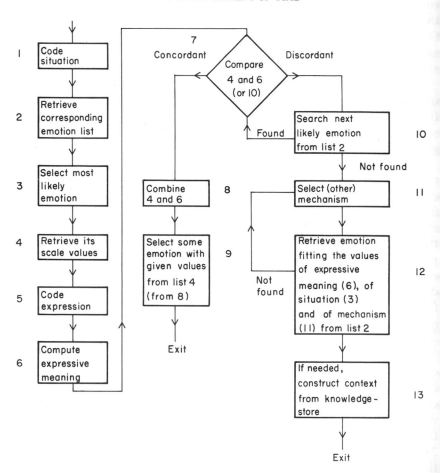

grease spot, and a grease spot on an evening dress must be recognized as something probably preventing its owner from going to a party. Evidently, extent and nature of this coding ability and corresponding store of knowledge are sources of variance for recognition-of-emotion performance.

2. It must be assumed that the store contains not only factual implications, but emotional implications as well. Not being able to go to a party must be known to be unpleasant, disappointing, or causing anger. We can represent this store of information as containing all situations known to the system. Each situation will possess a list containing all emotions which it may elicit with, for each, the corresponding likelihood of occurr-

ence, and the conditions for occurrence. Obviously, this is a crude and arbitrary representation of what probably is, to a large extent, a set of rules of inference and combination. For each situation there may be more than one list of emotions or of emotion probabilities corresponding to different kinds of people, e.g., girls about 22 years of age with a personality such as suggested by the photographs. There may be differentiation corresponding to all the kinds of contextual cues mentioned at an earlier point.

3. It is assumed that when confronted with a person in a situation, one will expect that person to experience the emotion most likely under these circumstances. One will be "set" for that emotion. It may be assumed, however, that one has in readiness the entire range of possibilities given under 2.

4. We assume a store of knowledge of emotion such that the "positional aspects" (see Section V,B), that is, their dimensional scale values, can be read off. We know that anger usually is an active, partly unpleasant, unfriendly emotion of variable degree of controlledness. This same store permits us our expressive behavior (or is the cognitive reflection thereof) and our own emotional introspection. It should consist of a complex set of emotions and corresponding scale values such that for each emotion many different sets of scale values are represented (there are different forms of joy), and such that to each set of scale values many different emotions correspond (see Section V,B). Some emotions or other motivational states may point to rather undefined sets of scale values; self -control, as an intention, may correspond to about every kind of behavior.

The store should be readable in both directions. Given an emotion, one can derive scale values; given a set of scale values, one can derive one or more emotions. Note that the same "list" will be used in several connections (in 9, 10, and 12). Processes 1 through 4 allow the system, when confronted with situational cues, to expect a certain kind of emotional behavior. It may be that under real-life conditions, processes 1 and 2 are the only ones which occur. This would suffice, with slight modifications, for the processes further on (7 and later).

5. The system must be able to register expressive behavior and to discriminate among its various features. There could be individual differences in the acuteness with which this can be done.

6. The system must be in possession of something equivalent to the multiple regression equations discussed in Section IV, C. The meaning of expression as such can then be inferred in a simple way.

7. Expressive meaning and situational suggestions can be compared by comparing their scale values. Whether or not expressive behavior conforms to the expectations based upon situational cues depends upon the tolerance permitted. To judge from the experiments, agreement as to scale half seems a sufficient condition.

8. About the rules of combination of concordant cues we have to be vague. Whether or not the resulting emotion is considered more extreme, or a compromise, depends upon factors as yet unclear.

9. An emotion is selected from the store mentioned under 4, now read in the opposite direction. The selection should involve an emotion which occurs with reasonable likelihood on the list for the situation in‑ volved (see 2). This may or may not be the same emotion as originally expected (in 3), depending upon the whims of the system and the possible shifts resulting from 8. With this, the system responds and has "recognized" an emotion. From the point of view of expression, "specification" as discussed in Section V, B has occurred.

10. If behavior does not correspond to expectations, it may be easy to adjust the expectations. A person may respond to a given situation in several ways, emotionally as well as overtly. The observer may simply shift to a different plausible interpretation from list 2. The majority of type IV interpretations (Section VI, F) will thus be conditioned. After the adjustment, discordance no longer exists.

11. If discordance persists, the discordance-resolving "mechanisms" are called into play: divorcing emotion from the given situation (type I), divorcing emotion from the situation while accepting the situation as such (type II), divorcing expression from emotion (type III), or simply denying the situation (included in type IV). It is assumed here that the subject has free choice in the type of resolution he wants to achieve. To some extent, this is probably true; most or all types occur with every cue combination. Still, it seems likely that some types of hypothesis are more plausible than others under certain circumstances. This is what may be reflected by the asymmetries mentioned (Section VI, E,3) and for the reasons given there.

12. The selected mechanism defines, to some extent, whether the final interpretation should correspond to the values of expression or should be on the list (2) corresponding to the situation. However, the selection process becomes rather involved here, since for most mechanisms the divorce of emotion from either expression or situation is not entire. If the subject decides to invent a new aspect in the situation, or some private thought or recollection, he usually tries to think of something which still fits the situation.

At any rate, the outline of what happens seems reasonably clear. An emotion is sought from the list corresponding to the expression values, possibly with the restriction that it should be an emotion which can be controlled, masked, or suppressed by the expression. It should be one which, in its turn, is either on the list of the situation or on a "list" of situational components compatible with the given situation. It is conceivable that a process of successive approximation in involved, whereby the selected situational component, in its turn, modifies the selected emotion to obtain a better fit.

If no idea comes to the system, it may select a different mechanism and start anew with 12.

13. Finally, the situational components may be concretized, using list 2. If "a fearful recollection" is needed, one may be found in the subjects' imagination.

The description given is meant to explain the recognition of an isolated expressive act. It is, however, easily extended to the perception of expressive sequences and of durable components in the stream of behavior in a given situation (see Frijda, 1965b). It contains the necessary ingredients for the expectations, the self-corrections, and the averaging as they occur under those conditions.

VIII. Conclusions

Much concerning the problems we have touched on is, as yet, unclear. The question of the number of expressive dimensions, or aspects, or categories, has yet to be decided. The studies on expression dominance and situational influences constitute mere beginnings. Nevertheless, some conclusions seem warranted concerning the main question: How is it possible to recognize other people's emotions?

It would seem that there exists some degree of immediate intuitive perception of expressive meaning, as claimed by Gestalt psychologists (Köhler, 1929; Arnheim, 1949) or by writers of a phenomenological bent (Klages, Scheler, Merleau-Ponty). The inherent meaning of expressive movement can be immediately evident; it can be instantly "read off" as tendency toward approach or withdrawl, opening or closure, activity or passivity, on the basis of general perceptible principles, as suggested in Section V,B.

Yet this immediately evident basis does not explain recognition of emotion. It may explain physiognomic characteristics of other people's behavior. It may be the basis, together with strong imaginative or symbolizing endowment, for perception of the unverbalized, and often unverbalizable, meaning attached to movement patterns, either human, as in dancing, or nonhuman, as in Michotte's (1946, 1950) experiments. It does not suffice to explain that understanding of emotion which leads to the expectation or appreciation of a fearful event when the other person looks fearful, or to our ideas about other people's inner experiences.

For that, large stores of knowledge need to be acquired: situational meanings, one's own emotional categories, and experience concerning the movements and actions of other toward one's self and the environment. There is evidence that physiognomic perception and recognition of emotions do not constitute inborn, immediately available givens. Physiognomic perception and recognition of emotion seem to increase with age (Dashiell, 1929; Gates, 1923; Honkavaara, 1961; Levy-Schoen, 1964). Even the intuitive recognition of emotion upon which, we may assume, a monkey's recognition performance is based, depends upon social experience and is absent in monkeys reared in isolation (Miller, Caul, and Mirsky, 1967).

Recognition of emotion may be intuitive and immediate; this does not preclude the intervention of much knowledge and experience, as the observations by Hebb (1946) and the training experiments reviewed by Mittenecker (1961) indicate. Recognition of emotion may consist of phenomenally immediate integrations in simple or well-known situations; it often consists of conscious hypotheses and self-corrections, and it often involves explicit inferential activities, utilizations of former experiences, and reasonings by analogy. Based in large part upon immediate appreciation of the positional, relational meaning of expressive behavior, recognition of emotion is a complex process which may vary from the immediately evident to the fully conscious making of plausible guesses.

This applies, in particular, when one understands, or tries to understand, other people's inner experiences. To explain this puzzling human possibility, the classical theories of reasoning by analogy or empathy were developed. Critics of these theories have objected that in most instances nothing of the sort seems to occur. They were right, because perceiving the positional aspects of behavior seen in a situation does not involve attribution of inner experience or the cognitive activities necessary for it. However, when a gap exists between behavior and the meaning of the environment, such attribution may occur. "Inner experience of others" is a hypothesis to bridge a gap in intelligible relations. If such a gap occurs and is indeed bridged, one is far away from the simple situations in which the phenomenal immediacy of physiognomic perception holds.

REFERENCES

Abelson, R. P. Modes of resolution of belief dilemmas. *Journal of Conflict Resolution,* 1959, 3, 343-352.

Abelson, R. P., and Sermat, V. Multidimensional scaling of facial expressions. *Journal of Experimental Psychology,* 1962, 63, 546-554.

Ahrens, R. Beitrag zur Entwicklung des Physiognomie und Mimik-Erkenntnis. *Zectschaft für experimentelle und angewandt Psychologie,* 1954, 2, 412-455.

Argyle, M., and Kendon, A. (1967). The experimental analysis of social performance. In L. Berkowitz (Ed.) *Advances in experimental social psychology.* Vol. 3. New York: Academic Press.

Arnheim, R. The gestalt theory of expression. *Psychological Review,* 1949, 56, 156-171.

Bain, A. *Emotions and the will.* London: Longmans, Green, 1895.

Benesch, H. Der Ausdruck im Momente des Versagens. *Verhandlungen Kongress der deutsche Gesellschaft fur Psychologie, 1959,* 1960.

Blake, W. H. A preliminary study of the interpretation of bodily expression. *Teachers College Contributions to Education,* 1933, No. 574.

Boucher, J., and Ekman, P. A replication of Schlosberg's evaluation of Woodworth's scale of emotion. Paper read at the Western Psychological Association, Honolulu, 1965.

Bruner, J. S., and Tagiuri, R. The perception of people. In G. Lindzey (Ed.) *Handbook of social psychology.* Vol. 2. Cambridge: Addison-Wesley, 1954. Pp. 634-654.

Brunswik, E. Perception and the representative design of psychological experiments. *Berkeley: University of California Press, 1956.*

Brunswik, E., and Reiter, Lotte. Eindruckscharaktere schematisierter Gesichter. *Zeitschrift fur Psychologie,* 1938, **142,** 67-134.

Carmichael, R., Roberts, S. O. and Wessel, N. Y. A study of judgment of manual expression. *Journal of Social Psychology,* 1937, **8,** 115-142.

Cline, M. G. The influence of social context on the perception of faces. *Journal of Personality,* 1956, **25,** 142-158.

Coleman, J. Facial expression of emotion. *Psychological Monographs,* 1949, **63,** 1.

Dashiell, J. F. A new method of measuring reactions to facial expressions of emotions. *Psychological Bulletin,* 1927, 24.

Davis, R. C. The specificity of facial expression. *Journal of General Psychology,* 1934, **10.**

Davitz, J. *The communication of emotional meaning.* New York: McGraw-Hill, 1964.

Dittmann, A. T. The relationship between body movements and moods in interviews. *Journal of Consulting Psychology,* 1962, **26,** 48.

Dittmann, A. T., Parloff, M. B., and Boomer, D. S. Facial and bodily expression: A study of receptivity of emotional cues. *Psychiatry,* 1965, **28,** 239-244.

Duffy, E. *Activation and behavior.* New York: Wiley, 1962.

Fistel, A. Der Eindruck der mimischen Erscheinungen in seines Bedingthief vom physiognomischen Umfeld. *Psychologische Rundschau,* 1953, **4,** 236-261.

Ekman, P. Body position, facial expression, and verbal behavior during interviews. *Journal of Abnormal and Social Psychology,* 1964, **68,** 295-301.

Ekman, P. Communication through nonverbal behavior: A source of information about interpersonal relationships. In S. S. Tomkins and C. E. Izard (Eds.) *Affect, cognition and personality.* New York: Springer, 1965. Pp. 390-442. (a)

Ekman, P. Differential communication of affect by head and body cues. *Journal of Personality and Social Psychology,* 1965, **2,** 726-735. (b)

Ekman, P. Personality, pathology, affect and nonverbal behavior. Paper read at Western Psychological Association, Honolulu, 1965. (c)

Ekman, P., and Friesen, W. V. Head and body cues in the judgment of emotion: a reformulation. *Perceptual and Motor Skills,* 1967, **24,** 711-724. (a)

Ekman, P., and Friesen, W. V. Origin, usage and coding: The basis for five categories of nonverbal behavior. Paper given at the Symposium on Communication Theory and Linguistic Models, Buenos Aires, 1967. (b)

Ekman, P., and Friesen, W. V. Nonverbal behavior in psychotherapy research. In J. Schlien (Ed.) *Research in psychotherapy.* Vol. 3. Washington: American Psychological Association, 1967. (c)

Elshout, J. J. Computation of factor scores by complete regression. *Technical Reports,* Psychology Laboratory, Amsterdam University, 1967.

Engen, T., Levy, N., and Schlosberg, H. A new series of facial expressions. *American Psychologist,* 1957, **12,** 264-266.

Engen, T., Levy, N., and Schlosberg, H. The dimensional analysis of a new series of facial expressions. *Journal of Experimental Psychology,* 1958, **55,** 454-458.

Exline, R. V. Explorations in the process of person perception: visual interaction in relation to competition, sex and need for affiliation. *Journal of Personality*, 1963, **31**, 1-20.

Exline, R. V., and Winters, L. C. Affective relations and mutual glances in dyads. In S. S. Tomkins and C. E. Izard (Eds.) *Affect, cognition and personality*. New York: Springer, 1965. Pp. 319-350.

Exline, R. V., Gray, D., and Schuette, D. Visual behavior in a dyad as affected by interview content and sex of respondent. *Journal of Personality and Social Psychology*, 1965, **1**, 201-209.

Féléky, Antoinette. The expression of emotions. *Pscyhological Review*, 1914, **21**, 33-41.

Fernberger, S. W. False suggestion and the Piderit model. *American Journal of Psychology*, 1928, **40**, 562-568.

Flores d' Arcais, B. Forming impressions of personality in situations of contrast between verbal and mimic expressions. Proceedings of the 16th International Congress of Psychology, Bonn, 1960. *Acta Psychologica*, 1961, **19**, 494-495.

Frijda, N. H. The understanding of facial expression of emotion. *Acta Psychologica*, 1953, **9**, 294-362.

Frijda, N. H. Het Begrijpen van Gelaatsexpressies. Amsterdam: Van Oorschot, 1956.

Frijda, N. H. Facial expression and situational cues. *Journal of Abnormal and Social Psychology*, 1958, **57**, 149-154.

Frijda, N. H. Facial expression and situational cues: A control. *Acta Psychologica*, 1961, **18**, 239-244.

Frijda, N. H. Mimik und Pantomimik. In R. Kirchhoff (Ed.), *Handbuch der Psychologie*. Vol. 5. *Ausdruckskunde*. Göttingen: Hogrefe, 1965. Pp. 351-421. (a)

Frijda, N. H. Computer simulation as a tool for social psychology. Paper read at the Second European Conference on Experimental Social Psychology, Frascati, 1965. (b)

Frijda, N. H. Expressive behavior. In *International encyclopedia of the social sciences*. New York: Macmillan, 1968, 263-268.

Frijda, N. H., and Philipszoon, E. Dimensions of recognition of emotion. *Journal of Abnormal and Social Psychology*, 1963, **66**, 45-51.

Frijda, N. H., and Van de Geer, J. P. Codability and recognition. *Acta Psychologica*, 1961, **18**, 360-367.

Gates, G. S. An experimental study of the growth of social perception. *Journal of Educational Psychology*, 1923, **14**, 449-461.

Gibson, J. J. , and Pick, A. D. Perception of another person's looking behavior. *American Journal of Psychology*, 1963, **76**, 386-394.

Giedt, F. H. Comparison of visual, content and auditory cues in interviewing. *Journal of Consulting Psychology*, 1955, **19**, 407-416.

Gladstones, W. H. A multidimensional study of facial expression of emotion. *Australian Journal of Psychology*, 1962, **14**, 95-100.

Goldberg, H. D. The role of "cutting" in the perception of motion pictures. *Journal of Applied Psychology*, 1951, **35**, 70-71.

Goodenough, F. L., and Tinker, M. A. The relative potency of facial expression and verbal description of stimulus in the judgment of emotion. *Journal of Comparative Psychology*, 1931, **12**, 365-370.

Gottschaldt, K. Handlung und Ausdruck in der Psychologie der Persönlichkeit. *Revista di Psicologia*, 1958, **10**, 161-175.

Gottschaldt, K. Methodologische Perspektiven der Ausdrucksforschung. Proceedings of the 16th International Congress of Psychology, Bonn, 1960. *Acta Psychologica*, 1961, **19**, 475-481.

Guilford, J. P. *The nature of human intelligence*. New York: McGraw-Hill, 1967.

Harrison, R. Pictic analysis: toward a vocabulary and syntax for the pictorial code. Ph.D. Thesis, Michigan State University, 1964.

Hastorf, A. H., Osgood, C. E., and Ono, H. The semantics of facial expressions and the prediction of the meanings of stereoscopically fused facial expressions. *Scandinavian Journal of Psychology*, 1966, **7**, 179-188.

Hebb, D. O. Emotion in man and animals: an analysis of the intuitive process of recognition. *Psychological review*, 1946, **53**, 88-106.

Hofstätter, P. R. Dimensionen des mimischen Ausdrucks. *Zeitschrift für experimentelle angewandte Psychologie*, 1956, **3**, 505-529.

Honkavaara, S. The psychology of expression. *British Journal of Psychology*, 1961, *Monogr. Suppl.* 32.

Hulin, W. S., and Katz, D. The Frois-Wittman pictures of facial expressions. *Journal of Experimental Psychology*, 1935, **18**, 482-498.

Jaanus, H. *Het Aspect Activiteit by de Beóordeling van Gelaatsexpressies*. M.A. Thesis, Amsterdam University, 1966.

Jarden, E., and Fernberger, S. W. The effect of suggestion on the judgment of facial expression of emotion. *American Journal of Psychology*, 1926, **37**, 565-569.

Kaila, E. Die Reaktionen des Säuglings auf das menschliche gesicht. *Annales Universitatis Aboensis*. 1932, **17**, 13-32.

Kalina, W. Badania nad rozpoznawaniem wyrazów mimicnych uczuć u ludzi. *Przeglad Psychologyczny*, 1960, **4**, 177-185.

Kanner, L. Judging emotions from facial expressions. *Psychological Monographs*. 1933, **41**, (186).

Karsten, Lien. *Dimensies van de Gelaatsexpressie: Een Replicatie met de Marjorie Lightfoot Photos*. M.A. Thesis, Amsterdam University, 1965.

Kirchhoff, R. Die Umfelder des pathognomischen Ausdrucks. *Jahrbuch für Psychologie, Psychotherapie und medizinische Anthropologie*, 1962, **9**, 42-55.

Klages, L. *Grundlegung der Wissenschaft vom Ausdruck*. Leipzig: Barth, 1935.

Kline, L. W., and Johannsen, O. E. The comparative role of face and face-body-hands as aids in identifying emotions. *Journal of Abnormal and Social Psychology*, 1935, **29**, 415-426.

Knapp, P. M. (Ed.) *Expression of the emotions in man*. New York: International Universities Press, 1963.

Köhler, W. Zur Psychologie der Schimpansen. *Psychologische Forschung*, 1921, **1**, 2-46.

Köhler, W. *Gestalt psychology*. New York: Liveright, 1929.

Krout, M. Autistic gestures. *Psychological monographs*, 1935, **46**(208).

Kühnel, E. M. *Ueber den Eindruckswert schematisierter Gesichter*. Ph.D. Thesis, University of Vienna, 1954.

Landis, C. Studies of emotional reactions. II. General behavior and facial expression. *Journal of Comparative Psychology*, 1924, **4**, 447-509.

Landis, C. The interpretation of facial expression in emotion. *Journal of Genetic Psychology*, 1929, **2**, 59-72.

Landis, C., and Hunt, W. A. *The startle pattern*. New York: Farrar, 1939.

Langfeld, J. S. Judgments of facial expression and suggestion. *Psychological Review*, 1918, **25**, 488-494.

Langfeld, J. S. *The aesthetic attitude*. New York: Harcourt Brace, 1920.

Levy, L., Orr, T. B., and Rosenzweig, S. Judgments of emotion from facial expressions by college students, mental retardates and mental hospital patients. *Journal of Personality*, 1960, **28**, 342-349.

222   NICO H. FRIJDA

Lévy-Schoen, Ariane. L'Image d'Autrui chez l'Enfant. *Publications de la Faculté des Lettres et Sciences Humaines, Paris. Recherches,* 1964, 23.

Lewin, K. Kindlicher Ausdruck. *Zeitschrift für paedagogische Psychologie,* 1927, 28.

Lipps, Th. Die Erkenntnis von fremden Ichen. *Psychologische Studien,* 1905, 1.

Mahl, G., Danet, B., and Norton, N. Reflection of major personality characteristics in gestures and body movements. *American Psychologist,*1959, 14, 357.

Michotte, A. E. *La Perception de la Causalite.* Louvain: Editions de l'Institut Supérieur de Philosophie, 1946.

Michotte, A. E. The emotions as functional connections. In *Feelings and emotions: The Mooseheart Symposium.* M. Reymert (Ed.), New York: McGraw-Hill, 1950. Pp. 114-126.

Miller, R. E., Murphy, J. V., and Mirsky, I. A. Nonverbal communication of affect. *Journal of Clinical Psychology,* 1959, 15, 155-158.

Miller, R. E., Banks, J. H. J., and Ogawa, N. Communication of affect in "cooperative conditioning" of rhesus monkeys. *Journal of Abnormal and Social Psychology,* 1962, 64, 343-348.

Miller, R. E., Banks, J. H. J., and Ogawa, N. Role of facial expression in "cooperative avoidance conditioning" in monkeys. *Journal of Abnormal and Social Psychology,* 1963, 67, 24-30.

Miller, R. E., Caul, W. F., and Mirsky, I. A. Communication of affects between feral and socially isolated monkeys. *Journal of Personality and Social Psychology,* 1967, 7, 231-234.

Mittenecker, E. On the significance of the phenomenally nonmediated "understanding" of expression. Proceedings of the 16th International Congress of Psychology, Bonn, 1960. *Acta Psychologica,* 1961, 19, 485-490.

Munn, N. L. The effect of the knowledge of the situation upon judgment of emotion from facial expressions. *Journal of Abnormal and Social Psychology,* 1940, 35 324-328.

Numenmaa, T., and Kauranne, U. Dimensions of facial expression. *Report Department of Psychology, Institute of Pedagogy, Jyväskyla,* 20.

Osgood, C. E. Fidelity and reliability. In H. Quastler *Information theory in psychology.* Glencoe: Free Press, 1955. Pp. 374-384.

Osgood, C. E. Dimensionality of the semantic space for communication via facial expressions. *Scandinavian Journal of Psychology,* 1966, 7, 1-30.

O'Sullivan, M., Guilford, J. P., and de Mille, R. Measurement of social intelligence. *Reports of the Psychological Laboratory, University of Southern California* No. 34.

Rosenberg, B.G., and Langer, J. A study of postural-gestural communication. *Journal of Personality and Social Psychology,* 1965, 2, 593-597.

Royal, D. C., and Hays, W. L. Empirical dimensions of emotional behavior. *Proceedings of the 15th Internation Congress of Psychology, Brussels, 1957,* 1959, 419.

Rump, E. E. Facial expression and situational cues: demonstration of a logical error in Frijda's report. *Acta Psychologica,* 1960, 17, 31-38.

Sainsbury, P. Gestural movement during psychiatric interivew. *Psychosomatic Medicine,* 1955, 17, 458-469.

Sarbin, T. R. Role theory. In G. Lindzey (Ed.), *Handbook of social psychology.* Vol 1. Cambridge: Addison-Wesley, 1954.

Schachter, S. The interaction of cognitive and physiological determinants of emotional state. In L. Berkowitz (Ed.), *Advances in experimental social psychology.* Vol. 1.New York: Academic Press, 1964. Pp. 49-80.

Scheflen, A. E. Communication systems such as psychotherapy. In J. H. Masserman (Ed.), *Current psychiatric therapies.*New York: Grune & Stratton, 1965. Pp. 33-41.

Schlosberg, H. A scale for the judgment of facial expression. *Journal of Experimental Psychology*, 1941, **29**, 497-510.

Schlosberg, H. The description of facial expression in terms of two dimensions. *Journal of Experimental Psychology*, 1952, **44**, 229-237.

Schlosberg, H. Three dimensions of emotion. *Psychological Review*, 1954, **61**, 81-88.

Shepard, R. N. The analysis of proximities: Multidimensional scaling with an unknown distance function. *Psychometrica*, 1963, **27**, 125-140.

Sherman, M. The differentiation of emotional responses in infants: I. Judgments of emotional responses from motion pictures views and from actual observation. *Journal of Comparative Psychology*, 1927, **7**, 265-284.

Spitz, R. A., and Wolff, S. The smiling response. *Genetic Psychology Monographs*, 1946, **34**, 57-125.

Stringer, P. Cluster analysis of non-verbal judgments of facial expressions. *British Journal of Mathematical and Statistical Psychology*, 1967, **20**, 71-79.

Stringer, P. *Personal communication.*

Stringer, P. *Sequential proximity as the basis for similarity judgments of facial expressions.* Mimeo, University College, London, 1968. (b)

Tagiuri, R. Movement as a cue to person perception. In *Perspectives in personality research.* H. David and H. Brengelmann (Eds.), London: Crosby, Lockwood & Sons, 175-195.

Thompson, D. F., and Meltzer, L. Communication of emotional intent by facial expression. *Journal of Abnormal and Social Psychology*, 1964, **68**, 129-135.

Thompson, J. Development of facial expression in blind and seeing children. *Archives of Psychology*, 1941, **264**.

Tomkins, S. S., and McCarter, R. What and where are the primary affects? Some evidence for a theory. *Perceptual and Motor Skills*, 1964, **18**, 119-158.

Triandis, H., and Lambert, W. W. A restatement and test of Schlosberg's theory of emotion with two kinds of subjects from Greece. *Journal of Abnormal and Social Psychology*, 1958, **56**, 321-328.

Turhan, M. Ueber die Deutung des Gesichtsausdrucks. *Psychologische Beiträege* 5.

Vandenberg, S. G., and Mattson, E. The interpretation of facial expressions by schizophrenics, other mental patients, normal adults and children. Proceedings of the 16th International Congress of Psychology, Bonn, 1960. *Acta Psychologica* 1961, **19**, 495-497.

Van Wijk, L. J. *Dimensies van de muziekbeoordeling.* M.A. Thesis, Amsterdam University, 1964.

Warries, E. *Situatie en expressie.* M.A Thesis, Amsterdam University, 1963.

Woodworth, R. S. *Experimental psychology.* New York: Holt, 1938.

Woodworth, R. S., and Schlosberg, H. *Experimental psychology.* (Rev. ed.) New York: Holt, 1955.

STUDIES OF STATUS CONGRUENCE

Edward E. Sampson

DEPARTMENT OF PSYCHOLOGY
UNIVERSITY OF CALIFORNIA
BERKELEY, CALIFORNIA

I. Introduction

All social systems differentiate the individual members of the system along several different dimensions. Individuals may be differentiated, for example, on the basis of their age, their sex, their income, their education, and their occupation. These dimensions are often referred to as *statuses*, a term which not only suggests the existence of a quality or performance by which individual differentiations are made, but in addition, a ranking of persons along that differentiated dimension. Thus, for example, individuals in this society are differentiated in terms of their income and education; in addition, they are ranked relative to other individuals along these same two dimensions. Some of these differentiations are based on *ascribed characteristics* (e.g., race, age, and sex), whereas others are based on *achieved characteristics* (e.g., education, occupation, and income).

II. Sociological Approach to Status Congruence

In the sociological literature on social class, differentiations based primarily on achieved statuses have been employed to obtain either a single summary index of an individual's class position in society *or* to obtain an index which has variously been referred to as status crystallization, status consistency, or status congruence. This latter approach to the study of social class assumes that the *patterning of ranks* across the several dimensions which are differentiated within any social system is an important social variable. Early concern with this multidimensional view of social structure and the importance of patterning can be traced to Max Weber's distinction between class, status, and party (1946).

Early theorizing (e.g., Benoit-Smullyan, 1944) maintained that an individual's status ranks tend toward a state of equilibration. A state in which an individual's rank position along one status dimension differed from his rank position along another position was assumed to produce forces toward the equilibration or balancing of these two rank positions. Therefore, the proper, balanced state, would be a man, for example, who ranked highly along an economic dimension and who was ranked highly along a dimension of prestige, or power, and so forth, as well. Disequilibrium in status positions within a social system was thought to be a discomforting state of affairs both for the individual and for the social system itself. Lack of status equilibration or consistency of ranks across status dimensions was seen as a precursor to societal revolution through which action one would achieve a change in the balancing of status positions.

In an interesting examination of one aspect of this derivation, Goffman (1957) asked a national sample of the U.S. population to rank several groups (e.g., state government, big business, labor unions, small businesses, and the national government) first in terms of their present influence over national life and policy, and second in terms of how the respondents would like to see their relative influence. Goffman then correlated the discrepancy between the perceived actual and the desired arrangements of influence with an index of the individual's status consistency. To obtain this index of status consistency, he selected the three dimensions of income, education, and occupation. An individual was defined as consistent if his income and education ranks were *both* consistent with his occupational rank and inconsistent if either income or education was higher or lower than his occupational rank. In general, Goffman found support for the expectation that those persons whose status consistency was low showed greater desire to see a change in the distribution of influence within the society. By controlling for occupational level and making comparisons of consistents with inconsistents within three occupational strata, Goffman further found that the relationship between inconsistency in status ranks and desire for a change in the influence hierarchies was strongest for the higher occupational stratum and weakest for the lower occupational stratum. Goffman offered several *post hoc* interpretations of this latter finding. He suggested, for example, that where status inconsistency can be reduced by upward mobility within the system — a condition which is possible for those of lower occupational rank — then this mode of equilibration will be sought in preference to the more revolutionary mode of wishing to see an upheaval in the power arrangements of the society.

In addition to his own work, Goffman cited several observations which support the notion that status inconsistency can lead to a desire for change in the distribution of power within a social system. For instance, Edwards (1927) reported that those most interested in social change in several revolutions which he studied were drawn from groups with discrepancies between their political and economic power. Ringer and Sills (1952-1953), studying political extremists in Iran, found that such extremists, both on the right and the left, were more inconsistent in their education, occupational, and income ranks than were political moderates. The studies by Lenski (1954, 1956) suggest that individuals low in status crystallization (his term for this same concept) more frequently had liberal political orientations and tended to vote for the political party which favored the greatest amount of general social innovation and change. A recent cross-national analysis (Lenski, 1967) in which the voting behavior in Australia, Britain, Canada, and the United States was related to an index of status inconsistency (i.e., the discrepancy between one's occupational class and one's religious group affiliation) provided additional support for this same thesis. Inconsistents, for example, working-class Protestants and middle-class Catholics, exhibited more liberalism or left-of-centerism in their voting behavior across nations (except for Britain) and elections than did the consistents; i.e., working-class Catholics and middle-class Protestants.

An earlier, by now classic study of voting patterns (Lazarsfeld, Berelson, and Gaudet, 1948) conceptualized the situation discussed above in terms of "cross-pressures" rather than in terms of status congruence. From this study, it is difficult to tease out a true liberal — conservative voting pattern (unless one equates Democrat with liberal and Republican with conservative). However, their data do suggest that the voter who is subjected to cross-pressures, in that his religion pushes him one way and his socioeconomic status (SES) pushes him another — the inconsistents in Lenski's analysis — *delay* their voting decision and show generally *less interest* in the election as compared with the voters lacking cross-pressures (i.e., the consistents). By reanalyzing the data presented by Lazarfeld *et al.* in Fig. 4 of their article in the text by Freedman, Hawley, Landecker, and Miner (1952, p. 19), in which voting behavior by religion and SES is presented, this author has found further confirmation for the Lenski argument. Thus, for example, of those who voted Democratic in the 1940 election, approximately 45% were consistent while 55% were inconsistent. The reverse relationship holds in examining the Republican voters. Here we find that 59% were consistent and 41% were inconsistent. Thus, it appears as though the early discussion of cross-pressures in voting behavior can be updated and usefully reconceptualized in terms of a congruence model.

In a more recent work Lasswell and Lerner (1966) described the social characteristics of several revolutionary elites. In discussing the elites of both the Chinese Communists and the Kuomintang, Lasswell and Lerner noted that while both groups have high status derived from well-to-do fathers and a high education, the individual soon concluded that had he been born in the West, "he would have a job (given his education) and command a factory, but that short of a thoroughgoing revolution, he can look forward to no better prospect than unemployment in his own backward country" (Lasswell and Lerner, 1966, p. 381). That is, the revolutionary of China was a person who had a high ranking on income, general familial prestige and education, but was ranked low in power: a condition of status incongruence.

The Lasswell and Lerner examination of the Nazis suggests the degree to which the leadership of the movement as well as its followers were men who were marginal in that they deviated from a substantial number of predominant attributes of the German society; that is, they ranked similarly to others of the German society on several attributes but differed (i.e., were inconsistent in their ranks) on several other attributes.

Even more recently, Rush (1967) examined the relationship between status incongruence as measured by income, occupation, and education, and right wing extremist attitudes. In general, he found a positive relationship with those persons whose status positions were inconsistent being more extremely right wing in their attitudes. In their study of the relationship between status consistency and political attitudes, on the other hand, Kelley and Chambliss (1966) reported that status consistency was not as good a predictor of political attitudes as social class and minority group membership taken alone. Clearly, the problem becomes one of determining, through the use of appropriately controlled comparisons, whether it is the consistency or inconsistency of the pattern of status ranks that is producing the political attitudes, or whether it is simply one *key* dimension (e.g., occupation or ethnic status) that accounts for the variance. Lenski (1954, 1956), Rush (1967), and Goffman (1957), in controlling on occupation or education, still reported an effect attributable to the consistency factor itself. In addition, however, as Lenski himself argued (1967), only certain kinds of inconsistency appear to produce an effect on political attitude and behavior. In particular, he suggested that the inconsistency between an achieved status (e.g., occupation) and one with more ascribed characteristic (e.g., religious affiliation) produces the greatest effect.

In a particularly biting and insightful critique of much of this type of work, however, Mitchell (1964) has reexamined some of the Lenski data and techniques of single-factor control and concluded that *ethnicity* taken alone seems to explain most of the variation in one set of voting behavior results. At best, the issue must remain open, although even the most severe critics cannot ignore the growing body of data which shows a status congruence effect. The debate may rage on, however, concerning the magnitude of that effect.

Perhaps more on the conceptual than the methodological side are the especially useful comments of Kasl (undated report). As it has been employed throughout the literature of sociology and more recently, of psychology, status congruence is a variable which purports to be a property of the individual, the dyad, the small group, as well as of a collectivity or of the entire social system. Kasl recommended that we differentiate these referents, both for clarity of reference and, as importantly, in order to examine what might turn out to be differing antecedents and consequents which vary as a function of the particular unit whose property is defined as inconsistent. He suggested referring to the status inconsistency (the general term) of a single individual by the term "status incongruence," that of dyad by the term "status discrepancy," of a small group by the term "status equilibrium," and of a collectivity by the term "status crystallization." Unfortunately, the present state of systematic study of the variable of status consistency does not permit us at this time to do more than accept as reasonable and potentially useful the kinds of distinctions which Kasl suggested. As we study this variable in the latter part of this article, however, it is important to note that we are involved primarily with a unit property of a relatively small, interacting group, sometimes a dyad; i.e., either status discrepancy or equilibrium in Kasl's terms.

The more general notion that status inconsistency is a displeasing state of affairs has been used in connection with topics other than political attitudes and behaviors. The work of Jackson (1962), for example, was based on the assumption that incongruence produces psychological stress which in turn should be reflected in various psychological disturbances. Using national survey data, he found that high symptom levels were associated with inconsistency between the individual's ascribed statuses of race and his achieved statuses of occupation or education. He concluded that while all kinds of status inconsistency are psychologically disturbing, the manner by which the individual responds to the inconsistency varies as a function of relative positions of his achieved and ascribed statuses.

The monograph by Kasl and Cobb (1967) is in this same tradition of relating status consistency to health-related variables but employing a rather important new approach. Their study sought to relate the effects of parental status discrepancy, involving the variables of father's education and occupation and mother's education, upon several physical and psychological indices of health. Their findings generally indicated support for the negative (i.e., contrary to good health) consequences of intergenerational inconsistency, with parental status inconsistency having consequences for the physical and psychological health of their offspring. In order to explain their rather interesting and here-to-fore unstudied findings, Kasl and Cobb focused primarily upon the psychological family environment which is provided by status inconsistent parents. The factors of conflicting expectations and general family instability and uncertainty are seen to play a major role in their interpretative scheme.

III. Small-Group Studies of Status Congruence

Within the area of small group research, several studies suggest a relationship between status inconsistency, on one hand, and measures of group satisfaction or morale or group productivity on the other. Stuart Adams (1953) studied air force flight crews and computed an index of status congruence for each crew based on such dimensions as age, rank, and amount of flight time. He related this index to measures of friendship, trust, and general satisfaction, finding a positive relationship between congruence or consistency and satisfaction. Using several indices of crew performance, including such things as optical bombing scores, crew coordination, radar bombing scores, and instructor ratings of over-all performance, Adams reported a curvilinear relationship between these indices of technical performance and status consistency; that is, as status consistency moves from minimum to maximum, crew performance first shows improvement, then undergoes some deterioration. Apparently, there is an optimal level of status consistency for technical performance.

Exline and Ziller (1959), in an early laboratory study, varied the degree of status consistency in small discussion groups on the dimensions of voting power and task ability. Someone with high task ability (as experimentally manipulated) and low voting power was said to occupy inconsistent status positions within his group. Exline and Ziller reported that congruent groups were more congenial and showed greater discussion agreement than incongruent groups.

More recently, Burnstein and Zajonc (1965) sought to examine a group's tendency to reduce incongruent or inconsistent status ranks as a function of the prior history of task success or failure. In a controlled experimental situation, the researchers examined status consistency based on a dimension of performance status, involving the subject's apparent task ability, and control status, involving his influence over the groups' product. As they set up their experimental situation, each group began with a perfect congruence between performance and control status; over time, experimental manipulations produced discrepancies between these two status dimensions. The experimental induction of status incongruence produced along with it a deterioration in task performance. Burnstein and Zajonc observed the rapidity and manner by which the incongruent structure was changed toward congruence as a function of the group's history of past task success or failure. They reported finding that "members of groups with a history of successful outputs are more ready to reduce an incongruence in status ranks than members of unsuccessful groups" (p. 360). Furthermore, their data for individuals suggest that those persons who were involved in especially large incongruities in status ranks were more responsive to the need for restructuring the group's status hierarchies. In their experimental situation, in which incongruity was linked with relatively poor task performance, congruity in status ranks thereby became instrumental to the attainment of the rewards of successful group performance.

IV. The Mechanisms of Status Congruence

One of the explanatory models used in interpreting status congruence effects assumes congruence is instrumental to group goal attainment. According to this type of analysis, consistent statuses within a group may facilitate group goal attainment under certain specifiable conditions. It is not clear, however, that this same type of interpretation would deal satisfactorily with the effects of status inconsistency on the individual. One might, of course, maintain that if the individual's goal is to be free of tension and stress, then consistency of status ranks might better serve that end than would inconsistency. This interpretation is in part a broader statement of several of the more specific ideas which follow.

This then brings us to a more general discussion of the *mechanisms* which have been assumed to account for the status congruence effect. In his early work in this area, Benoit-Smullyan (1944) suggested that status disequilibrium was frustrating to the individual especially in that he *expected* certain of his rankings to go with other rankings; i.e., power and prestige should accord with wealth. When this matching did not exist, the individual became frustrated and sought to change the system toward greater equilibration of status ranks. Lenski (1954) suggested that the poorly crystallized individual was a *marginal man* who combined two roles of discrepant status, thus increasing the likelihood of his having unpleasant or frustrating social experiences. With the work of Sorokin (1947, 1959), Jackson (1962), Goffman (1957), and Homans (1961), the focus of the explanation begins to shift increasingly toward a specfication of a "conflicting demands" explanatory model. Sorokin (1947, 1959) saw an incongruent system as creating a situation of role conflict in that persons occupying different ranks positions were faced with conflicting demands for their behavior.

Jackson (1962) proposed several bases for the stress and difficulty which status incongruent individuals are assumed to experience. The major problem, however, presumably was the ambiguity and uncertainty of the social relationships resulting from the occupation of positions containing conflicting role expectations. Likewise, Goffman (1957) suggested a role-conflict interpretation of status incongruence effects, focusing especially on the difficulty of holding two rank positions which are simultaneously salient and conflicting. As noted by Mitchell (1964) in his methodological examination of some of the status congruence work (especially that of Jackson and Lenski), the model employed by Homans (1961), while appearing at first very similar to the conflicting-expectations notions of Goffman and Jackson and to some extent, Lenski, emphasizes the *relational* character of status congruence. Mitchell took Lenski and the others to task for using an inappropriate method to test a theory which emphasizes social relationships. Homans (1961) drew our attention to the fact that a given *social relationship* between two people, P and O may be incongruent and give rise to tension. This focus of Homans is related to the more recent work of Adams (1965) on equity theory. Although more will be said about this later, it is important at this point to note that equity theory, as Adams presented it, uses the explanatory model of cognitive dissonance to derive its behavioral predictions. Rather then insisting that the status incongruent person is subjected to conflicting demands which produce tension, this reasoning emphasizes that the individual who is status incongruent feels that he is not getting what he deserves (i.e., expects) given his positions relative to the positions of other persons within the relationship. Homans discussed this latter condition as involving the issue of *distributive justice*; Adams discussed this under the rubric of equity theory. Later, the author will attempt to relate these two approaches to his own program of research on status congruence.

The work of Lenski, Jackson, and Goffman, based primarily on analyses of national survey data, directs our attention more toward the individual who is status incongruent than toward the *relationship* between persons which may be status incongruent. The explanation for the effect of incongruence advanced by these writers, however, is rather similar to the more directly relational views of Homans. Homans, for example, suggested how a condition of *social incertitude* may result from a status incongruent social relationship. This concern with problems of establishing predictable social relationships, which forms a key part of Homans' interpretation of the status congruence effect, is, as we have seen, also a central part of several other accounts of incongruence. Nevertheless, the work of Homans and the critique by Mitchell suggest a direction in which investigations in this area should move. To study the means whereby status incongruity is seen to operate, especially given an explanatory model which emphasizes the notion of uncertainty, ambiguity, and conflicting expectations, one should move toward an examination of social relationships and encounters within small groups. It was toward this aim that the author's program of research on status congruence was undertaken.

V. The Research Program[1]

There are two important aspects of this research program which, by way of preface, should be noted. First the research was guided by a conceptual framework which sought to link the sociological work on status congruence with the psychological investigations of cognitive consistency or balance. Second, the work attempted to provide empirical support for several parts of this general framework through systematic, controlled laboratory experimentation rather than through survey methods.

In an article appearing in 1963 (Sampson, 1963), the author noted that certain conclusions based on the more sociological studies of status congruence were similar to the ideas embodied in the psychological theories of cognitive consistency, including Festinger's notion of cognitive dissonance (1957), Heider's (1946, 1958a), Newcomb's (1953, 1959), and Cartwright and Harary's (1956) notions of cognitive balance, and the Osgood *et al.* view of congruity (1957). A model of *expectancy congruence* was developed to bring the similarity in these two seemingly different topics into clearer focus. Let us assume that each position along a status hierarchy carries with it a set of expectations pertaining to the behavior of the occupant of that position. If we are dealing with a situation in which one

[1] The several experimental studies of status congruence discussed as part of the research program were conducted under Grant No. MH-06506 of the Public Health Service; Principal Investigator, Edward E. Sampson.

person is placed on two dimensions, then a state of incongruence exists when the expectations for the position along one status hierarchy are in conflict with the expectations for the position on the other status hierarchy. Clearly, the emphasis in this formulation is upon conflicting expectations associated with different positions along several status hierarchies. Unlike the idea of rank inconsistency which maintains that status incongruence exists whenever the pattern of ranks across several status dimensions is variable, the model presented suggests that status incongruence exists *only* when rank positions define conflicting expectations for one's behavior. Thus, according to the model, one might occupy a high rank along status dimension A and a low rank along status dimension B and *not* be status inconsistent if the expectations for one's behavior for the rank position on A were not in conflict with the expectations for one's behavior for the rank position on B. The sociological finding that variable rankings along the dimensions of occupation, education, income produce a status incongruence effect (i.e., tension, stress, and desire to change) suggests that, in our society at least, the behavioral expectations for rank positions along these selected dimensions are positively correlated. We learn to expect a positive correlation between ranks on education, occupation, and income, and thus regard similar rankings on these dimensions as appropriate and without conflict. In theory at least, one could be ranked high on one status dimension and low on another and not experience the status incongruence effect because the behavioral expectations for A and B were not positively correlated.

Relating this interpretation of status congruence to the psychological theories of cognitive consistency becomes possible by assuming that a state of consistency is a learned preference having broad social and individual survival value and that tendencies toward status congruence are of the same sort as tendencies toward cognitive balance, consistency, or consonance. These tendencies were termed "expectancy congruence," and status congruence was viewed as a *special case* of this more general theory. This in brief outlines the major thesis of the 1963 article. It provided the basis for a series of major laboratory studies which sought to examine several facets of the expectancy congruence model.

The introduction of status variables into the relatively controlled setting of the laboratory presented several initial problems to be overcome. The author and his associates were faced with the matter of having either to create status hierarchies in the laboratory, entirely through manipulation, or if possible, to deal with "real" status dimensions. Several months of preliminary pretesting, during which time subjects were given tests and false feedback to "create in them" a status variable, led to a rejection of these experimental manipulations as too artificial and ineffectual. The establishment of an effective degree of status incongruence could not be accomplished through these entirely manipulative means. Reality always seemed to loom larger than the small world we sought to create. These efforts, some of which were admittedly and immodestly highly ingenious, but most of which resulted in failure, led us to look increasingly toward the use of "real" status factors. What were the real kinds of status differentiations that the university-student population of experimental subjects actually make in their day-by-day dealings with each other? First and most clearly, there does exist within the university community a status hierarchy based on year-in-school. Roughly speaking, graduate students have higher ranking along this dimension than do lower division undergraduates; and seniors have higher ranking than freshman, etc. Second, but perhaps less clearly, sex defines a relevant status dimension, even within the theoretically egalitarian halls of academe. Males often are seen to have a higher status, especially vis-a-vis certain kinds of task situations, than are females. Given these two real dimensions, it seemed possible to employ them in a controlled laboratory setting to create various conditions of status congruence and study the effects.

A. POSITIONAL CONSISTENCY VS. EXPECTANCY CONGRUENCE

One of the first derivations to be studied involved what appeared to be a distinction between the typical sociological application of status congruence and the conception presented in the model of expectancy congruence. As we have seen, expectancy congruence emphasizes that one must define status incongruence in terms of a conflict of expectations rather than solely in terms of rank position differences. A person who is highly ranked on one dimension and low on a second is not thereby automatically status incongruent. The determination of whether or not this is the case depends on the nature of the expectations defining behavior appropriate to his rank position on each dimension. If these expectations are inconsistent, then we have an instance of status incongruence or, in our more general terms, of expectancy incongruence. On the other hand, should the expectations not be inconsistent with each other, then the mere descriptive fact of differential ranking on the two dimensions does not produce the status incongruence effects.

Brandon (1965) set up a rather ingenious experimental situation to test these alternative conceptions. Although an article dealing with this study has appeared in print, it will nevertheless be useful to describe her procedures and ideas in some detail since they provided a model which was maintained throughout the other studies in the research program. To test the expectancy congruence model of status congruence against the model which we shall term "positional consistency" (because its emphasis is upon the rank positional pattern across several status dimensions), it was necessary to select status dimensions, some of which were linked together by the expectations of a strong positive correlation and some of which either were not linked through expectation, or for that matter, linked by a significantly weaker positive correlation.

Brandon selected three status dimensions for her study:

(1) *Personal status* defined in terms of the individual's position within the academic community and based upon the person's year in school, age, and sex. It was assumed — and later verified — that a high-to-low status dimension existed with an older male graduate student being high, a male undergraduate (usually a junior), being in the middle, and a young female undergraduate being low.

(2) *Job difficulty and responsibility* defined in terms of the number of items on the experimental task which were under the direct control of the subject. The task involved the subjects in groups of three in a small-scale assembly-line factory production. They were provided a limited set of materials out of which they were to produce certain items which they would then "sell" to the experimenter. They were informed that the experimenter would "buy" good products for $100 each, but "fine" them $150 for each faulty product they tried to "sell." It was made clear to the subjects that the money figures were only a means of score-keeping and that no actual money would be used. Three specific jobs were defined by the experimenter and taken on by the subjects. (a) Cutter: The job of the cutter involved the greatest difficulty and responsibility in that he was to use a model pattern and a large paper cutter to cut out six patterns at one time. Any slip of the paper cutter and six products were ruined out of a limited resource pool. (b) Draftsman: This job, intermediate in both difficulty and responsibility, involved the subject in using carbon paper and a ruler to draw three 3-inch squares at one time. A slip of the ruler and three products from the limited supply could be ruined at once. (c) Folder: This job involved the least amount of difficulty and responsibility. All the person had to do was fold one piece of paper at a time into quarters.

(3) *Representative leader position.* The third status dimension involved administering three cards from the Thematic Apperception Test (TAT) to the subjects and then, presumably on the basis of a rather rapid scoring of their stories, selecting one member of the group of three as group representative, one as understudy, and the third as nothing. All groups had been told that if further work were available — a relevant issue to these subjects, all of whom had been hired through the University Placement Center and were being paid to serve as experimental subjects — depending on how well their group worked together, a liaison person

would be needed linking their group with the experimenter and liaison personnel from other groups. It was emphasized that this person should be one who was especially adept at getting along with others. The group representative was to be this person.

It was assumed by Brandon that dimensions one and two (personal status and job responsibility) and one and three (personal status and representative leadership position) were linked together by a relatively strong expectation of positive correlation; but that dimensions two and three (job responsibility and representative leadership position) were either not linked or only weakly linked by any expectation of positive correlation. Both the assumptions pertaining to the existence of each status dimension as well as these assumptions concerning their interrelationship were validated either on the actual sample studied in the experiment or on a similar student sample. Thus, for example, students in the university do see a status ranking system with the older male graduate at the top and the younger female undergraduate at the bottom. Furthermore, when asked, subjects indicated that the older male graduate *should get* the most responsible position on the job (i.e., cutter) and the young female should get the least responsible position (i.e., folder). Similar positive linkage was established between personal status and representative leadership position; i.e., subjects again felt that it would be appropriate for the graduate male to get the position of group representative. By contrast, the relationship between job status and representative leadership position was seen as being slight.

Given this situation, it was possible to create experimental groups which varied status congruence in ways that permitted a comparison between the expectancy model and the positional model. Five separate treatment conditions were created, with six groups run under each condition.

(i) *Completely Consistent* (CC). The pattern of status positions was entirely consistent across all three dimensions. The older male (rank 1) was the cutter (1) and the group representative (1); the younger male (rank 2) was the draftsman (2) and the understudy (2); the female (rank 3) was the folder (3) and had no position (3) of representative leadership.

(ii) *No Consistency* (NC). The attempt here was to create a maximally incongruent arrangement. The older male (1) was the folder (3) and the understudy (2); the younger male (2) was the cutter (1) and had no leadership position (3); the female (3) was the draftsman (2) and the group representative (1).

(iii) *Expected Consistency* (EC). This condition is one of two in which the dimensions which are linked by expectation are examined. The older male (1) is the cutter (1) but has no position on representative leadership (3); the younger male (2) is the draftsman (2) and the group representative (1); the female (3) is the folder (3) and the understudy (2). It is to be noted that in this condition consistency obtains between personal status and job status, the two dimensions which are expected to go together, with "inconsistency" existing with the third status dimension (representative leadership position), in which there is no strong expectation of linkage. This condition would be inconsistent by the positional theory but is perfectly consistent according to the expectancy congruence model: There are no conflicting expectations because the so-called misrankings between dimensions one and two with three are not based upon any expectation of linkage.

(iv) *Expected Consistency* (EC). This is the second condition in which two status dimensions which are expected to go together are linked (one and three). The older male (1) is the folder (3) and the group representative (1); the younger male (2) is the cutter (1) and the understudy (2); the female (3) is the draftsman (2) and has no representative leadership position (3).

(v) *Unexpected Consistency* (UC). In this condition, the two dimensions which are correlated are those which are not expected to go together (job status and representative leadership position). The older male (1) is the folder (3) and has no leadership position (3); the younger male (2) is the cutter (1) and the group representative (1); the female (3) is the draftsman (2) and the understudy (2).

Although with only these three status dimensions it would have been possible to create other arrangements, it was felt that these five would be adequate for testing the expectancy model. Data consisted of behavioral observations made by the experimenter, using both a notational system and tape recordings of group conversations, and questionnaires completed by the subjects at several time points during the experiment. Perhaps the best manner of summarizing what is a rather long and detailed series of findings is to examine a cumulative ranking of the five experimental conditions on several self-report mood and opinion variables (i.e., semantic differential ratings of the situation, felt tension and hostility, pleasantness of group atmosphere, and concern for quality task performance). Table I presents this data summary.

Using this summary notation, Brandon reported two main clusters of experimental conditions, with the Completely Congruent condition falling between the two. The first cluster was composed of the two Expected Consistency conditions (iii and iv) and involved generally *positive* feelings about the situation. The second cluster, composed of the Unexpected Consistent and the No Consistency conditions (v and ii), involved generally more *negative* feelings about the situation, with the most negative

TABLE I[a]

RANK ORDER OF FIVE EXPERIMENTAL CONDITIONS ON FIVE MEASURES OF AFFECT[b]

Affect measures	Experimental conditions				
	4EC	3EC	CC	UC	NC
Total semantic differential	1	3	2	4	5
How much tension or hostility did you feel?	1	2	3	5	4
How much tension or hostility was there in the group?	1	3	2	4	5
How much did you care whether the items were up to standards?	3	1	4	2	5
How pleasant was the group atmosphere?	1	3	2	4	5
Sum of ranks	7	12	13	19	24

[a] From Brandon (1965, p. 284).
[b] *Note:* Rank 1 = high positive affect; Rank 5 = low positive affect.

condition being condition ii in which no consistency was present. Falling between these two clusters, however, Brandon found the Completely Consistent condition (i). Except for this latter finding, Brandon's results support the expectancy model of status congruence rather than the more simplistic positional model. Her finding that the presence of rank consistency *when it is expected* (as in conditions iii and iv) produces positive feelings within the group, whereas rank consistency that is unexpected (v) does not have this effect, is especially important support for the expectancy model. Quite striking, in fact, in this regard, is a comparison of conditions iii and iv with v. These three conditions have exactly the same over-all amount of rank or positional consistency in that two out of the three dimensions are consistent. They differ, however, in that conditions iii and iv are consistent on those dimensions which are linked by an expectation of consistency; their inconsistency exists on those dimensions in which there is no linkage based on expectancy. Condition v, on the other hand, is consistent only on the unexpected linkages. The finding that the first two conditions produce a pleasant setting and the last condition produces an unpleasant situation thus adds considerably to the expectancy interpretation of status congruence.

Embarrassing, however, both to the positional model and the expectancy model, are the data for the Completely Consistent condition. *All* theories of status congruence predict that this condition should be the most pleasant in that all status dimensions are positively correlated. The failure to uphold this prediction, plus the findings of a study which will be discussed shortly, led to the formulation of a more complex model of status congruence and group functioning.

In a first effort to deal with the unexpected data for the Completely

Consistent condition, the argument was advanced that *distributive justice* was not present in this condition and that its absence produced the less positive over-all ratings for these groups. As Homans (1961) used the concept, distributive justice involves distributing resources in a situation in proportion to an individual's investments in the situation; i.e., giving greater resources or rewards to the person who puts in the greatest amount of effort or has the greatest amount of prior training or is given the greatest amount of responsibility. This notion of justice is akin to the Adams (1965) notion of equity in that equity is said to obtain when the investment-to-outcome ratio for one person in a relationship is equivalent to the investment-to-outcome ratio for another, comparison person in the relationship. Thus, for example, if P has a highly difficult and responsible job (investments or input) and receives higher pay (outcome) than O whose job and pay are relatively lower, a situation of equity or distributive justice may be said to prevail. Inequity or injustice would exist in this situation, on the other hand, if for his investment of high job difficulty and responsibility P received the same amount of pay (or other such outcomes) as O, whose job was of much lesser difficulty and responsibility.

Another criterion, on the other hand, whereby justice may be achieved, involves the concept of *equality* rather than *equity*. Whereas equity emphasizes a Protestant ethic philosophy in which one should get out of life rewards proportional to what is put into it, equality suggests either (or both) that some kinds of outcomes should receive equal distribution to all persons regardless of their investments or that under certain conditions outcomes should receive equal distribution, again disregarding the nature of the investments. For example, the fact of existing as a person (which hardly appears to fit a notion of differential inputs or investments) may be seen as guaranteeing, in theory at least, the equal distribution of some kinds of rewards; i.e., rights to freedom, equality of opportunity and education, etc. Injustice in this case occurs when the distribution of rewarding resources follows the principle of equity rather than equality. The point is that certain kinds of outcomes may not be tied to investments. All men have certain rights merely because they exist (and live within a particular society). A simple equity notion ignores this fact by overemphasizing the input — output model and ethical framework. We shall return again to a more lengthy discussion of this extremely important matter, including a normative view of equity vs. equality. Suffice it to indicate for now that the equality notion of justice proved useful for interpreting the results of Brandon's study.

Whereas the one meaning of justice as equality stresses the fact that some kinds of rewards or outcomes are distributed equally regardless of the individual's investments, the other meaning suggests that certain circumstances (e.g., situational norms or rules of conduct) urge equality rather than equity of distribution. As Brandon stated this latter point, "Justice implies that whenever fairness cannot be defined, the costs and rewards which are to be distributed should be distributed equally among all persons" (1965, p. 286). In relating this notion to her own study, Brandon suggested that within the limited resource structure of her situation, "... since leadership rank is not expected to be linked with any particular job rank, then leadership should be assigned such that persons who have a low rank on the other dimensions will be compensated by being given more leadership" (p. 286).

The Completely Congruent condition in Brandon's study is one in which the older male held all the desirable positions and the young female held none. In terms of the rewards available for distribution within this situation, the male received all of them and the female none of them. In the other two conditions in which expectancy was met (conditions iii and iv), the distribution of persons along the remaining dimension was such that each was the recipient of something rewarding in the situation. The female, for example, rather than having nothing of importance as far as outcomes go, was either made the understudy along the representative leadership dimension or given the job of draftsman. Under these conditions, both justice and expectation are served. In the Completely Congruent condition, however, while expectation is met, justice is ignored. Brandon interpreted the satisfaction results for the Completely Congruent condition in these terms.

At this point in the research program, it was just beginning to appear as though the study of status congruence, which had been understood *solely* in terms of a model of conflicting expectations, would be in need of some modification in order to include this matter of justice.

B. Two Sources of Incongruity: Self and Status

A second study, conducted by Bunker (1966), sought to examine the status congruence effects in more detail and, in addition, to add to the issue of a social or interpersonal incongruity a more directly intrapersonal incongruity. The expectancy model conceptualizes the problem produced by status incongruence in terms of a conflict of expectation both on the *intrapersonal* and on the *interpersonal* level. One facet to status, especially to those status positions which one achieves in occupational roles, pertains to the potential conflict between self and status. A person's job status presents certain requirements, functions, obligations, responsibilities, etc., which may be in and of themselves in conflict with the person's personal, self-characteristics. A person, for example, may be in a position of some authority which he personally finds incompatible with his self-characteristics: He may be a quiet, submissive individual, one who thinks poorly of himself, who nevertheless is put into a position of leadership.

Status congruence is viewed as a dimension which is independent of self-status congruence. In theory at least, one may be in a position of status incongruence, experiencing conflicting expectations for his behavior, but experiencing no conflict between the status positions and his self-characteristics. In practice, however, especially when the expectations linked to the incongruent statuses are mutually exclusive and thereby severely in conflict, one might expect one of the status expectations to define behavior which is also imcompatible with one's self-characteristics. To examine the theoretically independent effects of status congruence and self-status congruence, Bunker set up a laboratory experiment in which he independently manipulated self-characteristics, job-role behavior, and general community status.

The electric train board originated by Ghiselli and used in several studies (Ghiselli and Lodahl, 1958; Smelser, 1961) was selected for the experimental task. In this task, subjects were required to use push buttons and levers controlling the movements of two trains and two sidings, to maneuver one train from Position A on the board to Position B, while moving the second train from its home at Position B to Position A. The task required good coordination of effort among the participants in order to avoid accidents and other kinds of derailings. As Bunker set it up, the task permitted a job-role assignment to be made such that one position was of high responsibility and involved considerable decision making (this role was referred to as "the dispatcher"), while the other position involved considerably less responsibility [this position was called "the freight train operator" (FTO)]

For experimental subjects, Bunker selected persons who would "bring with them" one of the status variables: college-bound high school seniors and actual college students. All subjects were male. It was expected that the college student would be seen as having higher social status than the high school student. It was further assumed that one would normally expect the higher status college student to be given the higher status job-role (dispatcher) and the lower status high school student to be given the FTO job role. This type of assignment would produce a condition of status congruence.

All prospective subjects were given a short form of the California Psychological Inventory (Gough, 1964) which was used to measure the self-characteristics thought to be of relevance to this task situation, dominance-submission. An assignment of a dominant subject to the dominant role of dispatcher and a submissive subject to the submissive role of FTO was assumed to provide a condition of self-status congruence. Reverse assignments, on the other hand, would produce self-status incongruence.

Dyads were composed and scheduled for the experiment in order to meet the required conditions of status congruence-incongruence and self-status congruence-incongruence. The experiment proper consisted therefore of four conditions, with 10 dyads being run in each condition.

Data were analyzed both with regard to task performance and self-report measures of satisfaction, tension, desire to change the structure, etc. Somewhat contrary to the prediction that the best performing condition would be Completely Congruent (both self-status and status-status congruence) and the worst would be the Completely Incongruent, the data presented in Table II suggest support for the over-all *better* performance of both the *most* congruent and the *least* congruent conditions; that is, if anything, the completely Congruent *and* the Completely Incongruent conditions performed better than the conditions in which only one source of incongruence was present (i.e., either self-status or status-status). However, as Table II clearly shows, the Completely Congruent group, as predicted, performed best of all. A check on the success of the experimental manipulations suggested that they had been effective, and therefore the interaction effect results could not be attributed to ineffective experimental treatments. Satisfaction measures provided general support for the original predictions in that the self-status congruent conditions and the status congruent conditions were more satisfied with the over-all situation, including themselves, their team's performance, their partner, etc., than were the parallel incongruent conditions.

The puzzlement, however, involved the unexpectedly good performance of the Completely Incongruent condition. In an effort to explain this finding, Bunker sought to demonstrate that an actual change in social

TABLE II
MEAN NUMBER OF SUCCESSFUL TRIPS[a]

	Self-role	
Status	Congruent	Incongruent
Congruent	29.2	22.2
Incongruent	20.6	24.6

[a]This is a summary table of means abstracted from a larger analysis of variance table. The F values for the interaction effect represented by the means presented above were 3.62 ($p < .10$)

structure had occurred during the course of the experiment. If this change could be demonstrated, then we would have additional support for the theoretical model from which this work has been derived. The theory suggests that incongruities provoke tendencies toward their reduction. One manner of achieving such a reduction is to change an incongruent structure toward greater congruity. In a rather intensive reexamination of the Completely Incongruent condition, Bunker found evidence for a job-role change on the part of the members of the dyads. In this condition, the high school student who was submissive on the CPI had been assigned the dominant role of dispatcher, while the college student who was dominant on the CPI was given the relatively subservient role of FTO. If the FTO, in this condition, however, were shown to have played a more active and directive role while the dispatcher served more as a yes-man, then the initially incongruent social structure would have changed toward congruity. In this case, the change would have produced both a status congruence and a self-status congruence. Behavioral ratings which supported this possibility were found by Bunker's analysis. For example, the high school dispatchers in the Completely Incongruent condition rated themselves as significantly less involved, more submissive, and less autocratic than dispatchers in the other three conditions.

Equally interesting in this regard is the argument *against* any similar structural change occurring in the other two conditions in which only one source of incongruity was present. Quite simply, a change in the social structure in these conditions would only *exchange* one form of incongruence for another. For example, in the condition in which statuses were incongruent (college student − FTO and high school student − dispatcher) but self-statuses were congruent (dispatcher-dominant and FTO-submissive), a change in job-roles would have supplanted status incongruence with self-status incongruence. In essence, one source of strain would have been exchanged for another with what we assume would be the consequence of continued disruption.

Taken as a whole, Bunker's study provides support for the expectancy model of congruence, but more significantly it suggests a balancing of forces which limits the extent to which status incongruence will lead to action to reduce it. Brandon demonstrated that status congruence rather than being so absolutely desirable a state may in itself provide a problem of justice. Bunker has suggested that status incongruence will not inevitably lead to forces toward its reduction; one must also take into consideration other sources of strain within the system.

C. POWER AND INCONGRUITY

Bunker's study suggested how self-status incongruence operated to influence the usually expected status congruence effects. The author was led to a consideration of the variable of *power* as another limiting factor. It seemed plausible, for example, to suggest that the power structure of a situation would be important in influencing the intensity of the status incongruence effect by altering the *salience* of one of the status dimensions under consideration. Up to this point, it had been assumed, and perhaps rightly so given validating data, that each status dimension under consideration enters with equal saliency in any given conflict of expectations. That a person was a graduate student, for example, was thought to be as salient to him and to those with whom he interacted as was his assigned task role of low-status folder. Both these dimensions were thought to enter with equal degree to produce the conflicting expectations of status incongruence. What happens, however, in a situation in which one of the status dimensions under consideration is more salient to the relationship? Does this heightened salience serve to minimize the conflict by focusing attention and concern upon one of the several sets of status-linked expectations? Or, does the salience serve to increase the level of the strain produced by the status incongruent situation?

In order to examine this matter further, Sampson and Bunker (1966) selected reward-and-punishment power as the variable to be employed in increasing the salience of one of the status dimensions investigated. More specifically, they built their manipulation of status congruence upon Brandon's earlier work, using sex, age, and year in school as the defining ingredients for one status dimension (personal status in the university community) and job-role as the second status dimension. As with Brandon's study, Sampson and Bunker assumed that a lower division female student had generally lower status than an upper division male student, and that assigning her to a job-role which had authority and responsibility over upper division male students would produce a condition of status incongruence. Status congruence could be achieved by assigning this responsible job-role to a male student of comparable age and year in school. The heightened salience of one status dimension, job-role, could be accomplished by giving the individual occupant either very high or relatively low reward and punishment power over the others in his or her group. It was assumed that high job-role power, either reward or punishment, would increase the salience of that status dimension by comparison with low job-role power.

Groups were composed of two male subjects hired through the Placement Center for a 2-hour experiment, and either a male (for Congruent conditions) or a female (for Incongruent conditions) accomplice, who pretended to be just another subject sent over for the experimental session. All groups were given as their experimental task a variation of a test of alternative uses. A pile of 50 cards was put before them. In each work period of the assigned series they were to select one or more cards, read the object listed on each card, and offer as many alternate uses for the named objects as they could think of during that work period. They could decide either to continue naming alternate uses for the object indicated on one card or skip on to the next card in the deck. The subjects were told that one of the three group members would be selected to play the role of "evaluator." This role was defined as being responsible for both judging the worth of the team's task performance and using a system of rewards or fines to motivate better performance. The evaluator, selected through a rigged election, was always the accomplice. In this manner it was possible to employ precisely the same array of inductions and threats of fine or promise of rewards to all subjects. Power was varied by allowing the evaluator to have either a great amount or a very small amount of control over the group's monetary supply. Under the high power condition, for example, the evaluator threatened or levied fines in amounts of 20¢ or 40¢ per work period; under conditions of lower power, the fines threatened or taken were in amounts of 4¢ or 8¢ per work period.

Data were collected both from observations made of subject interaction and subject task performance as well as from projective sentence-completion measures and more traditional paper-and-pencil self-report measures. Results of most of the data analyses demonstrate rather strong effects of the power variable in contrast to the very weak or nonexistent status incongruence effects. This is especially so with respect to task performance. Here we find that high power produced a significantly greater increment in performance over time than did low power. Analyses of both projective data and the more structured questionnaire data, indicated that the status congruence of the situation did influence general work attitudes (e.g., feeling the task was more difficult and serious), but that far fewer differences attributable to congruity were found here than in previous work of a similar nature. It appears, therefore, that the effects of status incongruence can be minimized under conditions which maximize the salience of one of the conflicting status positions. In other words, a condition of status incongruence does *not* inevitably motivate efforts toward its reduction.

In one sense, a condition of status incongruence had been viewed as somewhat like a conflict situation with equally valent alternatives. However, it is now clear that all status-linked expectations are not equally important. The conflict between opposing status expectations can be lessened by introducing anything that weights one set of expectations more heavily than the other, opposing set. In the case of the Sampson and Bunker study, the conflict over status incongruence was reduced through the introduction of the power linked to one's job-role.

Clearly, a similar mechanism must operate in the larger social system in which incongruity between one's occupation, education, and income can be reduced by values which make one of these dimensions more salient to the person in any given social situation or which make one dimension of greater over-all importance and value. In either case, one would expect to find few, if any, status congruence effects in that the conflict of expectations is reduced by overvaluing the expectations from one of the several potentially conflictful sources. It seems plausible to suggest that this is what actually occurs in many situations. Situations, roles, and personal values, therefore, can reduce the theoretical conflicts of status incongruence prior to one's actually experiencing such conflicting demands. It is probable that such a process occurred in the Sampson and Bunker study just described.

D.   Status Congruence: Expectancy and Justice

The final major study to be reported here was undertaken in an effort to shed further light on the independent operation of the two issues of conflicting expectations and distributive justice which were raised by Brandon's study.

In his discussion of status congruence and its effects, Homans (1961) suggested that a condition of status congruence was one which produced *both* social certitude (i.e., nonconflicting expectations) and distributive justice. Thus, for example, according to Homans, in a status congruent dyad, all the stimuli which A presents to B are nonconflicting, there are no conflicting demands present, the stress of an ambiguous social relation is minimized and social certitude prevails. Homans argued further, however, that this same type of situation is one in which distributive justice also prevails. Although Homans suggested (through some rather confusing prose) that distributive justice and social certitude are different phenomena, he most clearly regarded both as deriving from a condition of status congruence. If one is dealing with a status congruent group, therefore, he has a group in which both certitude and justice exist.

As we have seen, however, Brandon's results suggested that while a condition of complete status congruence did provide a situation in which the social certitude of nonconflicting expectations was present, rather than justice prevailing, there was a situation of distributive *injustice*. The work of the author and his associates differed from Homans' work in this area in two ways. In the first place, social certitude and distributive justice are viewed as relatively independent consequences of status congruence. Rather than both following so directly from a condition of status congruence, as Homans implied, it is suggested that certitude may exist without justice and vice versa. In the second place, Homans' conception of justice differed from the author's, in that, as was pointed out earlier, justice can refer either to equity *or* equality. Where Homans equated justice with equity, the entire matter was left open to discover conditions (e.g., situational norms and individual personality preference) under which equity *or* equality prevail.

Although the many facets of this matter have not yet been experimentally studied, an attempt was made in this fourth study to create a situation in which the certitude effect of status congruence varied somewhat independently of the justice effect. In a rather interesting and valuable contribution to this research program, Kardush (1968) introduced the variable of social mobility as a means whereby *certitude* and *justice* effects could be separated. For her study, Kardush hired 84 males varying in age and year in school from the University Placement Office. She composed groups of three persons each, with each group containing one graduate student, one upper division student, and one lower division student. This variation was assumed to involve one status dimension. As we have already seen from the previous work, this manner of introducing a status difference into a group is effective. When subjects arrived they were interviewed so that each person's position on this personal status dimension would be recognized. They were then given a rather long training session involving the complex experimental task on which they were to work. The task itself consisted of a war game which this three-person team was to play against a mythical enemy. The game involved a contour map divided into numbered areas and containing a starting position for the team's forces and a goal region which was defined as the enemy headquarters. Each group's aim was to reach that goal and destroy as much of the enemy forces as possible on the route to the goal. The map itself was divided in advance by the experimenter into a multitude of numbered regions. Each region on the map was represented by a 3 × 5 card which indicated the fate of the team's troops should they pass over or through that region. Enemy troops had already been deployed around the map in several regions and thus should the team select certain routes to the goal, they would be met with stiff resistance and losses to their own forces.

All details of the game had been specified in advance by the experimenter, including the nature of the action in each region of the map, the number and location of enemy troops, and the actual rules of the entire game. Thus, all groups were presented with a standardized situation. Each team was given a maximum of six decision periods or a total of 1 hour's actual decision time, whichever came first, in order to win the game. A decision period was well defined in terms of a definite sequence of *jobs* to be carried out by each member of the team. These jobs, varying in difficulty and responsibility, formed the basis of the second status dimension. The jobs, by title, were Captain, Sergeant, and Private.

The map used in the game was placed in a corner of the experimental room and concealed from the subjects by a screen. The only person who could have access to the map, as part of his scouting mission, was the Sergeant. The Captain was provided with a rough sketch of the terrain with only the contours, the starting, and the goal positions represented. The Captain was given the job of chief decision maker; the Sergeant was the scout; and the Private did the clerical work of recording victories and losses as the game progressed. As chief decision maker, the Captain was to decide what areas of the map were to be scouted, how many of a limited supply of forces should be moved out of the starting region and into the map proper, where they should be moved, and when they should be moved. He gave his orders to the Sergeant concerning the part of the map which he wished to have scouted. Based on the Sergeant's reports, the Captain then made his decisions, wrote them down on paper and submitted them to the experimenter. She then pulled out the relevant 3 × 5 cards (i.e., cards dealing with the regions over or through which the Captain had decided his troops should be moved) which defined the outcome of that move. As the scout, the Sergeant was given a 2-minute period for each decision period to go behind the screen and to report as accurately as possible the information that his Captain wanted. Usually, he tried to reproduce that part of the total map that the Captain asked for. The Private's only job was to take the feedback given to the group by the experimenter after the Captain had decided on their move for that decision period and compute losses and gains, to write these down on a form provided, and to hand them to the Captain. He was then the clerk in this venture.

A single decision period or trial therefore involved the following several steps: (1) the Captain's deciding on the regions to be scouted, (2) the Sergeant's doing the scouting and giving the Captain his report, (3) the Captain then deciding on the actual movement of his troops and handing this decision to the experimenter, (4) the experimenter's selecting the relevant 3 × 5 battle cards and giving the outcome information to the Private, and (5) the Private's computing the gains and losses and returning these to the Captain. At this point, one decision period had been concluded and a new one could begin.

A supposedly random selection of persons for jobs was held for the first game. The experimenter drew slips of paper with each subject's name written on it, stating that the first name drawn would be the Captain, the second, the Sergeant, and the third, the Private.

In status congruent groups, the assignment of people to job-roles was based on the expected ordering: the graduate student was made Captain;

the upper division student, Sergeant; and the lower division student, Private. In the status incongruent groups, a reverse ordering was maintained: the lower division student was made Captain, the upper division student was Sergeant, and the graduate student was made Private. Data analyses of nominations made prior to the start of the game confirmed the success of this manipulation.

Social mobility was introduced into this experimental situation by indicating to the subjects that after they completed this first war game they would take a break and then play another, similar war game. For that second game, half of the groups were told that the positions they presently had would be maintained. This is referred to as the *closed* condition. The other half of the groups were told that their jobs might be changed in the second session, as before beginning that second game there would be another "random" drawing of slips of paper fom a hat, and thus jobs were likely to be different.

Psychologically, in terms of the variables of social certitude and distributive justice, just what does this open vs. closed group structure mean? In the first place, open vs. closed essentially indicates that between the present and the future there will (open) or will not be (closed) a change in the social structure. Second, the anticipation of a change away from a presently negative situation is seen to be positively motivating to the subjects, whereas a change away from a presently positive situation is seen to be negatively motivating.

Based primarily on the lead provided by Brandon's work, a working assumption was adopted that a congruent status structure provides the positive value of certitude and the negative value of injustice, while an incongruent status structure provides the positive value of justice and the negative value of incertitude. It was further assumed that whereas injustices intensify over time and become more negative to a group, increased contact serves to decrease the over-all import of the issue of certitude since there is increased knowledge about the other individuals. Anticipating a possible change from injustice to justice therefore is more positively motivating (or the reverse more negatively motivating) than is anticipating a change from incertitude to certitude.

From the preceding assumptions it is possible to predict a statistical interaction effect in the Kardush study. We would expect both the Status Congruent – Open System and the Status Incongruent – Closed System to perform better on the task and have more positive attitudes about the situation than the two other conditions. The groups in both of these former conditions are presumably positively motivated yet for somewhat different reasons. The open structure with its anticipation for change is "motivationally positive" for the Congruent condition because it holds out the possibility that the present state of injustice will be alleviated by the future reassignment of jobs (which are seen to be one of the few tangible rewards available in this limited experimental situation). The closedness of the social structure for the Incongruent condition is "motivationally positive," on the other hand, because it maintains the justice that presently exists. The one negative feature of the Incongruent condition, involving incertitude, is diminished in importance over time simply because, as has been indicated, through interaction people come to know each other well enough to minimize certitude as a key issue.

The Status Congruent — Closed System, on the other hand, is one in which the already negative state of injustice will remain. Further, as already suggested, time presumably will only intensify the negative value of this injustice. By contrast, the Status Incongruent — Open System is one in which the justice which exists and is a positive feature of the situation can be lost through a change in structure. In both of these latter cases, then, one is exchanging a positive for a negative or retaining a negative feature. In the former two conditions, however, one exchanges a negative for a positive or retains a positive feature. Thus, we would expect an interaction effect with the former two conditions (Status Congruent — Open and Status Incongruent — Closed) superior to the latter two conditions (Status Congruent — Closed and Status Incongruent — Open).

Data from the Kardush study came from an analysis of actual team performance on the war game's task and self-report measures of feeling and attitude taken on several questionnaires given to the subjects. Since the results from the study are very numerous and complex, the summarizing of some of the essential findings is intentionally selective.

Several separate indices of team performance could be constructed, varying from, for example, the actual number of decision periods completed within the 1 hour time limit to the amount of losses inflicted on the enemy forces. For each of these performance indices, a two-by-two analysis of variance was conducted. Table III presents a summary of findings obtained for several major performance indices yielding significant main effects for the congruence or incongruence of the status structure. In general, across all indices, the status congruent groups performed more effectively than the status incongruent groups. The difference is most striking for the major performance measure of closeness to the enemy goal. Apparently, at least with regard to performance, the open or closed nature of the system has little effect and predictions of an interaction effect were not borne out.

Analyses of the self-report questionnaire data, on the other hand, did yield results consistent with the prediction of an *interaction* effect, with the Status Congruent — Open System and the Status Incongruent —

Closed System scoring "more affectively positive" than the two other experimental conditions. Table IV summarizes several of the findings obtained with these measures. For example, with regard to preference for a second game, we find a very significant interaction effect, with both the Congruent-Open and the Incongruent-Closed groups showing the greatest desire for a second game. The results with this measure together with those for a measure of present satisfaction (e.g., How much did you like working in this group?), in which an interaction effect of high statistical significance also was found, support the expectation that for the Congruent-Open and the Incongruent-Closed conditions, the problems of certitude or justice, although of immediate importance, are diminished by the anticipation of a second game in which things will become even better.

Other rather strongly significant *interaction* effects involve such measures as:

(1) If you were asked to come back for other experiments, how much would you like to be with the same group of people you are with now? $F_{AB} = 6.81, p < .025$.

(2) How much did you like the war game? $F_{AB} = 6.01, p < .025$.

(3) How much hostility did you personally feel? $F_{AB} = 2.83, p < .10$. In both the Congruent-Open and the Incongruent-Closed, less hostility was reported.

(4) If you felt any hostility, to what extent did you feel free to express it? $F_{AB} = 8.30, p < .01$. Although they felt less hostility in general, those in the Congruent-Open and the Incongruent-Closed groups felt relatively freer to express any they may have had. This appears to indicate the over-all more pleasant atmosphere in these two conditions.

(5) To what extent was it important for you to be liked by the other members of the group? $F_{AB} = 3.53, p < .10$. Both the Congruent-Open and the Incongruent-Closed groups felt this to be relatively important to

TABLE III

MEAN PERFORMANCE SCORES ON SELECTED
MEASURES FOR THE CONGRUENT AND
INCONGRUENT CONDITIONS

Measure	Condition		
	Congruent	Incongruent	p value
Decisions periods completed	4.82	4.80	NS
Closeness to goal	6.07	4.14	< .005
Number of battles planned	5.30	3.57	< 05

TABLE IV
SUMMARY OF SELECTED SELF-REPORT DATA SHOWING
AN INTERACTION EFFECT

	Congruent	Incongruent	
1. Like working in the group:			
Open system	8.00	7.14	$F_{AB} = 7.01^a p < .025$
Closed system	6.76	7.47	
2. Like to have a second game:			
Open system	7.90	6.07	$F_{AB} = 7.46^a p < .01$
Closed system	7.02	7.71	
3. Like the war game:			
Open system	7.62	6.24	$F_{AB} = 6.01^a p < .025$
Closed system	6.86	7.34	
4. Personally felt hostile:			
Open system	2.33	3.67	$F_{AB} = 2.83^a p < .10$
Closed system	3.14	2.95	
5. Freedom to express hostility:			
Open system	6.23	4.85	$F_{AB} = 8.30^a p < .01$
Closed system	3.58	5.30	
6. Summary rating of group atmosphere:			
Open system	6.61	5.99	$F_{AB} = 3.71^a p < .10$
Closed system	5.97	6.10	

^{a}The data reported are based on the representation of two of the three factors involved in the study; F and p values are based on the significance level of the analysis of variance for the interaction effect conducted on the more complex table. High scores indicate a more positive attitude.

them, again suggesting the more positive tone and atmosphere of mutual concern and caring which these conditions evoked. Other measures of the groups' mutual concerns and desires to work together, involving responses to questions about the importance of pulling the various ideas and suggestions together, $F_{AB} = 3.39$, $p < .10$, and the importance of equal sharing in decision making, $F_{AB} = 3.22$, $p < .10$, also showed interaction effects which approached statistical significance.

In response to a question concerning the reaction to the open or the closed system (depending on what had been announced to the group by the experimenter), we find a significant interaction effect, but in this case, unlike the preceding, the Congruent-Open groups reported being most satisfied rather than frustrated by this opportunity, while the Incongruent-Closed group reported feeling most frustrated by its closed system ($F_{AB} = 3.75$, $p < .05$). The significance of the interaction effect, in this case, occurs primarily because of the high degree of satisfaction at being in the open system expressed on the part of the Congruent-Open groups. As a general main effect, being in the open system is more pleasurable than being in the closed system ($F = 19.78, p < .001$). Although this measure does not offer unequivocal support for the predictions, the strikingly high satisfaction score of the Congruent-Open groups suggests that the anticipation of a change (which allows for justice to occur) is seen by them as a good thing. The group in this condition, therefore, which by the standards of social certitude is in fine shape, still is pleased by the chance for there to be a redistribution of jobs for the second game. Although, as argued, such redistribution could produce slight incertitude, on the more positive side, it also allows for justice.

Semantic differential ratings of the situation indicated significant interactions effects on such measures as, "the situation was exciting rather than dull," $F_{AB} = 4.73, p < .05$; and "the situation was conducive to work rather than of the sort making it difficult to work, $F_{AB} = 4.06, p < .05$. As with preceding measures, in both cases, the Congruent-Open and the Incongruent-Closed groups found the situation relatively more exciting and more conducive to work. Several semantic-differential ratings of "self-during-the-game" also led to a series of interesting findings which, as before, indicated an interaction effect. Those in the Congruent-Open and the Incongruent-Closed groups rated themselves as relatively more *assertive* rather than submissive, $F_{AB} = 7.58, p < .01$; more *critical* than easy going, $F_{AB} = 4.50, p < .05$; more *bossy* than friendly, $F_{AB} = 2.84, p < .10$; and more *ambitious* than *unambitious*, $F_{AB} = 4.53, p < .05$. Clearly, they did not view themselves in an entirely positive light; on the other hand, their descriptions suggest a more involved, competitive orientation.

As presented in Table IV, one final, *summary* measure of member's evaluation of the entire situation, an index composed of several of separate items, indicates an interaction effect which approaches significance; the Congruent-Open and the Incongruent-Closed groups both rated the over-all situation in relatively more positive terms, $F_{AB} = 3.71, p < .10$).

Numerous other findings, for example, main effects for Congruence — Incongruence and for Open—Closed, were also obtained. Of course, given the rather substantial number of interaction effects, such main effects become somewhat difficult to interpret. Their number, this difficulty in interpretation, and finally their somewhat lesser relevance to the model we are moving toward, has led to deleting them from this article. The interested reader will find much fuller discussion of this entire project in Kardush (1968).

VI. Toward a Two-Factor Conception of Status Congruence

The work just reviewed on status congruence—especially the studies of Brandon and of Kardush—suggests a two-factor model. In the initial approach to status congruence, as we have seen, it was assumed that the *major issue* involved in status incongruence was one of conflicting expectations. This was a view shared with most workers in this area of study. The research program, then, began by viewing the effects of status congruence *only* in terms of this one-factor theory. As previously discussed in terms of the four studies examined, we learned, first, that there are limitations to the typically observed status congruence effects and, second (and for the author's purposes more important), another factor, namely, justice, appeared to be contributing significantly to the findings. Although the work to date has really not adequately tested the complex functioning of expectancy congruence (the first factor) and justice (the second factor), the research program has suggested that the original model was in need of change. The implication, of course, is that all of the approaches to the study of status congruence are likewise in need of review and probable revision. Whereas the initial understanding of status congruence effects centered entirely on the issue of conflicting expectations, developing ideas urged that the effects of justice be considered as well.

For the sake of simplicity, the essential ingredients of the new model in diagrammatic form is outlined in Fig. 1. As the figure indicates, the nature of the social structure which defines the relationship between two or more persons—its congruence or incongruence in status structure as *one* example—embodies two classes of issue or two types of problems. The first class of problems involves situational (including interpersonal) control or mastery. The second class of problems involves an issue of justice. The manner by which each of these problems is handled, in turn, is seen to influence, directly or indirectly, the outcomes for the persons involved

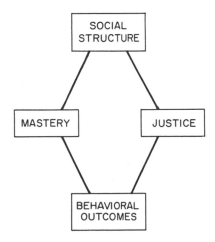

Fig. 1. A two-factor model of interpersonal behavior.

in the relationship. In general, it is suggested that whenever two or more people come together, presumably for some purpose, they face two kinds of interpersonal issues with which they must deal. Furthermore, it is suggested that the success or failure they experience in dealing with these two basic issues will in turn influence the task and affective outcomes of their relationship.

A. FACTOR I: MASTERY

In the last several years the concept of mastery has taken its place as a significant part of several conceptualizations of motivation. Perhaps more than any other recent writer in this area, Robert White (1959) has placed the entire issue of "becoming competent in one's world" into its proper place in psychological theory. The idea here is a rather simple one. The individual is assumed to be motivated importantly by a need to know about himself and about his world so that he may engage in more effective and competent transactions with his physical and social environments.

The concept of mastery and the issues it raises are in themselves somewhat differentiated phenomena. We may speak about three general meanings or types of mastery:

(1) Cognitive mastery or knowledge about the physical and social environment. This form of mastery may exist in the form of specific knowledges about aspects of our environment or in the form of expectations—anticipatory foreknowledges—about the environment and its manner of functioning.

(2) Physical mastery primarily involving skills, talents, or abilities. Mastery of this second sort is centered for the most part on the various abilities which one comes to acquire through transactions with the environment rather than more simply upon the knowledges or expectations which one possesses.

(3) Resource and outcome control or power. In this third sense of mastery, the focus is upon the actual mediation of resources that allows one to exercise power through the manipulation of the outcomes available to others and which are under one's own direct control.

In all three senses of mastery outlined above, the theme of prediction and control is most evident. The man who has specific knowledges about his environment, who has a set of anticipatory foreknowledges or expectations, who possesses specific skills and abilities, or who is able to mediate resources and thus govern outcomes, is able, through any of these channels, to understand his environment and to operate more effectively and competently within it.

The use of general mastery concepts can be examined from either a psychological or a more sociological perspective. From psychology we have ideas within ego psychology and White's notion of competence motivation, work in the area of cognitive development, and various conceptions of consistency theory. From sociology, the emphasis shifts toward the broader social system issues of the coordination and integration of interaction, the role of norms and of a complimentarity of expectation in guiding social relationships and in making a social order possible.

Newcomb's (1953, 1959) development of his A-B-X balance theory is rooted heavily in a context of environmental mastery. Heider (1958a,b), to whom Newcomb's system owes a great deal, was also explicit on this same point. For Heider as for Newcomb, one major function of perception is environmental control. Heider also suggested how the perception of constancies in the environment, which exist, for example, when we "see only the positive traits in a person we like" (1958b, p. 25) – a balanced cognitive structure – allows us to know and predict what will happen. Balanced cognitive structures therefore provide us one means of exercising the power or control function of perception.

Somewhat along these same lines are the several studies of De Soto and his colleagues (De Soto, 1960, 1961; De Soto and Bosley, 1962; Wunderlich, Youniss, and De Soto, 1962); De Soto sought to study the cognitive structure of a social structure, but particularly what he assumed to be the individual's "predilection for the real-world counterpart of halo, for a high correlation between the variables on which people are ranked" (1961, p. 16). His work in general suggests that people do prefer single orderings of social structural phenomena, i.e. one ordering of a set of data rather than multiple orderings. De Soto has used this fact of individual cognitive life to interpret some of Lenski's work on status congruence as well as to indicate more clearly another aspect of the cognitive balance mechanism. In an effort to explain the fact of individual preference for single orderings of social phenomena, De Soto first suggested and then demonstrated that multiple orderings are more difficult and take a longer time to learn: "it is hard to handle two organizations of the same set of the same kind" (1961, p. 20). He then sought to uncover the source of this difficulty. By viewing individual ordering behavior as a function of an ordering schemata, De Soto suggested how such schema contribute to our environmental cognitions and may in fact be an ability with evolutionary survival value. He ceased speculation at that point, however, and urged that more research be conducted. Nevertheless, it seems apparent from his work that individual cognitive functioning, especially with regard to ordering phenomena, has relevance to our own concerns with status congruence as well as with our more general concerns with environmental control and mastery. It is an easy, though an admittedly speculative step, to suggest, as De Soto implied, that multiple orderings can often (though clearly not always) thwart environmental control and mastery as they provide the individual with potentially conflicting or ambiguous arrangements of his environment. The preference for single orderings therefore is a preference for a mode which may facilitate environmental control and mastery.

In a 1963 article (Sampson, 1963), the author tried to indicate how several of the psychological theories of cognitive consistency were applicable to the understanding of status incongruence by outlining several assumptions concerning the relationship between one's expectations about interpersonal encounters, the effective coordination of human interaction, and the outcomes of a successful transaction with the physical and social environment. Some of the thinking in that article and in the several assumptions presented was based upon sociological concepts, especially the ideas of G. H. Mead (1934) and some of the structural-functional theory of Talcott Parsons (Parsons and Shils, 1951).

It is assumed that for any coordination of action between two or more persons, each must have some anticipatory foreknowledge, some expectations, about the behavior of those others with whom he is involved in a particular interactive encounter. The absence of such expectations or the presence of a conflicting set provides a problem which must be resolved before the relationship can proceed. The need to know what to expect from others, the need to predict in advance, within a tolerable margin of error, what is likely or probable in a given interpersonal encounter, allows one, in its fulfillment, to gain some degree of mastery and control over his interpersonal environment. Broadly speaking, the existence of a social order, built as it is upon a complex set of normatively regulated coordinations and integrations among its elements, requires minimally conflicting anticipatory foreknowledge for its own maintenance and development. The norms of a society, its patterns of role relationships and expectations, provide a set of guide lines to action which make order rather than chaos the reigning reality.

In role-theoretical terms (Sarbin, 1954), an interactive encounter with another person involves an initial defining process in which ego seeks to discover alter's role in order to know his reciprocal role and thereby have sufficient knowledge of the situation to act effectively within it. Ego's concerns, then, are to use these societal labels and norms together with his naive faith that people will fulfill the expectations held for them in order to gain mastery of the situation. From the perspective of the larger social system itself, the satisfaction of each person's demands for mastery permits the entire enterprise to progress.

What do we have at this point in the discussion? In the first place, we have an individual who is concerned with learning about his environment, clarifying ambiguities within it, seeking predictibility and control. He seeks to master and become competent in his world. In the second place, this person moves out into interpersonal encounters in which this issue of mastery is most salient to coordinated and effective interaction.

Mastery in the several usages outlined thus become a theme which is central to many human endeavors. It is a theme which characterizes the developing child as well as the adult, the individual as well as the social system: All come to develop and organize strategies for achieving mastery and thus for effective functioning. It is not surprising therefore to expect that this issue of mastery in one or more of its forms would compose one of the major dimensions characterizing all interpersonal relationships, including those produced by the congruity or incongruity of the status structure.

B. Factor II: Justice

Whereas the author's initial theoretical approach to status congruence centered entirely on the general issue of mastery — i.e., in terms of a conflicting expectations interpretation — research strongly suggested that he (and other researchers as well) had missed the other equally important part of the picture. As indicated in earlier discussions, justice is not a single issue but rather a series of issues around a common theme: the form of the distribution or allocation of resources. Although one of the aspects of mastery presented involves resource control, the two underlying issues, mastery and justice, focus on different root purposes which may be served by roughly the same class of behaviors. Thus, one could be said to gain some mastery over the environment through the control of valuable resources (e.g., wealth, industrial or human technical-energy control, and military might). On the other hand, the allocation of these resources can be viewed from the perspective of the justice involved. It appears at this point, then, that it is valuable to maintain the distinction between mastery on the one hand and justice on the other.

Justice as a concept, as we have seen, has at least two essentially different meanings when referring to an interpersonal relationship.

1. Equity

A condition of justice obtains when the person gets what he deserves, when, to be more specific, his outcomes (i.e., what P gets) relative to the outcomes of other (O) are in proportion to their respective investments or inputs. The recent work of Adams (1965) and of Weick (1966) on equity theory builds upon this conception of justice. Using a dissonance theory framework, Adams posited several kinds of response to inequity which can occur; all responses, however, are directed toward reducing the dissonance which inequity is assumed to produce:

(1) One may vary the investments or inputs, as, for example, by

working harder or better or—when the outcomes are relatively low—by working less hard or doing work of poorer quality.

(2) One may try to vary the outcomes, as, for example, by seeking to move upward in some status hierarchy, or gain greater rewards, or for that matter, in theory even move downward or gain lesser rewards.

(3) One may engage in a psychological distortion of either the investments or the outcomes.

(4) One may psychologically or even physically "leave the field."

(5) One may seek to act on O as in trying to influence him to change his investments.

(6) Finally, one may change the object of comparison and cease focusing on one's proportionality relative to *that* O.

These several reactions to inquity are of the same sort as those listed by Newcomb (1953, 1959) and Heider (1958a) as techniques whereby one may reduce cognitive imbalance. They are also comparable to reactions described by Festinger (1957) as approaches to dissonance reduction. These response modes follow, however, from an exchange theory of justice based upon the view that justice in a relationship hinges on equity.

There are several problems within equity theory proper, as Weick so aptly pointed out (1966), but few as keen as that involved in determining just what are inputs or investments in a relationship and what are outcomes. The typical list includes such investment items as education, age, experience, training, skill, sex, ethnic background, social status, effort, and seniority. This list clearly covers a broad range extending from items as ascribed status (sex, age, and ethnic status) to items of achieved status. For outcomes, the listing typically includes, on the positive side, pay, intrinsic job reward, fringe benefits, affection, respect, status symbols, etc., and on the negative side, poor working environment, monotony, insult, rejection, etc. The range of outcomes then extends from job-centered benefits to more directly interhuman concerns of respect, affection, and rejection. As presented, equity theory also suggests that what may at one time be viewed as an investment may at another time be viewed as an outcome and vice versa. This does indeed further complicate the entire picture; it does not appear too helpful merely to suggest that inputs and outcomes are to be understood as P defines them.

Somewhat limiting also to the entire equity notion is its rootedness in job contexts. As Weick suggests in his discussion of the theory:

> ... equity theory may be relevant to a more limited range of problems than investigators have realized .... Equity theory appears to be among the more useful middle-range theories of organizational behavior (1966, p. 439).

There may in fact be a substantially greater usefulness to such an exchange theory concept as equity in a setting which itself works upon an economic model such as an employment situation. In such a setting, both managers and employees readily think in terms of investments and outcomes, and thus justice may be meaningfully defined in the exchange language of equity. Whether or not *this* meaning of justice applies beyond the job context, however, may better be left as an open issue. As will be suggested, the *general issue* of justice applies in all human relationships. The specific reference to justice in terms of equity, however, may only apply to a more limited range of human encounters; i.e., primarily to the job situation or other situations which are normatively defined in terms of an economic or exchange model.

Not all of our interpersonal life is based upon an economic or exchange framework. And this brings us to a consideration of a second, equally valid conception of justice. As suggested earlier, the notion of justice as equity appears to involve a particular social ethic summarized years ago in Weber's discussion (1930) of the Protestant Ethic. One gains rewards through his effortful investments. Resources are then allocated on the basis of one's hard work and other such investments in earning them. A religious ethic may in turn become a social norm governing interpersonal relationships. In this case, an equity norm would appear.

2. *Equality*

Another ethic, perhaps most commonly associated with a political rather than a religious philosophy, argues, on the other hand, that all men should share equally in all resources. Hard work as an investment is not eliminated from this particular viewpoint, but rather the relationship between investment and outcome is less highly correlated under this system than under the equity approach. For equity theory, "it is precisely because of imperfect correlations (between inputs and outcomes) that problems of equity arise" (Weick, 1966, p. 421); for this other perspective, however, this same imperfection of correlations between inputs and outcomes is normatively appropriate. Those who invest a great deal and those who invest little are presumed to share equally in the distribution of resources. Welfare state ideas and recent programs of Medicare and probable future programs involving the negative income tax and guaranteed minimal wage for all people follow much more from a version of this latter ethic which equates justice with equality rather than with equity.

A less extreme view of the equality approach to justice would maintain that *certain resources* in certain contexts are to be allocated on the basis of equality of distribution rather than in proportion to one's investments. In this somewhat more moderate view there are some areas of life in which it is appropriate for outcomes to be proportional to investments, whereas there are other areas in which it is appropriate to distribute outcomes according to an equality principle. Thus, for example, in the area of employment or the marketplace in general, perhaps investments and outcomes are to be linked as equity theory maintains, while in other areas of human endeavor, equality is the basic rule or norm for achieving justice. When we come to think of such outcomes as affection, love, courtesy, and respect, it becomes difficult to maintain that equity rather than equality should be the prevailing principle. The unequal distribution of these types of outcomes as would occur if one followed a principle of equity produces a condition of felt injustice. The obvious relevance of this conceptualization to contemporary matters of civil rights hardly needs further specification.

In this connection, it is interesting to note Bales' (1955) earlier analysis of two sources of strain within any social system. One source of strain follows from the system's efforts to adapt to its outer environment. In following through this process, Bales suggested that adaptation of this sort involves a division of labor which in turn creates a condition of unequal access to, and distribution of, desired resources. In his account of this process, Bales next suggested that this inequality or injustice which results lies at the base of the second or integrative (socioemotional) source of strain for a social system. That is, an interpersonal strain arises out of the *equitable but unequal* distribution of resources according to one's functional position in the division of labor (i.e., one's job). In a not too dissimilar manner, Marx (Bottomore, 1966) argued his class struggle view of history and society. The equitable distribution of economic outcomes by risk investments (rather than by energy expenditure) produced a condition of inequality between the classes and laid the groundwork for their presumed class struggle. In both of these cases, justice in a relationship is defined primarily in terms of equality of resource distribution. As Bales stated most explicitly in his argument, "As solidarity between persons having different advantage in the distribution of property rights increases, strains are created toward a more 'communal,' 'equalitarian' distribution of property rights . . . ." (Bales, 1955, p. 130).

Related to this entire matter of justice as equity and justice as equality is Gouldner's discussion of the norm of reciprocity (1960). In the author's approach, as in Gouldner's and several others, the emphasis has been upon the *justice norms* which govern any given interpersonal encounter. The author views situations as varying in the kinds of social norms governing their functioning, some stressing an equity norm, others, an equality norm. It appears that as Homans or as Adams, for example, conceive of it, equity is a psychological process regulated by an intrapsychic mechanism of dissonance reduction rather than as a social process regulated by norms or rules of procedure. Viewed in an entirely psychological manner, one all too readily comes to overlook the role played by social norms in regulating interpersonal behavior. Thus, equity theory becomes too vastly overgeneralized as a description of all interpersonal encounters rather than a picture of a normatively regulated process in one kind of social engagement.

In his interesting discussion of interpersonal relations, Heider (1958a) added his contribution to the discussion of justice. He examined justice in both equity and equality terms. A recent study, although not deriving directly from Heider's considerations, is nevertheless relevant both to several of the points he made and to the more general issue of equity vs. equality. Morgan and Sawyer (1967) created a bargaining situation involving friends in one condition and nonfriends in the other. Their rationale for involving friends — nonfriends is best captured in the following quote from their article:

> The above analysis[a review of several bargaining ideas and studies]assumes, as nearly all analyses of bargaining have, that you are interested strictly in maximizing your direct return on this particular occasion. Wise persons, however, do not treat every encounter like a used-car transaction where they never expect to see the other again; friends, instead, also take care that the other obtains an outcome sufficiently rewarding so that he is willing to interact again (p. 140).

Several bargaining strategies were possible for their subjects, including an equality choice — sharing monetary rewards equally with one's partner — and an equity choice — giving the lion's share to the person who occupies the stronger position within the bargaining game set up. Their data, interestingly enough, rather strongly pointed to equality over equity as the outcome. And this preference for equality held whether or not one's partner was his friend. The authors concluded:

> Among boys of this age (10 — 12) — friends or not — strict equality, it appears, is a highly attractive outcome. Its attraction is strong enough that a boy with much better possibilities is willing to forego them for the sake of equality, and is expected to do so by the other (p. 145).

Gamson's discussion of coalition formation (Gamson, 1964) provides still another body of material from a bargaining situation in which equity is not the unequivocal preference. We would clearly expect an exchange model of social behavior to operate in the usual bargaining situation. Gamson discussed several theoretical alternatives to understanding what occurs in a "mixed-motive" game situation in which there exist elements of both conflict and coordination. One model was most similar to Adams' equity notion or to Homans' notion of distributive justice and was described as the "minimum resource model." Behavior, according to this model, seems to be governed by a *parity norm:* "This is the belief by the participants that a person ought to get from an agreement an amount proportional to what he brings into it" (p. 88). By contrast, another theoretical model, which Gamson labeled the "anticompetitive theory," emphasized equal sharing presumably in order to maintain harmonious social relationships within the group and keep to a minimum the disruptive consequences of bargaining. The research which Gamson reviewed indicates some support for this anticompetitive theory: Several studies by Vinacke and his colleagues (Vinacke and Stanley, 1962; Uesugi and Vinacke, 1963), emphasized sex differences in preference for parity over greater equality or sharing of resources; males tended more toward parity, females toward harmonious social relationships and hence equality. Other studies also reported this more altruistic strategy. One interpretation which Gamson suggested for this anticompetitive game strategy is quite similar to the quoted statement from the Morgan and Sawyer study (1967): Long-run personal benefits may be gained through establishing good relationships with another; equal sharing may in the long run, therefore, maximize everyone's gains. It is apparent, nevertheless, from an examination of Gamson's review that *both* equity and equality are strategies or normatively regulated preferences within bargaining situations in which one might have supposed an input-outcome equity exchange model would best apply. To define justice, therefore, only in terms of a parity norm or via the concept of equity, appears to be both too limiting and not to encompass adequately several bodies of empirical data.

What is being argued for, therefore, is a consideration of the concept of justice in at least its two major senses. In the one, justice in a relationship exists when resources are allocated on the basis of investments. This the author and others have referred to as *equity.* In the other, justice exists when resources are allocated independently of investments and according to a norm or principle of *equality.* It is suggested, furthermore, that both senses of justice in human relationships can be and have been demonstrated. To speak of equality as a special case of equity overlooks more than it reveals and is a move toward unwise parsimony.

C. MASTERY AND JUSTICE: COORDINATION OR CONFLICT?

The general model with which we have been dealing is based upon the assumption that *both* mastery and justice are issues involved in any social relationship. Whatever is taken to be the outcomes of the relationship, whether it be in terms of task performance or matters of satisfaction and morale, is influenced by the manner in which these two issues are dealt. It is assumed that mastery and justice are not the sort of issues that bring themselves to final resolution in any viable human relationship; they swing cyclically up and down, at one moment approaching a satisfactory level, at the next, responding to changed internal or external conditions of the relationship, moving upward toward a new point of salience and tension. It is likely, in fact, that viable relationships build and develop and experience their moments of pleasure and pain on the basis of shifts and conflicts within these two areas of interpersonal contact.

Nevertheless, when placing calipers around a slice of time and examining the frozen relationship, one is led to the conclusion that successful groups have worked out some reasonable resolution to the mastery and justice issues. It is to the nature of this resolution which we now turn our attention. On the basis of some evidence we are led to conclude that a viable relationship is one which strikes a *balance* between the forces seeking resolution of the issue of mastery and those seeking resolution of the issue of justice. Brandon's study appears to fit this interpretation as do the major results of Kardush's work. In addition, both the theoretical framework and Bales' empirical research reach a rather similar conclusion. In each of these cases, the argument suggests that across time one must balance perfection of mastery with excellence of justice; at any one point in time one gives up some mastery in order to achieve some justice, or gives up some justice in order to achieve some mastery. In Bales' equilibrium model the process extends through time so that at any one point imbalance exists within the system (e.g., more mastery than justice), leading to pressures to move toward the other pole. A relationship then would be characterized by its swings from one extreme to the other—from mastery to justice and back again—finding full equilibrium only when viewed through the lengthy perspective of time.

Another conception, by contrast, argues that one can have both issues resolved simultaneously. For example, Homans maintained that both social certitude and distributive justice derive from the same quality of the social structure, namely, its congruence of status positions. Although a choice between these two contrasting conceptions would best be made on empirical grounds, when it comes to a consideration of status congruence, we cannot help but be struck by the interpretative aid which the balancing conception provides. In that situation, at least, status congruence has consequences for mastery and justice. These are sufficiently inversely related so that the optimal solution is a balancing of pressures toward mastery with pressures toward justice. In a parallel fashion, Bales argued that system solutions to adaptive task problems are roughly inversely related to solutions to integrative socioemotional problems, and that only a balancing solution will be optimal.

To argue precisely as Bales does, we would have to maintain that solutions to the problems of mastery are inversely related to solutions to the problems of justice, or more simply, that with mastery comes injustice. Although this appears to be the case with regard to status structures within groups in *minimal* resource situations, could it be the more general case as well? Clearly, if justice means equality and only that, then mastery and justice are at odds with each other. This is especially the case where mastery is resolved through differential access to resources, i.e., power. The equity notion of justice, however, does not bear the same negative relationship to mastery. In fact, where an equity norm prevails, differential mastery solutions are justified as being legitimate. It is therefore at least plausible to suggest that where justice is achieved through a principle of equality, within a given time period some mastery must be sacrificed for the sake of justice. Where justice, however, is achieved through a principle of equity, then both mastery and justice can be obtained simultaneously. One immediate and rather interesting implication of this formulation suggests that to the extent that task performance is directly affected by the problems of mastery, task performance will suffer *more* (at least for a time) where justice is to be accomplished through equality than where justice can be achieved through equity. On the level of the small laboratory group brought into a psychological experiment, this formulation and implication is probably not readily apparent. On the level of the society, however, it appears somewhat more clearly and is heard in particular in the arguments of those who claim that equality as a means of achieving justice will bring with it a lessening of productive capacity (i.e., of industrial, technological mastery).

An individual, a small group, or for that matter, a society has values which point strongly toward one or the other of these contrasting solutions. For some, taking a larger time perspective, the immediate sacrifice of a little mastery in order to gain equality is seen as appropriate: for them, justice as equality is a prime value. For others, by contrast, mastery is of primary importance and regardless of arguments embedded in terms of short vs. long term losses and gains, their values opt for mastery and its immediate justice-partner, equity. Could time and space permit, the examination of some of the broader social implications of this formulation would perhaps in itself be an interesting and valuable extension of the model.

VII. Summary

We first examined the concept of status congruence as it has appeared in both the social psychological small-group literature and the survey research literature from sociology. Several interpretations of the status congruence effects were presented, with a general agreement emerging in which status incongruence was conceptualized in terms of a model of conflicting expectations. We next looked at several key studies dealing with status congruence that were conducted as part of the author's over-all research program. In progressing through these studies, it was noted how in each case either a limiting condition for the operation of the congruity effect was found, or more importantly for this article, a second, nonexpectancy factor was found to be operating. The language of Homans was used and this second factor was called justice. In examining the two factors that emerged from studies of status congruence, the author was struck by the apparent parallels between the first factor of expectancy (which was part of the initial explanatory model of the status congruence effects) and the second factor of justice and the commonly discussed two factors of interpersonal behavior; e.g., power and affiliation, task and socioemotional. In examining and attempting to explicate this parallel and these two factors, we were led to discuss the outlines of a more general model of status congruence and interpersonal behavior. The general model which was outlined dealt with the two factors of mastery and justice and viewed status congruence as a specific case example of the functioning of these two factors. Some literature was reviewed which lent credence and significance to the discussion of mastery and to the pinpointing of mastery, in its several meanings and usages, as one of the key factors involved in all interpersonal encounters. Next, several discussions of the factor of justice were reviewed suggesting two separable meanings for the concept. The one refers to a notion of justice as equity in which justice prevails when the relative investments and outcomes of a relationship are proportional. The other refers to justice as equality and exists when resources are allocated equally to all participants in a relationship rather than on the basis of investments. After examining some of the theoretical and the empirical literature, the conclusion was reached that whereas the issue of justice characterizes all interhuman encounters, norms specific to certain social contexts determine whether justice will be realized by means of an equity principle or an equality principle. The article concluded with a brief discussion of the modes of operation of justice and mastery, considering whether they should be conceptualized according to an equilibrium or conflict-balancing model, an alternative, coordination model, or a mixed model. The tentative conclusion was offered that the equilibrium model applies when justice functions by an equality norm but that the coordination model applies when justice functions by an equity norm.

REFERENCES

Adams, J. Stacy. Inequity in social exchange. In L. Berkowitz (Ed.), *Advances in experimental social psychology*. Vol. 2. New York: Academic Press, 1965. Pp. 267-299.

Adams, Stuart. Status congruency as a variable in small group performance. *Social Forces*, 1953, 32, 16-22.

Bales, Robert F. Adaptive and integrative changes as sources of strain in social systems. In A. Paul Hare, Edgar F. Borgatta and Robert F. Bales (Eds.), *Small groups*. New York: Knopf, 1955. Pp. 127-131.

Benoit-Smullyan, Emile. Status, status types, and status interrelations. *American Sociological Review*, 1944, 9, 151-161.

Bottomore, T. B. *Classes in modern society*. New York: Pantheon Books, 1966.

Brandon, Arlene C. The relevance of expectation as an underlying factor in status incongruence. *Sociometry*, 1965, 28, 272-288.

Bunker, Gary L. Self-role congruence and status congruence as interacting variables in dyadic behavior. Unpublished doctoral dissertation, University of California, Berkeley, 1966.

Burnstein, Eugene and Zajonc, Robert B. The effect of group success on the reduction of status incongruence in task-oriented groups. *Sociometry*, 1965, 28, 349-362.

Cartwright, Dorwin, and Harary, Frank. Structural balance: A generalization of Heider's theory. *Psychological Review*, 1956, 63, 277-293.

De Soto, Clinton B. Learning a social structure. *Journal of Abnormal and Social Psychology*, 1960, 60, 417-421.

De Soto, Clinton B. The predilection for single orderings. *Journal of Abnormal and Social Psychology*, 1961, 62, 16-23.

De Soto, Clinton B., and Bosley, John J. The cognitive structure of a social structure. *Journal of Abnormal and Social Psychology*, 1962, 64, 303-307.

Edwards, L. P. *The natural history of revolutions*. Chicago: University of Chicago Press, 1927.

Exline, Ralph V., and Ziller, Robert C. Status congruency and interpersonal conflict in decision-making groups. *Human Relations*, 1959, 12, 147-162.

Festinger, Leon. *A theory of cognitive dissonance*. Evanston, Ill.: Row, Peterson, 1957.

Freedman, Ronald, Hawley, Amos H., Landecker, Weiner S., and Miner, Horace M. *Principles of sociology*. New York: Holt, 1952.

Gamson, William A. Experimental studies of coalition formation. In L. Berkowitz (Ed.), *Advances in experimental social psychology*. Vol. 1. New York: Academic Press, 1964. Pp. 81-110.

Ghiselli, E. E., and Lodahl, M. Patterns of managerial and group effectiveness. *Journal of Abnormal and Social Psychology*, 1958, 57, 61-66.

Goffman, I. W. Status consistency and preference for change in power distribution. *American Sociological Review*, 1957, 22, 275-281.

Gough, H. G. *Manual for the California Psychological Inventory* (Rev. ed.) Palo Alto, Calif.: Consulting Psychologist Press, 1964.

Gouldner, Alvin, W. The norm of reciprocity: A preliminary statement. *American Sociological Review*, 1960, 25, 161-178.

Heider, Fritz. Attitudes and cognitive organization. *Journal of Psychology*, 1946, 21, 107-112.

Heider, Fritz. *The psychology of interpersonal relations*. New York: Wiley, 1958. (a)

Heider, Fritz. Perceiving the other person; and consciousness, the perpetual world, and communications with others. In Renato Tagiuri and Luigi Petrullo (Eds.), *Person percep-

tion and interpersonal behavior. Stanford, Calif.: Stanford University Press, 1958. Pp. 22-32. (b)

Homans, George C. *Social behavior: Its elementary forms.* New York: Harcourt, Brace & World, 1961.

Jackson, Elton F. Status inconsistency and symptoms of stress. *American Sociological Review,* 1962, 27, 469-479.

Kardush, Marcelle. Status congruence and social mobility as determinants of small group behavior. Unpublished report. University of California, Berkeley, 1968.

Kasl, Stanislav V. Conceptual and methodological considerations in research on status inconsistency. Institute for Social Research. The University of Michigan, Undated report.

Kasl, Stanislav V., and Sidney Cobb. Effects of parental status incongruence and discrepancy on physical and mental health of adult offspring. *Journal of Personality and Social Psychology,* 1967, 7 (Whole No. 642), pp. 1-15.

Kelley, K. D., and Chambliss, William J. Status consistency and political attitudes. *American Sociological Review,* 1966, 31, 375-382.

Lasswell, Harold D., and Lerner, Daniel. *World revolutionary elites.* Cambridge, Mass.: M.I.T. Press, 1966.

Lazarsfeld, Paul F., Bernard Berelson, and Hazel Gaudet. *The peoples choice.* New York: Columbia University Press, 1948.

Lenski, Gerhard. Status crystallization: A nonvertical dimension of social status. *American Sociological Review,* 1954, 19, 405-413.

Lenski, Gerhard. Social participation and status crystallization. *American Sociological Review,* 1956, 21, 458-464.

Lenski, Gerhard E. Status inconsistency and the vote: A four nations test. *American Sociological Review,* 1967, 32, 298-301.

Mead, George H. *Mind, self, and society.* Chicago: University of Chicago Press, 1934.

Mitchell, Robert E. Methodological notes on a theory on status crystallization. *Public Opinion Quarterly,* 1964, 28, 315-325.

Morgan, William R., and Sawyer, Jack. Bargaining, expectations, and the preference for equality over equity. *Journal of Personality and Social Psychology,* 1967, 6 139-139.

Newcomb, Theodore M. An approach to the study of communicative acts. *Psychological Review,* 1953, 60, 393-404.

Newcomb, Theodore M. Individual systems of orientation. In Sigmund Koch (Ed.), *Psychology: A study of a science.* Vol. 3. New York: McGraw-Hill, 1959.

Osgood, Charles E., Suci, Georrge J., and Tannenbaum, Percy H. *The measurement of meaning.* Urbana, Illinois: University of Illinois Press, 1957.

Parsons, Talcott, and Shils, Edward A. (Eds.) *Toward a general theory of action.* Cambridge, Mass.: Harvard University Press, 1951.

Ringer, B. B., and Sills, D. L. Political extremists in Iran. *Public Opinion Quarterly,* 16 (Winter, 1952-1953), 689-701.

Rush, Gary B. Status consistency and right-wing extremism. *American Sociological Review,* 1967, 32, 86-92.

Sampson, Edward E. Status congruence and cognitive consistency. *Sociometry,* 1963, 26, 146-162.

Sampson, Edward E., and Bunker, Gary L. The effects of power and congruity on small group behavior. Unpublished report. University of California, Berkeley, 1966.

Sarbin, Theodore R. Role theory. In Gardner Lindzey (Ed.) *Handbook of social psychology.* Vol. 1. Cambridge, Mass.: Addison-Wesley, 1954.

Smelser, W. T. Dominance as a factor in achievement and perception in cooperative problem solving interaction. *Journal of Abnormal and Social Psychology,* 1961, 62, 535-542.

Sorokin, P. A. *Society, culture and personality.* New York: Harper, 1947.

Sorokin, P. A. *Social and cultural mobility.* Glencoe, Ill.: Free Press, 1959.

Uesugi, T. K., and Vinacke, W. E. Strategy in a feminine game. *Sociometry,* 1963, **26,** 75-88.

Vinacke, W. E., and Stanley, S. Strategy in a masculine quiz game. Technical Report No. 2, University of Hawaii, 1962.

Weber, Max. *The Protestant ethic and the spirit of capitalism.* Translated by T. Parsons. New York: Scribner, 1930.

Weber, Max. Class, status, party. In Hans H. Gerth and C. Wright Mills (translators and Eds.), *from Max Weber: Essays in sociology.* New York: Oxford University Press 1946.

Weick, Karl E. The concept of equity in the perception of pay. *Administrative Science Quarterly,* 1966, **11,** 414-439.

White, Robert W. Motivation reconsidered: The concept of competence. *Psychological Review,* 1959, **66,** 297-333.

Wunderlich, Richard A., Youniss, James, and De Soto, Clinton B. Schemas and kinship, *Psychological Reports,* 1962, **11,** 495-498.

EXPLORATORY INVESTIGATIONS OF EMPATHY[1]

Ezra Stotland

DEPARTMENT OF PSYCHOLOGY
UNIVERSITY OF WASHINGTON
SEATTLE, WASHINGTON

I. Introduction

For centuries, ordinary people and extraordinary people, like poets and novelists, have known that it is possible for one person to experience an emotion because he perceived that another person is experiencing an

[1]The preparation of this article and all of the initially reported studies were supported by a grant from the National Science Foundation.

271

emotion. John Donne wrote, "I am involved in all mankind." Dostoevski described the youngest of *The Brothers Karamazov* as responding to the feelings of all his friends and relatives. When ordinary people read novels, poetry, or just newspaper accounts of emotional experiences, they will often become emotionally aroused. Of course, not all of the arousal results from sharing emotional experiences with the protagonists in the written account; at least some may simply be the result of the excitement or drama of the story. On the other hand, some of the arousal is doubtless the result of identifying with the protagonists. The same is obviously true with respect to television, theater, movies, etc. Not infrequently, a person will report that he has become emotionally exhausted from watching the performance.

The same phenomenon is evident in everyday life. A mother will share the joys and sorrows of her children; friends often feel each other's emotions; the sight of a sick or injured person will sometimes upset us; and we are sometimes elated at another person's success. Our sharing of the feelings of another does not, however, *necessarily* imply that we will act or even feel impelled to act in a supportive or sympathetic way when we are reacting to another's sorrows. We might avoid the other person because he makes us feel bad; how often have we heard a person say that he does not like someone because he is so sad. Likewise, people sometimes avoid certain books, plays, movies, etc., because they induce sadness, and are attracted to others which exude joy. Nevertheless, on other occasions, a person may be moved by another's pain to help the other, or to help another attain and sustain a happy experience. In short, sharing another's feelings should be distinguished from acting sympathetically and helpfully toward him. The relationship between action and the sharing of feelings is obviously not a simple or direct one.

II. Definition of Empathy

The phenomenon referred to rather loosely in the previous paragraphs as the sharing of another's emotions can be described as "empathy," but a more precise definition is needed. For purposes of the studies to be described in the body of this report, empathy is defined as follows: It is an observer's reacting emotionally because he perceives that another is experiencing or is about to experience an emotion. The present report summarizes some recent work in which empathy has been taken into the experimental laboratory for closer study. Before these studies can be described, however, it is first necessary to explicate this still rather broad and ambiguous definition.

A. EMOTION

First, the term "emotion" needs some elaboration. For purposes of this research we have defined emotions as having two ingredients, physiological and subjective. It is a physiological state of arousal which has subjective affective concomitants. Neither the physiological nor the subjective states separately is sufficient to define an emotion, although it is not always possible to obtain adequate measures of both. There are great differences among people in the particular physiological system in which they are most likely to manifest a state of arousal (Lacey, 1950). Some people evidently exhibit heart-rate increases where others will show, say, blood pressure as manifestations of states of arousal. Thus, even though the same direction of change in each physiological system may be shown by all people who are becoming aroused, they may vary in the magnitude of the change in any given system. With respect to the subjective ingredient, problems of varying awareness of feelings and ability to interpret them, of willingness to report affective states, of different referents of the words used to report them, retrospective distortions of affective experience, all make such reports potentially unreliable. Nevertheless, arousal as a physiological condition is broader than emotion. A state of arousal would not be referred to as an emotion if it can be reasonably assumed not to have an affective subjective correlate. The individual may be aroused to act, to work, to attend, etc., but this general alerting state is not necessarily an emotional state. The person may simply be getting set to act or may be actually acting, and many actions can occur without the person's being in an emotional state. Hopefully, people are quite alert while driving, but not very emotional.

Second, a question arises as to the degree of similarity between the emotions of the observer and the person he is watching. (The latter will be referred to as the "other.") In the above discussion of the literary and real-life occurrences of empathy, it was implied that the emotions of the other person and the observer are at least highly similar. Furthermore, in the research reported below, cases in which there is similarity between the observer's and the other's emotions are the central concern. Yet the given definition includes the possibility of the observer and the model having different and even opposite emotions. For example, a sadistic person might feel joy at another's pain; or a jealous person might become depressed when his rival is elated.

Unfortunately, there is little or no research on the basis of which we can readily develop a measure of the degrees of similarity of emotions. Physiological measurement of emotions has not even provided us with clear distinctions among the various emotions which we subjectively experience. Only some beginnings have been made, such as Ax's (1953) findings of the difference between anger and fear. But even in this work, the differences are quite subtle and do not occur in all of the physiological systems. Furthermore, the distinctions are not so sharp that it is possible to infer, from a given physiological index, what the person's emotional state is.

Nevertheless, differences among the various emotions do exist subjectively, regardless of the difficulty of measurement. This dilemma has been tentatively resolved in the present research, first by making a simple dichotomy of emotional states into positive and negative ones, with little attempt to differentiate among the various types of positive and negative emotions. Examples of positive emotions are joy, pleasure, elation, etc. Examples of negative emotions are depression, anxiety, pain, etc. The second aspect of the resolution of the dilemma is to differentiate between the positive and negative emotions on the basis of subjective reports from the observers or empathizers.

B.   ANTICIPATING FUTURE EVENTS AND PREDICTING ANOTHER'S BEHAVIOR

Another point of elaboration of the definition of empathy concerns cases when the other person's experience has implications for the observer's welfare. These are related in a trivial way to the phenomenon of empathy as described in the opening paragraphs. For example, the observer may have learned that when a certain other person or class of persons feels bad (or good), the observer can reasonably expect some painful (or pleasurable) experience; he then experiences some negative (or positive) emotion. Some examples are as follows. The soldier who receives an injection may wince in pain; the other soldiers lined up behind him to receive their injections become anxious just watching him. The boss comes to work in an obviously good mood; his workers look forward joyfully to an easy day. The other's emotion then acts as a kind of signal of what is about to occur to the observer. Although such cases do in fact fit the definition of empathy, they are of no great moment here. They can easily be explained as instances of an anxious (or joyful) reaction having been conditioned to certain stimuli. Thus, it makes little difference whether these conditioned stimuli are other peoples' emotions or are lights, words, buzzers, or any other physical entity. The other person's feelings are simply a source of information about one's own probable fate. The much more interesting cases of empathy are those in which the other person's fate does not indicate anything about one's own. For example, a prosperous farmer who raises much of his own food might positively empathize with a starving child in Brazil about whom he reads. In fact, from the material point of view, the food shortage in Brazil might prove advantageous to the farmer, since it might lead to a raise in the demand for some of his crops — yet he might strongly empathize with the child — or, at the least, he probably would not feel happy that the child was starving.

We must also recognize the distinction between the term "empathy" as used here and its use as a description of an individual's tendency to make an accurate prediction about the behavior of another person. Let us refer to the latter type of empathy as "predictive empathy." (We prefer not to call this empathy but will use the term since it has become common parlance. It is not empathy because the observer does not have to experience the emotion he perceives in order to make this prediction.) Typically, studies of predictive empathy involve predicting the responses of the other to a personality inventory or an attitude scale. Predictive empathy has had a very troubled history because of all sorts of artifactually determined results and the difficulty of avoiding them. Cronbach (1955) clearly demonstrated that accurate prediction of another's response to an inventory could be the result of (1) sharing the same response bias as the other and assuming that others will respond similarly to one's self; or (2) knowledge of the type of person the other is and inferring accurately how such people tend to respond; of (3) from "actually" being the same type of person as the other and then assuming the other's responses are like one's own. Since Cronbach's critique, much less work has been done using this definition of empathy, partly because the attempts to devise ways of avoiding these artifacts have not been very successful.

Nevertheless, the relationship between predictive empathy and the present conception of empathy needs to be made clear. Empathy as defined here involves the observer perceiving the other's emotions. Whether his perception is accurate or not is a secondary matter, since he will respond to the other's experiences as he perceives them. Thus, if there are cues which suggest a feeling, it is possible to empathize with "nonexistent" emotions both in face-to-face situations and in literature. The factors which influence the perception of another's emotional state therefore are very important in determining the degree of empathy. Thus, some of the artifactual processes which confound the study of predictive empathy are directly relevant to empathy. Empathy might even have an influence on the predictive empathy in the following way. The observer may first positively empathize with another whom he perceives at first to be experiencing a given emotion to a moderate degree. The observer might then come to experience this emotion with greater intensity than he at first perceived in the other. The increased emotional level in the observer may, for example, result from his gradually recalling experiences of his own which are similar to the other person's emotionally arousing experiences. The observer may then generalize from his own newly elevated emotional level to the emotional level he perceives in the other; predictive empathy has been influenced by positive empathy. Such a process might have occurred in an old study by Allport (1924) in which subjects enhanced their ability to judge the emotional state of another "accurately" by imitating his facial expressions. This interactive process between positive and predictive empathy might continue even further, so that the observer might come to empathize with the higher level of emotion he now perceives in the other, thereby intensifying his own experience, and so forth.

C. The Influence Direction

Yet another point of clarification of the present definition of empathy concerns its relationship to the kind of process described so brilliantly by Schachter and Singer (1962). The basic process described by them is that of an individual who experiences proprioceptive sensations induced by epinephrine, but does not have any basis for understanding the nature or significance of these sensations. In such cases, Schachter's research indicates that the individual will feel "sad" or "happy," depending on how he perceives the emotional state of another person, who has ostensibly also received epinephrine. If the other person is happy, the subject will act happy and report that he feels so; likewise for sadness. The basic proposition in Schachter's work is that the individual uses the other person's reactions as a way of evaluating his own already present, rather uninterpreted sensations.

In the case of empathy, however, the process is in the reverse direction. The individual perceives the other's emotional state first, and his own reactions, both subjectively and physiologically, are an outcome of his perception of the other person. There is no necessary inconsistency between the phenomenon described by Schachter and empathy. Both processes undoubtedly occur, but the conditions under which they arise are different. In the Schachter phenomenon, the process starts when the person has a proprioceptive sensation which he cannot understand and turns to the other for understanding; in empathy the process starts with the perception of the other. Of course, both processes might occur in sequence; e.g., the individual may be in a state of arousal because he has observed another in an emotional state, but then turn to the other as a way of subjectively defining his emotional state. The complexities resulting from such sequences had best be examined after more research is done both on empathy and the Schachter phenomenon.

III. Significance of Empathy and Related Research

The next questions are: Of what significance is empathy? Why study it? Where does it fit into the larger scheme of psychological processes?

A. EMPATHY IN PERSONALITY DEVELOPMENT

The concept of empathy has been at least theoretically significant in the area of personality development, most notably in the ideas of Harry Stack Sullivan (1953). Sullivan postulated that the infant almost automatically empathizes with its mother, feeling euphoric when she does, and anxious when she is. How this process occurs is not made clear. Nevertheless, his analysis is not materially altered by making the assumption that the mother's emotional state may be communicated by her touch, her movements, her voice, her facial expressions, etc. This, of course, raises the researchable question of how the infant "knows" that, for example, a harsh tone of voice signifies negative affect, and so forth. In any case, Sullivan maintained that the infant associates the positive and negative states which it empathizes from its mother with certain of its acts, perceptions, etc. Those actions, impulses, perceptions, and the like, which are associated with the mother's negative affect then are incorporated in the "bad-me," i.e., the infant's conception of the bad things about himself. If the child empathizes from its mother extremely severe anxiety, the acts, feelings, and ideas that occur concomitantly with this anxiety are left out of awareness, are pushed off into the "not-me." The individual can become aware of the "not-me" only as a so-called "uncanny" emotion — which cannot be defined in ordinary language. On the other hand, those actions, impulses, etc., which are associated with empathized euphoria from the mother become part of the "good-me," the positive self-concept. The good and bad "me's" then form the basis of the individual's subsequent development. If the child has a large proportion of his experiences associated with the bad-me, he will, for example, not be able to satisfy many of his needs since they are not available to him. On the other hand, the impulses, actions, etc., which are incorporated in the good-me are given freer rein, are more readily expressed and experienced, etc.

One would have imagined that Sullivan's rather provocative ideas would have stimulated much research in empathic processes in infants, but not a great deal has been done. Escalona (1945) showed that children of imprisoned mothers were more upset on the days that the mothers were anxiously waiting to appear before a parole board. Similarly, in a study of nursery school children, Murphy (1937) observed behavior which she interpreted as empathy.

Aronfreed and Paskal (unpublished manuscript) have attempted to show that empathy in children can be treated as a special case of associative learning. In an ingenious experiment they were able to suggest at least one of the conditions under which a child learns to empathize. Six- to eight-year-old girls in all of the experimental conditions, were given a choice of pressing one of two handles on each of a number of training trials. Pressing one of the handles led to a receipt of candy on 60% of the trials and the other handle led to a red light 60% of the time. The child's job was to predict when the light would go on. In the experimental condition, when the light did go on, the female experimenter showed many signs of joy and was very warm and affectionate to the child. In one of the control conditions, the experimenter only showed signs of "joy" when the red light went on, but was not warm to the child. In the other control condition, the experimenter was warm and affectionate to the child whenever the light went on, but did not show any joy. In the test situation for all the children the experimenter was seated some distance from the child, but facing her. The red light was no longer visible to the subject. The child then made a series of choices between the two levers, with the experimenter displaying positive affect whenever the light went on, but not attending to the child at all. Thus, the only potential "reward" for the child's pressing the noncandy lever was the experimenter's "joy." It was found that the children in the experimental condition were more likely than those in the two control conditions to choose to act to give the adult a pleasurable experience. In short, the adult's pleasurable experience had acquired rewarding qualities for the children mainly after it had been associated with the "primary" reward of receiving affection. Aronfreed did not measure empathy itself, but assumed that an empathetic process occurred in the children in the experimental condition and that this process led to the children's altruistic behavior.

In addition to suggesting some of the conditions under which children learn to empathize with positive affect in another, Aronfreed (Paskal and Aronfreed, 1965) also investigated children's learning of empathy to negative feelings. In the first phase of the key experimental condition, the children experienced a painfully loud noise through earphones; three seconds after that the experimenter showed signs of hearing the painful noise in her earphones. In the second phase, the child experienced a painful noise which the experimenter showed the child how to turn off by pressing a lever; in the third, a test phase, another child wearing earphones showed signs of distress. The dependent variable was whether the child then acted to turn off the loud noise that presumably caused the other child's distress. In one control condition the temporal association between the subjects' and the experimenter's pain was random in the first phase. In the second control condition, the noise terminated by the experimenter in phase two was not painful. It was found that the children showed the sympathetic behavior of shutting off noise more in the experimental condition than in any of the others; that is, when the child's own pain had been associated with another's pain and when the experimenter had shown the child what to do to shut off painful noises. Again, Aronfreed did not measure empathy directly, but assumed that it occurred because of the association between the child's own pain and the experimenter's pain in phase one.

B. EMPATHY, ALTRUISM, AND SOCIAL EXCHANGE

Aronfreed's data and the opening discussion indicate that empathy sometimes gives rise to sympathetic or helpful, i.e., altruistic, behavior toward another person. As Berger (1962) pointed out, empathy can lead to avoidance of the other, if the empathy causes one to experience negative affect. Nevertheless, empathy can also provide the basis of altruism. In fact, Aronfreed's research described above might even suggest that all moral or altruistic behavior is based on empathy. Until further research delineates the conditions under which avoidance and altruism occur as a consequence of empathizing with negative affect, however, the most reasonable position to assume is that empathizing provides the basis of at least some altruistic behavior. For example, an individual may act to reduce the anxiety of another because he empathizes with him and therefore can reduce his own anxiety by reducing the other person's. Or an individual may seek to enhance or sustain a state of joy or euphoria in another because he empathizes with such a person.

Berkowitz and his associates (Berkowitz, 1957; Berkowitz and Daniels, 1963, 1964) have shown that an individual will work to help another person, even when the latter cannot even know or find out who is helping him or how much he is being helped. Berkowitz' explanation for this is that the individual has learned an ideal of social responsibility which leads him to act in an altruistic way. If we assume that there can be more than one cause for such altruistic behavior, it is possible to hypothesize that the subjects in Berkowitz' studies empathized with the persons who were dependent upon them. They may have empathized with his anxiety about getting the prize offered for doing well and may have expected that they would empathize with his joy if he received the prize, this expectation leading them to work harder for the other person. Since Berkowitz reports that many of his subjects resented working for their dependent peer, it seems likely that the first of these two processes, the one based on reducing empathized anxiety, is probably the more prevalent one in these studies.

Some recent work by Hoffman and Saltzstein (1967) is relevant to the distinction just made between a learned ideal of social responsibility and empathy. They compared (1) children to whom moral behavior was explained in terms of the possible consequences of their own behavior for other people's welfare, (2) children who were punished for transgressions, and (3) children who were simply told that such and such behavior was wrong. The researchers found the first group, who were told of consequences to others, behaved in a more moral manner. Thus, Aronfreed's argument that empathy is the basis of morality may find some support in Hoffman's study, but the process is not the direct one of empathizing with another person. Instead, what seems to be important is talking about, symbolizing, or cognizing the reactions of other people. It is possible, of course, that parental communications about consequences to others may take on meaning only for those children who have had direct experience of empathizing with another person in the manner suggested by Aronfreed.

The possible relationship between altruistic behavior and empathy raises some questions about the exchange theory approach to human interaction as set forth by Thibaut and Kelley (1959). Their interpretation of social relationships essentially assumes the individual seeks to maximize his own gains and minimize his losses. Social interaction is viewed as a situation in which people adjust their behaviors toward one another until they reach at least some degree of surplus of gains over costs. As Deutsch and Krauss (1965) have pointed out, this exchange theory is "ruthlessly selfish"; the person is assumed to react to another person no differently from the situation in which he reacts to a machine, and in both cases he is supposedly primarily oriented toward getting as much as he can from the interaction.

The possibility of the individual empathizing with his "opponent" introduces a somewhat different flavor to the Thibaut and Kelley social exchange approach. An individual could be playing both on his own side and on the other person's, since he empathizes with him. The possibility of empathizing with the other person can of course be handled by exchange theory by simply incorporating the empathized feelings, good or bad, into the gain-cost "computations" attributed to the people involved. This is essentially what was done above in linking empathy with altruism. Nevertheless, the possibility of empathizing makes the exchange theory formulation much more complex; questions have to be raised at all times about one person's reaction to the other person's gains and losses. Exchange theory as now stated does not provide a way of predicting when a person will or will not empathize and to what degree.

C. EMPATHY IN CLINICAL PRACTICE

Another area of psychological concern with empathy is that of clinical and counseling psychology. The oft-repeated maxim that a therapist should be able to empathize with his patient has been expounded at length by Katz (1963). A therapist who empathizes presumably will be better able to understand his client, to communicate with him better, and to establish better rapport with the patient, who in turn may feel close to a therapist who appears to share his feelings. Katz argues that the therapist cannot simply engage in some instrumental act of empathizing, that he cannot just decide to empathize and then simply do so. Instead the therapist must open himself to the experiences of his client; he must lower the psychological barrier. Then empathizing will result. The first study by the author and Stanley Sherman to be described below has a strong bearing on this issue, although on the face of it, the idea of deliberately empathizing does appear to be a bit far-fetched. Another issue raised by Katz is whether, at the time the therapist is empathizing with his client, the empathized affect is the only affect the therapist can experience or whether he can keep the empathized emotion at some distance from his own feelings. This problem is also dealt with in the first study.

In sum, then, empathy has been postulated to be significant in understanding personality dynamics and development in very young children, in the motivation of altruistic behavior, and in therapeutic situations. Yet, very little experimental work has been devoted to determining the conditions which influence empathy.

D. THE WORK OF BERGER

We have already mentioned Aronfreed's research which is based on secondary reinforcement notions. Another researcher who approached empathy from a learning theory point of view is Berger (1962). He used a classical conditioning paradigm in his experiments. In the experimental condition male college students observed another male college student ostensibly receive an electric shock in his arm a few seconds after a buzzer sounded. The model jerked his arm as if he really were receiving a shock. In the control condition, the model moved his arm, but the subjects were told he wasn't receiving a shock. Berger found that the subjects in the experimental condition showed greater galvanic skin responses (GSRs) to the buzzer than did those in the control conditions. Berger explicitly avoided making the assumption that the observers were empathizing, since it is possible that they experinced positive affect because the model was in pain, i.e., the observers were sadistic or negatively empathizing. However, if the assumption can be made that most subjects experienced negative affect, they can then be described as empathizing, presumably with the fear that the model experienced while awaiting the shock.

In a second experiment, Berger repeated the same two conditions as in the first, but added two more control conditions: In one, the model was supposed to receive a shock but did not move his arm; in the other, there was neither shock nor arm movement. Again, Berger found that when the model moved his arm to a "shock," the subjects did show more GSR to the buzzer than in any of the control conditions. A cognitive basis of GSR is strongly suggested by Berger's report that the subjects in the shock-no-arm-movement control condition frequently did not believe that the model was receiving shock, and this "may account for the relatively low frequency of instigations in this condition" (p. 460).

Berger was thus able to demonstrate a process that could be referred to as empathy, but his analysis is devoid of any explanation of why the observer empathizes. Basically, he has demonstrated only that empathy can be produced in the laboratory. This is mainly of methodological significance, since it is hardly a new fact that people can empathize. The problem is to find the determinants and conditions of such empathy. It might be argued that Berger has begun to solve the problem, but his control conditions appear to demonstrate primarily that if the observers do not believe that the other is experiencing negative affect or is about to experience pain, they will not react emotionally; i.e., there is no emotion with which to empathize.

Berger's results raise an interesting question about one of the control conditions in the Aronfreed and Paskal study (unpublished manuscript). The children in one of Aronfreed's groups simply observed that the adult experienced pleasure, but they did not receive any affection from her. Although Aronfreed did not measure their empathized reactions directly, he did infer that the youngsters in this condition experienced less empathy than those in the experimental condition. This condition is analogous to the experimental condition in Berger's study, since the latter's subjects also simply observed the model having an emotional experience. The question thus arises as to why Aronfreed's control subjects did not experience empathy. This question is especially pertinent because in both studies the pain or pleasure of the model or adult was signaled in advance. A possible explanation is that children may be unable to empathize with the experiences of adults unless these experiences have been associated by contiguity with positive (or negative) experiences of their own, as in Aronfreed's experimental condition, while adults do not require this contiguity. But this explanation raises the further question as to why this difference should exist; perhaps it is a matter of the adults' wide range of experience, so that they are able to understand the feelings of another merely on the basis of their past experiences.

Another possible explanation concerns the nature of the relationship between the observer and the model. In Aronfreed's study, the relationship was adult-child; in Berger's it was a peer relationship, since the model was simply another student. However, since the relationship between the observer and the model was constant in all conditions, there was thus no opportunity to discover if the nature of the relationship had any effect on the results.

IV. Measurement of Emotions in Studies of Empathy

Most of the studies reported below deal with this very problem of the influence of the relationship between the observer and the other on empathy. These studies serve two functions: the primary one being exploratory, and the secondary, theory testing. The most pertinent function is that of exploration. First, the research program sought ways in which empathy could be produced in the laboratory so that its determinants could be studied. Second, the exploration consisted of varying the types of social relationships existing between the observer and the other in order to determine what the effects of these relationships are. Some of the questions that could be asked, then, are as follows: Is there more empathy between peers than between people at different status levels? Is empathy enhanced if the other is dependent in some way on the observer? How much does one empathize with someone who has views opposing one's own on matters not relevant to the emotion involved in the empathy? The questions about the effects of the social relationships are not posed in a random fashion. Since they are related to a theory about social relationships, these questions serve both to give a better understanding of the empathetic processes and to provide support for the theory. Furthermore, since hypotheses about these processes are embedded in a theory about social relationships which has ramifications and empirical implications beyond the phenomenon of empathy, it becomes possible to view empathy as one particular type of process systematically related to many others. Finally, the theory has implications for individual differences in empathy under specified conditions, a problem that we have not touched on this far. The theory will be presented later after the concrete nature of the studies have been described in more detail.

Typically, in these studies a number of subjects, usually five or six, observed another person, usually a pseudo-subject, undergo either a positive or negative experience. The observer's emotional reactions were generally, but not always, measured by using two physiological measures, palmar sweating and vasoconstriction, and by the subjects' ratings of their own feelings. The measure of palmar sweat was used in all of the studies of empathy reported below, but the apparatus for measuring the vasoconstriction was developed after the program of studies was under way. Since the studies are not presented in chronological order here, the reader should not be surprised at the appearance and disappearance of the measure of vasoconstriction from study to study.

A. PALMAR SWEATING MEASURE

The measure of palmar sweating used here was a chemical one introduced to psychology by Mowrer (1953). The subject sat at a table with the following apparatus before him: an envelope containing Kleenex and cotton daubers; a jar containing acetone with ferric chloride in solution; a postal scale with an upright metal piece attached to the back. The top of this upright metal piece was level with the weighing surface of the scale when depressed by 1 pound of pressure. Attached by Scotch Tape to the weighing surface of the scale were one or more sheets of vellum, about 2 inches square. This vellum had been treated in advance by soaking it in a mixture of tannic acid and water so that it was impregnated with tannic acid.

The subject administered the measure himself. He was instructed first to take one of the Kleenexes from the envelope and clean off the pad of whichever finger of his nonpreferred hand he was going to use. The purpose of this was to remove some of the excessive dirt and moisture from the fingers. Next, the subject removed one of the cotton daubers from the envelope, opened the jar of acetone, dipped the dauber into the solution, and smeared some of the fluid on the pad of the finger he had just dried. Holding these fingers in the air, he replaced the cover on the jar. In 20 seconds all the acetone had evaporated, leaving the ferric chloride behind on the pad of the finger. At the end of this 20-second period, the subject pressed his finger down on the scale until his finger rested on the tip of the upright metal piece attached to the scale. Thus, the subject pressed his finger with 1 pound of pressure on the piece of vellum attached to the scale, keeping it there for 3 minutes. During this time, the ferric chloride on the subject's fingers dissolved into any perspiration the subject generated. The perspiration with the ferric chloride was absorbed into the vellum. The ferric chloride combined with the tannic acid in the paper to produce an ink. The darkness of the ink fingerprint was proportional to the amount of perspiration. The pressure was kept at a constant 1 pound for the 3-minute period because the amount of perspiration absorbed by the vellum is also affected by the pressure of the contact. Kuno (1956) reported that the palmar sweat reaction has a very brief latency, but the full impact of the palmar sweating reaction either does not occur until a number of seconds later or cannot be fully measured without the 3-minute period. The darkness of the ink-fingerprint was measured by means of a densitometer. The basic measurement was the difference between the amount of light absorbed by the fingerprint and the amount absorbed by the vellum not touched by the subject's fingers.

This procedure was carried out once just before a critical stimulus and then repeated with the adjoining finger as the stimulus was presented. Ferreira and Winter (1963) found that the amount of sweating is consistent among the fingers of the same hand. The difference between the densities of two fingerprints was computed and this difference was divided by the density of the first, base-line fingerprint. The reason for dividing by the base-line period is that the amount of change of palmar sweat from base-line period to stimulus period appears to be roughly proportional to the amount of base-line sweating. If the darkness of the fingerprint increased from the first to second finger used, the amount of the increase, in standard units, was the person's score. If it did not change, his score was zero. If the fingerprint was lighter in the second administration, a score of zero or no change was also given. The rationale for this procedure is that palmar "drying," reflected in the lighter second print, has no psychological meaning; there is no such psychologically meaningful reaction as "palmar drying." Any change in a lighter direction must therefore reflect either unreliability of measurement or a recovery from a palmar sweat reaction which occurred prior to the second fingerprint measure. In either case, the amount of palmar drying can only reflect error variance for a measure of palmar sweating in response to neutral stimuli and was therefore disregarded.

On the other hand, there are any number of studies which have shown that palmar sweating is indeed a measure of emotional arousal (Mowrer, 1950; Beam, 1955; Gladstone, 1953; Winter, Ferreira, and Ransom, 1963; Davis, 1957). It has been found to reflect a subject's state of anxiety as well as his reaction to pain. As in the case of many physiological measures, its relationship to pleasure is unknown.

B. Vasoconstriction Measure

Vasoconstriction is a very quick reaction consisting of a tightening of the capillaries of the fingers, thus reducing the amount of blood present in the fingers. Vasoconstriction has also been found to reflect emotional arousal (Ackner, 1956; Hovland and Riesen, 1940; Nafe and Wagoner,

1936, 1938; Teichner, 1965; Sturup, Bolton, Williams, and Carmichael, 1935; Marquis and Williams, 1938). Vasoconstriction was measured by means of light plethysmographs placed on the thumb of the nonpreferred hand. The plethysmograph consisted of a small bulb whose light was focused by a lens on the subject's finger. Directly on the opposite side of the finger from the bulb was a photocell which was sensitive to the amount of light penetrating the finger. The amount of light penetrating the finger is inversely proportional to the amount of blood in the finger. Accordingly, the person's pulse in his finger was recorded on an oscillograph connected through an amplifying system to the photocell. With apparatus constructed for this series of research projects, it was possible to record the pulse of six subjects simultaneously. Details of the construction and operation of the apparatus are reported elsewhere (Crawford, Stotland, and Shaver, 1967).

The measure of vasoconstriction was modeled somewhat after the procedures of Davis (1955), and was derived as follows from the oscillographic recording of the pulse. The amplitude of the heartbeat was measured for each heartbeat occurring during a relevant period. The amplitudes of these heartbeats during a specified time period was averaged. The first relevant period was the $2\frac{1}{2}$ seconds prior to the onset of the critical stimulus, i.e., the base-line period. The second relevant period was the $7\frac{1}{2}$ seconds subsequent to the critical stimulus. Following Lacey's (1950) suggestions for the construction of an autonomic lability score, a correlation was computed between the base-line average amplitude and the poststimulus average. This correlation was used in a regression equation to predict poststimulus amplitudes. Each subject's vasoconstriction score was then the algebraic deviation from his predicted score. Thus, this procedure does not entail dividing the poststimulus mean amplitude by the base-line amplitude, and it differs from the procedure used for palmar sweating. The reason that vasoconstriction was handled differently is that it was found that changes in amplitudes are not proportional to the base-line amplitude. This is in contrast to the case of palmar sweating in which such proportionality was found (see above).

Two physiological measures were used rather than one because, according to Lacey (1950) and others, people differ in the degree to which they show states of emotional arousal in any given physiological system such as vasoconstriction, palmar sweating, or heart-rate changes. Thus, any particular measure will not necessarily reflect increased arousal in all of the subjects. In the most ideal of methodological worlds, one would either measure a variety of physiological reactions for each subject, or one would develop some way of predicting in which system a person shows the most change under arousal. Multiple measurement was not possible because several subjects were run simultaneously in each of the experimental sessions, and it would have been impossible to assess a series of different physiological reactions on all the subjects at the same time. The two measures that were used could easily be obtained on several subjects; the palmar sweat measure is simple and self-administering, so that as many as 30 subjects have used it simultaneously in other research (Gladstone, 1953). The size of the groups used in the present study was dictated by the fact that the available oscillograph could read from six subjects maximally. Also, it is possible to take palmar sweat and plethysmograph recordings from the same hand simultaneously, since the plethysmograph is placed on the thumb and the palmar sweat measures are taken from the other fingers.

The second approach to the problem of individual differences in the "preferred" system of physiological reactivity is that of getting some measure of the subjects' "preferred" system in advance of the critical period. The practicalities of research, however, limit the possibility of getting large numbers of subjects to come to the laboratory twice. Furthermore, it is not certain that individual differences in system "preference" are not confounded by general tendencies to react to certain types of stimuli with certain physiological systems. Nevertheless, in the present research program, attempts are being made to circumvent these problems by administering some sort of stimulus early in the experimental session and by measuring reactions to that stimulus. The reactions to that stimulus can be used as a basis for predicting reactions to the critical stimuli. One unsuccessful attempt to follow this procedure is illustrated in the first study reported below. Further attempts are presently being made to resolve the problem. Part of the difficulty seems to be that it may be necessary to present stimuli similar to the critical stimulus, but not so similar as to have artifactual consequences.

C. QUESTIONNAIRE RESPONSES

The third type of measure used in these studies was the subjects' reports of their feelings during the critical parts of the experimental period. These reports were obtained immediately after the emotionally arousing stimulus had ceased being administered to the person with whom the subject might have empathized. The subjects rated their feelings on 7- or 9- point scales. The questions asked differed somewhat from study to study, since it became increasingly apparent through the course of the program that more and more differentiated questions were necessary. In general, separate questions were asked concerning the subjects' feelings of tension or relaxation before, during, and after the person was subjected to the emotional stimulus, and separate questions about the subjects' feeling "good" or "bad" during these periods. In addition, the subjects in each study were asked about their liking for the other person, their perception of his experiences, their feelings about the experiment, etc., in order to get a more complete picture of their reactions.

The questionnaire responses were viewed primarily, but not exclusively, as ways of gaining further clarification of the subjects' physiological reactions. Since it is not possible to differentiate the various emotions on the basis of physiology alone, further differentiations can be made on the basis of these subjective reactions. Thus, if subjects in condition X showed more physiological arousal than those in condition Y, differences between the two conditions with respect to the subjects' subjective ratings were examined. By using this approach it is possible to learn whether the subjective quality of the observer's reactions is positively or negatively correlated with the other's ostensible emotional reaction. The possibility also exists that the affective quality of the observer's reactions may not be readily classified as simply being positive or negative; other subtle emotional reactions may be occurring, such as jealousy, envy, pity, etc. These more subtle states are sometimes reflected in the additional questions that the subjects are asked, as mentioned at the end of the previous paragraph. But a full answer to these questions awaits better physiological differentiation of the emotional states. In some instances, no differences in the subjective reports may be found between conditions which differ in physiological reaction. Our assumption here is that more subtle questioning or probing would have elicited the verbal differences and that empathy may well have occurred. The basis for inferring whether it has occurred or not then becomes broader, e.g., the experimental context and other relevant studies.

Nevertheless, the subjects' reports of their feelings were not given the same status as measures of emotional reactions as were the physiological measures; the subjects may have given socially desirable descriptions of their own feelings. They may have thought it socially desirable to respond that one empathizes. Unless their autonomic nervous systems are involved, it is not wise to assume they really have empathized with the other person. Of course, it is possible that they were showing their emotions in some physiological system not measured in the studies, but it would not be prudent simply to make the assumption that this was occurring.

V. Imagine-Self Study

Both laymen and psychologists commonly assume that empathy

entails an individual's putting himself symbolically or imaginatively in another's place. George Herbert Mead (1934) has called this process "taking the role of the other." In the usual description of this process the implication is that the person does so in order to better predict the other's behavior. In that sense, it is a cognitive process closely akin to predictive empathy as described above. The problem thus is whether taking the role of the other has empathetic emotional consequences as well as predictive value. The first study to be reported is related to this problem. This investigation is also significant for the theory to be presented below about the effects of the relationship between the observer and other on empathizing. One of the assumptions made in applying the theory is that the relationship between observer and other influences the degree to which an individual will place himself in another's position and therefore empathize with him.

A. PROCEDURE

In general, the design of the study (performed by the author and Stanley Sherman) involved inducing three different mental sets in the subjects as they observed another person undergo a painful, neutral, or "pleasurable" experience, i.e., a 3×3 design. The first set was that as they observed the other, they were to imagine how they themselves would feel if they were in the other's position ("imagine-self" condition). The second set was that they were to imagine how the other person felt ("imagine-him" condition). The remaining subjects were asked to watch the other person's physical movements very closely ("watch-him" condition). The general hypotheses were, first, that more empathy would occur in the imagine-him condition than in the watch-him condition; second, that more empathy would occur in the imagine-self condition than in the watch-him condition; third, that more empathy would occur in the imagine-self condition than in the imagine-him condition. Empathy is defined here as a negative emotional reaction in the condition in which the other undergoes pain, and as a positive emotional reaction in the condition in which the other undergoes "pleasure." However, the pleasure aspect of empathy is less salient, since it is difficult to communicate pleasure clearly and definitely in the laboratory.

These hypotheses are based on the assumption that empathy is the result of a cognitive or symbolic process. If the individual imagines himself to be in an emotionally moving situation, he presumably will have the emotion to some degree, although his emotion would be of much less intensity than if he really were in the situation. On the other hand, when he imagines how someone else feels in an emotion-arousing situation, part, but only part, of his imagining process will involve placing himself symbolically in the other's position, since he will project himself in this way to gain a better understanding of the other's experience. Since only part of the process in imagining the other person's experience involves the self, the intensity of the empathized emotion should be less than in the imagine-self set. Now, when a person is instructed just to watch the other closely, he will have little tendency to place himself in the other's position and thereby will not do much empathizing.

This study will be described in detail because it is as yet unpublished research, and because many of the experimental procedures are the same as for some of the subsequently described studies.

The subjects were 128 male undergraduates at the University of Washington who were expected to participate in research as part of their introductory course in psychology. Four, five, or six subjects were run at each session of the experiment. The subjects, plus one paid assistant trained to act like a subject, sat at three tables, two or three to a table, all facing the front of the room. On the tables before each subject were the apparatus for measuring palmar sweating, a plethysmograph, and a questionnaire placed face down. At the front of the room was a table with a chair beside it. On this table was a diathermy machine and a large dial facing the subjects. The diathermy machine was so placed that all the dials and controls, etc., could be seen by the subjects.

The experimenter, Stanley Sherman, first introduced the experiment briefly as a study of the "process of social observation as it occurs in small groups with a minimum of information." He then instructed the subjects to place the plethysmographs on the thumbs of their nonpreferred hands, telling them that it measured their heartbeat and assuring them that it could not shock them. Following this, he instructed them in the use of the palmar sweat measurement apparatus and started the first 3-minute period of measurement on their index fingers. During this period he gave the subjects instructions about a questionnaire asking their opinions of psychological research. The purpose of this administration was to provide a base line for the next period in which palmar sweating was measured. As soon as the 3-minute period was up, a second measure of palmar sweating was begun, using another finger. The subjects then started to fill out the questionnaire. At 10 seconds into the 3-minute period, a blank pistol was fired in the next room in order to get some indication of the reaction to this unexpected stimulus in the two systems used for measuring—vasoconstriction and palmar sweating. These physiological responses were related to the subjects' reactions in the empathy part of the study. In this way, it was hoped to overcome the problem underlined by Lacey (1950) of individual differences in reactive systems. However, the results showed that this technique did not work, possibly because the gunshot was too different from the empathy situation.

In any case, a few seconds after the gun went off, the experimenter said briefly that the noise was from a neighboring experiment. The subjects then went on to fill out the questionnaires. This was used as a more or less neutral task during the second 3-minute period involved in the palmar sweat measurement.

When the 3 minutes were up, the experimenter continued as follows:

> Now since this is an experiment in social observation, there must necessarily be something for you to observe. And what we are going to have you observe is a demonstration by one of you on this diathermy machine. Before anyone entered the room this (afternoon), the laboratory assistant, using a table of random numbers, selected one of the chairs to be the chair of the demonstrator. This position was marked by putting a red "X" in the lower left hand corner of the next page of your questionnaire. So could you all turn to the next page of your questionnaire, and look in the box for the red "X." Now if you received a red "X," that means that you are to be the demonstrator for this session. If you did not receive a red "X," that means that you are not to be the demonstrator for this session. You will simply sit in your seat and observe the actual demonstrator as carefully as you can, trying to remember all of your reactions for purposes of filling out the questionnaire at the end.

The paid assistant (now called the "demonstrator") then raised his hand and was instructed to sit in the chair beside the table at the front of the room, his back to the other subjects. The experimenter then explained the workings of a diathermy machine and indicated that the heat is generated between the two rubber pads lying on the table beside the machine. After turning on the warm-up switch, the experimenter strapped the demonstrator's hand in the rubber pads. (Needless to say, the machine was not in working order, although all the lights and dials worked as if it were.) The subjects were then instructed to start another 3-minute period of palmar sweat measurement.

The experimenter then explained that by turning a knob visible to the subjects the machine could be set to give any one of three levels of intensity of heat with the following explanation:

> Either it is set at the low level of intensity, which results in a sensation of warmth in the hand of the demonstrator that is quite soothing and quite pleasant; or it is set at the intermediate level which results in a sensation of heat in the hand of the demonstrator that is neither pleasurable nor painful; or it is set at a high level of intensity, higher than used by physical therapists, which results in a sensation of pain. However, for a period of 30 seconds, it is neither physiologically nor psychologically damaging. Now whichever level is used for a given session is determined by a random device.

The experimenter then told them that they each had received written instructions concerning the way in which they were to observe the demonstrator. They were told that they would be asked questions afterwards to measure how well they carried out their instructions. By this time, a 3-minute palmar sweat period had elapsed. As soon as the subjects had put their fingers on the scales, again for another palmar sweat reading, they were instructed to read and re-read the instructions which they found on the next page of the questionnaire. The palmar sweat recording was made while they read the instructions to see if the different instructions would lead to any differences in arousal. The immediately preceding recording was taken as a base line for this. No differences were found among the subjects reading the three different instructions. The three different sets of instructions were as follows:

Imagine-Self Condition

In a few moments you will be watching the actual demonstration. While you are doing so, please imagine how you yourself would feel if you were subjected to the diathermy treatment, whether it turns out to be painful, pleasant, or neither. While you are watching him, picture to yourself just how you would feel. (You are to keep clearly in mind that you are to react as if it were *you* who got the red check mark and stepped forward in anticipation. You are to react as if it were you who will have the experience that is pleasant, painful, or neither.) While you are watching him, you are to concentrate on yourself in that experience. You are to concentrate on the way you would feel while receiving the treatment. Your job will be to think about what you reactions would be to the sensations you would receive in your hand. In you mind's eye, you are to visualize how it would feel to you to be the demonstrator in this experiment.

Since the success of the experiment depends on how well you carry out the instructions, please re-read them now.

Imagine-Him Condition

In a few moments you will be watching the actual demonstration. While you are doing so, please imagine how the demonstrator feels as he is subjected to the diathermy treatment, whether it turns out to be painful, pleasant, or neither. While you are watching him, picture to yourself just how he feels. (You are to keep clearly in mind that it is he who got the red check mark and stepped forward in anticipation. It is he who will have the experience that is pleasant, painful, or neither. While you are watching him, forget yourself.) While you are watching him, you are to concentrate on him in that experience. You are to concentrate on the way he feels while receiving the treatment. Your job will be to think about his reaction to the sensations he is receiving in his hand. In your mind's eye, you are to visualize how it feels to him to be the demonstrator in this experiment.

Since the success of the experiment depends on how well you carry out these instructions, please re-read them now.

Watch-Him Condition

In a few moments you will be watching the actual demonstration. While you are doing so, please watch exactly what the demonstrator does. You are to watch all of his body movements that you can see. Your job will be to watch his leg movements, arm movements, foot movements, head movements, hand movements. You are to watch his bearing and posture. You are to notice anything that he does, whatever it is. (While you are watching him, don't try to imagine how you would feel in his place or how he is feeling. Don't think about how he feels or how you would feel. Just watch him very closely.)

Since the success of the experiment depends on how well you carry out these instructions, please re-read them now.

These instructions were randomly distributed among the subjects at any given session, one or two in each condition.

When 3 minutes of studying the instructions had elapsed, another palmar sweat recording was begun. The experimenter then picked up a 3×5 card from a deck lying behind the machine, on which were written either "high," "low," or "neutral." (The experimenter did not know which of these he would pick up, since the deck had been shuffled in advance by an assistant. Thus, experimenter effects were minimized.)

As he picked up the card, the experimenter said, "Now for this session, we will use the (high, low, or neutral) level of treatment, which most people find (painful, pleasurable, neither painful not pleasurable)."

During the next 7 seconds, the experimenter adjusted the knobs controlling the level of heat that was to be administered, the 7 seconds being used to allow time for recovering from any vasoconstrictions which might have occurred as a result of the announcement of the level of heat to be administered. He then turned on the heat, the needle on the diathermy machine dial and the large adjoining dial swinging a distance proportional to the level of heat. When the experimenter turned on the machine for the "high" treatment, the demonstrator jerked back and then squirmed moderately in his seat as if he were receiving a painful stimulus; for the pleasurable treatment he started slightly and then relaxed slowly moving his hands as if "sopping up" the warmth; and for the neutral condition, he hardly gave more than a slight start. The reason for having the demonstrator keep his back to the subjects is that it was judged to be quite impossible for a student assistant to do a convincing job of expressing feelings facially and to do so for some 20 sessions. The model's keeping his back to the subjects was justified by the initial instructions, i.e., that the study concerned social perception "with minimal information." The machine was "kept on" for 30 seconds, and when it was shut off, the demonstrator relaxed appropriately and the experimenter told the subjects to fill out the questionnaires. After completing the palmar sweat recording and the questionnaires, the entire experiment was explained to the subjects. Vasoconstriction measures were made at the point when the heat level was announced and 7 seconds later when the machine was turned on.

B. RESULTS

We now turn to the results of the study. To determine whether the subjects perceived the demonstrator "accurately," the first item on the final questionnaire concerned the subjects' perception of the degree of pain or pleasure the model received. The data indicate clearly that the subjects perceived that the demonstrator experienced more pain in the high than in the neutral condition, and more pleasure in the low condition than in the neutral, although the latter difference is not nearly as great as the former. Furthermore, no differences were found among the conditions in palmar sweating while the subjects were reading their instructions for the three different sets.

The first hypothesis is that the subjects in the imagine-him—pleasure condition would show more positive emotion than those in the imagine-him—neutral or in the watch-him—pleasure conditions and that the subjects in the imagine-him—pain condition would show more negative emotion than those in the imagine-him—neutral or in the watch-him—pain conditions. No significant differences in vasoconstriction were found among the relevant conditions in response to the experimenter's announcement of the heat treatment. As for vasoconstriction when the machine was turned on, subjects in the imagine-him—pleasure condition vasoconstricted more than those in the imagine-him—neutral conditions (Table I). They also showed a nonsignificant trend to vasoconstrict more in the imagine-him—pleasure than the watch-him—pleasure condition. On the other hand, the subjects in the imagine-him—pain condition vasoconstricted more than those in the watch-him—pain or those in the imagine-him—neutral condition. Furthermore, in keeping with expectations, the three watch-him conditions did not show any significant differences, nor was there any difference between the imagine-him—neutral condition and the watch-him—neutral. Although no significant Walker-Lev tests of interactions were found, all of the differences were in the expected direction. Nevertheless, the measure of palmar sweating did not show any significant differences among the relevant conditions nor did the subjects' ratings of their own feelings.

The second major hypothesis is that the subjects would show more negative emotion in the imagine-self—pain condition than in the imagine-self—neutral condition and the watch-him—pain condition. Our reasoning also predicted there would be no differences among the three watch-him conditions. This time, neither vasoconstriction to the announcement nor to turning the machine on showed any significant differences. But palmar sweating tended to support the expectation. Table II shows that the subjects in the imagine-self—pain condition sweated more than those in the

TABLE I

MEAN VASOCONSTRICTION[a] TO TURNING ON THE MACHINE
IMAGINE-SELF STUDY

	Heat treatment		
Induced set	Painful[b]	Neutral[b]	Pleasurable[b]
Imagine-him	A .774 (14)	B −.435 (16)	C .906 (15)
Watch-him	D −.293 (14)	E −.145 (16)	F .201 (15)
Imagine-self	G −.179 (13)	H −.501 (14)	I −.294 (16)

Significant t Tests and Walker-Lev t Tests for Interaction[c]

A vs. B $t = 1.602$ $p < .07$ (one tail)
A vs. D $t = 1.369$ $p < .10$ (one tail)
B vs. C $t = 1.808$ $p < .05$ (one tail)

[a]The higher the score, the more vasoconstriction. Negative scores mean average vasoconstriction below the level predicted from the correlation between base line and post-stimulus pulse volumes.

[b]Number of subjects, indicated in parentheses.

[c]The error term for these tests and all those in subsequently reported ones are based on a pooling of within-cell error terms of all of the conditions. Where both sexes were used, separate poolings were made for each sex.

imagine-self — neutral condition and the people in the watch-him — pain condition. On the other hand, the imagine-self — pleasure condition did not show much palmar sweating. In fact, there was an unpredicted but significant difference between the imagine-self — pain and imagine-self — pleasure conditions. And the interaction of this difference with the corresponding watch-him conditions was also significant. Thus, it appears that the subjects in the imagine-self — pain condition showed more palmar sweating than those in the imagine-self — neutral, imagine-self — pleasure, and watch-him — pain conditions. On the other hand, as expected, the watch-him conditions were not significantly different from one another.

The subjects' self-reports of their feelings just before and just after the machine was turned on tend to be consistent with the palmar sweat data in the imagine-self conditions. The subjects in the imagine-self — pain condition reported the following feelings more than in the imagine-self — neutral condition or in the watch-him — pain condition: tension while anticipating the machine to be turned on; experiencing the study as unpleasant; and feeling nervous after the machine was off. All interactions of these three variables among the imagine-self – pain and imagine-self – neutral conditions and the watch-him – pain and watch-him – neutral conditions were significant. Furthermore, the subjects in the imagine-self – pleasure condition found the study more pleasant than those in the imagine-self – pain condition, while no such difference was found between the corresponding watch-him conditions.

The third major hypothesis is that there would be more empathy in the imagine-self conditions than in the imagine-him conditions. We have already seen that the imagine-him conditions show more empathy with respect to vasoconstriction, while the imagine-self groups exhibit more with respect to palmar sweating. In fact, the amount of palmar sweating in the imagine-self – pain condition was also significantly greater than in the imagine-him – pain condition, the interaction with the corresponding neutral conditions being significant (Table II). The fact that the imagine-him condition generated differences with respect to vasoconstriction as the machine was turned on suggests that these subjects were reacting to the feelings they perceived the model as having at a given moment. In fact, after the machine was turned off, they did not report any affect related to

TABLE II
MEAN PALMAR SWEAT SCORES[a] IN IMAGINE-SELF STUDY

Induced set	Painful	Neutral	Pleasurable
Imagine-him	A	B	C
	.386	.971	.909
Watch-him	D	E	F
	.708	.543	.883
Imagine-self	G	H	I
	1.559	.665	.453

Significant t Tests and Walker-Lev t Tests for Interactions

G vs. H $t = 2.409$ $p < .02$ (one tail)
G vs. D $t = 2.267$ $p < .02$ (one tail)
G vs. A $t = 3.161$ $p < .005$ (one tail)
G vs. I $t = 3.197$ $p < .01$ (two tail)
G vs. H vs. D vs. E Walker-Lev $t = 1.429$ $p < .08$ (one tail)
G vs. H vs. A vs. B Walker-Lev $t = 2.947$ $p < .005$ (one tail)
G vs. I vs. D vs. F Walker-Lev $t = 2.562$ $p < .02$ (two tail)
G vs. I vs. A vs. C Walker-Lev $t = 3.608$ $p < .001$ (two tail)

[a]The higher the score, the more palmar sweating.

the model's level of heat treatment. There were even slight hints in the self-reports that the subjects in the imagine-him—pain condition felt somewhat relieved that the pain was over. On the other hand, the fact that the imagine-self condition generated differences in palmar sweating suggests that the emotional reactions of these subjects were not quite so tied to the experience of the model. Palmar sweating as measured here is a less time-bound measure than is vasoconstriction; it could reflect emotional arousal beginning at any time during the approximately 60 seconds from the time of the announcement to the time when they were filling out the first four questions of the questionnaire. Thus, the reactions of these subjects were less likely to be reflected in vasoconstriction measured at any point in time than were the reactions of those in the imagine-him condition. This interpretation is supported by the fact that the subjects in the imagine-self—pain condition reported that they were experiencing a high level of negative affect both before and after the machine was turned on. In the imagine-him—pain conditions, there was, if anything, some positive affect after the machine was turned off.

The key point is that on none of the physiological measures was there any significant differences among the watch-him—pain, watch-him—neutral, and watch-him—pleasure conditions, while there were differences on the physiological measures in the two imagining conditions. This indicates empathy is related to the set that the person has in viewing the other person. A "superficial" set of just watching him does not lead to empathy.

These results also suggest that any interpersonal process, symbolic or overt, which causes an individual to imagine himself in another's position would lead him to empathize with the other person. One process which may lead a person to develop this set is indicated by a theory about social schemas, or the cognitive structures that people have about the forms of social relationships. While it is a general theory of perception, it can be used to clarify the empathetic process and so will be described in some detail.

VI. Perceived Similarity, Empathy, and Birth Order

A. SOCIAL SCHEMAS AND BIRTH ORDER

The basic assumption of the theory is that an individual in perceiving a social situation attends to certain aspects or dimensions of it, while he tends to ignore other features. The aspects given attention can vary from person to person. In his somewhat similar formulation, Kelly (1955) referred to these attended to aspects as "personal constructs." The difference between personal constructs and dimensions is that the former refer to individuals perceived as such, rather than to the type of social relationship in which the persons are involved. On the other hand, the present notion of dimension refers to the social relationships *per se*, independently of the particular people concerned. For example, two people may be perceived as communicating with one another to a high (or low) degree. The dimension here is communication, and the person can be either high or low on the dimension. Or, one person will be perceived to help another; the dimension is helping, one person being higher on that dimension than the other.

We also assume here that individuals vary in these perceptual dimensions because of their experiences in their families of birth. The child learns to perceive his relationships with others in terms of certain dimensions. This learning is assumed to occur in the following fashion. In each situation or occurrence in which a child perceives himself and others, certain dimensions are more likely to be available for perception. For example, if a child is being physically moved from one place to another by his parents, the dimension of controller-controlled is highly available for perception. The dimension of the degree of similarity between parent and child is less obvious and not likely to be perceived. The child then selectively attends to the more available dimensions, perceiving the situation in terms of one or more of these dimensions. In our example, the child perceives that the parent is controlling his location in the room. Among the available dimensions, the one which the child is most likely to perceive is probably the one which is most related to his need for satisfaction. Being carried around the room may be quite closely tied in with the opportunity to play with certain pieces of furniture.

Typically the child perceives himself and each other person, e.g., his father, in a variety of situations and occasions and perceives him often in terms of the same dimensions. Furthermore, the child will perceive his, say, parents as holding much the same position on these dimensions; e.g., they will most frequently be on the high end on the dimension of power. The child then will learn to conceive that he and these others occupy certain relatively stable positions on these dimensions; parents are *generally* high in power. This learning involves basically the same type of process as in any concept learning situation in which the individual learns first which dimensions to attend to, and then places certain entities at appropriate places on this dimension. If a given entity is placed at a certain position on this dimension in a variety of situations, the individual will come to expect that the entity will be at that position in future occasions as well, and will tend to structure new situations to fit his expectancies.

Furthermore, the child does not necessarily perceive a given social situation in terms of only one dimension. The child who is being carried around the room by his parents may perceive the situations in terms of power and degree of nurturance, too; the parents may bring him closer to or further from the desirable piece of furniture. In addition, on different occasions certain dimensions may be more salient to the child. He may come to conceive of the other people in terms of their positions in several different dimensions; e.g., power, nurturance, and communication. Accordingly, through a complex process of association, the child will come to conceive of a correlation between positions in these various dimensions; e.g., powerful people are nurturant.

The key step in this process is that the child generalizes these conceived correlations to situations outside his immediate family; that is, instead of the conceived correlations which he develops being restricted to his family, he will tend to perceive extrafamilial situations in terms of what he has learned in his family. We have labeled the cognitive structures which are assumed to underly this process of generalized perception social schemas. The assumption that the child will tend to perceive extrafamilial relationships in terms of the social schemas developed within the family is based on the same type of reasoning as that employed by Bruner (1957), who argues that the categorizing process in perception functions to reduce surprise; Heider (1958), who emphasizes the tendency to find stabilities in the environment; and Festinger and his followers, who maintain that the individual seeks cognitive consonance, i.e., avoids the unexpected. Unless the individual encounters many situations which are obviously contradictory to his social schemas, he will be set to perceive situations in accord with his schemas, thus strengthening them through repetition. Further, an adult will tend to perceive situations in line with his schemas derived from early childhood. The more ambiguity in a situation the greater will be the structuring in terms of personal schemas.

One way of indexing the difference in family experience is through a person's birth order. The situations encountered by an only child are obviously going to be different from those encountered by a middle-born child in a large family. It is not possible or necessary to present here an interpretation of the research on birth order to support the present theory (cf. Stotland, unpublished manuscript). The reader is referred to Sampson (1965), however, for a thorough documentation of the fact that birth order does make a substantial difference in an adult's social schemas.

The general hypothesis that emerges from this discussion is that a person's order of birth will tend to determine the situations in which he will empathize. This proposition follows from the assumption, supported in the imagine-self study, that a person's set in perceiving himself and others, such as his set to imagine himself to be in the other's position, will determine how much he empathizes with the other. This set is in part a reflection of the person's social schemas, which in turn are presumably influenced by his order of birth.

B. PERCEIVED SIMILARITY AND BIRTH ORDER

The social schema which is the focus of attention in the next three studies is one which holds that other people who are similar to one's self in one respect are similar to one's self in other ways as well. It will be presented as an example of how schemas operate to determine empathetic relationships. This schema is assumed to be especially characteristic of later borns (LBs). Later borns enter the world in a situation in which there are at least some others, their siblings, who are similar to themselves in a variety of respects, e.g., size, status in the family, duties at home, patterns of activities, and illnesses. The LBs cannot help but perceive that they are more similar in these and other ways to their siblings than to their parents. Furthermore, it becomes quickly apparent through words and fact that the younger child must follow in the footsteps of the older in clothing, school, size, privileges, etc. Thus, the LB has many occasions through which he can learn that those who are similar to him in one dimension probably are similar in others as well. Obviously, these broad statements need some modification. The age gaps between siblings, their sexes, and the ways the parents treat them will all have an influence. Yet, in general, this schema will be learned more by LBs than first borns (FBs) (first borns include oldests and onlies).

The FBs are born into a situation which is quite hierarchical, in which the differences between himself and his parents, in power, status, independence, knowledge, etc., are constantly emphasized. Even if he later acquires a sibling, he will tend to view the sibling in the light of the schemas that he had acquired earlier, i.e., a hierarchically centered one, rather than those based on similarity.

The argument leads to the proposition that LBs will empathize more with someone similar to themselves than with someone different. That is, if they perceive themselves as similar to the other in one respect, they will be set to perceive themselves as similar in other respects as well. These "other respects" may consist of being in an emotionally arousing situation. Thus, they will be set to imagine themselves in another's emotional situation, if the other is already perceived to be similar to them.

C. RESEARCH ON BIRTH ORDER, SIMILARITY, AND EMPATHY

1. Similarity Created by Prior Work Experience

This reasoning receives support from a study by Stotland and Dunn (1962). Male and female undergraduate subjects were gathered in large groups and told that they were to help the psychology department to evaluate the interest value of a number of tasks which had been developed for use in research. The subjects were told that since there were so many different types of tasks, each subject would receive a different and randomly assigned set of tasks. After the subjects completed performing the rather simple paper and pencil tasks, they then read about another subject who had participated in a similar study a year earlier. Some of the subjects read that this person had, by chance, been assigned the same set of tasks they had been given, while others read that he worked on a different set. Then half of all the subjects read that this person had, independently of the study, been found to be quite good at clerical tasks, while the other half read that he was quite poor. The subjects then worked on a clerical task themselves.

Later borns who had read that the other subject had worked on similar tasks the year before performed on the clerical tasks in accord with the model's supposed ability; they did better when he was ostensibly better; and poorer when he was ostensibly poorer. If the model was different from them in tasks he had worked on, they were uninfluenced by his clerical ability level. On the other hand, the FBs were not affected by the experimental manipulations. The initial experimentally induced similarity to the model evidently aroused a schema in the LBs to the effect that they were probably similar in other respects as well, and the resultant set affected their performance level.

2. Work-Induced Similarity, Birth Order, and Empathy

This experimental paradigm was carried into the problem of empathy in a study by Stotland and Dunn (1963). The same technique for inducing similarity was used, except that the model was present. The 132 male and female undergraduate subjects were assembled in groups of 9 – 12 subjects of the same sex and were all given the same tasks as in the above study and on the same pretext. After they had finished, they were informed that one of them selected by chance in the same manner as in the imagine-self study was to come to the front of the room to take a test while the others observed. (The true subjects were assured that they would not take the test.) The perennial paid assistant was selected, but before he took the test, the experimenter asked him to tell the others something about himself, so that the others could know him better. He (or she) then described the tasks on which he had ostensibly just worked. For half the subjects present, these tasks were identical to their own; for the other half, quite different.

The model then took a test of logical thinking which was described as a good predictor of success in a variety of situations and consisted of listening to a series of syllogisms over a set of earphones, and then making a quick judgment of the validity or invalidity of the syllogisms. The watching subjects could not hear the items but could hear the model's answers as he went through the 20 items. The experimenter then reviewed the subjects' answers orally, indicating whether each was right or wrong. For half the sessions, the model did quite well, for the other half quite poorly. The subjects' palmar sweating was measured while they observed the model take the test and then again while learning of the model's level of performance. (Vasoconstriction was not measured in this study, since the study was done before the apparatus was built.)

At the time of the original publication of this study, the statistical technique described above to eliminate "palmar drying" had not yet been invented and the results with respect to palmar sweating were reported as nil. More recently, however, the data have been reanalyzed using the new technique. The new findings are given in Table III. Later-born males showed more palmar sweating when a model who did poorly was similar to themselves than when he was different. The FBs did not show this tendency, and the interactions of the experimental treatments with the birth order groups was significant. Females showed this same trend but to a nonsignificant degree.

The subjects were also asked to rate their feelings while observing the model on four rating scales, which were pooled to provide an index of affect, the lower the number the more positive the feelings (Table IV). Consistent with the hypothesis, both the male and female LBs reported that they felt better when the similar model did well than when he did

TABLE III
PALMAR SWEATING IN ARBITRARY SIMILARITY STUDY

	Males		Females	
Model	Model similar	Model different	Model similar	Model different
	First Borns			
Good	.096	.216	.055	.192
	A	B		
Poor	.032	.587	.357	.256
	Later Borns			
Good	.467	.120	.408	.500
	C	D		
Poor	.893	.331	.612	.144

Significant t Tests and Walker-Lev t Tests

C vs. D $t = 1.448$ $p < .09$ (one tail)
A vs. B vs. C vs. D   Walker-Lev $t = 2.270$ $p < .025$ (one tail)

TABLE IV
SELF-REPORT[a] OF TENSION WHILE OBSERVING MODEL IN
ARBITRARY SIMILARITY STUDY

	Males		Females	
Model	Model similar[b]	Model different[b]	Model similar[b]	Model different[b]
	First Borns			
Good	13.55	12.25	12.29	14.36
	(9)	(12)	(7)	(11)
Poor	13.33	14.50	14.863	15.11
	(6)	(10)	(7)	(9)
	Later Borns			
Good	A	B	E	G
	11.57	13.00	10.38	17.40
	(7)	(4)	(8)	(5)
Poor	C	D	F	H
	15.43	14.67	16.13	13.67
	(7)	(9)	(8)	(6)

Significant t Tests and Walker-Lev t Tests

A vs. C $t = 2.132$ $p < .03$ (one tail)
E vs. F $t = 2.882$ $p < .01$ (one tail)
E vs. G $t = 3.142$ $p < .005$ (one tail)
E vs. G vs. F vs. H Walker-Lev $t = 3.0789$ $p < .005$

[a]Sum of self-ratings of affect; the higher the score, the more negative the affect.
[b]Number of subjects indicated in parentheses.

poorly. For the female LBs the interaction among the four conditions is significant. Thus, in general, these results are consistent with the proposition that LBs will empathize more with someone similar to themselves that will FBs.

However, some of the impact of the study is lost with respect to the female LB subjects. The subjects also rated their own abilities on the logical reasoning task, the female LBs rating themselves as much higher in the similar-good condition than in the similar-poor, as would be expected from the theory. Accordingly, their more positive feelings in the former condition may reflect the fact that they now have a higher estimate of their abilities. Although the male LBs did not show a parallel difference, a question is raised about this study as to how much the resultant feelings were influenced by self-evaluation of abilities. (An interpretation of this study and those reported below in terms of a higher level of arousal in the FBs is not supported by the fact that the two groups show no *over-all* consistent tendency to react differentially physiologically.)

3. Personality Similarity, Birth Order, and Empathy

The hypothesis that perceived similarity to the other determines empathy more among LBs than among FBs was tested again in another study conducted by the author, Kelly Shaver, and Robert Crawford. This study was designed to determine, first, whether a basis of similarity other than prior experience in the same laboratory session could lead to empathy. This other basis of similarity was a set of scores on a personality inventory. Second, this study was designed to refine the dimension of similarity by using three points on this dimension—similar, intermediate, and different—rather than just the extreme positions employed in the two previously described studies. Third, the cause of the model's affective experience was to be completely divorced from any implications for the observer's self-evaluations. Accordingly, in this study, the diathermy treatment was used on the model rather than having him work on a test. The observer's self-evaluation could not obviously and directly be influenced by his imagining himself going through a diathermy treatment. A fourth objective of this study was to have a model undergo a neutral experience as well as the positive and negative experiences. The observers' reactions to positive and to negative affective experiences in the others could thus be compared to their reactions to the neutral experiences. In this way, it could be determined whether the similarity hypothesis applies to positive as well as negative affect.

The basic method of this study was the same as the one used in the first experiment described in Section V, including the diathermy treatments of the model. Again, three heat treatments were used, high (painful), neutral, and low (pleasant), only one of these at each experimental session. Both vasoconstriction and palmar sweating were measured. Both males and females were subjects, though at separate sessions. Instead of giving the subjects any instruction as to which set they were to take in observing the other, the subjects were given a description of their degree of similarity or difference in personality to the other in the following manner: Before the model was selected by a "random" method, the experimenter told the subjects that in order to make the laboratory groups more like real-life groups in which people have some knowledge of one another, he would give them certain information about each other. This information was their degree of similarity or difference from one another as indicated on personality tests which they had taken in their introductory course in psychology some weeks before. The subjects were handed sheets with their own name at the top and with the names of the other subjects listed in three categories—similar to themselves, different from themselves, or intermediate. For one-third of the subjects, at a given session, the model-to-be was listed as simi-

lar, for one-third he was described as different, and for the others was said
to be intermediate. The model was then "chosen" by the same procedure
as in the "set" study, i.e., by having the subjects look under their questionnaires for the check mark. All through this process, the model's name
was repeated several times so that the subjects would notice his degree of
similarity to them. In short, the experimental design had three levels of
similarity and three levels of diathermy machine heat: painful, neutral,
and pleasant. The subjects were 105 males and 91 females.

Let us first examine the results related to empathizing with pain. The
hypothesis that LBs would empathize with someone similar to themselves
who has experienced pain more than with someone different was supported for female subjects but not for the males. The support for the
hypothesis among the females was obtained from the measure of vasoconstriction and from subjective reports but not from the palmar sweat
measure. Table V shows for females of each birth order group the mean
vasoconstriction to the announcement of which heat treatment the model
was to undergo. Among LBs, those in the similar-pain condition exhibited
more vasoconstriction than those in the similar-neutral condition, while
those in the intermediate-pain condition vasoconstricted more than those
in the different-pain conditions. All of these differences are consistent
with the hypothesis. Among the LB subjects who observed the model in
the neutral condition, the mean difference between the similar and differ
ent conditions is significant, but in a *reverse* direction from the difference
in the pain condition. This difference was and remains inexplicable since
it was expected that the three neutral conditions would not differ significantly. In any case, the predicted interaction between the similar-
pain, similar-neutral, different-pain, and different-neutral conditions is
significant.

No differences were found among LB females in vasoconstriction at
the time the machine was turned on, possibly because an insufficient time
was allowed for the subjects to recover from any vasoconstriction to the
announcement. (The time was lengthened in later studies, including the
study with effects of different perceptual sets reported earlier.)

In line with the results on vasoconstriction to the announcement,
female LBs who observed someone similar to themselves undergo pain
reported the following more than those who observed someone different:
tension after the treatment, nervousness after the treatment, unpleasantness of the study itself, perception of the model's distaste of the study,
and perception of the model's hostility to the experimenter. In short, the
LB females felt worse and more annoyed if the model was similar that if
she were different and they assumed more that the model shared their
feelings. If the model went through a neutral condition, no differences in

TABLE V
VASOCONSTRICTION OF FEMALE SUBJECTS TO ANNOUNCEMENT OF
HEAT TREATMENT IN PERSONALITY-SIMILARITY STUDY

Treatment	Model similar[a]	Model intermediate[a]	Model different[a]
	First Borns		
Painful	−.135	.727	−.740
	(4)	(1)	(4)
Neutral	−.392	−.104	−.208
	(4)	(5)	(4)
Pleasurable	.372	.005	−.070
	(5)	(6)	(7)
	Later Borns		
Painful	A	B	C
	.856	.307	−1.041
	(6)	(7)	(7)
Neutral	D	E	F
	−.783	.313	1.357
	(7)	(5)	(6)
Pleasurable	G	H	I
	1.678	−.099	−.892
	(3)	(5)	(5)

Significant t Tests and Walker-Lev t Tests

A vs. D $t = 1.720$ $p < .06$ (one tail)   A vs. C $t = 1.990$ $p < .04$ (one tail)
B vs. C $t = 1.473$ $p < .09$ (one tail)   C vs. F $t = 2.517$ $p < .02$ (two tail)
D vs. F $t = 2.246$ $p < .05$ (two tail)   D vs. G $t = 2.083$ $p < .04$ (one tail)
G vs. I $t = 2.056$ $p < .05$ (one tail)   F vs. I $t = 2.169$ $p < .04$ (two tail)

A vs. D vs. C vs. F   Walker-Lev $t = 2.996$ $p < .005$ (one tail)
B vs. C vs. E vs. F   Walker-Lev $t = 1.729$ $p < .10$ (two tail)
G vs. H vs. D vs. E   Walker-Lev $t = 1.793$ $p < .05$ (one tail)
G vs. I vs. D vs. F   Walker-Lev $t = 2.997$ $p < .005$ (one tail)

[a]Number of subjects indicated in parentheses.

self-reports were obtained, thus raising further questions about the meaning of the high level of vasoconstriction in the different-neutral condition. Another way of checking the hypothesis is to compare the LB females in the similar-pain condition with those in the similar-neutral condition. The former reported feeling more tense while the treatment was on and more nervous when it was over; further, they perceived the model as being more negative to the experimenter. None of these differences was found if the model was intermediate or different from themselves.

All in all, for females, the evidence from vasoconstriction to the announcement of the heat level to be administered and from subjective reports tends to support the hypothesis that the degree to which LBs empathize with pain is determined by the degree of perceived similarity to the model. Among FBs, on the other hand, there were no significant differences in vasoconstriction or palmar sweating between the similar-pain condition and any other condition; nor were there any significant differences on any of the subjective variables reported above. Although none of the Walker-Lev tests for interaction were significant between the FBs and LBs, the consistency of the results bears out the hypothesis that similarity determines empathy more for LBs than for FBs.

We can now turn to the hypothesis concerning pleasure. Let us refer first to female LBs. Again they show no difference in palmar sweating. As is indicated in Table V, however, they do show a higher level of vasoconstriction to the announcement of the heat condition in the similar-pleasure condition than in the similar-neutral condition, the neutral-pleasure condition and the different-pleasure condition. Moreover, the interaction between the similar-pleasure, similar-neutral, different-pleasure, and different-neutral conditions are significant as is the interaction between the similar-pleasure, similar-neutral, intermediate-pleasure, and intermediate-neutral conditions. These differences show that LB females react more when a person similar to themselves is experiencing pleasure than if the person is not similar or is not experiencing pleasure. On the other hand, the FBs showed no significant differences among any of the conditions. All of these differences are consistent with the hypothesis. Again, no significant differences were found in vasoconstriction among LBs when the machine was turned on. And, this time, no significant differences in subjective reports of affect were found.

For male LBs, no differences were found in palmar sweating nor in vasoconstriction to the announcement, but these subjects did vasoconstrict more when the machine was turned on in the similar-pleasure condition than in the intermediate- and different-pleasure conditions, and the interaction was significant among the similar-pleasure, similar-neutral, intermediate-pleasure, and intermediate-neutral conditions. All of these differences are consistent with the hypothesis. As in the case of the females, no differences were found with respect to the subject's self-reports. And the FB males showed no significant differences among conditions.

In summary, then, as predicted, both male and female LBs vasoconstrict more in the similar-pleasure condition, although the males do so when the machine is turned on, the females, when the announcement is made. Moreover, FBs do not show any differences. On the other hand, no differences were found in the palmar sweat reactions. The absence of significant differences in self-ratings of affect to the pleasure conditions may reflect the unwillingness of subjects in our society to admit to experiencing pleasure, especially when it is "given" to the model by a person of the opposite sex for the females and of the same sex for the males. Nevertheless, the possibility also exists that the subjects did not, in fact, share the other's pleasure, but felt negatively, e.g., enviously, about it.

In total, despite the unexplainable absence of differences in palmar sweating, and despite the curious lack of any sign of empathy among male LBs in the pain conditions, this study does provide several indications that the LBs, rather than FBs, empathize more with similar people than with different persons. This is the case even when the similarity and the source of the other person's pleasure were not directly related.

4. Similarity Based on Prior Experience

The process of empathy as formulated here is based on the individual's being able to perceive or imagine the feelings of another person. This perceptual or imaginative process will be enhanced by the individual's having been in a situation similar to the other's. Furthermore, in this case LBs will be more affected by the similarity of their own past and the other's present experiences than will FBs. This will occur because of the LB's generalizations from their own experiences to the other person and because of the LB's generalizations from the other's present experiences to their own.

These ideas were tested in a small follow-up study to the one just described, in which the same diathermy machine procedure was used. The subjects were all males. It was not feasible to give the subjects a full-blown pain experience similar to the model's. Instead, before the empathy part of the experiment began, the subjects were asked either to imagine how they themselves, or to imagine how someone else, would feel if they were subjects in a pain-inducing psychological experiment. (The pain treatment was the only one used in the empathy part of this study.) This was done by having the subjects read the following:

> To avoid any misunderstanding, we can tell you that you, *yourself* will not go through the psychological experiment described below, although someone else might.
>
> Try your best to imagine how you (someone else) would feel if you (he) were the person going through the experiment described below. While you read about it, try to imagine how you (he) would feel.
>
> #### Experiment
>
> This is an experiment which can do no permanent harm to you (him). You (he) place your (his) hands on a flat surface that is attached to some apparatus. At a signal, the experimenter turns the apparatus on, and you (he) feel a sharp pain in your (his) hands. Your (his) pain continues for as long as the apparatus is on. You

(he) feel it in all your (his) fingers and in your (his) palms. The apparatus is kept on for about 45 seconds, your (his) pain becoming sharper during this time. When the apparatus is turned off, your (his) pain subsides immediately.

After completing the reading of this passage, the subjects filled out a brief questionnaire in which they described their feelings while reading the passage. Next, the empathy part of the study was conducted in the same fashion as in the study just described. Two conditions of similarity to the model were used, similar and different.

Unfortunately, the distribution of the birth order groups in this study was lopsided, as can be seen from Table VI, making it difficult to compare the two groups. Nevertheless, there were enough LBs to provide some basis for testing the hypothesis. It was predicted that in the imagine-self—similar model condition, there would be more empathy than in the imagine-him—different condition, with the other two conditions intermediate. This prediction was born out by the level of palmar sweating, as can be seen in Table VI. The imagine-him—similar condition and the imagine-self—different condition manifest palmar sweating at a level intermediate between the two extreme groups. However, no parallel significant differences were found in vasoconstriction, possibly because in this study, the subjects in the imagine-self conditions were reacting more to their memories of their own "previous" experiences rather than to the experiences of

TABLE VI
PALMAR SWEAT IN IMAGINATIVE-SIMILAR PERSONALITY STUDY

Induced set	Model similar	Model different
	First Borns	
Imagine yourself	.000 (1)	.206 (4)
Imagine him	.3212 (4)	.046 (7)
	Later Borns	
	A	
Imagine yourself	.993 (7)	.642 (6)
		B
Imagine him	.619 (10)	.286 (4)

Significant t Test

A vs. B $t = 1.583$ $p < .08$ (one tail)

the other person. This explanation is consistent with the analysis from the imagine-self study reported above. In any case, this follow-up study suggests that it is possible to get LB males to empathize with the pain of a person similar to themselves, but it may be necessary to give them some, even if only symbolic or imaginary, experience similar to the other's experience.

In reviewing the totality of the evidence that LBs empathize more with people similar to themselves than with those different from themselves, it can be concluded that even in the face of the unevenness of the variables there is considerable evidence for this hypothesis. In none of the studies was there any evidence that the degree to which FBs empathize is influenced by perceived similarity. It should not be concluded erroneously that these studies indicate that FBs do not empathize. The theory of social schemas presented above suggests some of the conditions that would lead to empathy among FBs. Studies are now in progress to determine if these suggestions are valid.

5. Interaction, Empathy, and Birth Order

The social schema studied so far has been that of perceived similarity leading to more perceived similarity. Later borns may also develop social schemas of give-and-take interaction being associated with similarity. Later borns do much giving and taking with others who are similar to themselves in many respects, i.e., their siblings. They exchange clothes, ideas, blows, help, etc., over a long period of time; thus, there is ample reason for them to develop an interaction-similarity schema. On the other hand, FBs do not have as much opportunity to interact with equals as do LBs. Oldest children are often treated by parents and others as parental surrogates rather than as an equal part of the group of children. Evidence for the existence of such an interaction-similarity schema comes from a study by Stotland and Cottrell (1962). Groups of six male college students were formed to carry out a word-assembly task so arranged that one of the six would be the center of the interaction, the other subjects sending and receiving words only with this subject. These words had no communicative value, since they were simply part of the materials used in the task. Next, one of the subjects (the model) publicly took a test of listening through earphones to a passage in Hindi and counting the number of times that a certain phoneme occurred. For half the groups, this model was the "high"-interaction subject; for the other half, he was not. In half of each of these two groups, the model ostensibly did very well at the task. In the other half, he did quite poorly. Then all of the rest of the subjects took the same phoneme counting task, predicting their own levels of performance and evaluating them afterward.

In the high-interaction condition, the LBs predicted better performance and actually performed better when the model had done well than
when he had done poorly. In the no-interaction condition, there was not
only no tendency for the LBs to match the model's performance but also
there was even a tendency to react in a manner opposite to the model. The
FBs showed almost no differences among the conditions. In short, the
LBs tended to make themselves similar to others with whom they had interacted, even when they had hardly communicated with these others.

These findings lead to the hypothesis that when interacting with another, LBs rather than FBs are more likely to empathize with the other.
This hypothesis was tested in a study by Stotland and Walsh (1963) using
both male and female subjects, always in like-sexed groups. The first part
of the experiment was the same work-exchange task used in the Stotland
and Cottrell (1962) study. This time, however, only a high-interaction
model condition was employed. Instead of having the model take a test of
his ability to recall phonemes, this time he took the same test of logical
reasoning ability used in Stotland and Dunn (1963). Half the time the
model ostensibly did poorly; half the time he did well.

At the time the study was published, the vasoconstriction apparatus
was nonexistent and the presently employed analysis of palmar sweating
was not used. However, since that time, the palmar sweat data were reanalyzed using the new procedure, with the results reported in Table VII.
Among males, the LBs sweated more when the model did poorly than
when he did well, and male LBs sweated more when the model did poorly
more than did FBs. The condition by birth order interaction was
significant for males. As in the Dunn study, the females showed the same
trends as the males but to an insignificant degree. The male LBs also reported more negative affect when the model had done poorly than when
he had done well, with some trend among females in the same direction.
Inconsistent with the Stotland and Cottrell study, there are no differences
among any of the groups in their ratings of their logical reasoning ability,
possibly because of their "prior knowledge" of their own levels of ability.
Nevertheless, this lack of effect on the subjects' self-ratings of ability indicates that the negative affect among the LBs in the poor model condition
was not owing to their feeling anxious because of an unfavorable self-
evaluation. Again, the low level of palmar sweating does not appear to
reflect positive affect.

VII. Conclusions

In reviewing all the studies directly and indirectly related to empathy,
the following conclusions can be drawn. It is possible to study so subtle

TABLE VII
PALMAR SWEAT IN THE INTERACTION STUDY

Males[a]		Females[a]	
Model good	Model poor	Model good	Model poor
First Borns			
A	B		
.618	.177	.216	.314
(14)	(16)	(17)	(16)
Later Borns			
C	D		
.377	.931	.368	.477
(11)	(14)	(14)	(17)

Significant t Tests and Walker-Lev t Tests

C vs. D $t = 1.753$ $p < .05$ (one tail)
B vs. D $t = 2.600$ $p < .01$ (one tail)
A vs. B $t = 1.500$ $p < .08$ (two tail)
A vs. B vs. C vs. D   Walker-Lev $t = 2.278$ $p < .025$ (one tail)

[a]Number of subjects indicated in parentheses.

and important a phenomenon as empathy in the laboratory and to examine some of the determinants of empathy. The process leading to empathy can be understood in terms of cognitive variables such as the mental set that the person has when he observes the other. The form or type of social relationships between one person and another influences the amount of empathy, presumably because the form of the social relationship influences the manner of perceiving the other and thinking about him. Individual differences in reactions to social situations, in perceiving the other, and in thinking about him must be considered in predicting how much empathizing will occur. These individual differences appear to be determined in part by the birth order of the person. For example, LBs empathize more with someone similar to themselves than with someone different, while FBs' empathy is not affected by the degree of similarity. Further, LBs empathize more with someone with whom they have interacted than with someone else, while FBs are not sensitive to this difference.

The lack of consistency in the manifestations of empathy, both with respect to the physiological variables and the self-ratings, is quite troublesome. Work is proceeding to develop more reliable and more valid indices of the various emotions, as well as to study the effects on empathy of status, dependency, etc.

ACKNOWLEDGMENTS

The author wishes to thank Mr. Stanley Sherman, Dr. Kelly Shaver, Mr. Robert Crawford, Mr. James Buss, and Mrs. Judith Buss for their assistance in preparing the article and running the studies.

REFERENCES

Ackner, B. Emotions and the peripheral vasoconstriction system. *Journal of Psychosomatic Research*, 1956, 1, 3-20.

Allport, F. H. *Social psychology*. Cambridge, Mass: Riverside Press, 1924.

Aronfreed, J.,and Paskal, Vivian. Altruism, empathy, and the conditioning of positive affect. Unpublished manuscript.

Ax, A. F. The physiological differentiation between fear and anger in humans. *Psychosomatic Medicine*, 1953, 15, 433-442.

Beam, J. C. Serial learning and conditioning under real-life stress. *Journal of Abnormal and Social Psychology,* 1955, 51, 543-551.

Berger, S. M. Conditioning through vicarious instigation. *Psychological Review*, 1962, 29, 450-466.

Berkowitz, L. Effects of perceived dependency relationships upon conformity to group expectations. *Journal of Abnormal and Social Psychology*, 1957, 55, 350-354.

Berkowitz, L., and Daniels, L. R. Responsibility and dependency. *Journal of Abnormal and Social Psychology*, 1963, 66, 429-436.

Berkowitz, L., and Daniels, L. R. Affecting the salience of the social responsibility norm: Effects of past help on the response to dependency relationship. *Journal of Abnormal and Social Psychology*, 1964, 68, 275-281.

Bruner, J. S. On perceptual readiness. *Psychological Review*, 1957, 64, 123-152.

Crawford, R., Stotland, E., and Shaver, K. Set-up for obtaining plethysmographic recordings from several subjects simultaneously. *Psycho-physiology*, 1967, 3, 435-439.

Cronbach, L. J. Processes affecting scores on "understanding of others" and "assumed similarity." *Psychological Bulletin*, 1955, 52, 177-193.

Davis, R. C. Critique and notes – A further study of the effect of stress on palmar prints. *Journal of Abnormal and Social Psychology*, 1957, 55, 132.

Davis, R. C., Buchwald, A. M., and Frankman, R. W. Autonomic and muscular responses and their relation to simple stimuli. *Psychological Monographs,* 1955, 69 (9, Whole No. 405).

Deutsch, M., and Krauss, R. M. *Theories in social psychology*. New York: Basic Books, 1965.

Escalona, S. K. Feeding disturbances in very young children, *American Journal of Orthopsychiatry*, 1945, 15, 76-80.

Ferreira, A. J., and Winter, W. D. The palmar sweat print: A methodological study. *Psychosomatic Medicine*, 1963, 25, 377-384.

Gladstone, R. A group test of palmar sweating. *Journal of General Psychology*, 1953, 48, 29-49.

Heider, F. *The psychology of interpersonal relations*. New York: Wiley, 1958.

Hoffman, M. L., and Saltzstein, H. D. Parent discipline and the child's moral development. *Journal of Personality and Social Psychology*, 1967, 5, 45-57.

Hovland, C., and Riesen, A. Magnitude of galvanic and vasomotor responses as a function of stimulus intensity. *Journal of General Psychology*, 1940, 23, 103-121.

Katz, R. L. *Empathy: Its nature and uses*. Glencoe, Ill.: Free Press, 1963.

Kelly, G. A. *The psychology of personal constructs*. New York: Norton, 1955. 2 vols.

Kuno, Y. *Human perspiration*. Springfield, Ill.: Charles C. Thomas, 1956.

Lacey, J. J. Individual differences in somatic response patterns. *Journal of Comparative and Physiological Psychology*, 1950, 43, 338-350.

Marquis, D. C., and Williams, D. J. The central pathway in man of the vasomotor response to pain. *Brain*, 1938, 61, 203-220.

Mead, G. H. *Mind, self and society*. Chicago: University of Chicago Press, 1934.

Mowrer, O. H. *Learning theory and personality dynamics*. New York: Ronald Press, 1950.

Mowrer, O. H. *Psychotherapy: Theory and research*. New York: Ronald Press, 1953.

Murphy, Lois B. *Social behavior and child personality: An exploratory study of some roots of sympathy*. New York: Columbia University Press, 1937.

Nafe, J. P., and Wagoner, K. S. V. The effect of thermal stimulation upon dilation and constriction of the blood vessels of the skin of a contralateral hand. *Journal of Psychology*, 1936, 2, 461-477.

Nafe, J. P., and Wagoner, K. S. V. The effect of pain upon peripheral blood volume. *American Journal of Psychology*, 1938, 51, 118-126.

Paskal, V. and Aronfreed, J. The development of sympathetic behavior in children: An experimental test of a two-phase hypothesis. Oral presentation for paper session on internalization and social control, biennial Soc. Research in Child Development, Minneapolis, 1965.

Sampson, E. E. The study of ordinal position: Antecedents and outcomes. In B. A. Maher (Ed.), *Progress in experimental personality research*, New York: Academic Press, 1965. Vol. 2.

Schachter, S. and Singer, J. E. Cognitive, social and physiological determinants of emotional state. *Psychology Review*, 1962, 69, 379-399.

Stotland, E. Social schemas, birth order, and adult social behavior. Unpublished manuscript, University of Washington, 1966.

Stotland, E., and Cottrell, N. B. Similarity of performance as influenced by interaction, self-esteem, and birth order. *Journal of Abnormal and Social Psychology*, 1962, 64, 183-191.

Stotland, E., and Dunn, R. Identification, oppositeness, authoritarianism, self-esteem and birth order. *Psychological Monographs*, 1962, 76 (9, Whole No. 528).

Stotland, E., and Dunn, R. Empathy, self-esteem and birth order. *Journal of Abnormal and Social Psychology*, 1963, 66, 532-544.

Stotland, E., and Walsh, J. Birth order in an experimental study of empathy. *Journal of Abnormal and Social Psychology*, 1963, 66, 610-614.

Stürup, G., Bolton, B., Williams, D. J., and Carmichael, E. A. Vasomotor responses in hemiplegic patients. *Brain*, 1935, 58, 456-468.

Sullivan, H. S. *The interpersonal theory of psychiatry*. New York: Norton, 1953.

Teichner, W. H. Delayed cold-induced vasodilatation and behavior. *Journal of Experimental Psychology*, 1965, 69, 426-432.

Thibaut, J. W., and Kelley, H. H. *The social psychology of groups*. New York: Wiley, 1959.

Winter, W. D., Ferreira, A. J., and Ransom, R. Two measures of anxiety: A validation. *Journal of Consulting Psychology*, 1963, 27, 520-524.

THE PERSONAL REFERENCE SCALE: AN APPROACH TO SOCIAL JUDGMENT[1]

Harry S. Upshaw

DEPARTMENT OF PSYCHOLOGY
UNIVERSITY OF ILLINOIS AT CHICAGO
CIRCLE
CHICAGO, ILLINOIS

I. Introduction

A number of topics in social psychology involve the application and extension of theoretical principles imported from other areas of psychology. Chapter headings in textbooks call attention to this relationship between individual and social psychology by phrases such as "social per-

[1]This article and all the original work reported in it were supported by a grant from the National Science Foundation.

ception," "social learning," and "social judgment." This article is concerned with one of these areas in which general psychology is related to social psychology: that of judgment. The fundamental aim of this article is to establish a framework for representing social judgment as part of the general psychology of judgment.

What is commonly regarded as the general psychology of judgment is a literature based on research in psychophysical laboratories. As in any other field, certain conventions have developed in psychophysics regarding experimental tasks, methods of data analysis, and types of theoretical constructs. There is no reason to impose these conventions on social psychology. There must be found a level of analysis by which social psychological and psychophysical principles can be interchanged such that both areas are fairly represented. It is hoped that this article will help to establish this level.

A variety of theoretical concepts have been employed by psychologists referring to a subjective representation of objective events and stimuli. For example, Lewin (1935) talked of the "life space" of a person, Koffka (1935) of the "behavioral environment," and Sherif (1935) of the "frame of reference." These concepts call attention to individual differences in perception, cognition, and judgment. They serve to challenge the feasibility of a psychology that treats human subjects as interchangeable samples from an undifferentiated universe. Perhaps because of the subjectivity which they imply, these concepts have not generally been treated in a rigorous fashion. Instead, they have functioned as tenets of a faith that in the stimulus-organism-response (S-O-R) paradigm of psychological activity O is equal to or greater in importance than S. That faith has been scientifically productive. Nevertheless, there is need to temper it with the realization that it is as arbitrary to assume that people are always different as it is to assume that they are always the same. A criterion is needed by which to decide whether sameness or difference is indicated.

In the following discussion the judgment process will be discussed as the means by which a person measures certain of his cognitions and perceptions. The concept of the personal reference scale will be introduced as a device for subjectively representing a set of stimuli. Any scale measures something; a reference scale measures a subjective quantity. Logical criteria will be developed for inferring sameness and difference of quantity and scale. A heuristic model of the reference scale will be described for application in those situations in which it can be assumed that a reference scale and a physical scale measure the same quantity, or (in a somewhat different form) that two reference scales measure the same quantity. Theories of judgment will be discussed in terms of that model.

II. The Judgment Process

In recent years information theorists have promoted an analogy between the human judge and a channel for the transmission of information, an analogy which calls attention to three aspects of judgment. First, it points to the fact that judgment involves the matching of a response to a stimulus. Second, it suggests that some information that is present in an input may be lost in the channel. Thus, a judge may not be capable of processing all the information to which he is exposed. Furthermore, the communication demands that are made upon the person, whether in research or in real life, may be such as to permit or encourage less than optimal information transmission. A third consideration suggested by the information-transmission view of judgment is that the output sometimes contains information that was added by the channel. The task requirements of many experiments as well as those of many interaction situations outside the laboratory often prescribe a type of information which the judge is to add to the input.

A. INPUT – OUTPUT

The input and output of the human judge are objectively observable. However, psychological processes referring to the transmission of input information, and the deletion from or addition to that information must be inferred. The logical nature of the constructs inferred on the basis of a comparison of input and output information has provided endless controversy in psychology. [Papers by Natsoulas (1967), Savage (1966) and Stevens (1966a,b) summarize modern views in this controversy.]

In this article it is assumed that a judge under certain circumstances compares stimuli, whether "real" or "hypothetical," and expresses quantitative relationships among them. The assumption that a judge expresses quantitative relationships among stimuli implies that the judgmental process, whatever it is, results in the classification of stimuli according to some perceptual or cognitive property. The present approach is one that focuses attention upon the existence of reliable quantitative relationships among the responses to a set of stimuli. Such relationships define a *subjective* (cognitive or perceptual) *quantity*. The question of the identity of a subjective quantity and that of its scientific utility are here considered to be separate from the question of its existence.

B. THE CONCEPT OF QUANTITY

Guilford (1954) has distinguished among three classes of continua that are commonly assumed in psychological scale construction. One is a physical continuum, referring to an objectively observable property in terms of which the judged stimuli differ. Another is subjective, referring to the perception (or, presumably, the cognition) of the stimuli. The third is the response continuum, referring to the judgmental output. Guilford's distinction suggests a major point of emphasis in this article: A single, fundamental relationship among the three continua may result in sets of data which superficially appear to reflect different relationships resulting from nonessential variations in response language. It is important to distinguish between variation which is attributable to an arbitrary choice of response language and that which is attributable to the inferred perceptual or cognitive process. (Although the choice of language may be viewed as arbitrary with respect to the process expressed by the judgments, it is not conceived here as arbitrary in any other sense. In fact, a basic concern of the present work is to formulate theoretical approaches to judgmental language.)

1. The Nature of Quantities

As commonly understood the term "quantity" appears to be synonymous with "quantitative variable." These terms imply the ordering of a class of objects according to a specifiable property. Furthermore, it is the relative magnitudes of the objects, not their absolute values, which seem to be essential in defining a quantity. Thus, the height that is measured in inches is considered to be the same quantity as that measured in feet, even though the numerical magnitudes assigned to the objects are different. The concept of a quantity appears not to require a metric; or perhaps it would be more accurate to say that the concept of a quantity allows a choice of metrics.

A quantity refers to an entire population of elements, or objects, not just those that are present in an experiment. Furthermore, a quantity refers to a single, specifiable property in terms of which implicit comparisons are made among the elements in the class. A subject's judgments of a series of stimuli are not, therefore, to be automatically considered to reflect a subjective quantity. If the concept is to be useful in the judgmental context it must be demonstrated or assumed that any set of judgments which is to be interpreted as representing a subjective quantity results from implicit or explicit rules that are generalizable by the judge to all members of a class of stimuli. It must be further assumed that these rules refer to a single property, which, at least from the point of view of the individual judge, characterizes in variable degree all stimuli in the class. Methodologically, these restrictions in the application of the concept of quantity to a set of judgments suggest the appropriateness of some measure of internal consistency reliability (see Nunnally, 1967, pp. 206ff.) as evidence of the existence of a quantity in a concrete case.

It was argued earlier that a single quantity might be expressed in any of several alternative metrics. Thus, a transformation from one unit to another does not affect the identity of the quantitative variable. Similarly, the procedures employed to assign values to a sample of elements do not determine the identity of the quantity. In support of the contention that quantities are not inextricably tied to measurement procedures, Ellis (1966, p. 33) discussed two logically independent procedures for measuring mass. One involves balancing pairs of stimuli on a beam balance, and the other involves substituting pairs of stimuli which are balanced against a reference stimulus. The order relationships resulting from the two procedures cannot be derived one from the other, a fact which establishes their logical independence. Yet, few would demand that mass measured by the two procedures be considered two different quantities.

The argument of the above paragraph is extremely important in the effort to view human judgments as measures of psychological quantities. First, it admits the possibility that a judge using subjective procedures might accomplish the measurement of a physical quantity. This possibility means that the question of whether, for example, "perceived length" and "physical length" are the same variables is amenable to experimental evidence, and need not be settled by definition. A second implication of defining a quantity independently of its associated measurement procedures is that it is logically possible to assume on the basis of empirical evidence that two sets of judgments refer to a single quantity. Because the psychological processes involved in judgment are not directly observable, any conception of quantity which is tied to measurement procedures would be difficult to apply to comparisons of two sets of judgments. The question of whether two sets of judgments represent one quantity or two (or none) under such a conception would require information concerning the nature of the unobservable, underlying processes. With the present conception, on the other hand, the question is answerable by means of internal evidence in the judgments.

2. The Criterion for the Identity of Quantities

It has been argued above that neither the particular measurement procedures nor the resulting metric is essential to the existence of a quantity. Every quantity entails *some* measurement procedures and *some* metric, but both of these facets of quantity permit a degree of substitution among alternatives. The essential facet of any quantity is the order relationships among the measured objects. As long as these relationships are not altered, the quantity itself is unaltered.

If invariance in the ordering of objects is the essence of the concep of quantity, then obviously, the decision concerning whether a set of judg ments represents the same quantity as a physical measure or as anothe set of judgments depends upon the equivalence of ordering. Ellis (1966, p 48) has stated the criterion for the identity of quantities precisely: ". . two procedures are ones for ordering things in respect of the same quan tity if and only if they would always generate the same order amongst th same particulars under the same conditions."

It should be noted that the criterion adopted here for the identity o quantities depends in no way upon any special type of language for th expression of order relationships. Thus, applying this criterion to judg ments, a single quantity might be expressed in any judgmental language Cross-modal matching in psychophysics may be viewed as the translatio of quantitative terms from one language to the other. In this regard the us of numbers to express quantitative relationships among stimuli is to b viewed as an arbitrary choice of judgmental language (cf. Stevens 1966b). The height of a column of mercury reveals the order among ele ments with respect to temperature whether or not that height is expresse as a number. Similarly, any magnitude controlled by a subject can b used to express quantitative relationships with respect to subjectiv magnitudes.

Methodologically, the criterion for the identity of quantities implie correlational analysis. The linear correlation between two measures of single quantity is required to be high, whereas that between measures o different quantities is required to be low. In research that emphasizes th identification of quantities, an adaptation of the multitrait-multimethod matrix analysis proposed by Campbell and Fiske (1959) is appropriate Such an adaptation, amounting to a multiquantity-multimeasurement procedure matrix, would structure the inquiry concerning the identity an difference of quantities into a pattern of correlations reflecting divergen cies as well as convergencies among various measures. For example suppose that an experiment consisted of four tasks: (1) the categorica ratings of a set of attitude statements according to how pro or anti each i toward a target object, (2) the squeezing of a hand dynamometer wit variable force to indicate the same attribute, (3) the categorical ratings o the statements according to how acceptable each is as an expression o the subject's own attitude, and (4) the squeezing of the dynamometer t indicate degree of acceptability. Evidence that the pro-anti judgment represent a quantity that is distinct from that of the acceptability judg ments would be provided by the finding that the linear correlation coeffi cients are higher between measures associated with the same property but different judgmental language, than those between the same language but different properties.

C. THE CONCEPT OF SCALE

It has been noted that a single quantity can be expressed in a variety of languages, including numbers, and in a variety of different magnitudes within a given language. Any expression of a quantity in terms of a set of magnitudes constitutes a *scale*. Any scale consists of a set of tripartite elements: an object sampled from the population of objects to which the quantity refers; a magnitude (a number or an amount of some other quantity with which the object is matched); and a rule, or a group of rules, relating the object and the magnitude to express the quantitative status of the object (cf. Suppes and Zinnes, 1963; Upshaw, 1968a). The criterion for the identity of quantities that has been adopted here permits any single quantity to be measured by a variety of different scales. Scales that measure the same quantity may differ in at least three ways. They may involve different modes of expression (e.g., numbers, strength of grip, amount of electrical current). They may involve different levels of precision in the quantitative relationships to which they refer. Finally, they may represent insignificant transformations of metric. Another way of describing the last type of difference is that the two scales may involve different magnitudes within a common mode of expression to represent the same quantitative relationships.

It has become commonplace in discussions of measurement within the social sciences to note that numbers permit a variety of interpretations, not all of which are appropriate in every case. Various "scale levels" are often distinguished following the classification system suggested by Stevens (1951). Although this system was developed and has been most often discussed in terms of numbers as the indicators of quantity, it is apparent that it can be easily generalized to refer to any type of quantitative language. The classification system refers to the degree of precision of the scale. Thus, what Stevens called a "nominal scale" consists of a set of quantitative designations which serve to identify classes of objects which are alike. Designations which serve both to identify classes of objects and to reflect the quantitative order among the classes are called an "ordinal scale." "*Interval*" and "*ratio scales*" refer to measurement of a property with a constant unit and an origin which is arbitrarily (in the case of the interval scale) or rationally (in the case of the ratio scale) established.

In the literature some attention has been given to judgmental precision as a dependent variable. Sherif and Hovland (1953) produced some evidence that ego involvement in the judgmental issue affects the precision level (see also Sherif, Sherif, and Nebergall, 1965). Some of the research done within the framework of information theory which was recently reported by Bieri, Atkins, Briar, Leaman, Miller, and Tripodi (1966) may be interpreted as referring to differences in scale precision.

Variable scale precision underlies the interpretation offered by White and Harvey (1965) and White, Alter, and Rardin (1965) for data relating own attitude to judgments of how favorable statements are toward a target object.

At the base of the Stevens system for classifying scales is the notion that any scale can be transformed by an appropriate function without any loss of information. The scale levels which Stevens described correspond to different types of transformations which preserve all of the essential information of the original scale. Thus, any transformation of unit which maintains the linear order of scaled objects, but which does not affect the origin is said to be a permissible transformation of a ratio scale. The interval scale is said to be invariant with respect to transformations of both origin and unit, whereas the permissible transformations of an ordinal scale are those that maintain the rank order of objects. Any transformation that retains the identity of classes is a permissible transformation of a nominal scale.

The rules which link magnitudes to objects in the process of measurement serve to map those objects into a mathematical system. The level of precision of a scale is determined by the types of arithmetical formulas that can be meaningfully applied to the objects under the mapping rules. The type of evidence required to establish the level of precision in a concrete instance is not simple, even in measurement involving objective quantities. With subjective quantities, there is an additional complication because the mapping rules and their application are not directly observable. For this reason, intuitive cues concerning appropriate arithmetical operations, which might be suggested by the mapping rules, are not available to the scientist who studies the judgments.

An important function of what are called "psychological scaling models" is that they provide the rationale for various arithmetical operations and, therefore, theoretical evidence of the precision level of the judgmental scale. Despite the availability of an impressive variety of scaling models (see Torgerson, 1958), the prevailing practice in psychophysics and in social psychology is to collect data without apparent concern for the underlying psychometric theory. The nature of the assumptions made concerning the level of precision of the judgmental scale can often be inferred only indirectly, based upon the type of interpretation of the data which the investigator makes. In a recent paper Manis (1967) noted that the phenomenon that is often called "contrast" (that is, the shift in judgment of stimuli away from the value of an experimentally introduced stimulus) has been interpreted by some people as a perceptual phenomenon (i.e., a change in quantity) and by others as a change in scale. In anticipation of the detailed discussion of this issue which will be presented in a ater section, it is relevant to make the point here that the two types of interpretation require different assumptions concerning the level of precision of the subjective scales which comprise the fundamental data. Specifically, the scale hypothesis attributes the shift in the typical judgment, which characterizes the contrast effect, to a difference in scale origin. Because an interval scale permits any transformation of origin without loss of quantitative information, the interval scale level is all that must be assumed to support the scale hypothesis. On the other hand, the claim that a difference in origin is evidence of a difference in quantity is reasonable only if it can be assumed that the two scales are ratio scales, for only with data at this level of precision is the level (or location) of a scale nonarbitrary.

D. THE PERSONAL REFERENCE SCALE

When a person judges a series of stimuli, he assigns a magnitude to each according to rules that he may or may not be able to verbalize. If, and only if, the assigned magnitudes are internally consistent is it to be said that they correspond to a subjective quantity. The particular numerical or other values reflect the individual's reference scale for measuring the underlying quantity. According to this conception of judgment, the comparison of judges who respond to a common series of stimuli might reveal differences in subjective quantities or differences in reference scales. If the latter, the differences may be in the level of quantitative precision, or they may be in the values of the scale parameters which will be discussed in the next section.

The concept of the personal reference scale is introduced into the study of judgment in order to call attention to the many interpretations possible for any given difference between experimental groups. The time has surely come both in psychophysics and in social psychology to inquire into features of data other than the mere difference in mean scores of experimental groups. The most generally useful level of analysis for such an effort appears to be the individual judge.

The traditional hazard of employing the single subject as the analytic unit in psychology has been the tendency to assume that all individual differences are differences of quantity and never scale. Somehow a value system has developed in psychology which views linguistic or scale variation as trivial and perceptual or cognitive-quantity variation as profound. It may be that in their eagerness to pursue issues of high status according to this value system, investigators have overlooked a potentially rewarding set of research issues concerned with judgmental language.

In the next section a heuristic model will be presented which focuses attention upon several dependent variables, all of which correspond to aspects of a judge's personal reference scale. In the current literature many of these variables are treated as though they required for explanation some theory relating to quantities, whereas the analysis here suggests that a theory relating to scales would be adequate.

III. A Heuristic Model of the Reference Scale

Historically, judgmental research began as an adjunct of the psychology of perception. Many of the methods employed today and much of the scientific terminology reflect the original concern of psychophysicists to measure "pure" sensations. Judgmental methods and terminology, however, have been applied to a variety of problems that have nothing more than an analogical relationship to sensory phenomena. Examples of the use of psychophysical methods may be found in almost every area of psychology, e.g., mental testing, personality functioning, learning and thinking, attitude measurement, and attitude change, as well as perception. Not only have the methods of judgmental research been extended beyond the area of sensory psychology, but judgmental theories have likewise been applied to a variety of content areas.

The concept of the personal reference scale is applicable without regard to the perceptual or cognitive processes underlying judgments in a particular case. The reference scale describes a subjective quantity. Research issues involving such quantities are of two types: those that concern the comparison of a subjective quantity with the objective quantity upon which it is assumed to be based, and those that concern the comparison of two subjective quantities (or two scales that measure the same subjective quantity).

A major example of an issue that concerns the comparison of subjective and objective quantities is provided by the search in sensory psychology for "the psychophysical function." The goal of that search is the discovery of a class of equations that will transform reference scale values into physical scale values or vice versa. Outside of the sensory domain, probably the best known example of an issue that concerns the comparison of objective and subjective quantities is the so-called utility function of economics. That function relates an objective scale of wealth (number of dollars, amounts of commodities, etc.) to a reference scale of personal satisfaction.

Probably most judgmental issues in social psychology and many in other areas (including the sensory area) concern the comparison of two reference scales. Research dealing with judgmental differences owing to stimulus context, personal involvement, own attitude, and the requirements of cognitive consistency (see Upshaw, 1968b) provides examples of the comparison of reference scales.

According to the criterion for the identity of quantities which was discussed above, two quantities are to be considered identical if for a given set of conditions the linear order of any sample of appropriate objects is the same. For over 100 years the nature of the psychophysical function relating reference and physical scales has been disputed in sensory psychology. Fechner (1966) argued that the reference scale is a logarithmic function of the corresponding physical scale. Various other functions have been suggested from time to time (see Guilford, 1954), but none of the proposed functions seems to be as well supported by data as the power law advocated by S. S. Stevens (see Ekman and Sjoberg, 1965). Strictly speaking, therefore, it appears that seldom will a reference scale and a physical scale be found to be linear transformations, one of the other. It should be noted, however, that regardless of the particular psychophysical function, two sets of judgments of a given stimulus series will be linearly related provided that the same psychophysical function applied for both sets.

In formulating a model of the reference scale it is convenient to assume that two measures of a single quantity are to be compared. Such an assumption appears generally reasonable only in comparison of two reference scales. However, for expedience in the case of comparison of reference and physical scales the model to be described will be thought of as applying to a comparison of whatever transformations of the two scales are necessary to produce a linear relationship between them. Thus, if the psychophysical law is truly logarithmic, then any person's judgments are linearly related to the logarithms of the physical stimulus values. If the power law holds, then the logarithms of the judgments are linearly related to the logarithms of the physical values. Since the purpose of the model is to delineate various facets of reference scales, no harm will be done by restricting its application in the suggested manner.

A. COMPARING PHYSICAL AND REFERENCE SCALES FOR A SINGLE QUANTITY

For expository purposes imagine an experiment in which a single subject responds to each of a series of stimuli several times. The judged value of a stimulus s on trial t will be represented as J_{st}. The physical value of the same stimulus will be designated P_{st}. One way to compare the judgment with its corresponding stimulus is to subtract one from the other, thus defining the "error" of judgment, or more accurately, the discrepancy between the reference scale and the physical scale. Following Cronbach (1955), who developed the basic model for the analysis of empathy scores, the following identity can be written:

$$
\begin{aligned}
J_{st} - P_{st} = &(\bar{J}_{..} - \bar{P}_{..}) \\
&+ (\bar{J}_{s.} - \bar{P}_{s.}) - (\bar{J}_{..} - \bar{P}_{..}) \\
&+ (\bar{J}_{.t} - \bar{P}_{.t}) - (\bar{J}_{..} - \bar{P}_{..}) \\
&+ (J_{st} - P_{st}) - (\bar{J}_{..} - \bar{P}_{..}) \\
&- [(\bar{J}_{s.} - \bar{P}_{s.}) - (\bar{J}_{..} - \bar{P}_{..})] \\
&- [(\bar{J}_{.t} - \bar{P}_{.t}) - (\bar{J}_{..} - \bar{P}_{..})]
\end{aligned}
$$

where $\bar{J}_{s.}$ is the mean judgment of stimulus s over trials, $\bar{J}_{.t}$ is the mean judgment over stimuli for trial t, and $\bar{J}_{..}$ is the mean judgment over all stimuli and all trials, etc.

An inverse measure of the similarity of the judge's reference scale and the physical scale is provided by the mean square discrepancy between judgments and physical values. This score is defined as

$$
S^2_{JP} = 1/n_s n_t \sum_{s,t} (J_{st} - P_{st})^2
$$

Squaring and summing the identity, S^2 is resolved into the four additive components listed in Table I. Each of these components has a particular meaning, assuming a linear relationship between judgment and physical values (or transformations of these values, as discussed above) and assuming that the reference scale is an interval or ratio scale. The first component is simply the squared difference between the grand mean

TABLE I

FOUR COMPONENTS OF S^2 FOR THE COMPARISON OF A REFERENCE SCALE AND A CORRESPONDING PHYSICAL SCALE[a]

Component designation	Composition
Origin	$(\bar{J}_{..} - \bar{P}_{..})^2$
Unit	$1/n_s \Sigma_s [(\bar{J}_{s.} - \bar{P}_{s.}) - (\bar{J}_{..} - \bar{P}_{..})]^2$
Origin over trials	$1/n_t \Sigma_t [(\bar{J}_{.t} - \bar{P}_{.t}) - (\bar{J}_{..} - \bar{P}_{..})]^2$
Unit over trials	$1/n_s n_t \Sigma_{s,t} [(J_{st} - P_{st}) - (\bar{J}_{s.} - \bar{P}_{s.}) - (\bar{J}_{.t} - \bar{P}_{.t}) + (\bar{J}_{..} - \bar{P}_{..})]^2$

[a]Note — In the hypothetical experiment implied by the model the physical scale value for a given stimulus is the same on every trial. Hence, $\bar{P}_{s.} = P_{st}$ and $\bar{P}_{.t} = \bar{P}_{..}$. These simplifications of the terms in the model have *not* been made, in order to preserve the similarity of the terms in the present application with the corresponding terms of Table II.

of the distribution of judgments and the mean physical value of the stimuli. The size of this component is increased by shifts of the reference scale origin above or below the origin of the physical scale. In this sense, the component may be described as a "constant error."

The second component is a differential stimulus factor. This component as defined is the variance of the differences between the mean judgments (over trials) and the physical values of the stimuli. Accordingly, the expression in Table I can be rewritten as

$$\sigma_{\bar{J}_{s.}}^2 + \sigma_{\bar{P}_{s.}}^2 - 2r_{\bar{J}_{s.}\bar{P}_{s.}}\, \sigma_{\bar{J}_{s.}}\, \sigma_{\bar{P}_{s.}}$$

where $r_{\bar{J}_{s.}\bar{P}_{s.}}$ is the linear correlation between the mean judgment over trials for each stimulus with the corresponding physical value. With a fixed stimulus series the size of the second component reflects two features of the distribution of judgments: the dispersion of judgmental values and the extent to which differences in the physical values of stimuli are matched by differences in judged values. The first of these subcomponents is the expansiveness of the judgmental language, and the second may be viewed as an index of the extent of discrimination in the judgments relative to that on the physical scale. These two subcomponents correspond to the two facets of judgmental unit discussed by the present author in an earlier paper (Upshaw, 1965). It can be shown that the second component as a whole becomes smaller in value as $\sigma_{\bar{J}_{s.}}$ approaches $r_{\bar{J}_{s.}\bar{P}_{s.}}\, \sigma_{\bar{P}_{s.}}$, that is, as the judge matches the distinctions that he makes among stimuli to his ability to discriminate. In the special case in which the correlation is perfect this component reflects only the dispersion of judgments relative to that of the physical values, and it can, therefore, be interpreted entirely in terms of unit size.

The third component is a differential trial factor. With a constant stimulus series, $\bar{P}_{.t} = \bar{P}_{..}$. Thus, the third component reduces to $\sigma_{\bar{J}_{.t}}^2$, or the variance over trials of the mean values assigned to the stimuli. The component is, in other words, a measure of the fluctuation of the reference scale origin over trials.

The last component in Table I is a residual factor reflecting differences between the reference scale and the physical scale which are not accounted for by the constant error or the differential stimulus and trial factors, taken as "main effects." It is, essentially, an interaction effect involving stimuli by trials. With a constant stimulus series, the fourth component may be rewritten as

$$\sigma_{Jst}^2 - \sigma_{Js.}^2 - \sigma_{\bar{J}_{.t}}^2$$

As an interaction between stimulus and trial (from which the variance owing to the characteristic expansiveness of language and that owing to origin over trials have been removed), the last component may be viewed as a measure of the fluctuation of unit over trials.

B. Comparing Two Reference Scales for a Single Quantity

Because of its dependence on physical values, the model that is represented in Table I is not generally applicable to problems in social psychology, where usually the physical values are not known. A more appropriate model for social psychology would be one in which the comparison is between pairs of judges, or one judge on two occasions. The model under discussion can be generalized to serve this purpose in a simple, straightforward way. For comparing the reference scale of a single judge with the physical scale, the following equation was written:

$$S_{JP}^2 = 1/n_s n_t \sum_{s,t} (J_{st} - P_{st})^2$$

An analogous expression can be written for the comparison of two judges in terms of the fundamental model:

$$S_{J1J2}^2 = 1/n_s n_t \sum_{s,t} [(J_{1st} - P_{st}) - (J_{2st} - P_{st})]^2$$

$$= 1/n_s n_t \sum_{s,t} (J_{1st} - J_{2st})^2$$

where J_{1st} is the response of judge 1 to stimulus s on trial t.

By algebra equivalent to that employed earlier for the fundamental model, the general model for comparing two sets of judgments is resolved into the four components described in Table II. An important feature of the generalized model is the fact that physical values of the stimuli do not enter the calculations at all. The model assumes that the judges respond to the same stimulus series, and that whatever psychophysical function applies to one judge also applies to the other. Thus, the model is one that links the stimulus and its corresponding judgment closely, even though the physical value of the stimulus is of no concern in the application of the model.

The generalized model described in Table II provides a framework for studying two sets of judgments that refer to the same psychological quantity and differ only "by scale." In the earlier discussion of the basic model the first component was described as referring to the origin of a judge's reference scale relative to the physical scale. In the generalized form, the first component refers to the difference between the origins of the two scales. If the two scales that are compared are centered at the same place on the physical scale, this component will have the value of zero.

TABLE II

FOUR COMPONENTS OF S^2 FOR THE COMPARISON OF TWO REFERENCE SCALES
FOR A SINGLE PSYCHOLOGICAL QUANTITY

Component designation	Composition
Origin difference	$(\bar{J}_{1..} - \bar{J}_{2..})^2$
Unit difference	$1/n_s \, \Sigma_s \, [(\bar{J}_{1s.} - \bar{J}_{2s.}) - (\bar{J}_{1..} - \bar{J}_{2..})]^2$
Difference in origin over trials	$1/n_t \Sigma_t [(\bar{J}_{1.t} - \bar{J}_{2.t}) - (\bar{J}_{1..} - \bar{J}_{2..})]^2$
Difference in origin over trials	$1/n_s n_t \, \Sigma_{s,t} \, [(J_{1st} - J_{2st}) - (\bar{J}_{1s.} - \bar{J}_{2s.})$
	$\qquad - (\bar{J}_{1.t} \;\; \bar{J}_{2.t}) \mid (\bar{J}_{1..} \;\; \bar{J}_{2..})]^2$

The second component in the generalized model refers to the difference between two reference scale units. As discussed earlier, there are two important aspects of the scale unit, the relative expansiveness of the judgmental language (the metric), and the accuracy with which stimulus differences are matched by judgmental differences. In the generalized form considerations of accuracy are, of course, not relevant to the model. Instead, concern is directed to the extent to which two judges agree in the distinctions which they make among the stimuli. An alternative expression for the second component as listed in Table II is

$$\sigma^2_{\bar{J}_{1s.}} + \sigma^2_{\bar{J}_{2s.}} - 2r_{\bar{J}_{1s.}\bar{J}_{2s.}}\,\sigma_{\bar{J}_{1s.}}\,\sigma_{\bar{J}_{2s.}}.$$

Thus the comparison of two reference scales with respect to unit involves an examination of the relative spacing of the stimuli (range of the two metrics, implying a comparison of $\sigma^2_{\bar{J}_{1s.}}$ and $\sigma^2_{\bar{J}_{2s.}}$) and the extent of agreement between the judges in regard to discrimination among the stimuli (implying an interpretation of $r_{\bar{J}_{1s.}\bar{J}_{2s.}}$). The correlation term in the unit component can be expected to be less than perfect when any one of three conditions obtains: (1) the values of the stimuli in the series are imperfectly discriminable to the human organism; (2) one judge is more astute in discriminating the magnitudes of the stimuli than is the other, perhaps because of motivational, sensory, or intellectual factors; and (3) the true relationship between the two sets of judgments is nonlinear, indicating that they do not refer to a single psychological quantity, as the model requires. If the value of the correlation is 1.00, and if scale units are the same (i.e., $\sigma_{\bar{J}_{1s.}} = \sigma_{\bar{J}_{2s.}}$), then the value of the second component is zero.

The third and fourth components described in Table II refer to differences in the fluctuation of origin and unit over repeated judgments of the same stimulus series. The third component, as defined in Table II, is actually the variance computed over trials of the differences between judges in the mean judgment of all of the stimuli in the series. Therefore, an equivalent expression for that component is

$$\sigma^2_{\bar{J}_{1.t}} + \sigma^2_{\bar{J}_{2.t}} - 2r_{\bar{J}_{1.t}\bar{J}_{2.t}} \, \sigma_{\bar{J}_{1.t}} \, \sigma_{\bar{J}_{2.t}}$$

In the form of the equivalent expression the component referring to fluctuation of origin over trials (O/T) is seen to reflect two separately interesting aspects of data. First, $\sigma^2_{\bar{J}_{1.t}}$ and $\sigma^2_{\bar{J}_{2.t}}$ measure the fluctuation of the scale level over trials. Second, the covariance term reflects the extent to which the origins are affected alike by trials. In any given experiment, the factor of trials may be conceived either as a random or a fixed effect (Green and Tukey, 1960; Winer, 1962) depending upon whether they are thought of as representing mere replications of the stimulus series or as a temporal variable. In the latter case, one might expect a substantial correlation over trials for measures of two reference scale origins. When trials are not assumed to be time-related, the correlation term in the O/T component is expected to have a value near zero. Hence, depending upon the specific issues involved in an experiment, data relating to the O/T component are amenable to analysis in terms of two types of questions.

The last component in Table II, unit over trials (U/T), reflects the discrepancy between judges which is not accounted for by differences in origin, in unit, or in the fluctuation of origin over trials. The size of this component in any experiment is an index of the extent of interaction between stimuli, trials, and judges. Such an interaction, assuming that it has been established that the two sets of judgments reflect a single psychological quantity, would reflect differences between judges in trial-to-trial fluctuation in the dispersion of judgments computed over all stimuli in the series, i.e., the scale unit. The component is expected to have a value near zero when the following conditions are met: (1) the dispersion of judged values is consistent over trials for each judge; (2) the extent to which each judge matches the stimulus discriminations of the other judge is consistent over trials; and (3) the judged position of each stimulus relative to all others in the series is consistent over trials for each judge, individually, and for any given trial between judges. The third condition is, of course, equivalent to the fundamental assumption of the model that the two scales correspond to a single quantity. If that assumption is granted, and if it is assumed that the judges are on every trial equally astute in stimulus discrimination, then the U/T component is interpretable in terms of the relative variation over trials of unit size.

As previously discussed, the logical criterion for the identity of quantities implies a linear correlation between scales which, except for measurement error, is perfect. In terms of the model described in Tables I and II, the comparison of two scales which do not measure a single quantity results in large values of the second and fourth components because of less than perfect correlations. Thus, the total value of $S^2_{J_1J_2}$ (the sum of the four components) provides an index of the dissimilarity of two reference scales, whether the dissimilarity is attributable to differences in quantities or to differences in scale. For present purposes the interpretations that have been suggested for components of the model are the desired ones. For that reason it will henceforth be assumed in this article, unless specifically noted, that any application involves a single quantity and two scales that are nearly perfectly correlated.

Although it is feasible to compute the value of S^2_{JP} (or $S_{J_1J_2}{}^2$) and each of its components, the principal use of the model is as a heuristic device to delineate various aspects of reference scales. Furthermore, the fact that the component scores sum to the value of S^2 provides logical proof that the various research issues implied by each component are all problems of scale not quantity. This demonstration has potential implications concerning the nature of theories that might account for phenomena associated with each component.

In the next section several theoretical approaches to problems in social judgment will be surveyed. Only one of these "theories" (the variable perspective model) has been treated explicitly as a theory of the reference scale. Each was formulated to account for particular judgmental phenomena without apparent concern for the distinction made here between quantity and scale. For this reason there is some danger that the following discussion in terms of the distinction will not adequately represent the theories. Misinterpretation will be minimized if the reader will regard the next section not as an attempt to integrate theories of judgment but as an effort to specify on the basis of prior research and theory the determinants of quantity differences and scale differences in judgments. It is, in short, a groping toward a new theory of judgment which separates psychological quantity and reference scale phenomena in social psychological data.

IV. Theoretical Approaches to Social Judgment

A. HYPOTHESIZED DIFFERENCES IN QUANTITY

The criterion for the identity of quantities which was discussed earlier specifies that any sample of two sets of judgments is significantly related linearly and not significantly related by any more complex function. Theories that predict only differences in the central tendency and dispersion of the distribution of judgments are therefore considered to be theories of reference scales. Those that predict bilateral shifts or the inversion of order among some stimuli because of experimental factors are considered theories of subjective quantities. Only one of the major theories of social judgment clearly refers to quantity differences. This is the assimilation-contrast formulation of M. Sherif and his associates. Other investigators have addressed research to the question of whether various particular judgmental phenomena represent quantity or scale effects. In the following discussion of theories of quantity, those studies dealing with isolated phenomena will be reviewed even though they do not constitute a single theory.

1. The Assimilation-Contrast Model

The theoretical orientation suggested by Sherif and his colleagues (Hovland, Harvey, and Sherif, 1957; Sherif, Sherif, and Nebergall, 1965; Sherif and Hovland, 1961) has been influential in the design of research on a variety of social-psychological problems of judgment and social attitudes. The approach represents an attempt to identify in the realm of social behavior certain judgmental phenomena that were originally observed in research on sensory processes, and to specify some antecedent conditions of their occurrence. These phenomena, assimilation and contrast, involve a shift in the judged values of a constant series of stimuli toward or away from experimentally introduced stimuli known as "anchors." In order to represent the theoretical approach in terms of the reference scale model developed in this article it is desirable to consider the phenomena of assimilation and contrast independent of the interpretation made of these phenomena by the theory.

Assimilation and Contrast as Judgmental Phenomena. The assimilation-contrast approach was formulated on the basis of a particular interpretation of a psychophysical study by Sherif, Taub, and Hovland (1958). In that research anchors were supplied at varying positions relative to the series; some near an end of it, and others successively more remote. Averaging over the stimuli in the series, the investigators found that the frequency distribution of judgments, hence the modal category used in judging stimuli in the series, shifted from the control condition (no anchor) toward an adjacent anchor and away from a remote anchor. On the basis of a demonstrated shift in the average judgment toward an anchor stimulus which is near the end of the series (assimilation) and away from an anchor stimulus that is relatively far from the end of the series (contrast), Sherif *et al.* concluded that either assimilation or contrast occurs with anchoring, depending upon the distance on the physical scale between the stimulus that is judged and the anchor.

In interpreting the Sherif *et al.* study it is well to take note of the following features of the experiment:

(1) As previously mentioned, the independent variable was the physical scale value of the anchor stimulus. In one condition there was no anchor; the other conditions represented successively more remote anchoring.

(2) The experimental task of the subject was to judge each stimulus on a six-category rating scale.

(3) In those conditions in which there were anchors, the anchor stimulus preceded each stimulus in the series.

(4) The subjects were told that the anchor stimulus was to be considered an example of a stimulus to be assigned to either the minimum or maximum value of the rating scale.

(5) The same subjects participated in all conditions.

(6) The dependent variable in the study was the frequency of category usage in each experimental condition, these frequencies representing sums over subjects and stimuli.

The shifts in the modal category that were designated assimilation and contrast were accompanied by reduced dispersions of the distribution of response. Thus, the shift that was designated assimilation was, in fact, a modal response nearer to the anchor than was the modal response in the no-anchor condition, and a reduced dispersion of responses. That which was designated contrast was a modal response that was further from the experimental anchor than was the modal response in the no-anchor condition. The so-called contrast phenomenon was also accompanied by a reduced dispersion compared to that in the no-anchor condition.

In terms of the reference scale model, the phenomena of assimilation and contrast as observed in the Sherif *et al.* study might be described as a shift in reference scale origin toward or away from an experimental anchor, accompanied by an increase in size of the unit of judgment. The criterion for the identity of quantities cannot be applied to the data of the Sherif *et al.* study because their dependent variable did not retain information about the matching of physical and judged values. Thus, although it is plausible to think of assimilation and contrast effects in the study as reference scale phenomena, the critical data bearing on this point were not analyzed.

Parducci and Marshall (1962) produced evidence in support of their contention that the effects called assimilation and contrast by Sherif *et al.* represented artifacts of judgmental language. Specifically, they proposed that the remembered value for the hypothetical stimulus defining a boundary of the category associated with the anchor was displaced in a manner predictable from adaptation-level theory (to be discussed later), and that this displacement accounted for the results of the Sherif *et al.* study. This interpretation, which will be discussed more fully in a later section, implies that the data of the Sherif *et al.* study represent scale origin and scale unit phenomena rather than differences in psychological quantities.

   Assimilation and Contrast as Theoretical Terms. In formulating their theory of social-psychological effects in judgment, Hovland *et al.* (1957) and Sherif and Hovland, (1961) interpreted the psychophysical experiment as providing evidence that the perception of any given stimulus is displaced toward a near anchor and away from a remote anchor. According to this interpretation, some of the stimuli in any particular stimulus series might be displaced in one direction while others in the same series are displaced in the opposite direction. (This bilateral displacement within a single series was *not* observed in the data of the Sherif *et al.* experiment; it is a logical consequence of one interpretation of that experiment.) In applying their interpretation of assimilation and contrast phenomena to social attitudes, Hovland *et al.* and Sherif and Hovland assumed that a person anchors his reference scale by means of his own attitudinal position. Therefore, for each person assimilation and contrast effects are relative to his own position. In the comparison of the reference scales of subjects whose own positions are at opposite ends of a series of attitudinal positions, the bilateral displacements representing assimilation and contrast to own position would lead to a nonlinear relationship between the two scales.

   The fact that the theory predicts nonlinearity implies that the data collected to test the theory must be precise enough to warrant interpretation of the relative spacing of stimuli on the judgment scale. According to the earlier discussion of scale precision, an interpretation of differences in the spacing of stimuli which are judged in the same rank order requires interval or ratio scales. With two interval or ratio reference scales corresponding to a single stimulus series, the assimilation-contrast model of social judgment predicts the disconfirmation of the criterion for the identity of quantities. The predicted nonlinearity, however, has not generally been found in relevant experimental data (Hinckley, 1932, 1963; Ostrom, 1966; Upshaw, 1964, 1965; Ward, 1965, 1966).

   The Reference Scale Model Applied to the Assimilation-Contrast Theory. The basic principles of assimilation and contrast which underlie the theory are assumed to refer to general judgmental phenomena occurring with sensory as well as cognitive judgments. Although the theory has been applied mainly to the judgment of social stimuli, the basic processes that it assumes appear to apply as well to the judgment of other classes of stimuli. In principle, therefore, it is reasonable to imagine the comparison of a physical scale with its corresponding judgmental scale. Given appropriate anchor conditions, such a comparison would be expected by the theory to reveal that some of the stimuli are judged more or less accurately, whereas some stimuli are overvalued and others undervalued because of assimilation and contrast (a suitable data transformation corresponding to the psychophysical function is presupposed in this discussion as explained in the presentation of the reference scale model in the early part of section III). If the reference scale model were applied in such a comparison, even though its assumption of a single quantity is not met, the component of greatest interest would be that referring to unit. (The origin component, if it attained a significant value, would reflect failure of the over- and undervaluation because of assimilation and contrast to balance each other.) The unit component, as noted earlier, comprises two separate aspects of data. One of these, in the case of the comparison of a reference scale with a physical scale, involves the variance of the mean reference scale values and the variance of the physical values of the stimuli in the series. The variance of judgments might be larger or smaller than that of the physical values, depending upon the particular pattern of assimilation and contrast. A specific prediction can be made, however, for the second aspect of the unit component, the covariance term. The assimilation-contrast theory, because it specifies nonlinearity between an anchored reference scale and its corresponding physical scale, leads to the expectation of a correlation coefficient between these variables which is less than unity.

No effects are predicted on the basis of the assimilation-contrast theory for the origin-over-trials or the unit-over-trials components of the reference scale model.

In the comparison of two reference scales based upon a single stimulus series, the differences of quantity predicted by the assimilation-contrast theory would be manifested in the correlation term of the unit component. If any other component attained substantial value, it would be attributable to differences in anchor stimuli or in differential tendencies on the part of the judge to assimilate or contrast judgments to the anchor stimuli.

The assimilation-contrast theory allows for individual differences in degree of assimilation and contrast. Some evidence has been reported suggesting that a judge's degree of involvement in the judging task affects the tendency to assimilate and contrast (Sherif, Sherif, and Nebergall, 1965). Involvement is assumed to affect judgment by means of the size of the "latitude of acceptance." The construct of latitude of acceptance appears to be equivalent to that which Thurstone and Chave (1929) called "attitudinal tolerance," referring in the context of attitude measurement to the range of positions on an attitude scale that a judge endorses. In the work of Sherif and his colleagues the latitude of acceptance is generally defined operationally in terms of the response of a judge to the instruction to check all of a set of stimuli which he finds acceptable. In addition to the latitude of acceptance, Hovland *et al.* (1957) suggested a latitude of rejection, referring to the range of scale positions that the judge finds objectionable. It is the position of the anchor stimulus relative to the latitude of acceptance which is said to determine the pattern of assimilation and contrast. Specifically, an anchor stimulus with a scale value that is relatively close to the range of values representing the latitude of acceptance is, according to hypothesis, likely to be displaced in the direction of the latitude of acceptance. On the other hand, if the anchor stimulus is sufficiently removed from the acceptance region of the scale, thus falling within the latitude of rejection, it is supposed to be displaced still farther in the direction opposite to the acceptable region of the scale.

The formulation linking latitudes of acceptance and rejection to assimilation and contrast is not satisfactory for several reasons. First, this formulation requires the interpretation of assimilation and contrast as displacements from some true position. The anchor stimulus is supposed to be displaced toward or away from the latitude of acceptance, a phenomenon that can be observed only if a point of reference is established by which to assess displacement. One possibility is that the physical scale provides the basis for assessing displacement of anchors. However, when one considers the physical scale in this regard a fundamental difficulty with the conceptions of latitude of acceptance and latitude of rejection becomes apparent. In order to be meaningful, a latitude of acceptance or a latitude of rejection must be defined in terms of stimuli that are contiguous on a scale. Any set of stimuli can be ordered to virtually an infinite number of scales, according to the variable property that is isolated for consideration. Those stimuli that a particular judge likes or dislikes, accepts or rejects, etc., can be expected, in principle, to be arrayed contiguously only on a scale of preference. Thus, a set of attitude items might be scaled according to the extent to which a judge finds them acceptable as statements of his own convictions. (The respondent's task in Thurstone scaling is of this nature, as is the manner in which the latitudes of acceptance and rejection are determined in studies based upon the assimilation-contrast model.) The same items might be ordered to other scales, as, for example, the pro-anti scale commonly employed in attitude measurement (the judge's task in Thurstone scaling). No particular relationship between values on these two types of scales can be assumed, unless it is known that the judge based his preference ratings on the stimulus attributes in terms of which the attribute scale was constructed. In the absence of this assurance one should expect to find that stimuli evaluated as acceptable (when more than one stimulus is chosen) are likely to have values that are greatly scattered over the various attribute scales in which an investigator might have an interest.

Related to the problem of defining latitudes of acceptance and rejection as contiguous regions of a scale, the Thurstone theory of attitude measurement includes a provision for removing items from the final measurement instrument for which there is not a high correlation between the endorsement of the item and the endorsement of other items of similar scale value. This feature of the model, called the "criterion of irrelevance," was intended by Thurstone to insure a high correlation between the scale of acceptability and the scale of favorability toward the attitude object. The criterion of irrelevance was apparently never used in the construction of Thurstone scales except in the prototype instrument provided by Thurstone and Chave (1929). Studies by Dudycha (1943), Jones (1942), and Miller (1934) indicated that in the attitudinal measurement instruments constructed without use of the criterion of irrelevance the typical respondent endorsed statements that were not contiguously located on the scale of favorability toward the attitude object. The present point is that the results obtained by Dudycha, Jones, and Miller could have been predicted a priori, since there was no reason to believe that latitudes of acceptance constitute contiguous regions on any scale except one that corresponded to the variable of acceptability. The same difficulty appears to be a serious problem with the assimilation-contrast model as presently formulated.

Related to the difficulty of conceiving latitudes of acceptance and rejection as contiguous scale regions is the problem of identifying the nature of the scale property in terms of which assimilation and contrast are assumed to occur. For the sake of argument, let us imagine that a hypothetical respondent finds lifted weights acceptable according to their heaviness. It may be imagined that the respondent partitions the stimulus series into those weights that he finds acceptable (the relatively heavy stimuli) and those that he finds objectionable (the relatively light stimuli). An anchor stimulus which is outside the boundary of his acceptable subset is supposed to be displaced in the direction of the latitude of acceptance. It is difficult to tell from the present formulation whether in a case of this sort the judged heaviness of the anchor stimulus is expected to be changed, or merely its judged desirability (perhaps necessitating a change in preference criterion to incorporate considerations other than heaviness).

A final difficulty with the assimilation-contrast formulation is that the phenomena that were observed in the Sherif *et al.* (1958) experiment, however they are interpreted, appear to refer to the change of judgments of a series of stimuli owing to the introduction of an anchor. On the other hand, the assimilation-contrast theory is concerned with the judgment of the anchor stimulus, not the series stimuli.

The assimilation-contrast theory has been an influential approach to certain social-psychological problems of judgment. By and large, however, it has served as an orientation to research problems not as an explicit theory to be tested. [Indeed, its proponents have specifically disclaimed any intention of formulating a formal theory of judgment at this point in time (Sherif *et al.*, 1965).] As indicated in the above review, neither the logical constructions nor the available empirical data provides convincing evidence of the differences of quantity that are implied by the theory. From the perspective of the reference scale model the hypothesized differences of quantity refer to the most important feature of the theory. It is regrettable that very little research effort has been directed toward that aspect of the theory.

2.   *Quantity vs. Scale Interpretations of Context Effects*

The bilateral displacements because of anchoring which the assimilation-contrast theory predicts represent a special case of phenomena known as "context effects." Any systematic shift in the judgment of a subset of stimuli that can be attributed to an addition to or deletion from the total set of stimuli with which the subject deals is a context effect. Most often all of the judged values of a constant stimulus subset are found to be inversely related to the physical values of anchor stimuli (contrast effect), although a direct relationship (assimilation effect) has sometimes been reported. [Sherif and Hovland (1961) present a review of all but the most recent studies of context effects.] The question of whether the particular, bilateral context effects expected on the basis of assimilation-contrast theory represent quantity or scale phenomena was discussed in the previous section. Here the same question is raised concerning the typical demonstration of context effects involving all stimuli alike, as opposed to the differential stimulus effects predicted by assimilation-contrast theory.

Related to the issue of quantity vs. scale interpretations of context effects is the question of whether, or to what extent, they represent artifacts of an inadequate response language. Campbell, Lewis, and Hunt (1958), Harvey and Campbell (1963), and Krantz and Campbell (1961) have produced experimental evidence suggesting that the data of many studies of context effects may reflect two distinct processes. One process refers to the judge's accomodation of a limited categorical response language to alterations in the range of stimulation. The other refers to some implied psychological process that has nothing to do with "vocabulary exhaustion."

The use of a restricted, categorical response language in judgmental research might be justified if the topic under investigation concerns how a person copes with an inadequate vocabulary. Otherwise it appears difficult to justify the continued practice both in psychophysics and social psychology of collecting data in which the dual processes described by Campbell and his associates are almost certain to be confounded. If knowledge is to be gained about the psychological process in judgment that does not refer to coping with an inadequate vocabulary, then this extraneous consideration must be eliminated or controlled in experiments. Even when the limits of the vocabulary are not obviously called into question by the experimental plan, the categorical response language apparently triggers certain processes that are not instigated by limitless modes of expression. The work of Campbell and others, which has already been cited, as well as that of Stevens and Galanter (1957) and Parducci (1963, 1965) make it clear that the frequency of category usage is determined by other factors as well as by subjective magnitudes.

In methodological discussions within psychology and sociology it has become commonplace to use the term "scale" to refer to nothing more than a set of response categories which the investigator provides for the subject. A "scale" in this sense may, of course, measure nothing. The reference scale model described in this article is based upon a very different conception: one that views a scale as an expression of the quantitative relationships among objects. Under the present conception the issue of whether any particular phenomenon refers to scale or quantity presupposes an adequate response language. Artifacts of vocabulary exhaustion and response biases concerning the frequency of category usage are *neither* quantity nor scale phenomena.

The linearity criterion for the identity of quantities which was developed earlier in this article specifies a scale interpretation of any differences between two linearly related sets of judgments. This criterion is implicitly challenged by two recent studies of context effects. In both of these studies, one by Hicks and Campbell (1965) and one by Bevan, Maier, and Helson (1963), an attempt was made to demonstrate a change in origin of a ratio scale as a function of the manipulation of context. Presumably a change in absolute origin would be interpretable as a change of quantity, rather than scale.

The data of the Bevan *et al.* study were estimates of the number of beans in a jar. Because the subject's response was made in terms of an estimated count, and because counting implies cardinal numbers, the investigators assumed that the observed contrast effect represented a change of absolute origin. Their argument is not compelling, however, since it implies that scale level is determined by the judge's vocabulary. In fact, as was noted earlier, the precision level of any scale is established by the types of arithmetical operations that can be performed meaningfully with the scale values. For example, as a measure of a perceptual quantity the judgment in inches of line length has no special properties because the corresponding physical quantity is measurable on a ratio scale in terms of units of the same name. Guesses of how many beans are in a jar, when interpreted as a measure of a perceptual quantity, must be evaluated by the same criteria as any other scaling procedure.

Hicks and Campbell studied the effects of context on values assigned to three sets of stimuli by a procedure designed by Thurstone and Jones (1959) to provide a ratio scale. Clear evidence of a shift in origin was found for all three judged attributes: the desirability of birthday gifts, the seriousness of traffic offenses, and the bizarreness and eccentricity of behavior symptoms. These results suggest either that the scale construction procedures did not, in fact, yield a ratio scale, or that the effect of context was to generate a family of subjective quantities, each measureable by a ratio scale, each with a different origin, and each linearly related to every other one. The investigators expressed reservations about the latter interpretation, and performed analyses to test several alternative interpretations in terms of methodological artifacts. Their data failed to confirm such artifacts. More recently, Jones (1967) reanalyzed part of the Hicks and Campbell data by a modified version of the Thurstone and Jones procedure. The original scaling method incorporates an assumption that the discriminability of stimuli is unrelated to their scale values, whereas the modified version assumes a systematic relationship between these two variables. (The revised version, it should be noted, is in closer accord with current psychometric theory than is the original.) The results based on the new method of scale construction indicated that the origin was invariant with changes of context.

Neither the Bevan et al. nor the Hicks and Campbell study presented convincing evidence of shifts in absolute origin. Apart from the question of experimental evidence, it is relevant to consider whether it is logical to imagine that context could determine the absolute origin. In the physical sciences it seems utterly impossible to think of any experimental manipulation that would alter the absolute origin of a ratio scale. The origin of a scale at this level corresponds to zero quantity. Zero height means no height, hence no object, since all objects have height. There are not many instances of ratio scales of subjective quantities. Consequently, it is difficult to grasp intuitively the full implications of a true zero point in the measurement of the quantities with which social scientists deal. Presumably, the possibility of defining two quantities that differ only in origin is as remote in the social domain as it is in the physical. It is probably logically possible, but exceedingly unlikely. The linearity criterion for the identity of quantities, therefore, will probably prove to be an adequate one. At the present time there is very little data by which to test the adequacy of the linearity criterion. Furthermore, that criterion has yet to be made explicit in terms of methodological procedures. It would, therefore, be premature to conclude that there can be no context effects on quantities.

Stevens (1958) has phrased the quantity vs. scale question concerning context effects as that of sensory adaptation vs. the relativity of judgment. According to Stevens' arguments the issue is resolvable, in principle, at the physiological level. Adaptation, he noted, traditionally refers to alterations of excitability, whereas judgmental relativity refers to the "modulus of the scale of judgment" (p. 646). The suggested resort to physiological indices has appeal. However, from the perspective of social psychology it is not entirely satisfying because it tends to assume that all differences in psychological quantities have physiological concomitants. In sensory scaling it may be reasonable to examine changes in excitability with shifting context. When, however, the scaling task refers to a cognitive, rather than sensory variable, the physiological criterion does not seem promising.

Manis (1967) employed an ingenious criterion in the case of a cognitive variable. He had subjects match descriptions of photographs with the stimuli to which they referred. Varying the context of photograph descriptions, he found that a constant subset of descriptions were attributed systematically to particular photographs in a manner suggestive of a contrast effect. Other experimental conditions involved rating the same descriptions by means of a numerical and a non-numerical language. These dependent variables also revealed a contrast effect, which Manis interpreted as a quantity phenomenon because of the parallel effect with the matching variable.

The development of criteria for the identity of quantities which will supplement the linearity criterion is very desirable. Indices such as those suggested by Stevens and Manis should be studied systematically. Before abandoning the linearity criterion in the face of data such as that which Manis presented, the possibility should be considered that results such as those he reported might be attributable to the responses made to the scale differences which were produced by the manipulated difference in context. Likewise, in the sensory domain, it may be that a shift in scale can, itself, produce physiological changes in excitability. At least this possibility should be explored. The possibility that scale differences may lead to subtle and substantively meaningful differences in other than judgmental behavior suggests extraordinary care in phrasing the quantity vs. scale issue in a particular instance.

B. HYPOTHESIZED DIFFERENCES IN SCALE ORIGIN

Two theories of scale origin will be discussed in this section, one a theory that has been applied very generally to sensory and cognitive quantities, and the other which applies to a more restricted class of cognitive variable. The first, adaptation-level theory was formulated by Helson (1947) to account for certain visual phenomena but has subsequently been applied to problems in psychophysics and perception, motivation, learning, thinking, personality, and interpersonal behavior (Helson, 1964). The widespread application has been challenged, particularly by Stevens (1958) who, as described in the preceding section, wished to distinguish between sensory adaptation and judgmental relativity in the study of context effects. As will be illustrated, Stevens' argument in this regard has important ramifications for social-psychological applications of the theory. Some of the difficulties inherent in generalizing the single theory of adaptation level to a variety of areas might be overcome by formulating special versions of the theory to meet the demands of particular domains. The question of the compatibility of the family of special theories is then amenable to subsequent research. The second theory to be discussed here can be viewed as one such special adaptation-level theory. It is the comparison-level theory which Thibaut and Kelley (1959) formulated to account for the evaluation of the utility of outcomes accruing to a person in social interaction.

1. Adaptation-Level Theory

Underlying adaptation-level theory is a view that human activity can generally be described in terms of its level and that for most psychological variables there is a level which corresponds in some sense to a point of psychological neutrality (Helson, 1964). This point constitutes the adaptation level (AL). In fashioning the concept into a theory of judgment, Helson assumed that the AL functions as the point of origin in terms of which a judge evaluates each stimulus. The theory refers to the determinants of AL. Viewed from the perspective of the present reference scale model and from consideration of the linearity criterion for the identity of quantities, adaptation-level theory can be described as a theory of reference scale origin.

Adaptation level is assumed to represent a weighted geometric mean of the values on a physical scale of all of the stimuli which the judge takes into account at the moment of rendering a judgment. Defining the AL as the geometric mean of the physical stimulus values amounts to accepting a logarithmic psychophysical function, as advocated by Fechner. Thus, the AL is defined as the mean of the assumed subjective stimulus magnitudes. The theory specifies, furthermore, that different weights are to be applied to three classes of stimuli: (1) those in the experimental series to be judged; (2) contextual stimuli which are physically present at the time of judging, but which are not judged; and (3) residual stimuli which are remembered from previous experiences.

Although procedures for the calculation of AL for the judgment of sensory qualities are available, in most applications to social-psychological problems and to many sensory problems, the theory of adaptation level serves primarily to formalize predictions of ordinal differences in the judgment of the same stimuli by judges with different experimental histories. Because the judgment of any given stimulus is assumed to be proportional to its distance above or below the AL, it is generally expected that the value assigned to a stimulus is inversely related to the level of stimulation (because the AL is directly related to stimulus level). Furthermore, it is assumed that the AL is assimilated to (that is, moves toward) the physical value of every stimulus to which the judge is newly exposed. The predicted effect of introducing an anchor stimulus is, then, to shift the AL in the direction of the anchor and, correspondingly, to shift the judgment of every stimulus in the series in the direction opposite to that of the anchor. In terms of the judgmental phenomena known as assimilation and contrast, adaptation-level theory posits a judgmental process that leads directly to contrast.

The basic adaptation-level theory described above refers to absolute judgments. Absolute judgments are responses designating the amount of some property which the judge attributes to a particular stimulus. Another type of quantitative response is what is known as a comparative judgment. This type of judgment represents the estimated difference between two stimuli with respect to the scale property. Thus, the judge may describe in his response how heavy a stimulus appears to be, or how much heavier it appears to be than some standard. His task in a social-psychological study, for example, may be to make an absolute judgment of how favorable toward an attitude object a particular course of action would be, or it may be to render a comparative judgment of how much more favorable toward the object some course of action would be than would the one advocated by the judge himself. Adaptation-level theory has been applied to comparative as well as to absolute judgments.

In classical psychophysics the so-called constant methods employ comparative judgments involving an experimentally established standard stimulus and a series of variable stimuli. Among the various scores associated with the constant methods is the point of subjective equality (PSE). The PSE is defined as the point on the physical scale which is judged to be equal to the standard stimulus. It has long been known that the PSE shifts with the distribution of stimuli, even though the standard stimulus is held constant. Helson, Michels, and Sturgeon (1954) suggested an application of adaptation-level theory that accounts for the dependence of PSE on the stimulus distribution. In this application the remembered value of the standard is assumed to be displaced toward the value of the AL which exists at the moment. This formulation amounts to a hypothesis regarding memory for the quantitative values of stimuli. According to this implicit hypothesis, the trace of each stimulus is displaced toward the adaptation level. When, therefore, a subject in a psychophysical experiment is called upon to judge the difference between a standard stimulus and a variable stimulus, presented successively and in that order, what he compares is the older trace of the standard with the more immediate impression of the variable stimulus. Extending the logic of this formulation, Helson and others have presented considerable evidence in support of the contention that the PSE is a special case of an adaptation level (Helson, 1964).

In the typical study of anchoring, the judge is not strictly instructed in how to use the information provided by anchors. It is conceivable that in many studies the anchor stimulus serves as a standard for comparative judgments. This possibility underlies the Parducci and Marshall (1962) interpretation of the Sherif et al. (1958) demonstrations of assimilation and contrast. The Sherif et al. study, it will be recalled, involved the experimental presentation of an anchor stimulus which was identified for the subject as an example of either the heaviest or lightest stimuli to be judged. The anchor stimulus always preceded the variable stimulus. Assimilation was observed in the condition in which the anchor stimulus coincided with the boundary of the experimental series. According to the Parducci and Marshall interpretation, the PSE corresponding to the anchor stimulus was, in all conditions, displaced in the direction of the AL (the geometric mean of the series of stimuli). Thus, when judgments were made in that condition in which the anchor was contiguous with the boundary of the series, the remembered value of the anchor was compared with stimuli which in no case exceeded it on the physical scale, but which sometimes subjectively did so because of the drift of the PSE toward the AL. This mechanism, which is entirely consistent with adaptation-level theory, can account for the assimilation phenomena of the Sherif et al. study. When, in the other conditions of that study, the anchor was sufficiently remote from the stimulus series, the displacement of its remembered value in the direction of the series adaptation level was assumed not to be sufficient to locate it below the value of any of the series stimuli. Thus, successively more remote anchoring is expected to produce contrast, and this was observed to be the case.

It is interesting to apply the logic of the Parducci and Marshall explanation of the Sherif *et al.* findings to an experimental situation in which the judgmental task is to estimate stimulus magnitude in terms of a continuous, unlimited language as distinguished from the categorical language used in earlier studies. For example, imagine that the anchors in a weight-judging experiment are correctly identified in terms of grams or ounces and that the subject's task is to judge each variable stimulus in terms of units of the same name. With only this change in the design of the Sherif *et al.* study, the PSE's corresponding to each anchor would represent a point on the physical scale which is remembered as that representing a given number of grams or ounces. Following Parducci and Marshall, the remembered value of the anchor would be expected to be distorted in the direction of the AL. This means that all anchors above the AL will be remembered as smaller than they truly are, and those below it as greater than they are. For purposes of argument, suppose that judges adopt a psychological unit which is exactly equal to the physical unit of gram or ounce, and that this unit does not vary as a function of anchoring. Thus, if stimuli x and y are separated by 50 gm on the physical scale, they will be separated by 50 gm on the psychological scale. If a 150 gm weight is remembered as 140 gm (for example), then according to the logic of the theory and the assumption of equal physical and psychological units, the stimulus that is judged to be 100 gm is one that has the physical value of 90 gm. Accordingly, the stimulus which physically is equal to 100 gm is expected to be judged as heavier than it truly is whenever it is compared to an anchor that is heavier than the AL, and lighter than it truly is when compared to an anchor that is below AL. This process is illustrated in Fig. 1. According to theory the stimulus AL is displaced toward each successively more remote anchor stimulus at the same time that the PSE for the anchor is displaced toward the AL. If the plausible assumption is made that the displacement of the PSE is greater than that of the AL for each new anchor stimulus, the Parducci and Marshall arguments, augmented by an assumption of an invariant judgmental unit (whether or not this unit is equal to the physical unit), imply increasing amounts of assimilation with increasingly more remote anchors. According to this rationale, then, the contrast effects reported by Sherif *et al.* were artifacts of a categorical response language.

The conclusion of the preceding paragraph depends upon several testable assumptions for which there is apparently no available data. Also

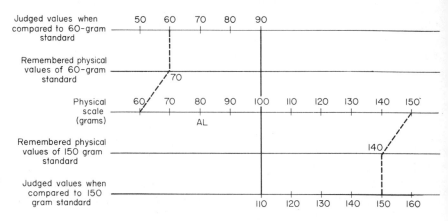

Fig. 1. Illustration of the process implied for comparative judgments by adaptation-level theory, assuming an unlimited language. (Broken lines refer to the hypothesized displacement in memory of the physical magnitudes of standards, the labels for which are accurately remembered. The solid line refers to the predicted judgment of a 100-gm weight in either of two anchor conditions.)

at the basis of the conclusion is the apparent dependence of the predictions of adaptation-level theory for comparative judgments on memory. If the standard (anchor) and variable stimuli had been presented simultaneously rather than successively, or if the order in which the standard and variable stimuli had been balanced, the Parducci and Marshall interpretation of the Sherif *et al.* results would apparently have been invalidated. Similarly, these design changes would invalidate the prediction of increasing assimilation with increasingly more remote anchors when judgments are made in terms of an unlimited language rather than a categorical one.

Obviously a great deal more research is indicated to determine the extent to which assimilation and contrast phenomena depend upon categorical language and successive presentation of anchors and variable stimuli. A still broader issue is that of the applicability of judgmental principles based upon studies of sensory processes to judgments based upon nonsensory, cognitive processes. Intuitively, it is plausible to imagine the distortion in memory of the perceived value of a sensory imput. If, however, the judge's task is to evaluate the utility of an outcome with which he is thoroughly familiar, it does not seem reasonable to expect that the outcome value would suffer the same type of distortion as that of an unfamiliar sensory event.

Inherent in the strategy of seeking explanatory principles outside one's own area of special competence is the hazard of building misleading analogies based upon arbitrary interpretations of research findings. As a case in point, adaptation-level theory has been imported into social psychology with benefit to the area. However, its successful application has generally not been at a very precise level. Most often, in fact, the theory has been invoked *post hoc* to account for phenomena which may be viewed as context effects. The present state of the theory is such that formal applications to social psychology are appropriate. However issues such as those discussed here (categorical vs. continuous language, comparative vs. absolute judgment, sensory vs. cognitive quantities, etc.) must be considered if the precise predictions of the theory are to be realized in practice. Unfortunately, very little attention to these matters appears to have been given, either in psychophysics or in social psychology.

2. Comparison-Level Theory

In their analysis of behavior in social groups, Thibaut and Kelley (1959) needed a judgmental concept by which to represent phenomena relating to a person's satisfaction with the outcomes he receives in a particular social interaction. For this purpose they formulated the concept of comparison level (CL), defining it as a special case of adaptation level (p. 82). Specifically, they defined CL as "some modal or average value of all the outcomes known to the person (by virtue of personal or vicarious experience), each outcome weighted by its salience (or the degree to which it is instigated for the person at the moment)" (p. 81).

As theory, comparison level is both more general and more specific than adaptation level. No attempt has been made to express CL mathematically, and no attention has been given from the perspective of this theory to the nature of the psychophysical function relating a reference scale to its corresponding physical scale. Furthermore, it is implicitly assumed by comparison-level theory that each judge has a single reference scale of outcome utility in terms of which he evaluates all outcomes, whatever their nature. The origin of that scale is presumably the CL, and it fluctuates with the salience of outcomes. This formulation contrasts with adaptation-level theory which assumes a different reference scale for each stimulus attribute that is judged, each with its particular AL. It appears that Thibaut and Kelley have effectively distinguished between estimates of the status of stimuli in terms of some attribute, on the one hand, and expressions of the desirability of stimuli, on the other. Scales of the first sort, i.e., attribute scales, presumably result from the subject's performance of what Coombs (1953, 1964) described as Task B. The utility scale would appear to involve Task A, the evaluation of stimuli according to their departure from the judge's ideal. However, the Thibaut and Kelley formulation does *not* explicitly suggest that judgment of utility is comparative rather than absolute.

The conception of a single utility scale implies that a nagging wife, a

10% salary raise, and a slice of apple pie are all evaluated in terms of a single CL. Therefore, the increased salience of outcomes that are objectively better than a person is currently receiving is expected to elevate the scale origin, and thereby reduce the enjoyment of current outcomes. Similarly, a shift of origin toward poorer outcomes is expected to increase the enjoyment of current outcomes. Clearly, Thibaut and Kelley anticipate contrast effects as a function of the change of context. Furthermore, context is defined quantitatively in terms of a hypothetical scale of objective value to the person and not in terms of qualitative aspects of outcomes. This conception of the judgment of utility can be tested, although it appears not to have been.

A straightforward application of adaptation-level theory to the judgment of utility would probably lead to the conception of the reference scale origin as a weighted average of the objective utility values of the series stimuli. Such a conception differs from that held by modern decision theorists (see Edwards, Lindman, and Phillips, 1965) in that it makes no provision in the measurement of utility for the subjective probability of attainment of the alternative outcomes. The comparison-level approach of Thibaut and Kelley, unlike classical adaptation-level theory, makes the probability of attainment an explicit determinant of reference scale origin. Subjective probability functions as a weight to be applied to the utility values of the series stimuli. According to this conception, therefore, the CL is to be thought of both as the origin of a scale of expected utility and as an approximation to a level of aspiration. Inherent in the formulation of CL is the possibility of bringing together several areas of psychological research. In this respect, the formulation is suggestive of further work along the lines of Siegel's (1957) endeavor to introduce the level of aspiration into the measurement of utility. The relevance of CL both to judgment and to decision making suggests that a full explication of the concept in regard to the issues of both fields would be greatly rewarding. At present, however, little empirical work has been directed to any aspect of CL.

Thibaut and Kelley recognized that most outcomes are complex, consisting of rewarding and costly features in combination. The notion of a single utility scale for the evaluation of all outcomes implies that a complex outcome can be represented on the scale for each of its components and for the total "bundle" as well. Individual differences in reactions to complex outcomes are predicted by Thibaut and Kelley. Specifically, people who are confident and outgoing are said to focus their attention more on the rewarding aspects of complex outcomes, while others who are fearful of failure attend primarily to the costly aspects.

Gumpert, Thibaut, and Shuford (1961) studied the hypothesized differences between reward- and cost-oriented people by means of an experiment in which girls evaluated the attractiveness of cosmetic kits. Subjects were selected on the basis of the Welsh A and R (Anxiety and Repression) Scales of the MMPI, under the assumption that those whose scores were relatively high on both of these traits are cost-oriented, and those relatively low on both are reward-oriented. The utility values of the stimuli were determined for each subject by means of a lottery technique that generates an interval scale. The arbitrary origin of the scale for each subject was defined as the utility of the particular outcome level to which she had been assigned by the experimenter. The hypothesized differential weighting of rewarding and costly aspects of unattained outcomes was assessed by determining the difference between the attained level (the arbitrary origin) and the judged value of the next best, unattained outcome. Reward-oriented people, since they are thought to weight rewards more heavily than costs, were expected to perceive the next best, unattained outcome as farther from the present level than did cost-oriented people. The data confirmed the hypothesis.

If it is true that reward- and cost-oriented people differ in the salience of rewarding and costly components of complex stimuli, it then follows that reward-oriented people have higher CLs than do cost-oriented people (since the CL is an average of outcomes weighted by their salience). This hypothesis was recently tested (Upshaw, 1967b) on the basis of ratings of hypothetical college instructors and hypothetical partners for social dating. Each subject rated the desirability both of instructors and dating partners based upon single-trait descriptions. Complex stimuli were constructed by pairing socially desirable and undesirable traits. The relative scale positions of the complex stimuli compared to the individual components served to define reward-cost orientation. Each subject was assigned two reward-cost scores, one for each set of stimuli. These scores were computed as the differences between the scale values of the individual components and of the composite for each complex stimulus, summed over the complex stimuli, and weighted inversely by the standard deviation of the ratings of the single-trait stimuli. (The inverse weighting according to dispersion of the single-trait stimuli represented an allowance for possible differences in reference scale unit.) The two measures of reward-cost orientation were significantly correlated.

The test of the hypothesis that the CLs of reward-oriented people are higher than those of cost-oriented people consisted of a comparison of the mean utility ratings of the single-trait stimuli for groups designated as reward- or cost-oriented. Three tests of the hypothesis were made: one for instructors, one for social dating partners, and one combining the two classes of stimuli by means of a standard score transformation. The first and third tests were clearly significant, whereas the second revealed a relationship in the expected direction that had a chance probability between .10 and .15. The net results were interpreted as confirmation of the hypothesis.

As a theory of judgment, comparison level has received very little attention. This is regrettable for it appears to be distinctly different in some of its implications from its acknowledged conceptual parent, adaptation level. These unique features derive from special considerations regarding utility judgments which are of less importance in judgments of stimulus attributes. Because the concept of CL was developed as an adjunct to a theory of social interaction, it offers a valuable potential link between the psychology of judgment, on the one hand, and the traditional social psychological domain, on the other.

C.   Hypothesized Differences in Scale Unit

According to the model of the personal reference scale, the judgmental unit encompasses two classes of phenomena: that referring to the degree to which stimulus differences are matched by judgmental differences (discrimination) and that referring to the expansiveness of the language in terms of which judgments are expressed. The relationship existing between two reference scales of the same quantity may be thought of in terms of a pair of linear regression lines, the coefficients of which are the product of the correlation coefficient for the two sets of values and the ratio of the two standard deviations. The correlation term refers to a comparison of the degree of discrimination underlying the two scales, and the ratio of the standard deviations refers to a comparison of the expansiveness of language (see Upshaw, 1965). It was noted earlier that the value of the correlation coefficient can be expected to be less than 1.00 under any one of three conditions: (1) the physical values of the stimuli are too close to permit perfectly reliable differentiation for even the most astute judge; (2) the judges differ in the extent to which they differentiate among stimuli, because of differences in motivation, ability, etc.; and (3) the true relationship between the two sets of judgments is nonlinear. The reference scale model is not likely to be informative if the first condition obtains. The model is intended for the study of factors that operate differentially according to characteristics of judges or of the situations prevailing at the time of judgment. The factors leading to the first condition are not of this sort. The model should not be applied if the third condition exists, because that condition entails a difference of quantity rather than scale. Only the second condition is truly relevant to the domain of the model.

The personal reference scale model implies a sequence of research questions related to scale unit. If the correlation terms in the unit and unit-over-time components have the value of 1.00 (or very closely approximate it), then these components can be interpreted unambiguously in terms of unit size. Any significant departure from perfect correlation necessitates additional analyses (and possibly new data) to determine which of the three conditions that were discussed in the preceding paragraph is responsible. If it is decided that there are genuine differences in discrimination underlying the two sets of judgments under comparison, then the reasons for this difference probably become the most important issue in the investigation.

There is a great deal of conceptual confusion in the literature concerning discrimination and unit size, and concerning processes bearing on each. The reference scale model indicates a particular relationship between discrimination and unit size which ultimately might be studied with profit. At the present time there is only a meager literature bearing on these phenomena considered in isolation, and none in which they are related.

1. A Note Concerning the Distinction between Discrimination, Stimulus Identification, and Scaling

In psychophysics the concept of discrimination refers to the sensitivity of the organism to differences of physical scale values. Thus, red—green color-blind people are those who cannot discriminate between red and green hues. They may, however, learn to identify which stimuli are red and which are green by means of cues such as differential brightness or, in the case of traffic lights, by conventions regarding position. There is a subtle distinction between discrimination and stimulus identification (or recognition) which has often been overlooked. The problem may derive from the excesses of the stimulus—response approach to psychology. Certainly the vocabulary of that approach invites a conception of discrimination as a process of distinguishing among stimuli rather than one of distinguishing among amounts of a variable property which characterize stimuli. If a subject holding weights in his left and right hands is asked whether he can discriminate between them, his task is that of deciding whether the stimuli are equally heavy, not whether they are different stimuli.

The discrimination problem is one of deciding whether two or more subjective magnitudes are the same, whereas the identification problem is that of deciding which of a set of stimuli is present. Discrimination is logically possible among absolutely novel stimuli and for quantities not previously experienced. In the case of identification, however, there clearly must be prior knowledge, at least with regard to a stimulus classification system.

The present article is devoted primarily to the psychophysical task of scaling (cf. Galanter, 1962; Luce, 1963; Luce and Galanter, 1963) whereby a judge indicates the subjective magnitudes associated with stimuli. The distinctions among identification, discrimination, and scaling are difficult to recognize in the fairly common experimental situation in which the judged stimuli differ in only one property. In such instances the judge whose task is stimulus identification has no basis upon which to perform that task except his judgments of the subjective magnitudes of each stimulus. Furthermore, his ability to discriminate differences of magnitude sets a limit upon his judgments of amount of difference among stimuli, and, in the unidimensional case, therefore, upon his ability to identify stimuli.

Although it is not always easy to tell whether a judge's task is to identify, discriminate, or scale stimuli, the difficulty often results from experimental conventions which needlessly confound the tasks. An identification task implies that the judge knows (or thinks he knows) exactly which stimuli might occur. Given that stimulation does occur, he must decide which stimulus event produced it. There is implicit in every identification task a criterion of "correct" performance. Correctness is an irrelevant consideration for discrimination and scaling, for in the performance of both of the latter tasks the judge is presumed to be an expert in conveying information about a subjective quantity. If a subjective quantity is involved at all in an identification task, it is as the means by which the judge estimates values of a corresponding physical quantity and thereby identifies stimuli.

Much of the confusion in the literature among the various judgmental processes is because of less than optimal methodological decisions on the part of investigators. The most straightforward way to treat identification is by means of information theory analysis or its equivalent (Luce, 1963).

Discrimination can best be studied by a paired comparisons schedule, in which the judge indicates which member of the pair of stimuli is of greater magnitude with respect to the subjective quantity. Scaling is appropriately studied by magnitude estimation or by the production of magnitudes in one domain to match those in another.

Often in the study of judgment the investigator prescribes a categorical response language without making it clear whether the judge is supposed to guess which category each stimulus belongs to (as determined by some presumably objective criterion), or whether his judgments were solicited in order to determine the status of each stimulus in terms of the categorical ratings of subjective magnitudes (whether, in brief, the investigator wants information *about* the subject or *from* the subject about the subjective magnitudes of the stimuli). If the latter, he may be forced by an inadequate number of response alternatives to convey his judgments less precisely than he is capable of doing, or than he would do if allowed a richer vocabulary. Therefore, the fact that a subject places two stimuli into the same response category is generally not *prima facie* evidence that he regards them to be of the same magnitude.

Categorical ratings, are, therefore, a bad methodological choice in the study of discrimination because they confound discrimination with a decision on the part of the judge that two magnitudes are close enough to warrant similar labeling. They are often an equally bad choice for studying identification when they do not provide enough distinct labels for the stimuli, thus confounding discrimination and scaling with identification.

In their theories of psychological scale construction, Fechner (1966) and Thurstone (1927) developed the idea that the probability of discrimination between two magnitudes is sufficient information for establishing their scale positions with respect to the measured quantity. The methodological procedures that have been based upon this fundamental premise abound in psychology and the social sciences. The fact that the premise has been institutionalized in the folkways of the discipline adds to the difficulty of maintaining a clear conceptual distinction among the judgmental tasks.

Failure to distinguish identification, discrimination, and scaling may be responsible for some of the reported difficulties in dealing experimentally with the concept of "equivalence range" or its presumed equivalent "category width" as a matter of style of categorizing (Fillenbaum, 1959; Tajfel, Richardson, and Everstine, 1964). In that line of research the subject is usually called upon to decide whether a particular stimulus is, or is not, an example of a specified class of stimuli. To be called an example of the class, the stimulus must be judged to have the characteristics which define the class. For example, all animals meeting a set of criteria that, in principle, can be made explicit are identified by the same response. They may all be considered, in one sense only, as equivalent. Although dalmatians, fox terriers, and bull dogs are labeled the same, most people could cite a number of differences among them. Equivalence in the phrase "equivalence range" appears, therefore, to refer to identification, not to discrimination or scaling. In many studies, however, equivalence range has been defined operationally by tasks that confound identification and discrimination. Bruner and Tajfel (1961), for example, presented slides containing variable densities of dots. A slide with 20 dots was correctly identified for the subject, and he was asked to decide for each subsequent slide whether or not it also contained 20 dots. Reliable individual differences in sensory discrimination are possible because of characteristic efficiency of physiological mechanisms, the motivation to report perceived differences, etc. However, the logical nature of the equivalence range construct does not seem to imply individual differences because of discrimination. Instead it implies differences because of identification. Insofar as reliable differences owing to both of these judgmental processes appear to exist, the failure to distinguish between them may have introduced considerable "noise" into the literature in this area.

Phenomena of identification, discrimination, and scaling warrant thorough investigation, both in sensory and cognitive domains. In light of the arguments of this section it appears that thoroughness of investigation implies the separation of the processes both conceptually and methodologically. A particularly valuable type of research would seem to be that in which a given set of independent variables are related to more than one type of dependent variable. An example of this research strategy was provided by Kelley, Hovland, Schwartz, and Abelson (1955) who studied the effects of judge's race (hence, presumed ego involvement) on categorical ratings and on paired comparisons of written statements of opinion with respect to the degree of implied favorable—unfavorable affect toward Negroes. They found a dramatic difference according to judgmental task. Based upon the paired comparisons data, the experimental groups appeared to have discriminated degrees of implied affect equally well. When the categorical ratings of the same statements were simply averaged (the method of equal-appearing intervals), the racially different groups were found to differ in what appeared to be reference scale origin, with the Negro group typically rating a statement as more anti-Negro than did the white group. The categorical ratings for the two groups were analyzed by the method of successive intervals, a scale construction method which is based upon Thurstone's premise that relative scale values are proportional to the probability of discrimination. These scale values correlated highly (.92) between the racial groups, suggesting two scales of a single quantity. Furthermore, they appeared to show both origin and unit differences between groups; the Negro subjects assigned generally less pro-Negro values to the items (as estimated from Fig. 3, Kelley *et al.,* 1955, p. 156) and a wider range of values.

It is apparent from the Kelley *et al.* study that the race of the judge has different effects upon different judgmental tasks. The following conclusions appear to be warranted by that study: (1) Negroes and whites discriminate equally well between degrees of sentiment toward Negroes as an attitude object (the paired comparisons data); (2) Negroes and whites define the attitudinal quantity in essentially the same way (the high linear correlation between successive intervals values, and an even higher correlation, .97, between paired comparisons values); and (3) Negroes, compared to whites, use a narrower judgmental unit in estimating the magnitudes of each stimulus (the wider range of successive intervals values).

In the social-psychological literature there is frequent mention of the term "discrimination." Most often, however, it is not possible to decide with reasonable confidence whether a particular set of data should be interpreted in terms of a difference in quantity between judges, a difference in the judgmental tasks performed by the judges, a difference in reference scale units between judges, or a true difference in discrimination. The confusion is increased by a tendency for investigators in this area to speak of the relative *ability* of judges to discriminate, rather than the relative discrimination that they attain in a particular experiment. Obviously ability cannot be measured except under conditions of maximum incentive, a consideration that is routinely overlooked. To rectify the current situation regarding the study of discrimination, investigators must phrase experimental issues more carefully than is the prevailing practice, and select appropriate experimental tasks. On the basis of the present literature it is doubtful that a single independent variable can be specified which is reliably related to a real discrimination dependent variable.

Although the correlation term in the unit components of the personal reference scale model is not an optimal statistic for studying discrimination, it does provide a sufficient criterion for a particular interpretation of the unit components. In comparing two judges if the correlations are virtually perfect, indicating both a single quantity and equal discrimination, it is appropriate to speak of differences in the size of the two reference scale units. In the next section these qualifying conditions will be assumed.

2. The Size of the Judgmental Unit

Volkmann (1951) described a judgmental theory that views the judge as partitioning the effective stimulus range into as many segments as are represented by his response repertoire. Confronting the task of scaling a set of stimuli, the judge presumably pays particular attention to those stimuli the magnitudes of which are the smallest and largest in the set. These stimuli define the judge's *perspective,* the psychological representation of stimulus range. In reporting the subjective magnitude of each stimulus, the judge apparently estimates its proportionate distance between the perspective parameters, and assigns it the appropriate categorical response. If the judge's perspective is extended by means of physically present, remembered, or imagined stimuli, the judgments of the original stimulus series will all be displaced in the direction opposite to that of the perspective expansion (provided, of course, that the number of available response categories is not changed). Volkmann's conception appears to be one of semantic adjustment whereby the judge fits a limited categorical language to his perspective.

A version of Volkmann's theory was generally supported in a study of the effects of stimulus range and judge's own attitude on the scale values of attitudinal statements (Upshaw, 1962). That version of the theory, called the "variable series model," assumes that a judge adds his own position to the series of positions that he is asked to judge. When his position exceeds the range of the experimental series, it serves to expand and anchor his perspective. Therefore, in effect, judges whose positions are within the series, and those whose positions exceed it, respond to different series (hence, the name of the model). In a design in which the range of the series and the attitudes of the judges are co-manipulated in order to render judges of differing positions in-range and out-of-range in various experimental conditions, the variable series model specifies a particular interaction which was observed in the study.

Much of the experimental work reported by Volkmann (1951) in relation to his theory seems to be directed to the question of the effects of a labeled anchor stimulus on the accuracy with which a subject judges a set of stimuli. The concern with judgmental accuracy suggests, in turn, that the theory is intended to account for stimulus identification rather than scaling. It was noted in the previous section that identification and scaling refer to different task sets on the part of the judge, identification being the set to choose the "correct" response from among discrete alternative responses, and scaling, the set to estimate stimulus magnitude in terms of a subjective quantity. It was also noted in the earlier discussion that with stimuli varying in one dimension only identification must be based upon scaling. This fact implies that a group of identifications in the unidimensional case, even though they are not based explicitly upon the scaling task, nevertheless might serve as a scale of subjective magnitude, provided that the identifications and a criterion scale of subjective magnitude can be shown to be linearly related. It is difficult to determine whether Volkmann's theory is primarily an identification or a scaling theory, but for much research on unidimensional stimuli, it may not matter.

If Volkmann's formulation is viewed as a scaling model, it clearly implies that unit size is a function of perspective. Assuming a fixed categorical language, the extension of perspective not only results in the displacement of the scale origin in the direction of the extension (and the displacement of scale values in the opposite direction), but also it results in an expansion of the physical scale distance between the boundaries of each response category. The expansion in the size of the categories is what is meant by an expansion of unit in the case of categorical ratings.

The consequence of an expanded unit is a reduced dispersion of scale values assigned to any subset of stimuli that are judged both in the original and expanded perspective conditions.

As a theory of the reference scale, Volkmann's formulation implies that the scale origin is a function of the sum (average) of the perspective parameters and that the unit is a function of the difference in these parameters. When applied to the specific problems of relating own attitude to the judgments of the attitudes of others, the theory was called "variable series" (Upshaw, 1962, 1964). In subsequent work, which will be discussed below, it has more often been referred to as the "variable perspective theory."

Data of the 1962 study referring to the least ambiguous items were later analyzed (Upshaw, 1965) to test the variable perspective predictions regarding judgmental unit. Those predictions were clearly confirmed for perspective manipulation by means of stimulus range. However, those based upon the assumed anchoring of perspective by means of the judge's own attitude were not confirmed. According to prediction, there should have been no differences in unit size among judges except as an interaction with stimulus range. In fact, the interaction was not found, and the judges did differ independently of stimulus range. Anti-Negro judges displayed the largest unit (smallest dispersion), neutral judges an intermediate unit, and pro-Negro judges the smallest unit. The differences in unit size among judges of varying attitudes were confirmed in another analysis involving the values assigned to all items by those subjects who participated in the full-range experimental condition (Upshaw, 1964).

The combined results of studies of attitude scaling seem to suggest that the variable perspective formulation of origin and unit is basically valid, even though some predictions relating unit to own attitude were not confirmed. Within the framework of the theory, there are two possible explanations of the unexpected relationship between attitude and unit size. First it may be that some determinant of unit size besides perspective operates differentially according to attitude, or according to some other factor that is nested in the grouping of judges according to attitude. A second possibility is that perspective is anchored in different ways (by different classes of stimuli that are remembered or imagined) according to the judge's own attitude. In any case, it should be noted that these findings relating unit size to attitude toward the social position of the Negro are consistent with data reported by Zavalloni and Cook (1965) and by Selltiz, Edrich, and Cook (1965), who also observed a wider range of scale values on the part of pro-Negro judges. If, furthermore, it is assumed that Negro judges generally have more pro-Negro attitudes than do white judges, then the smaller unit, hence wider range of values on the part of pro-Negro judges, is also consistent with data reported by Hovland and Sherif (1952) and by Kelley *et al.* (1955).

Ostrom (1966) applied the variable perspective model to the judgment of attitude statements relating to the race issue by Negro and white judges. Each judge wrote two attitude statements, similar to those in the stimulus series, expressing maximally pro- and anti-Negro sentiments. Another set of judges evaluated these perspective statements in terms of a pro — anti-Negro continuum. The Negro judging group was found by this index to have a typically narrower perspective than the white group. Both groups responded to alterations of stimulus range by narrowing their reported perspectives when the range was narrowed. On the basis of the information thus made available about the particular perspectives of the average judges in his various experimental groups, Ostrom then set forth specific hypotheses, based upon the variable perspective theory, relating to reference scale origin and unit. There were six experimental groups in a factorial design, corresponding to two races and three conditions of stimulus range (a total range and two restricted ranges, the restrictions being at either the pro- or anti-Negro ends of the ordered series). All predictions concerning the reference scale origins for the six groups were confirmed, as were most of those relating to unit size. (One of the two restricted range conditions was observed not to differ as predicted in the measure of unit size from that of the total range.) All told, Ostrom's study provided impressive evidence in support of the variable perspective model.

In a subsequent study, Ostrom and Upshaw (1964) examined data reflecting the scale origins and units for Negro and white judges in southern United States colleges with respect to a single series of attitudinal items administered on three occasions between 1930 and 1964. In terms of the variable perspective theory those data suggested that the perspectives of white judges had expanded in the pro-Negro direction during the time period, and that the perspectives of Negroes had not changed substantially. One interesting consequence of the apparent differential shift in perspectives of the two groups was that in the latest sample, as well as in Ostrom's earlier study (which he reported in 1966), the Negro judges generally viewed all statements as more pro-Negro than did white judges. The direction of this difference in origin is opposite to that found by Hinkley (1932) and by Hovland and Sherif (1952) on the basis of the same items. With respect to unit, in each of the time samples, the unit associated with Negro judges was smaller, hence the range of values greater, than that associated with white judges, thus replicating a highly reliable finding. (One of the three samples was that which Ostrom had previously studied and which was cited above.)

The hypothesis linking perspective and judgmental unit has received support from psychophysical, as well as from social-psychological, data. Parducci (1963), for example, has reported several studies which show the relationship. On the basis of these and other psychophysical data, Parducci (1965) formulated a range-frequency theory of categorical judgment. According to this theory, the judge establishes category limens (boundaries) by partitioning the stimulus range into as many segments as there are categories in his response language. This range principle is, of course, essentially the same as that in Volkmann's formulation. However, Parducci's statement of the principle is much more precise than that of Volkmann. For instance, Parducci acknowledges that psychological quantities and their associated physical quantities may not be the same. The partitioning under the range principle of the range-frequency theory is assumed to take place on the subjective, rather than the physical continuum. (Methodologically, Parducci assumes a "Thurstone scale of equal discriminability" as the locus of the partitioning process) (1965, p. 408). Thus, the category limens established by this process are assumed to result in subjectively equal categories. The scale values actually assigned to stimuli are assumed to reflect a compromise between the partitioning of the subjective continuum under the range principle, and another partitioning of the same continuum under a frequency principle. The latter principle corresponds to a hypothetical response bias leading to a tendency to use all categories equally often. As a partitioning rule, the frequency principle implies that categories are relatively narrow in regions of high stimulus density and relatively broad in less dense regions. The actual category limens underlying scale values are assumed by the range-frequency theory to be the means of the range and frequency limens.

Parducci's theory seems to suggest that judges typically confuse the identification and scaling tasks. The range-frequency compromise which lies at the heart of the theory may be interpreted as a compromise between the two tasks. The range principle may refer to the establishment of a reference scale unit, and the frequency principle to a device to maximize correct stimulus identifications. It is important to remember that the range-frequency theory as presently formulated is a theory of categorical judgment. A limited categorical language probably encourages an identification set on the part of subjects. To establish that identification and scaling are regularly confused by judges (as well as by investigators!) requires research on the effects of variable stimulus distributions, with clear instructions to scale rather than to identify and with an unlimited response language. This work has not been done.

The inverse relationship between perspective and the dispersion of judged values in both the Volkmann and Parducci theories is assumed to be mediated by the establishment of category boundaries. There is, therefore, some possibility that the range principle, as well as the frequency principle, functions only with a categorical language. Relevant to this issue is a study by Harvey and Campbell (1963) in which two parallel experiments were conducted testing the effects of stimulus range and other factors on categorical judgments in one case and a physical language (ounces) in the other. Of the dependent variables considered in that study, the one which is of interest in the present discussion is the difference between the scale values of the two stimuli that defined the range in the narrow-range condition. That difference was observed to be inversely related to perspective only with a categorical language.

Sandusky and Parducci (1965) studied judgments of the pleasantness of odors with two types of categorical language: one consisting of a fixed set of categories, and one that permitted the judge to add or to omit categories in order to express better the subjective quantity. Confirmation of the range hypothesis was found for both languages.

The range hypothesis was tested with an unlimited language in an experiment (Upshaw, 1969) in which judgments of moral outrage engendered by a set of statements describing offenses were rendered by placing an amount of sand into a bucket corresponding to the degree of censure for each statement. An item near the middle of the series, as determined in an earlier study, was selected as a modulus. A clear glass stein containing a standard amount of sand defining the modulus was visible to the judge at all times. Each subject participated in a wide- and in a narrow-range condition, half in each order. Range was manipulated by the inclusion of context stimuli which, in the narrow condition did not exceed the range of the series, and which in the wide condition exceeded the series at the serious end. The variable perspective theory produced three hypotheses: (1) the mean scale value for items in the common series is smaller (more trivial) in the wide (serious) context than in the narrow; (2) for each judge, the dispersion, computed over the stimuli of the common series, is smaller for the wide than for the narrow range; and (3) for each item, the dispersion, computed over subjects, is smaller for the wide than for the narrow range. The judgments of the subjects were quantified by weighing the sand which they placed into buckets. These data clearly confirmed all three hypotheses.

In numerous psychophysical studies (cited by Ekman and Sjöberg, 1965) a relationship has been found between the exponent of the psychophysical power function and the stimulus range. Thus, whether two reference scales of the same quantity are compared, or whether a scale of a subjective quantity is compared to a transformation of a physical scale based upon the psychophysical function, the unit of the reference scale seems to be affected by the stimulus range.

The process implied by both the Volkmann and Parducci theories to account for the perspective-unit relationship is one of a semantic adjustment to a limited, categorical language. However, the fact that the relationship has been observed with unlimited languages suggests that it is not an artifact of categorical ratings. The cross-modal study that was cited in which quantities of sand were used to express judgments of moral offense suggests, moreover, that the relationship is not a by-product of the subject's use of numbers, with or without experimentally imposed limitations. What, then, is the underlying psychological process acounting for the relationship? In order to set the limits for acceptable answers to that question it is necessary to know whether or not the relationship is directional; whether perspective determines unit as appears to be the case in some studies, or whether unit and perspective are merely correlated.

In a recently reported experiment (Upshaw, 1967a) subjects responded to 20 items similar in format to those of the Pettigrew Category Width Scale (Pettigrew, 1958). Each item consisted of the description of a class of objects in terms of an average scale value, e.g., "The average elephant can learn to spray himself with his trunk when he is 39 weeks old." The task of the subject was to estimate the largest and smallest values of the class, e.g., the slowest and fastest elephants. For each subject half of the items were expressed in relatively large units (e.g., weeks) and the other half in small units (e.g., days). Two forms of the questionnaire were constructed so that the small-unit items on one form were the large-unit items on the other. The information contained in matched small- and large-unit items was always the same. Hence, 12 inches in a small unit item was matched by 1 foot in a large-unit item, etc. This feature of the experiment entailed the introduction of number size as an extraneous variable, which will be discussed presently.

Since every person responded equally often in large and small units, personality factors which might interact with unit size were presumably controlled. In scoring, the minimum and maximum estimates for each item were first transformed to a common unit for all subjects. Then, each subject's minimum estimate was assigned a standard score in terms of the distribution of all minimum estimates, disregarding manipulated unit size. Similarly, maximum estimates were transformed to standard scores. The conversion to standard scores permitted direct comparisons of perspective measures as a function of unit size. Analysis of the data by t tests established that increasing unit size led to lower minimum estimates and to higher maximum estimates. Apparently, therefore, the relationship between perspective and unit is bidirectional.

Combining all the studies relating perspective and the dispersion of scale values, it appears that the size of a person's judgmental unit can be influenced by his perspective, and that under other circumstances his perspective can be influenced by his unit. The explanation of the apparently reversible relationship between judgmental unit and perspective is not immediately obvious. If the data had come from studies of stimulus identification instead of scaling, an explanation might be sought in terms of "channel capacity" (Attneave, 1959; Miller, 1956). The idea underlying the concept of channel capacity is that man has an inherent limitation on his immediate memory which restricts the number of stimulus-label combinations which he can use in stimulus identification. In the case of unidimensional stimuli, he might broaden the range of physical values assigned to each response category as a way of coping with an expanded range of the series. Because of the limitations imposed by channel capacity, the subject who performs an identification task, even without experimental restrictions on his language, presumably judges as though a categorical language had been prescribed. However, except in those cases in which a limited set of response categories are imposed, the scaling task does not appear to demand an identification set. The judge is generally instructed in scaling to evaluate each stimulus independently of all others and to base his judgment upon his subjective impression. Of course, the fact that he is not required to compare stimulus magnitudes with prejudged hypothetical magnitudes does not preclude the possibility that he does it. Whether by force of habit, superstition, or other causes, the judge may approach the scaling task with an identification set. Efforts to maintain consistency in use of the judgmental language, for example, might account for such a set, since consistency is likely to be expedited by means of committing to memory some stimulus-label combinations to which other stimuli could be referred for identification. Having approached the scaling task, for whatever reason, with an identification set, the subject may become restricted by his channel capacity to a small number of effective response categories.

The explanation of the relationship between unit and perspective in terms of a self-imposed identification set is unsatisfactory on two counts. First, it implies sharper differentiation among stimuli in a narrow range than in a wide range, hence, less than a perfect linear correlation between sets of judgments of the same stimuli which are presented in the context of different ranges. Second, it suggests that the relationship between reference scale unit and perspective should be observed only (or at least more strongly) in the judgment of unidimensional stimuli, since complex stimuli offer less of a challenge to the judge's channel capacity. The facts are, however, that the relationship has been observed with reference scales that have a virtually perfect linear correlation, and it has been observed with a variety of stimuli involving complex considerations (e.g., moral offenses) as well as with simple, sensory aspects. Channel capacity, therefore, should not be ruled out as an explanation of the phenomenon, even though at this time the available experimental evidence appears to contradict its implications.

The fact that unit size can be experimentally induced apparently without perspective as a mediating variable suggests that it may be determined by more than one factor. There is evidence, for example, that personality characteristics are reliably related to unit size. Data by White and Harvey (1965) and by Berkowitz (1961) may refer to this aspect of the reference scale, although other variables in the scale model were not controlled in either study. In the experiment relating comparison level and reward-cost orientation (Upshaw, 1967b), which was discussed earlier in relation to reference scale origin, evidence was found for individual differences in unit as well as in origin. The items of Pettigrew's (1958) Category Width (C-W) Scale appear to define a task that is essentially that which Ostrom (1966) used to obtain information about perspective. It may be, therefore, that individual differences on the C-W scale are really differences in perspective, or differences in unit which cause differences in perspective.

In an unpublished study, the present author compared the judgmental units (measured inversely by the standard deviations of scale values for a series of stimuli) and the perspectives (assessed by asking subjects to estimate low and high extreme values of a class of stimuli) in a scale setting for subjects who were classified as broad and narrow categorizers on the basis of the C-W scale. The results were unequivocal. Compared to narrow categorizers, broad categorizers described wider perspectives and reported scale judgments in terms of larger units.

In a pioneering study of the reference scale model that has been presented in this article, Murdoch (1965) investigated category width as measured by the C-W scale and a variable incentive for accuracy in estimating the lengths of lines in relation to the several dependent variables that are specified by the model. Murdoch assumed that the C-W scale actually measures tendencies toward broad and narrow perspective, and on that basis he made the following deductions from the variable perspective theory of judgment.

(1) The reference scale unit is directly proportional to perspective; hence, the dispersion of scale values, averaged over trials, is larger for narrow than for broad categorizers.

(2) Assume that scale origin fluctuates somewhat from trial to trial because of factors that operate at the level of the quantity (i.e., perceptual or cognitive, as opposed to linguistic factors), and that the amount of

fluctuation if measured on a hypothetical common scale would not differ according to C-W scores. When projected to the actual reference scales held by broad and narrow categorizers, however, the constant amount of fluctuation of origin over trials appears smaller for broad compared to narrow categorizers because of the larger scale units predicted for broad categorizers.

(3) As one might imagine a fluctuation of scale origin over trials, he might also conceive of the fluctuation of unit over trials. On the assumption that the degree of this fluctuation at the quantity level does not differ and that any difference is because of scale, it is expected that broad categorizers have smaller U/T components because of the hypothesized smaller units of their reference scales.

In addition to these predictions, Murdoch made others based upon the category width and equivalence range literature and concerned with the effects of the manipulation of incentive for accuracy. Because these aspects of the study are not directly relevant to the present discussion, they will not be treated here.

The experimental task for subjects in the Murdoch study was that of magnitude estimation of line length. Looking through a camera shutter the subject viewed two lines, one above the other in the visual field. The one on top was 16.43 cm long, and the one on bottom was one of the following (randomly ordered): 11.31, 13.88, 17.27, 23.47, and 29.00 cm. Each pair of lines was viewed for one-fifth of a second. Every stimulus in the series was judged 14 times. The standard stimulus was identified by the number 200, and the subjects were asked to assign proportional numbers to the six variable stimuli.

The reference scale model requires evidence that judgments under investigation differ only in scale and not in the nature of the subjective quantities which they measure. It is known that subjective length is related to physical length by a power function with an exponent that has an approximate value of 1.00 (Stevens and Galanter, 1957). For practical purposes this function is closely approximated by a straight line. As a test of the linearity requirement of the model, Murdoch computed a linear correlation between the scale values for each judge, averaged over trials, and the corresponding physical values. The mean correlation, over subjects, was .991, with a range of only .046. These results indicate the goodness of fit of the reference scale model, while at the same time they confirm earlier finding that subjective and physical length are related in almost a linear fashion.

The variable perspective model did not generate a hypothesis concerning scale origin as a function of C-W score. It did, however, for unit.

Specifically, broad categorizers were predicted to judge in terms of a broader unit than did narrow categorizers, leading to a smaller variance over scale values for stimuli in the experimental series. Such a variance measure was computed for each subject, and these measures were treated by the analysis of variance. The mean score for broad categorizers was found to be 250.1 compared to a mean of 344.5 for narrow categorizers ($p < .001$), thus confirming the prediction of unit size.

The variable perspective theory also led to the prediction that the fluctuations of both origin over trials and unit over trials are smaller for broad categorizers. Again individual variance measures were computed for each subject, and these scores were analyzed by two analyses of variance. The mean values for broad and narrow categorizers were 32.38 and 41.68 ($p < .05$) for O/T and 23.84 and 31.86 ($p < .001$) for U/T. All three predictions based on the variable perspective theory were, therefore, confirmed.

Given the apparently reversible relationship between unit size and perspective, it is difficult to decide whether the primary fact underlying the demonstrated individual differences in this area refer to unit, to perspective, or to both. Further research dealing with the personality characteristic may help to illuminate the issue with respect to situational inductions of unit size and perspective and vice versa.

Relevant to phenomena of unit size as observed both in the personality domain and as an experimental induction is the "central tendency effect" in psychophysics. This term refers to the tendency on the part of a subject to constrict the range of values which he produces in order to match those in a stimulus series. For example, if a judge is asked to move his hand a distance equal to the variable lengths of lines, he typically overestimates the short and underestimates the long lines (Guilford, 1954). In the classical case, such as that described, there is some suggestion that the judge's task implies an identification set. However, Stevens and Greenbaum (1966) have recently shown that the central tendency effect is found reliably in cross-modal scaling tasks in which the subject is not likely to interpret his job as that of identifying and reproducing the physical stimulus. Stevens and Greenbaum noted that the constriction of range which characterizes the central tendency effect occurs on whichever variable is placed under the control of the judge. When linear regression lines corresponding to the hypothesized power-law psychophysical functions were fitted to the log-log plots for paired modalities, the resulting slopes were found to differ according to which variable the judge adjusted in rendering his judgments. Furthermore, Stevens and Greenbaum reported reliable observer differences in the extent of the central tendency effect in cross-modal psychophysics.

The exact implications of the central tendency effect for the study of the reference scale are not clear. It does appear, however, that the effect is a unit phenomenon which occurs in the output rather than in the input phase of judgment. If the effect involves nothing but size of reference scale unit, it can then be said that subjects adopt a generally larger unit than that of the corresponding physical scale. Furthermore, the amount of discrepancy between physical and subjective scale units, by this view, constitutes a reliable source of individual differences, related perhaps to variables such as category width.

Only recently has systematic attention been given to phenomena relating to the reference scale unit. As indicated, current theoretical formulations are of two sorts, those that relate unit size to situational manipulations of stimulus range, and those that relate it to personality characteristics. Research directed to both types of theories has tended to involve categorical ratings which implicitly or explicitly confound the experimental tasks of identification, scaling, and discrimination. It is clear from available data, however, that unit effects attributable to perspective and personality variables occur with unlimited, continuous response languages. What is not clear are the psychological processes responsible for these effects.

The traditional concerns of the so-called psychology of judgment have been isolated empirical phenomena (e.g., assimilation and contrast), on the one hand, and "constant errors" or origin differences, on the other. It is possible that many of the isolated phenomena, and much that appears on the surface to refer to origin, will upon closer analysis be attributable to reference scale unit. For example, imagine two graphs plotted on one set of coordinate axes relating subjective and physical scale values for two subjects. Assume for purposes of illustration that the plots are linear and that the origins coincide. Finally, imagine that the units of the two scales portrayed by the graphs are different, resulting in different slopes for the two lines. The steeper slope of the judge with the smaller unit guarantees that any average value of judgments in the common series will have a higher value for him than for his counterpart with the larger unit, provided that the series contains mostly stimuli that are above the common origin. Thus, the attribution of judgmental effects to presumed differences in scale origin (adaptation level, comparison level, etc.) might be very misleading if the possibility that they are effects of unit is not tested.

V. Summary and Conclusions

This section has been concerned with judgment as studied both in the psychophysical and social psychological laboratories. An important problem in the work in both traditions is that of determining in a particular case whether the differences that are observed between sets of judgments correspond to perceptual and cognitive variation or whether they refer to differences of scale. A heuristic model of the reference scale was presented which serves to systemize numerous phenomena attributable to scale factors. The explication of that model led to a theoretical criterion for the identity of two quantities. Assuming suitable methodology, one could apply the criterion in a particular case to determine whether a given set of data should be interpreted at the level of scale or at the level of the quantity that underlies the scale. In those cases in which the scale level is deemed appropriate, the reference scale model provides several components in terms of which the locus of a particular experimental effect can be designated. Hopefully, therefore, the personal reference scale constitutes an orientation to judgment which will lead to precise phenomenal description and to a delineation of the theoretical issues in an area of application.

Theories of judgment, some of which have been contributed by social psychologists and some by psychophysicists, were surveyed in terms of the reference scale model. Most of them, it was revealed, can be viewed as theories of scale, rather than as theories of subjective quantities. Furthermore, all were seen to be fragmentary, referring primarily to one component of the reference scale model. An adequate theory of judgment would surely encompass all facets of the judge's reference scale. If the model described here does nothing more than to set the theoretical requirements for the study of judgment its primary purpose will be realized.

The model as formulated provides a structure for the theoretical analysis of judgment. Implied in the analysis are far more data that are usually collected in current judgmental studies. Some of these data refer to the criterion for the identity of quantities, and some refer to the various components of the reference scale. If the processing of such data is to be efficient, methods must be developed by which the relevant questions can be answered statistically. Methodology is clearly the next order of business in the study of the personal reference scale.

REFERENCES

Attneave, F. *Applications of information theory to psychology.* New York: Holt, 1959.
Berkowitz, L. Anti-semitism, judgmental processes, and displacement of hostility. *Journal of Abnormal and Social Psychology,* 1961, 62, 210-215.
Bevan, W., Maier, R. A., and Helson, H. The influence of context upon the estimation of number. *American Journal of Psychology,* 1963, 76, 464-469.
Bieri, J., Atkins, A. L., Briar, S., Leaman, R. L., Miller, H., and Tripodi, T. *Clinical and social judgment: The discrimination of behavioral information.* New York: Wiley, 1966.

Bruner, J. S., and Tajfel, H. Cognitive risk and environmental change. *Journal of Abnormal and Social Psychology,* 1961, **62**, 231-241.

Campbell, D. T., and Fiske, D. W. Convergent and discriminant validation by the multitrait-multimethod matrix. *Psychological Bulletin,* 1959, **56**, 81-105.

Campbell, D. T., Lewis, N. A., and Hunt, W. A. Context effects with judgmental language that is absolute, extensive, and extra-experimentally anchored. *Journal of Experimental Psychology,* 1958, **55**, 220-228.

Coombs, C. H. The theory and methods of social measurement. In *Research methods in the behavioral sciences.* L. Festinger and D. Katz (Eds.), New York: Dryden Press, 1953, Pp. 471-535.

Coombs, C. H. *A theory of data.* New York: Wiley, 1964.

Cronbach, L. J. Processes affecting scores on "understanding of others" and "assumed similarity." *Psychological Bulletin,* 1955, **52**, 177-193.

Dudycha, G. J. A critical examination of the measurement of attitude toward war. *Journal of Social Psychology,* 1943, **18**, 383-392.

Edwards, W., Lindman, H., and Phillips, L. D. Emerging technologies for making decisions. *New Directions in Psychology,* II, 1965, 259-325.

Ekman, G., and Sjöberg, L. Scaling. *Annual Review of Psychology,* 1965, **16**, 451-474.

Ellis, B. *Basic concepts of measurement.* London: Cambridge University Press, 1966.

Fechner, G. *Elements of psychophysics,* Vol. 1. Translated by H. E. Adler. New York: Holt, Rinehart, and Winston, 1966.

Fillenbaum, S. Some stylistic aspects of categorizing behavior. *Journal of Personality,* 1959, **27**, 187-195.

Galanter, E. Contemporary psychophysics. *New Directions in Psychology,* I, 1962, 87-156.

Green, B. F., and Tukey, J. W. Complex analyses of variance. General Problems. *Psychometrika,* 1960, **25**, 127-152.

Guilford, J. P. *Psychometric methods.* (2nd Ed.) New York: McGraw-Hill, 1954.

Gumpert, P., Thibaut, J. W., and Shuford, E. H. Effect of personality and status experience upon the valuation of unobtained statuses. *Journal of Abnormal and Social Psychology,* 1961, **63**, 47-52.

Harvey, O. J., and Campbell, D. T. Judgments of weight as affected by adaptation range, adaptation duration, magnitude of unlabeled anchor, and judgmental language. *Journal of Experimental Psychology,* 1963, **65**, 12-21.

Helson, H. Adaptation-level as frame of reference for prediction of psychophysical data. *American Journal of Psychology,* 1947, **60**, 1-29.

Helson, H. *Adaptation-level theory.* New York: Harper & Row, 1964.

Helson, H., Michels, W. C., and Sturgeon, A. The use of comparative rating scales for the evaluation of psychophysical data. *American Journal of Psychology,* 1954, **67**, 321-326.

Hicks, J. M. and Campbell, D. T. Zero-point scaling as affected by social object, scaling method, and context. *Journal of Personality and Social Psychology,* 1965, **2**, 793-808.

Hinckley, E. D. The influence of individual opinion on construction of an attitude scale. *Journal of Social Psychology,* 1932, **3**, 283-296.

Hinckley, E. D. A follow-up on the influence of individual opinion on the construction of an attitude scale. *Journal of Abnormal and Social Psychology,* 1963, **67**, 290-292.

Hovland, C. I., Harvey, O. J., and Sherif, M. Assimilation and contrast effects in reactions to communication and attitude change. *Journal of Abnormal and Social Psychology,* 1957, **55**, 244-252.

Hovland, C. I., and Sherif, M. Judgmental phenomena and scales of attitude measurement: Item displacement in Thurstone scales. *Journal of Abnormal and Social Psychology,* 1952, **47**, 822-832.

Jones, L. V. Invariance of zero-point scaling over changes in stimulus context. *Psychological Bulletin*, 1967, 67, 153-164.

Jones, V. The nature of changes in attitudes of college students toward war over an eleven-year period. *Journal of Educational Psychology*, 1942, 33, 481-494.

Kelley, H. H., Hovland, C. I., Schwartz, M., and Abelson, R. P. The influence of judges' attitudes in three methods of attitude scaling. *Journal of Social Psychology*, 1955, 42, 147-158.

Koffka, K. *Principles of Gestalt psychology*. New York: Harcourt Brace, 1935.

Krantz, D. L. and Campbell, D. T. Separating perceptual and linguistic effects of context shifts upon absolute judgments. *Journal of Experimental Psychology*, 1961, 62, 35-42.

Lewin, K. *Dynamic Theory of Personality*. New York: McGraw-Hill, 1935.

Luce, R. D. Detection and recognition. In R. D. Luce, R. R. Bush, and E. Galanter, (Eds.), *Handbook of mathematical psychology*, Vol. 1. New York: Wiley, 1963. Pp. 103-189.

Luce, R. D., and Galanter, E. Discrimination. In R. D. Luce, R. R. Bush, and E. Galanter (Eds.), *Handbook of mathematical psychology*. Vol. 1. New York: Wiley, 1963. Pp. 191-243.

Manis, M. Context effects in communication. *Journal of Personality and Social Psychology*, 1967, 5, 326-334.

Miller, G. A. The magical number seven, plus or minus two: Some limits on our capacity for processing information. *Psychological Review*, 1956, 63, 81-97.

Miller, L. W. A critical analysis of the Peterson-Thurstone war attitude scale. *Journal of Educational Psychology*, 1934, 25, 662-668.

Murdoch, P. H. J. The effects of categorization-style and cognitive risk upon judgment response language. Unpublished masters thesis, University of North Carolina at Chapel Hill, 1965.

Natsoulas, T. What are perceptual reports about? *Psychological Bulletin*, 1967, 67, 249-272.

Nunnally, J. C. *Psychometric theory*. New York: McGraw-Hill, 1967.

Ostrom, T. M. Perspective as an intervening construct in the judgment of attitude statements. *Journal of Personality and Social Psychology*, 1966, 3, 135-144.

Ostrom, T. M., and Upshaw, H. S. Race differences in the judgment of attitude statements as a function of historical events in race relations. Unpublished manuscript, 1964.

Parducci, A. Range-frequency compromise in judgment. *Psychological Monographs*, 1963, 77 (Whole No. 565).

Parducci, A. Category judgment: A range-frequency model. *Psychological Review*, 1965, 72, 407-418.

Parducci, A., and Marshall, L. M. Assimilation vs. contrast in the anchoring of perceptual judgments of weight. *Journal of Experimental Psychology*, 1962, 63, 426-437.

Pettigrew, T. F. The measurement and correlates of category width as a cognitive variable. *Journal of Personality*, 1958, 26, 532-544.

Savage, C. W. Introspectionist and behaviorist interpretations of ratio scales of perceptual magnitude. *Psychological Monographs*, 1966, 80 (Whole No. 627, Part 1).

Sandusky, A., and Parducci, A. Pleasantness of odors as a function of the immediate stimulus context. *Psychonomic Science*, 1965, 3, 321-322.

Selltiz, C., Edrich, H., and Cook, S. W. Ratings of favorableness of statements about a social group as an indicator of attitude toward the group. *Journal of Personality and Social Psychology*, 1965, 2, 408-415.

Sherif, C. W., Sherif, M., and Nebergall, R. E. *Attitude and attitude change: The social judgment-involvement approach*. Philadelphia: Saunders, 1965.

Sherif, M. A study of some social factors in perception. *Archives of Psychology*, 1935, New York, No. 187.

Sherif, M., and Hovland, C. I. Judgmental phenomena and scales of attitude measurement: Placement of items with individual choice of number of categories. *Journal of Abnormal and Social Psychology,* 48, 135-141, 1953.

Sherif, M., and Hovland, C. I. *Social judgment.* New Haven, Connecticut: Yale University Press, 1961.

Sherif, M., Taub, D., and Hovland, C. I. Assimilation and contrast effects of anchoring stimuli on judgments. *Journal of Experimental Psychology,* 1958, 55, 150-155.

Siegel, S. Level of aspiration and decision making. *Psychological Review,* 1957, 64, 253-262.

Stevens, S. S. Mathematics, measurement, and psychophysics. In S. S. Stevens (Ed.), *Handbook of experimental psychology.* New York: Wiley, 1951.

Stevens, S. S. Adaptation-level vs. the relativity of judgment. *American Journal of Psychology,* 1958, 71, 633-646.

Stevens, S. S. On the operation known as judgment. *American Scientist,* 1966, 54, 385-401. (a)

Stevens, S. S. Operations or words? *Psychological Monographs,* 1966, 80 (Whole No. 627, Part II). (b)

Stevens, S. S., and Galanter, E. H. Ratio scales and category scales for a dozen perceptual continua. *Journal of Experimental Psychology,* 1957, 54, 377-411.

Stevens, S. S., and Greenbaum, H. B. Regression effect in psychophysical judgment. *Perception and Psychophysics,* 1966, 1, 439-446.

Suppes, P., and Zinnes, J. L. Basic measurement theory. In R. D. Luce, R. R. Bush, and E. Galanter (Eds.), *Handbook of mathematical psychology.* New York: Wiley, 1963, Pp. 1-76.

Tajfel, H., Richardson, A., and Everstine, L. Individual consistencies in categorizing: A study of judgmental behavior. *Journal of Personality,* 1964, 32, 90-108.

Thibaut, J. W., and Kelley, H. H. *The Social Psychology of Groups.* New York: Wiley, 1959.

Thurstone, L. L. A law of comparative judgment. *Psychological Review,* 1927, 34, 273-286.

Thurstone, L. L., and Chave, E. J. *The measurement of attitude.* Chicago: University of Chicago Press, 1929.

Thurstone, L. L., and Jones, L. V. The rational origin for measuring subjective values. In L. L. Thurstone (Ed.), *The measurement of values.* Chicago: University of Chicago Press, 1959. Pp. 195-210.

Torgerson, W. W. *Theory and methods of scaling.* New York: Wiley, 1958.

Upshaw, H. S. Own attitude as an anchor in equal-appearing intervals. *Journal of Abnormal and Social Psychology,* 1962, 64, 85-96.

Upshaw, H. S. A linear alternative to assimilation and contrast: A reply to Manis. *Journal of Abnormal and Social Psychology,* 1964, 68, 691-693.

Upshaw, H. S. The effect of variable perspectives on judgments of opinion statements for Thurstone scales: Equal-appearing intervals. *Journal of Personality and Social Psychology,* 1965, 2, 60-69.

Upshaw, H. S. Category width as a function of judgmental unit. Paper presented to the annual meeting of the Midwestern Psychological Association, Chicago, 1967. (a)

Upshaw, H. S. Comparison level as a function of reward-cost orientation. *Journal of Personality,* 1967, 35, 290-296. (b)

Upshaw, H. S. Attitude measurement. In H. M. Blalock and A. Blalock (Eds.), *Methodology in social research.* New York: McGraw-Hill, 1968. Pp. 60-111. (a)

Upshaw, H. S. Cognitive consistency and the psychology of judgment. In R. P. Abelson, *et al.* (Eds.), *Theories of cognitive consistency.* Chicago: Rand McNally, 1968, in press. (b)

Upshaw, H. S. Stimulus range and the judgmental unit. *Journal of Experimental Social Psychology,* 1969, in press.

Volkmann, J. Scales of judgment and their implications for social psychology. In J. H. Rohrer and M. Sherif (Eds.), *Social psychology at the crossroads.* New York: Harper, 1951. Pp. 273-294.

Ward, C. D. Ego involvement and the absolute judgment of attitude statements. *Journal of Personality and Social Psychology,* 1965, 2, 202-208.

Ward, C. D. Attitude and involvement in the absolute judgment of attitude statements. *Journal of Personality and Social Psychology,* 1966, 4, 465-476.

White, B. J., Alter, R. D., and Rardin, M. Authoritarianism, dogmatism, and usage of conceptual categories. *Journal of Personality and Social Psychology,* 1965, 2, 293-295.

White, B. J., and Harvey, O. J. Effects of personality and own stand on judgment and production of statements about a central issue. *Journal of Experimental Social Psychology,* 1965, 1, 334-347.

Winer, B. J. *Statistical principles in experimental design.* New York: McGraw-Hill, 1962.

Zavalloni, M., and Cook, S. W. Influence of judges' attitudes on ratings of favorableness of statements about a social group. *Journal of Personality and Social Psychology,* 1965, 1, 43-54.

AUTHOR INDEX

Numbers in italics refer to the pages on which the complete references are listed.

373

SUBJECT INDEX

A